THEY FOUGHT BACK

Books by Yuri Suhl

One Foot in America (Novel)

Cowboy on a Wooden Horse (Novel)

Ernestine Rose and the Battle for Human Rights (Biography)

THEY FOUGHT BACK

The Story of the Jewish Resistance in Nazi Europe

Edited and translated by
Yuri Suhl

SCHOCKEN BOOKS · NEW YORK

Acknowledgments

I wish to express my deep appreciation to the Committee for the Book on Jewish Resistance sponsored by the American Federation of Polish Jews. Its generous assistance made the research for this book possible.

For their help with translations I am greatly indebted to Ben Gordon, Gisele Oster, Dr. Harold Kirshner, and the late Jakub Markovic (Prague).

I am grateful to Charlotte Pomerantz for valuable editorial suggestions; to Mrs. Gina Formiggini (Italy) for making available to me her unpublished manuscript Jews in the Italian Resistance Movement; to Auschwitz survivor Mrs. B. Liwschitz (Belgium), who spared no efforts in helping me obtain the full story of heroine Mala Zimetbaum; to Auschwitz survivor Gisa Weisblum (Israel) who, in addition to writing the Mala Zimetbaum story for this anthology, gave generously of her knowledge and time; to Alfred Grant (France), author of *Paris a City of the Front* (in Yiddish), for his friendly cooperation.

I am especially grateful to the YIVO Institute for Jewish Research for granting me permission to reprint material from the *YIVO Annual of Jewish Social Studies,* Vol. VIII, 1953.

My warmest thanks to Dina Abramowicz, librarian of the YIVO Institute for Jewish Research, who assisted me in every way possible to make full use of the splendid YIVO collection; to the efficient and courteous staff of the Zionist Archives and Library of New York; to Mr. Isaac Schneersohn, Director of the Centre de Documentation Juive Contemporaine (Paris), and to Mr. Lucien Steinberg for their generous cooperation; to the staff of the Jewish Historical Institute of Warsaw and its late Director, Professor Ber Mark, for their help and cooperation during my visits abroad, and by correspondence; to my wife, Isabelle, for undertaking the task of indexing this book; and last, but not least, I wish to express my indebtedness to Millen Brand, novelist and poet, whose deep concern for the truth in the subject of Jewish resistance is reflected in his meticulous editorship of this book.

My thanks to the following publishers and publications for permission to use material:

"The Bialystok Ghetto Revolt," by Reuben Ainsztein, from *The Jewish Quarterly* (London), spring 1956. © 1956, by The Jewish Quarterly (London). Reprinted by permission of The Jewish Quarterly (London).

"The Little Doctor—a Resistance Hero," by Leonard Tushnet, from *Jewish Currents* (New York), July, 1961, © 1961 by Leonard Tushnet. Reprinted by permission of *Jewish Currents.*

"The Revolt of the Jews of Marcinkonis," by Leyb Koniuchowski, from *The YIVO Annual of Jewish Social Science,* Volume 8, © 1954, by The Yiddish Scientific Institute (YIVO). Reprinted by permission of The Yiddish Scientific Institute.

"The Destruction and Resistance of the Jews in Italy," by Masimo Adolfo Vitale, from *YIVO Bletter,* Volume 37, © 1954 by The Yiddish Scientific Institute (YIVO). Reprinted by permission of The Yiddish Scientific Institute (YIVO).

Quotations from *I Cannot Forgive,* by Rudolf Vrba and Alan Bestic, © 1964, by Rudolf Vrba and Alan Bestic. Reprinted by permission of Grove Press, Inc.

First SCHOCKEN PAPERBACK edition 1975

10 9 8 7 6 5 4 79 80 81 82

Suhl, Yuri, 1908–   ed. and tr.
    They fought back.

Includes bibliographies.
    1. World War, 1939-1945—Underground movements—
Jews. I. Title.
[D810.J4S85   1975]   940.53′15′03924   74—26766

Manufactured in the United States of America

"Even in times of savagery the most brutish barbarians were not devoid of a human spark. For they did usually spare the children. This cannot be said of the Hitlerite beast who is out to devour the most precious ones, the ones who arouse the greatest compassion—innocent children."

EMMANUEL RINGELBLUM

This book is dedicated to the memory of the 1,200,000 Jewish children murdered by the Nazis in the ghettos and death camps of occupied Europe.

TABLE OF CONTENTS

page

INTRODUCTION — Yuri Suhl — 1

REVOLT IN SOBIBOR — Alexander Pechersky — 7

"LITTLE WANDA WITH THE BRAIDS" — Yuri Suhl — 51

THE HERBERT BAUM GROUP — Ber Mark — 55

THE STORY OF JEWISH RESISTANCE IN THE GHETTO OF CZESTOCHOWA — Dr. William Glicksman — 69

ZOFIA YAMAIKA — Esther Mark — 77

"CHIEF PHYSICIAN REMBA" — Yuri Suhl — 82

"COMRADE MORDECHAI" — Emmanuel Ringelblum — 85

THE WARSAW GHETTO UPRISING — Ber Mark — 92

UPRISING IN TREBLINKA — Samuel Rajzman — 128

THE BIALYSTOK GHETTO REVOLT — Reuben Ainsztein — 136

THE EVIDENCE — Yuri Suhl — 144

THE RESISTANCE MOVEMENT IN THE VILNA GHETTO — Abraham H. Foxman — 148

THE REVOLT OF THE JEWS OF MARCINKONIS — Leyb Koniuchowski — 160

REVOLT IN LACHWA — Aaron Schworin, Chaim Shkliar, Abraham Feinberg, Chaim Michali — 165

THE REVOLT IN THE TUCZYN GHETTO — Mendel Mann — 168

THE ESCAPE FROM KOLDYCZEWO CAMP — Joseph M. Foxman — 172

THE RESISTANCE OF THE SLOVAK JEWS — Emil F. Knieža — 176

THE ESCAPE AND DEATH OF THE "RUNNER" MALA ZIMETBAUM	Giza Weisblum	182
UNDERGROUND ASSIGNMENT IN AUSCHWITZ	Yuri Suhl	189
FIVE ESCAPES FROM AUSCHWITZ	Erich Kulka	196
ROSA ROBOTA—HEROINE OF THE AUSCHWITZ UNDERGROUND	Yuri Suhl	219
THE JEWISH PARTISANS OF HORODENKA	Joshua Wermuth	226
THE RESISTANCE MOVEMENT IN THE GHETTO OF MINSK	Yuri Suhl	231
CHILDREN—COURIERS IN THE GHETTO OF MINSK	Jacob Greenstein	241
THE STORY OF THE AMAZING OSWALD (SHMUEL) RUFEISEN	Jacob Greenstein	246
THE LITTLE DOCTOR—A RESISTANCE HERO	Leonard Tushnet	253
DIADIA MISHA (UNCLE MISHA) AND HIS PARTISANS: THE BLOWING UP OF THE SOLDIERS' HOME	Misha Gildenman	260
DIADIA MISHA AND HIS PARTISANS: THE ATTACK	Misha Gildenman	268
DIADIA MISHA AND HIS PARTISANS: DAVID OF YAREVITCH	Misha Gildenman	271
THE BULGARIAN JEWS IN THE RESISTANCE MOVEMENT	Matei Yulzari	275
DIARY OF A JEWISH PARTISAN IN PARIS	Abraham Lissner	282
THE DESTRUCTION AND RESISTANCE OF THE JEWS IN ITALY	Masimo Adolfo Vitale	298
THE JEWISH RESISTANCE MOVEMENT IN BELGIUM	Jacob Gutfreind	304
NOTES		312
INDEX		317

Introduction

SINCE THE end of World War II there has been a steady flow of documentary and fictional literature describing the genocidal means the Germans devised against the Jews in their relentless drive for the Final Solution. The first impulse of the survivors of Hitler's murder factories was to cry out their despair to the world, and so the documentation of horror began even while the war was still going on. As a result, the world quickly learned something about the long road of suffering that six million Jews traveled from the ghettos to the gas chambers.

But the world knows little or nothing about the other side of the holocaust picture: Jewish resistance—how the Jews struck back at their tormentors. The epic Warsaw Ghetto uprising is famous, but it is not generally known that in practically every ghetto and in every labor and concentration camp there existed a Jewish underground organization that kept up the prisoners' morale, reduced their physical sufferings, committed acts of sabotage, organized escapes, collected arms, planned revolts, and, in many instances, carried them out.

Who would have thought it possible for a Jewish underground organization to exist, let alone function, in the very heart of Nazi Germany— Berlin? Yet the *Baum-Gruppe,* an illegal group composed of young Jewish men and women of varied political persuasions, conducted anti-Nazi activities at the height of the war and under the very noses of the Gestapo. All but two were captured and either executed or later perished in concentration camps. This dramatic story of heroism and martyrdom is brought to the American reader here for the first time.

Every occupied country had its underground; and the French had their maquis, whose daring anti-Nazi activities have been widely recorded in books and films. But it is not generally known that besides the many French Jews who were members of the maquis there existed also an independent Jewish underground organization which called itself The Jewish Partisan Unit of Paris. Some of its members became legends in the French resistance movement. Their bold and spectacular operations are vividly described in the chapter of this book called "Diary of a Jewish Partisan in Paris."

Hitler did his utmost to conceal from the world the true nature of his concentration camps in Poland—they were death camps. He succeeded in muffling his victims' shrieks but he could not hide the smoke and flames belched into the skies by the crematoriums. As Hochhuth pointed out in *The Deputy*, "The pall of smoke and the glow of fires [were] visible to a distance of thirty kilometers. . . ." A perfect target for bombers, both day and night. The question that leaps to mind at once is: Why didn't the Allied Air Command bomb the gas chambers and crematoriums of the death camps out of existence? And why did they not bomb the railway lines that carried victims to these camps?

Louis Tursky asks these questions in his article "Could the Death Camps Have Been Bombed?" (*Jewish Frontier*, September, 1964), and presents a wealth of evidence to show that from a military standpoint it was possible to do so. Yet, early in 1944, when Chaim Weizmann,[1] acting on behalf of the Jewish Agency, asked the Western Allies to bomb the rail-lines leading from Hungary to the death camps of Poland, he was told that his request was "technically unfeasible." Tursky adds, with understandable bitterness: "It had not been previously unfeasible to drop weapons, explosives, and money into Poland for the Polish 'Home Army.' . . ."

What the Allied Command with its ample technical resources failed to do to halt the mass murder of Jews, the Jewish undergrounds, with their limited means and under conditions of unspeakable terror, attempted to do themselves and, in at least two instances, succeeded. Treblinka and Sobibor, two of the most notorious death camps in Poland, were put out of operation by the victims themselves, thanks to successful revolts. The stories of these revolts, how they were planned and carried out, are told here in firsthand accounts by those who took part in them. They rank with the most dramatic narratives in the annals of the human struggle for survival.

Rosa Robota and Mala Zimetbaum, who worked in the Auschwitz underground, were among the most courageous unsung heroes of the Jewish resistance. It was Rosa Robota's secret smuggling apparatus that provided the dynamite used to blow up an Auschwitz crematorium. And it was Mala Zimetbaum who found a way to save the lives of hundreds of women prisoners. Only fragments of their stories are scattered in various publications. Here, for the first time in the English language, is a full account of their underground activities and their martyrdom.

One of the most thrilling chapters in the history of the war is the story of the Jewish partisans in the forests of Eastern Europe. They numbered in the thousands—most were escapees from ghettos and camps. Not all who escaped reached their destinations, but for the Jew who made it to the forest, "the rifle, the cartridge belt, and the hand grenade took the place of the yellow badge that stung his body and violated his soul. . . . The once humiliated ghetto Jew now struck fear in the enemy's ranks." [2] The ghetto Jew, turned partisan, played an honorable role in the guerrilla movement that was vital to the Allied victory, and yet his story is almost entirely unknown.

Diadia Misha (Uncle Misha) was one such Jewish partisan who "struck fear in the enemy's ranks." His real name was Misha Gildenman. When he and sixteen other Jews escaped from the ghetto of Koretz, a small town in Volhynia, they had only one pistol and five rounds of ammunition. But before long, this small band of ghetto Jews grew into a mighty detachment of armed Jewish partisans numbering in the hundreds. Diadia Misha was their commandant. He and his partisans became a legend in the forests and villages of the Ukraine. Diadia Misha lived to tell his story, three episodes of which are included in this book. But many a Jewish partisan in Eastern Europe took his story with him to an unmarked grave.

The partisan movement in Soviet territories was a vital adjunct to the Armed Forces. But in the postwar Stalin period, when all Jewish cultural institutions in the Soviet Union were suppressed, the story of Jewish heroism was ignored by the chroniclers of the war. Fragments have only recently begun to emerge. As late as 1964 the following facts came to light:

1) Jews held leadership positions in over 200 partisan detachments, but many of them assumed Russian or Ukrainian names, and so their true identity was unknown.

2) The organizer of the first partisan units in the Smolensk region was known as Borisov. Actually he was a Jew from Yekaterinoslav-Dniepropetrovsk, whose name was Kleinman. He fell in battle.

3) The Soviet paper *Nowi Mir* (June 15, 1964) reveals that the organizer of the resistance movement among the prisoners of war and slave laborers in southern Germany was a Jew named Joseph Feldman who went under the name of Georg Pesenka. He perished at Dachau.[3]

The full dramatic story of Jewish resistance to Nazism during World War II has yet to be told, and the need for telling it is now more compelling than ever, not only to set the record down but also to set it straight. For there is a dangerous myth that the Jews did *not* resist; that, moreover, they willingly assisted in their own destruction. In his book, *The Destruction of the European Jews,*[4] in the main a valuable contribution to the growing body of holocaust literature, Raul Hilberg reconstructs from original German sources the monstrous machine of destruction the Nazis created for the implementation of the Final Solution. He then turns his attention to the victims of this machine, the Jews, and arrives at this conclusion: "The reaction pattern of the Jews is characterized by almost complete lack of resistance . . . the Jewish victims, caught in the straightjacket of their history, plunged themselves physically and psychologically into catastrophe."

Did Mr. Hilberg expect to find the true facts of Jewish resistance reflected in the reports of German officers to their superiors? Would those who were taught to believe that Jews were *Untermenschen* (subhumans) admit in print to Jewish heroism? Because Hilberg found no sign of Jewish resistance in official German documents, he concluded that none existed and then proceeded to buttress his conclusion with a theory of historic Jewish passivity. More recently Hannah Arendt, leaning heavily on Hilberg's conclusions, described Jewish resistance as ". . . pitifully small . . . incredibly weak and essentially harmless." [5]

Nothing could be further from the truth. The recorded facts present an entirely different picture of Jewish resistance. The true story is to be found in *Jewish* sources, mainly in the Yiddish language and, to a considerable extent, in Hebrew. It was written by the victims themselves before they perished, by survivors, and by historians who drew from these sources. One is compelled to agree with Elie Wiesel's observation: "The question is not why all the Jews did not fight, but how so many of them did. Tormented, beaten, starved, where did they find the strength—spiritual and physical—to resist?" [6] Only when assessed in the light of the inhuman conditions of life in the ghettos and camps does the full grandeur of Jewish resistance emerge.

Death by starvation was part of the German genocidal blueprint. The Jews resisted by smuggling food into the ghetto. The Germans decreed the death penalty for smuggling, but this did not stop the Jews. In the ghettos the smuggler was raised to the status of fighter, and the Warsaw Ghetto archivist, Emmanuel Ringelblum, proposed that a monument be erected to him.

The Germans established slave labor factories in the Warsaw Ghetto, forcing the Jews to sew military uniforms for the Wehrmacht. We find the following entry in Ringelblum's diary, *Notes from the Warsaw Ghetto*: ". . . the Jewish tailors working in the German commissary shops, wishing to do their part for the sabotage have sent off a transport of military uniforms with trousers sewed together, buttons on backwards, pockets upside down, and sleeves reversed (the left sleeve where the right should be). The transport was returned from Berlin, and now the Production Department is all agog. There are threats of drastic punishment."

Unauthorized departure from a ghetto was punishable by death, and yet Jews never ceased in their efforts to escape. There were two kinds of escapees—those who had made arrangements to live in hiding or on forged papers on the Aryan side (passive resistance), and those who escaped to the forests to join the partisans and fight (active resistance).

To further discourage escape from the ghetto, the Germans introduced "collective responsibility" which made whole families and groups responsible for the escape of a single individual. But this was not the only knotty problem Jewish underground fighters had to face. They had to grapple with the moral question of their responsibility to the collective. The underground fighters in various ghettos were torn between a desire to go to the forests and their duty to remain with those who could not escape, and prepare for the inevitable day when the Germans would march in to liquidate the ghetto. One choice held out the possibility of fighting the Germans with weapon in hand, and even of personal survival; the other meant dying with honor in a last and unequal contest. And of course it was always a torment to part from families even knowing that remaining with them could not save their lives. These were deep moral and personal dilemmas that only members of the Jewish underground had to face.

But whether the decision was to enter the forest or remain in the ghetto, the underground always needed weapons. Here, too, the Jews faced special difficulties. All other undergrounds in occupied Europe could, with regard to weapons, count on the support of Allied High Commands, but not the Jewish undergrounds.

Between July and September of 1942 over 300,000 Jews from the Warsaw Ghetto were forced into cattle cars and sent to Treblinka. Commenting on this mass deportation, Ringelblum writes: "We state firmly that had the responsible Polish authorities extended moral support and helped us with arms, the Germans would have had to pay for the sea of Jewish blood shed in July, August, and September, 1942." At the time of their deportation the Jews did not know their destination was Treblinka, nor did they know that Treblinka was a liquidation center for Jews. (As always, the Germans employed the euphemism "resettlement to the east for labor.") Moreover, the underground organization, then only several months old, was devitalized by the deportations. Still Ringelblum had the courage to say that had the Jews had arms, they would have fought back and resisted the deportations.

Between September, 1942, and January, 1943, the Jews learned the *real* destination of the deportees and the *real* meaning of Treblinka. This made a difference. Also, during the intervening months the underground was able to recover somewhat from the blow of the deportations. And so when the Germans marched into the ghetto on January 18, 1943, to deport the remaining 50,000 Jews, they were met with armed resistance. After four days of sporadic skirmishes between the poorly armed groups of the infant underground and the well-armed SS units, the Germans withdrew, paying with more than a score of their own dead.

Now the Germans knew that there was an armed force in the ghetto, and so did the Jews. Electrified by the January revolt, the ghetto population rallied round the underground and looked upon it as an authoritative body. But did the "responsible Polish authorities" also rally to the support of the ghetto underground? Not at all. After prolonged negotiations with the Polish underground under the command of the Polish Provisional Government in London, the late Philip Friedman wrote: "The Jewish underground received in February, 1943, only three months before the uprising, 50 revolvers, 50 hand grenades, and four kilograms of explosives." It should be added that some of the revolvers were defective and useless. (The *Armia Krajowa,* the Home Army, under the leadership of the Polish Government-in-Exile in London, was permeated with anti-Semitism. Undoubtedly, this is one of the reasons why the Jews received so little aid from the largest underground movement in Poland.)

And so, the Warsaw Ghetto fighters had to acquire their own weapons—painstakingly and as a result of tremendous sacrifice. They also manufactured their own bombs, hand grenades, and Molotov cocktails. But their most potent weapon was their deep sense of national pride and responsibility. As Ringelblum describes it: "We took stock of our position and saw that this was a struggle between a fly and an elephant. But our national dignity dictated to us that the Jews must offer resistance and not allow themselves to be led wantonly to the slaughter." And, in the early stages of the uprising, the ghetto fighters achieved some incredible victories. Even Hitler's Minister of Propaganda, Joseph Goebbels, was compelled to pay grudging tribute to them. He noted in his diary that "the joke cannot last much longer, but it shows what the Jews are capable of when they have arms in their hands." It could be said that long before Hitler suffered a military collapse on the combined battlefields of Europe and Africa, he suffered a moral defeat on the charred rubble of the Warsaw Ghetto.

But if not all the ghettos were as "lucky" as the Warsaw Ghetto in acquiring weapons, their courage was the same. The underground of the Lachwa Ghetto, for example, was unable to obtain a single revolver, yet the Jews of Lachwa staged a heroic revolt with hatchets, knives, and their bare hands.

The tales of Warsaw and Lachwa and the many stories of Jewish resistance that are presented here for the first time to the English-speaking reader are offered as contributions to a slowly emerging epic: Jewish resistance to Nazism in occupied Europe. In every detail, it is a tribute to the courage of a people and a celebration of the indomitable human spirit.

Revolt in Sobibor

By Alexander Pechersky

[EDITOR'S NOTE: *Of the six death camps the Nazis had set up in Poland, Sobibor is perhaps the least known, but it was the scene of one of the most dramatic revolts in the annals of Jewish resistance and, by and large, the most successful in its objective.*

Before the war Sobibor was a very small, obscure railway station situated between Wlodowa and Chelm, in eastern Poland. This relatively unknown spot Himmler chose as the proper site for a death factory. It was completed on May 8, 1942.

Transports arrived almost daily in Sobibor, numbering from 1,500 to 2,000 Jewish deportees from Poland, Czechoslovakia, Holland, France, Austria, and other occupied countries. In addition to the large number of SS men and Ukrainian auxiliary police that guarded the camp from the inside, Sobibor was surrounded by four rows of barbed wire fence over ten feet high, a ravine filled with water and a mined field. In July, 1943, Himmler himself came to inspect its operations. As a result of his visit, "production" was stepped up, reaching at times a high of 15,000 bodies burned in a single day.

But even in this heavily-guarded fortress of death, where escape seemed a human impossibility, the urge for freedom continued to live and the victims planned and schemed. One day a husband and wife tried to escape. They were caught and shot. In reprisal the Germans shot 150 Jews who worked in the same part of the camp as that couple. There was an unsuccessful attempt to make an escape route by digging an underground passage. Once a group of prisoners was working in a nearby forest; two of them strangled the guard and escaped. The rest were brought back to camp and shot. About seventy Dutch Jews tried to escape by bribing one of the guards. They were betrayed and executed by decapitation. From that day on the prisoners were counted three times daily; the comandant of the camp took the roll call.

One day in September, 1943, a transport arrived from Minsk, the first from the Soviet Union. On it was Alexander Pechersky, a Red Army officer captured by the Germans, and about seventy other Jewish prisoners

7

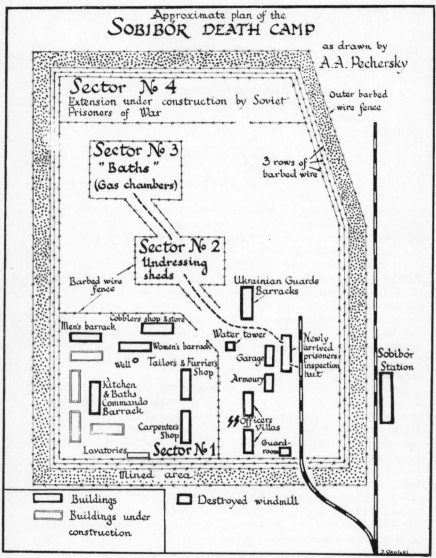

Approximate plan of the
SOBIBÓR DEATH CAMP

as drawn by
A.A. Pechersky

Sector № 4
Extension under construction by Soviet
Prisoners of War

Outer barbed
wire fence

Sector № 3
"Baths"
(Gas chambers)

3 rows of
barbed wire

Sector № 2
Undressing
sheds

Ukrainian Guards
Barracks

Barbed wire
fence

Men's barrack

Cobblers shop & store

Water tower

Newly
arrived
prisoners
inspection
hut

Sobibór
Station

Women's barrack

Well

Tailors & Furriers
Shop

Garage

Armoury

Kitchen
& Baths
Commando
Barrack

Carpenter's
Shop

Sector № 1

SS Officers
Villas

Guard-
room

Lavatories

Mined area

	Buildings
	Buildings under construction

Destroyed windmill

J. Okolski

Courtesy of **Jewish Observer and Middle East Review.**

of war. Three weeks later there was a spectacular revolt in Sobibor organized and led by Pechersky.

Soon after he returned from the war Pechersky wrote a pamphlet, The Revolt in Sobibor *(Yiddish translation by N. Lurie, Moscow: State Publishing House "Der Emes," 1946), in which he described the events in that camp from the day he arrived to the day of the successful revolt and his joining the partisans. This firsthand account of the Sobibor revolt is the most authentic report of that dramatic event. It is presented here in full in the editor's new translation from the Yiddish, and is brought up to date by a postscript giving additional related facts that have come to light twenty years after the event.]*

Alexander Pechersky About Himself

"I WAS BORN in Kremenchug in 1909. From 1915 we lived in Rostov-on-the-Don. I graduated from a seven-year school and a music school. I was a Soviet employee and was active in dramatic and musical circles. Before the war I was a leader of amateur groups.

On the very first day of the Fatherland war, I was mobilized as a junior commander. In September, 1941 I was promoted on the front to intendant second rank. I worked in both battalion and division staffs. In October, 1941, I was taken a prisoner of war. I became ill with typhus and by some miracle survived. Ordinarily the Germans shot all prisoners of war who came down with typhus, but I succeeded in concealing my illness.

In May, 1942, I made an attempt to escape. I was caught together with four others who had tried to run away. We were all sent to a punitive detachment in Borisov and from there to Minsk. On August 20, 1942, I was sent to the SS labor camp on Sheroka Street in Minsk where I was imprisoned until September 18, 1943. This, in brief, is my life up to Sobibor."

In September, 1943, the Germans hurriedly began to evacuate the remaining Jews from the ghetto of Minsk. They were herded into the camp on Sheroka Street in groups of 2,000, and from there were sent elsewhere. This SS labor camp on Sheroka Street maintainted a basic complement of prisoners consisting of 500 skilled Jewish workers selected from the ghetto of Minsk, about a hundred Jewish prisoners of war, and 300 non-Jews arrested for all sorts of petty crimes.

They rose at five in the morning and worked until eight in the evening. Twice daily they each received 150 grams of bread. Lunch consisted of a soup made of potato peelings, and that was all.

As if the daily backbreaking routine was not enough, the officers in charge of the camp would frequently indulge in certain "amusements." For example, when the bread rations were being distributed, the commander's assistant would order the prisoners to line up one behind the other, nose to neck. Then, pistol in hand, he would rest his elbow on the shoulder of the man heading the line and shoot along the length of the column. Anyone who was slow in lining up or who did not stand stiff as a ramrod would be hit by the bullet. Or sometimes at night when the prisoners were already huddling in their bunks, the commander would suddenly barge into the barracks with his two shepherd dogs and set them at the prisoners at random. The dogs would tear into the blankets and bodies, and one had to lie still or pay with his life.

One of the inmates was suspected of having pocketed 200 extra grams of bread. He was tied to a barrel and twenty guards, one after the other, beat him for exactly one minute on the soles of his feet with a pick-ax, When the man lost consciousness, they revived him with ice-cold water and resumed the beating.

Until September 18 the basic complement remained intact. But on that day all Jews were ordered to line up in the yard. It was four in the morning and still quite dark. Wrapped in darkness, bundles in hand, they were standing in line for the 300 grams of bread that was being issued for the journey. The yard was packed with prisoners but voices were kept low. Children clung to their mothers in fear. It was quieter than usual. On that morning no one was whipped, no one was scalded with boiling water, no one was set upon by the dogs.

Commandant Waks, twirling his whip, announced:

"You will soon be led to the station. You are going to Germany where you will work. Hitler makes it possible to spare the lives of those Jews who are willing to work faithfully for Germany. You may take with you your families and your more valuable possessions."

Women and children were taken to the station in automobiles; the men went by foot. As we marched past the ghetto, the people there recognized us and began to throw bread and other foodstuffs to us over the barbed wire. Farewells were shouted. Wailing and crying filled the air. Everyone knew full well what awaited us.

Men, women, and children were herded together, seventy in a car. There were no bunks, no benches. It was impossible to lie down. One barely managed to squat for a few minutes. Even when standing up, one felt crushed from all sides. The doors were bolted, the windows blocked with barbed wire. We were not given any food, not even a drink of water.

No one was allowed out to perform his natural functions. In this way we traveled for four days and nights without knowing our destination. On the evening of the fifth day, we arrived at a small deserted station. A white sign in big Gothic letters read SOBIBOR. To the right of the station was a forest, to the left a triple barbed wire fence three yards long. The train was switched over to a sidetrack. We were given water for the first time in five days, but we were still not given any food. We were locked up again in the cars overnight. On September 23, at nine o'clock in the morning, the locomotive slowly backed up our transport toward a gate within the barbed wire fence on which hung a sign: SONDERKOMMANDO.

As soon as the train had passed through the gate, it was shut. Hungry, broken in spirit, we began to get out of the cars. A group of eleven German officers with whips in their hands emerged from a white cottage. Their leader was a stocky, heavy-set German, Oberscharführer Gomerski, a former Berlin boxer. He planted himself in front of us, scrutinized us, and called out:

"Carpenters and cabinetmakers without families—forward!"

About eighty men, most of them prisoners of war, stepped forward. I was one of them. We were forced into a yard fenced off by barbed wire. From there we were led to a barracks with barren bunks and ordered to take our places. All the others in our transport remained on the other side of the fence and we never saw them again.

It was a warm, sunny day. I and several others went out into the yard. As we sat on the wooden logs that were there we began to talk. We talked of our homes, our dear and loved ones. I was from Rostov. I hadn't had any news from my family but I was certain they had been evacuated. Shloime Leitman was from Warsaw. When the Germans attacked the Soviet Union, his wife and children were in Minsk. They had no opportunity to flee and so they perished in the ghetto.

A short, stocky Jew sat down near us. He was about forty years old. He had just returned from work in some other yard. "Where are you from?" he asked me in Yiddish.

Shloime explained to him that I did not understand Yiddish because I was not raised in a Jewish environment. We continued our conversation with Shloime acting as interpreter. I noticed, to the northwest of us, gray columns of smoke rising and disappearing in the distance. The air was full of the sharp smell of something smoldering. "What's burning there?" I asked.

"Don't look in that direction," the Jew replied. "Your comrades' bodies are burning there; the ones who arrived together with you."

I almost fainted. He continued: "You're not the first and not the last. Every other day a transport of 2,000 arrives here, and the camp has been in existence for nearly a year and a half. So figure it out for yourself.

We had Jews from Poland, Czechoslovakia, France, Holland. But until you came we never saw here any Jews from the Soviet Union."

He was an old-time inmate who worked at sorting out the clothing of those who were killed. He was well-informed. From him we learned where our comrades had disappeared and how the whole thing operated.

He spoke simply, as though it were a conversation about ordinary matters, and we, the new arrivals, who had lived through some unusual experiences ourselves, shuddered as we listened to his story.

"As soon as you were separated from them," he said, "they were taken to a second yard where everyone, without exception, must gather. There they are told to lay down their bundles and undress before going to the 'bath.' The women's hair is cut off. Everything is done quietly and efficiently. Then the bareheaded women, wearing only their undergowns, and the children, go first. About a hundred steps behind them go the men, completely naked. All are heavily guarded. There is the 'bath,' " he pointed with his hand, "not far from where you see the smoke. Two buildings are standing there, one for women and children, the other for men. I myself have not seen what it looks like inside, but people who know have described it.

"At a first glance everything looks as a bath should look—faucets for hot and cold water, basins to wash in. . . . As soon as the people enter the doors are clamped shut. A thick, dark substance comes spiraling out from vents in the ceiling. Horrible shrieks are heard but they don't last long. They are soon transformed into gaspings of suffocation and convulsive seizures. Mothers, they say, cover their little ones with their bodies.

"The 'bath' attendant observes the entire procedure through a small pane in the ceiling. In fifteen minutes it is all over. The floors open up and the dead bodies tumble down into small wagons that are standing ready below, in the 'bath's' cellars. The full wagons roll out quickly. Everything is organized in accordance with the last word in German technology. Outside the bodies are laid out in a certain order. They are soaked with gasoline and set aflame. There is where they are burning," he pointed again. "We will also burn. If not tomorrow, then in a week or a month from now. . . ."

Though we were completely exhausted, we couldn't sleep that night.

"Sasha, what will happen?" Shloime, my bunk mate, demanded.

I couldn't tell him anything. I was too depressed to speak. I made believe I was asleep. Before my eyes stood Nellie, a two-year-old girl with curly hair. She was with us on the train. Now I saw her in that horrible 'bath' and it seemed to me that I, too, was there, suffocating together with them.

With these thoughts I dropped off, dreaming of flame, of hands aflame, and of little Nellie in flaming hands. Suddenly the flames changed into galloping horses. On the horses were Germans, chasing after someone. They were chasing after Elotchka, my daughter. There! There! They're catching up with her. . . . Seized with pain and terror, I began to scream. "Sasha, what's the matter? Wake up," I heard Shloime say, and I sat up on my bunk.

Soon after we arrived in Sobibor I began to jot down briefly and in deliberately distorted handwriting the most important events in our daily camp life. It was not until a year later that I deciphered these notes and rounded them out from memory. The first entry is dated September 24, 1943.

SEPTEMBER 24:

We arrived in camp yesterday and today we were roused at five in the morning. Each of us received a cup of hot liquid but no bread. At half-past six we were counted; at six we started out for work. The column was lined up three in a row. The Russian Jews who had arrived yesterday were placed in front of the column. Behind them were the Polish, Czech, and Dutch Jews. Oberscharführer Franz ordered the Russian Jews to sing Russian songs.

"We don't know which songs we're allowed to sing," I said.

The kapo (a prisoner with the status of a policeman) translated my words.

"Sing what you know," Franz replied.

"Sasha, what shall we sing?" Tsibulsky turned to me. He was a Jew from Donbas, tall and with a round face.

"Yesli Zaftra Voina." (If War Comes Tomorrow)

"What's the matter with you? They'll kill us."

"I say sing. We don't know any other songs."

Tsibulsky began:

> "If war comes tomorrow
> Tomorrow we march
> If the evil forces strike—"

All the others chimed in: .

> "United as one
> All the Soviet people
> For their free native land will arise."

The guards came running out of the barracks when our column passed. In this camp of death and despair the Soviet song rang out like a clap of spring thunder. We felt refreshed and exhilarated, as though we had received happy tidings, a promise of victory, and liberation.

We were taken to the so-called "Nord-Camp" which was in the process of being built. Nine barracks were already nearly finished. Some of us were assigned to various carpentry work, the rest were ordered to chop wood. The day passed more or less "smoothly." Only fifteen of us received twenty-five lashes each for not displaying enough zeal in our work. The prisoners had to do their own counting as they were whipped. If they made a mistake, the whipping began all over again.

SEPTEMBER 25:

Today our job was to transfer coal from one place to another. We were given twenty minutes for lunch. Throughout that time Franz stood near the cook, hurrying him on, with frequent proddings of the whip, to dish out more quickly the murky liquid that was called "soup."

Fifteen minutes had already passed and about 300 men had not yet received their rations. At that point Franz ordered the cook to go out into the yard and sit down on the ground. He was to sit erect with his hands straight down and his feet tucked under him. The cook did as he was told. Franz then started to beat the cook with his whip over the head and shoulders, methodically, to the rhythm of some march he was whistling. The body of the unfortunate cook would quiver from time to time. His face was covered with blood. He moaned inaudibly.

We witnessed the execution and had to keep silent. We choked on the bit of soup we swallowed. It tasted as thought it were mixed with blood. Hungry though we were, many spilled it out quietly.

SEPTEMBER 26:

An ordinary day. In the morning we received a cup of boiled water. At noon—a cup of water with moldy barley. In the evening—a piece of bread. About twenty-five men received twenty-five lashes each for various infractions. I was almost one of them. This is how it happened: Forty of our men were busy chopping wood. Hungry, emaciated, exhausted, they raised the heavy axes with great effort and dropped them on the chunky stumps. Franz kept hurrying them on: "Schnell! Schnell!"

Quietly he walked over to one of the Dutch Jews, a tall, skinny man with eyeglasses, and remained standing behind him. The near-sighted eyes apparently saw the stump in front as through a fog. The weakened hands could barely support the ax which fell haphazardly and unevenly on the stump without any prospect of ever completing the work.

Franz let him have one with his whip. The Dutchman moaned with unexpected pain, but did not dare to stop working. He continued hitting away at the stump as best he could, and the German, smiling, continued whipping the Jew over the head to the rhythm of the falling ax. By now the Jew's cap had fallen to the ground.

Franz was taking Gomerski's place who, it was said, rode off somewhere today. He was a pampered, self-indulgent German, very neatly dressed, his hands always gloved, his lips perennially smiling, his eyes, cold as ice.

I was standing nearby and althought I knew that for the interruption in my work I would get the same punishment I still could not control myself and behave as though nothing had happened. Franz noticed that I had stopped chopping. He called out to me: "Komm!" I thought to myself: Now I'm in for it. Well, the only thing to do is to show this low-life that I'm not afraid. I drew myself up erectly and met his sharp contemptuous stare with mine. He pushed aside the Dutch Jew and said to me in broken Russian:

"Russian soldier, you don't like the way I punish this fool? I give you exactly five minutes to split this stump. If you make it you get a pack of cigarettes. If you miss by as much as one second, you get twenty-five lashes."

He smiled again, stepped back a few paces, crooked his arm, and glanced at his wristwatch which was attached to a gold bracelet. I had an urge to seize this well-fed dog by the throat but I controlled myself. While he set the time I tried to figure out how best to tackle that knotty stump.

Franz gave the command: "Begin!"

Suddenly everything was in a haze. It seemed to me that the Fascist's mug lay on that stump. With all my strength and with a genuine hatred I hit it time and again until I nearly smashed the heavy ax. I broke out in a sweat. My back and hands hurt. My temples throbbed. I straightened up with great effort and saw that Franz was handing me a pack of cigarettes. "Four and a half minutes," I heard him say. "I promised so you're getting it."

My better judgment told me: Take it. Don't antagonize the commandant of the camp. You'll pay dearly for this. But I literally couldn't take the gift from this scoundrel's hand. "Thanks, I don't smoke," I said, and resumed working.

Franz went away quietly and returned in about twenty minutes, holding half a roll and a slice of margarine in his hand. His lips smiled as he stared at me penetratingly and coldly with his bulging eyes.

"Russian soldier, take it!"

Never in my life have I faced such a dilemma. I saw the envy in my comrades' eyes as they stared at me and at the commandant's handout. I inhaled the wonderful aroma of the fresh white bread; the amber colored margarine seemed so delicious! It had been such a long time since my palate had tasted such food. . . . But once again, a feeling stronger than logic compelled me to refuse. "Thank you. The rations we are getting satisfy me fully."

Naturally, the German could not let the irony of my reply pass unnoticed. For an instant his usual smile disappeared from his lips. Angry and somewhat confused, he asked: "Don't you want it?"

"Thanks, I'm not hungry."

I saw Franz clench the whip in his hand but he restrained himself, turned abruptly, and left the yard.

As soon as he had disappeared several of our men ran up to me and bombarded me with comments:

"Why didn't you take it?"

"For such a reply he could not only have broken your bones, he could have shot you on the spot."

"You could have caught hell and gotten us into trouble also."

But others said: "Well done."

I was tired. I thought I had done the right thing. We had to end the conversation. Schmidt, the kapo, was advancing toward us. All quickly went back to their places.

SEPTEMBER 27:

We were working, as on previous days, in the area of the Nord-Camp. Around ten in the morning I was approached by Kalimali (one of my comrades from the first transport, a young fellow from Baku, whose real name was Shubayev). He said to me: "Sasha, did you notice it? All the Germans are gone and only the kapo remained. What do you think this means?"

"I don't know," I said, "but as long as they're not here let's have a look around. It'll come in handy. You find out where the guards are stationed and when they change."

In the meantime one of the Polish Jews came over and said quietly: "A new transport has arrived."

Something tore at my heart.

"Where is the 'bath'?" I asked.

"Over there, behind that barracks. A little over a hundred yards from here. You see the high wire fence camouflaged with branches near the guards' booths at the corners? That's where it is." With shovels in hand we stood and looked in that direction. We didn't see any motion. All was quiet. But we continued to look and wait.

Suddenly we heard a horrifying cry from a woman, from many women, and children wailing, "Mama! . . . Ma . . ." The cries sounded like those in a nightmare from which one cannot awaken. Presently the frantic honking of frightened geese mingled with the human cries. Later we learned that three hundred geese were kept in the yard and that for the duration of the "bath" they were chased around so that their honking would drown out the shrieks of the people.

I felt as though I were paralyzed with fear. Not the fear of death. I was too stunned for that. What frightened me was the consciousness of my helplessness. I decided that something must be done! It was a decision born out of my fear.

Shloime Leitman and Boris Tsibulsky came up to me. Both were shaken and pale. Tsibulsky said, "Sasha, we must run from here. It is a little over two hundred yards to the woods. The Germans are now occupied. We can waylay the guards at the fence with our axes."

I replied, "We, perhaps, may succeed in running away. But what will happen with the others? They will all be finished off at once. If the plan is to run away, then we must all run together. Not a single one of us must remain here. Some will no doubt perish, but those who will survive will take revenge."

"You are right," Tsibulsky said, "but we must not delay too long. Winter is approaching. Footsteps leave marks on the snow. Generally it is more difficult to remain for too long in the woods in wintertime."

"If you trust me," I said, "wait and keep quiet. Don't mention a word of this to anyone. When the time comes, I'll tell you what to do."

I knew many of the Sobibor inmates quite well from the time when we were together at the camp in Minsk. I was especially friendly with Shloime Leitman, a cabinetmaker from Warsaw, a Communist. In Poland he had spent several years in prison. After the events of 1939 he came to Minsk. A man of medium height, skinny, and with deep-set eyes, he possessed both an inner drive and a keen native intelligence. He had an excellent way with people and could influence them with his talk. They trusted him and in time of need sought his advice. More than once we had talked of plans to escape and to make our way to the partisans. But now it was a matter of a mass escape. This was a serious undertaking which had to be thoroughly thought out and carefully prepared.

The arrival of Soviet prisoners of war created a big stir in camp. The inmates knew that somewhere a battle was being waged against the enemy and we, though it was a long time since we had been at the front, were battle-tried and had brought with us the breath of that struggle. They regarded us with curiosity and hope. They listened to what we said. They knew that among us there must be people who would take the initiative to act, and they expected these people to come forward.

From my talks with the old camp inmates and from my own observations I already had a general picture of the organizational layout of the camp. The section where our barracks stood was called Camp I. On these grounds were also located the tailors' and shoemakers' workshops, the cabinetmakers' shop, the smithy, and the kitchen. Further up was Camp II where the belongings of the murdered victims were sorted out, and the warehouses. Still further, and quite a distance to a side, stood Camp III with its gas chambers. And way up, at the very end was the Nord-Camp.

Later I found out where the arsenal, the sentries' quarters, and the garage were located; where the officers' quarters were and generally everything that was important to know. In addition to the large fence that surrounded the entire camp territory all other parts of the camp and all entrances were fenced off with barbed wire.

Later, when I was already free, in 1944, I heard reports from other Sobibor survivors. I believe it would be of interest to relate some parts of those reports. They may add important details to the general picture of the camp and may shed additional light on our escape.

Ber Feinberg, a Warsaw wigmaker, who spent seventeen months in Sobibor recounted the following:

"I worked in Camp II where the warehouses were located. As soon as those condemned to death had undressed we gathered up their belongings and took them to the warehouses: footwear separate, clothing separate, and so on. There we sorted out the things, packed them, and sent them off to Germany. Every day a trainload of ten cars filled with clothing, shoes, and sacks of women's hair left Sobibor for Germany. Photographs, documents, and other papers, as well as articles of lesser importance, we burned. When no one was watching we would throw into the fire money and jewelry which we found in the victims' pockets so that they would not fall into the hands of the Germans.

"Later I was transferred to other work. In Camp II three barracks were erected especially for women. In the first they took off their shoes, in the second their clothes, and in the third their hair was cut off. Being a wigmaker I was assigned to the third barracks. We were twenty wigmakers and we all cut the womens' hair and stuffed it into sacks. The Germans told the women that their hair was cut for hygienic reasons.

"While I was in Camp II I had the opportunity to observe many things. I witnessed the arrival of a transport from Bialystok made up entirely of naked people. The Germans apparently took this precaution to make sure that no one escaped. Throughout the journey they received neither food nor water. The dead in the transport were mingled together with the living. People were still conscious and breathing when they were covered with chloroformed lime. That was in June, 1943.

"Oh, what atrocities the SS committed! They stamped on small children and smashed their skulls with their boots! They sicked their dogs on defenseless people. The dogs tore chunks of flesh from their bodies! When someone became ill, the Germans did away with him at once.

"None of us was admitted to that part of Camp III where the 'bath' was located. But the camp inmates knew what was going on there. Reports reached us through various ways.

"One day the following incident occurred. When the people were already in the 'bath,' something went wrong with the apparatus supplying the gas. The victims broke down the door and started to run out. The SS killed some of them in the yard; the rest were driven back in again. The mechanic repaired the machine and everything proceeded according to schedule.

"On a sunny summer day an eighteen-year-old girl from Wlashov, as she was led to her death, cried out loud enough for the whole camp to hear: 'We shall be avenged. The Russians will come and you, bandits, will pay dearly for everything!' She was clubbed to death.

"One day a young Dutch Jew, while sorting the belongings of new arrivals in the warehouse, recognized the clothing of his own kin. He ran out into the yard and there, in the crowd of people being led to their death, he saw his entire family."

During the few days that we had been here, we had obtained a fairly clear picture of what the camp was like, but what interested me most was what we could do in order to escape.

On September 28 at lunchtime, Shloime was approached by the Jew who, on the day of our arrival, had told us about the camp.

"Sholem Aleichem. How is the work going?"

"So-so. Like a clock, you wind it up, it runs. There goes the first whistle. Time to get ready."

"Wait a minute. I must have a talk with your friend."

"Which one?"

"The one who doesn't understand Yiddish. Bring him this evening to the women's barracks."

"Why the women's barracks?"

"He's a handsome young man. Why shouldn't he spend a little time with our women?"

The second whistle blew and we all went back to our places.

During work Shloime whispered to me, "Ask for permission to go to the latrine right after me." I did so. There he told me of the talk he had with the Jew from Camp II.

"The girls are eager to meet you," Shloime said.

"Ah, let them go to the devil."

"And I think it's important. I don't think it was just idle talk."

"Who is he?"

"They say he's a tailor. His name is Baruch."

"All right. We'll go together."

That evening we went to the women's barracks. One hundred and fifty Jewish women and girls from various countries lived in that barracks. As soon as we entered, they surrounded us and we were deluged with questions about the Soviet Union and the front: Who were we? When would the war end? Who would win? We told them all we knew—how the Red Army drove the Germans from the outskirts of Moscow; how they routed them at Stalingrad; how they battered them at Kursk. We told them that the Red Army was already approaching the Dnieper and continued to advance.

"They say there are partisans in Russia who are continually harassing the Germans. Is it true?" one of them asked.

"It's true. The Germans, for instance, would not dare leave Minsk in less than ten vehicles, armed with machine guns and hand grenades. In the outskirts of Minsk, railway transports were being blown up nightly."

They listened with bated breath. For those who didn't understand Russian, Shloime translated into Yiddish. They translated for each other into German and Dutch.

"Tell me," a trembling voice came from a corner, "if there are so many partisans, why don't they attack our camp?"

"The partisans have their tasks. No one can do our work for us."

Baruch did not come. It was getting time to leave, so we said goodby and left.

On September 29, at 6 in the morning, all of the 600 men and women who were in the camp were lined up in columns and marched off to the interior railway line. There eight large platforms stood laden with bricks. We were ordered to unload them. We each had to take a load of 6 to 8 bricks, run with it a distance of over 200 yards, put it down on a designated spot, and quickly run back.

Near each platform, as well as all along the way, stood German overseers. They whipped us for the slightest mistake. Everything had to be done running. There were pushing and crowding. Each platform was worked by 70 to 75 men. They stepped on each other's toes. Anyone who failed to catch the brick as it was tossed to him and let it drop was given twenty-five lashes. Anyone who tarried a moment was whipped. The air continually resounded with the cracking of whips. Panting for breath, soaked with perspiration, eyes glazed, we ran with the bricks. In a matter of fifty minutes the platforms were empty. We were immediately lined up in a column and led away. The Germans were in a hurry. A transport of new victims waited behind the fence.

Eighty of us were taken to the Nord-Camp. There we were divided into two groups. Forty were put to work chopping wood; the rest, Shloime and myself among them, were ordered to work in the barracks. Before very long someone from the outside came in and announced: "We are escaping right now."

"How? Who said so?"

"We talked it over. There are only five guards now. We'll waylay them and make for the woods."

So irresponsible a step could only bring harm. I tried to convince the fellow why it should not be done. "It's easy to say," I said. "But the guards are not bunched together in one group. You kill one and another one will open fire on you. And with what will you cut the wire fence? And how will you cross the mine field? If you should tarry for just a few minutes the Germans will catch up with you. Perhaps some of you will succeed in breaking through, but what about those who work in the barracks? They know nothing about this, but they will certainly be shot. You say it's easy to escape. I don't know if it's that easy. But I think that with the proper preparation one can accomplish more even under difficult conditions than one can by acting precipitously under more favorable conditions. You can do what you like: I will not interfere with you, but neither will I join you."

It seemed that my words had the desired effect. They all returned to their work.

In the evening I met with Baruch. He began by saying that what I had said in the women's barracks the other night—no one can do our work for us—had made a deep impression on the women and that they understood the meaning of those words. But that nearby there had been standing a tall, skinny man, one eye always slightly closed, perhaps I had noticed him. "He is the kapo Brzecki, a vile creature. One has to be on guard against him."

"I have no reason to be on guard," I said, "because I do not intend to do anything other than what I am told."

"I can understand why you answer me that way," Baruch said. "We must, nevertheless, have a talk. Not so long ago Franz dropped a hint that Hitler had issued a decree to spare a certain percentage of Jews and that we, the laborers of this camp, were included in this percentage. And imagine, there are among us some fools who believe this! I understand you are up to something, but did you stop to consider what might happen to all of us if you should escape? The Germans cannot afford to have the secret of this extermination camp broadcast. As soon as one demonstrates that escape is posible, they will liquidate all of us at once. That is clear."

"Tell me," I asked, "have you been long in this camp?"

"Close to a year."

"So you, too, believe the Germans will not kill you. And I believe it as much as you do. What makes you think I am planning to escape?"

"Don't run off," Baruch held my arm. "Wait a minute. You wonder why we haven't escaped till now. So I'll tell you. We had thought about it more than once, but we didn't know how. You are a Soviet man, a military man. Take over. Tell us what to do and we'll do it. I can understand your misgivings. We hardly know each other. But be it as it may, we must talk it over. In the name of a group I come to tell you: We trust you. Act."

I looked at him as he stood before me. He was not a tall man but compact, with a clever, open face. I liked him.

"Anyway," I said, "I thank you for warning me against Brzecki. You are long in this camp. Would you, perhaps, know how the field behind the fence is mined? How thick and in what order?"

As it turned out, the camp inmates had dug the holes and Baruch was able to supply some valuable information about the field mines. We arranged that future contact between us would be made through Shloime.

After that I went to see the women.

The barracks dwellers sat on the lower bunks together with the "Easterners" (that's how we, who came from the Soviet Union, were called by the camp inmates). They were hungry, exhausted from hard labor, their bodies bruised from the whippings; they were doomed to death. But it sufficed to have a brief rest, a few peaceful moments, and one's spirit rose again. Especially here, in the company of women, backs straightened out, eyes sparkled, laughter was heard, and wherever you turned a lively discussion was in progress.

And what were they discussing here? They talked about the war and its prospects; about countries and cities; about science and technology; about the theatre, music, and literature; about the contradictions of human nature and about the future of humanity; here they sang, cried, and kissed; here the feelings of love and jealousy came into play; all the emotions that set the human heart aglow and quicken its pulse beat found expression here.

Yesterday I noticed a young girl in the barracks, with cropped chestnut hair. Her whole being exuded confidence. She was Dutch. I didn't know how we would communicate, but it occurred to me that this might even be an advantage in the beginning. I'd be sitting near her and still feel free to speak to others on whatever subject was necessary. Now Shloime and I walked up to her and we became acquainted. I spoke in Russian, she in German, Shloime in Yiddish. With his help we were able to conduct a conversation. Often this led to comical misunderstandings which evoked quite a bit of laughter from us and those who sat near us.

From then on we met every evening. The girl's name was Luka. Gradually we learned how to communicate with each other. From the meaning of a single word she would surmise what I wanted to say. Although she was still very young, she had lived through much.

Several difficult days had passed during which two new transports had arrived with more victims. Again the honking of the geese. One evening I was sitting with Luka outside on a heap of wooden boards. She smoked a lot.

"How old are you, Luka?" I asked.

"Eighteen."

"And I'm thirty-five. You could have been my daughter. You must obey me."

"Good. I shall."

"Then stop smoking. It makes me unhappy."

"I can't stop. Nerves. You know what it means?"

"In Russian it's also called nerves. It's not the nerves; it's the bad habit."

"Don't say that, Sasha. Do you know where I work? In the yard where the rabbits are. It is fenced off with a wooden fence. Through the cracks, you can see the naked men, women, and children as they are led to Camp III. I look and shake as in a fever, but I cannot turn my eyes from the sight. At times some call out, "Where are they taking us?" As though they knew that someone was listening and could answer their question. I tremble and remain silent. Cry out? Tell them they are being led to their death? Will it be of any help to them? On the contrary, like this, at least, they go without crying, without screaming, without humiliating themselves before their murderers. But it is so horrible, Sasha, so horrible!"

That evening Luka told me that she was not Dutch; she was a German Jew. They had lived in Hamburg. Her father was a Communist. When Hitler came to power her father's arrest was ordered, but he went into hiding. The Nazis beat her mother and demanded that she tell them where her husband was. Luka was threatened that she too would be beaten if she would not reveal her father's hiding place. She cried but she knew she must not say anything about her father and the people who used to visit them. Later they escaped to Holland. They had a short-wave radio.

In the evening people would visit her father and they tuned in on Moscow. When the Germans invaded Holland, her father had to escape again. She, her mother, and her two brothers were arrested and transported to Sobibor. Both brothers were killed. She and her mother were working.

"Tell me, Sasha, will this place be the end of our lives?"

On October 7, during a game of chess with Baruch, I told him through Shloime that I had to talk to him about something. We talked while playing. I was interested in the organization of the guards. Baruch gave me detailed information about this. I also asked him whether he knew of any reliable people working in the tailors', shoemakers', and cabinet-makers' shops in Camp II.

"Just tell me what, when, and where, and it shall be done," was Baruch's reply.

"I have a plan which we shall not discuss at present. The cabinet-makers' shop is about five yards away from the wire fence. What I want to tell you about now is the alternate plan in case the original one falls through. The three rows of wire take up four yards. The mine field occupies fifteen yards. Add an additional four yards past the mine field. Figure seven yards inside the cabinet workers' shop up to the stove. Altogether we have about thirty-five yards. We must dig a tunnel and begin from the stove. We must dig eighty centimeters deep, not more and not less. Above this height lie the mines, thirty centimeters deep. Below that we will strike water. If we dig 75/75 we'll shovel out twenty cubic meters of soil. The dug-up earth will have to be hidden, as much of it as possible, beneath the floor of the shop. In the course of the work we'll seek out other places to dispose of the earth. The digging must be done at night We must pick from among ourselves a specialist who would guard against digging too high, too low, or too much to one side. Under our conditions, digging twenty cubic meters should take from twelve to fifteen days.

"What are the drawbacks of this plan? I'm afraid that from eleven at night till dawn will not be sufficient time for 600 people to crawl, one behind the other, a distance of thirty-five yards. Because it is not a matter of just these thirty-five yards. It is important to get as far beyond them as possible, unnoticed. We must also bear in mind that in the course of the hours it will take to cover this distance fights may flare up. Everyone will want to be the first in line. On the other hand, those who believe Hitler's promise to spare their lives will hesitate to take the risk now. That is why I beg you to consider it carefully and consult with the others."

"All right. And what is your original plan?"

"I still have to think it through. It includes an attack on the German officers in charge of the camp. In the meantime I would like you to gather about seventy sharp knives or razors. I'll distribute them among the strong fellows. In case the plan fails we should at least have some weapons in our hands. Also, it is vital that Shloime and I should be assigned to work in the cabinetmaker's shop. From there it will be easier to observe things and do what is necessary."

"Good. Whatever is possible will be done. But I must tell you something. In our group there is Manny who is with the gang of young fellows who work on the barracks. Their kapo, Genick, approached him about being included. He said he wants to escape together with everybody. Naturally, Manny told him that he didn't know a thing. Personally Manny is of the opinion that it is all right to include the kapos, though Brzecki is a bastard."

"What did you tell Manny?"

"I told him that without you I cannot make any decision."

"Naturally, it would be to our benefit if the kapos were with us. The Germans trust them and they move about the camp more freely. But who knows whether they're not trying to worm their way in in order to betray us?"

Shloime said, "We'll tell you how we feel about the kapos some other time. Right now it's time to leave."

On October 8 a new transport arrived. In the morning Janek, the foreman of the cabinetmakers' shop, pulled three people out of the column for his shop. Two of the three were Shloime and myself. In the evening Baruch handed over to Shloime forty big, well-sharpened knives.

In the morning of October 9 Grisha received twenty-five lashes for chopping wood in a sitting position. This was a bad morning all around. By noontime about thirty people had been whipped.

In the evening Kalimali came running to us in a very agitated state. "You're asleep," he said, "and eight people are getting ready to escape today. They want me to join them. Whatever you plan to do, do it quickly."

"Are you out of your mind? Whose idea is this? Where is he?"

"It is Grisha's idea. He's in the women's barracks."

"I'm going there at once."

There were many people in the barracks. I immediately went over to Luka, took her by the hand, and asked her to come out and sit with me in the yard for a while. But leaving was not so simple. I was surrounded and besieged with questions: What was new? What would happen?

"I know as much as you do," I replied. And to Grisha I said, "Go out into the yard for a while. Luka wants to talk to you."

As soon as Luka and I had sat down in the yard Grisha arrived. "You wanted to see me, Luka," he said. "Do you have to tell me something?"

She looked at him surprised.

"It's not she," I said. "I have to talk to you. Kalimali says you are preparing to escape."

"Join us."

"How are you planning to do it?"

"Very simple. The area near the latrine is poorly lighted. There we'll cut the wire, crawl quietly through, waylay the guards and disappear."

"Very simple, you say. But supposing you are already on the other side, did you stop to think about those who will remain behind? As soon as you escape, the Germans will immediately finish off the rest."

"And who is to blame for that? Why are they sitting around, doing nothing?"

"Did you propose any plan to them?"

"I'm not long in camp. Why have they waited until now?"

"Listen, Grisha," I said. "Drop your plan. People are already working on this thing. Don't interfere."

"Who is working on it, you maybe?" he asked derisively.

"Maybe I."

"Where are you working on it? Here, with her on these boards?"

I tried to keep calm. "Cut out that tone," I said to him. "If you wish, I'll put you down on the leaders' list. You'll get an assignment. At the present that is all I can tell you."

"We're not waiting. We're leaving today."

"If that's the case," I said, "I'll talk to you altogether differently. You would be right if nobody did anything. But the preparations are practically completed. It's only a matter of days. The plan is to take out *all* the people. Do you, and your little group, want to destroy the plan, spit on everybody, because you think that you and your friends will succeed in your escape? No. That will not do. I'm warning you. I'll place lookouts all over. And if necessary . . ."

"What will you do, kill me?"

"If necessary, yes."

"In that case I have nothing to say to you," Grisha announced. He turned around and left.

I asked Luka to wait in the yard while I went back to the barracks. There I told Shloime briefly of my conversation with Grisha and ordered him to immediately post a strong fellow near the latrine to keep an eye on the fence. If he noticed any activity, he should inform us at once. Then I went back to Luka.

"Sasha, what did you talk to Grisha about?" Luka asked.

"Oh, nothing."

"It's not true. You had a heated quarrel. And what about your talks with all the others while you're sitting near me? You think I don't understand? I understand. You're using me for a cover-up. Yes, yes, that's clear."

"Well, all right. Let us say that it is so. But aren't you the daughter of a Communist? And didn't you yourself say you wished you could tear the Germans to pieces?"

"Yes. But I'm afraid, Sasha. What if the plan fails? Then they'll drive us all into Camp III. Oh, how I wish we could escape from here. But that's impossible, impossible . . ."

She trembled as she kept repeating, "Why us? Why don't they let us live? . . . Why? . . ."

I quieted and soothed her. "Luka," I pleaded, "promise me that you'll not utter a single word to anyone about what we've talked here."

"When I was a child," she said with resentment, "only eight years old, the police tortured me to make me tell them where Father was hiding and I kept silent. And now . . . Yes, you, Sasha . . ." With tears in her eyes Luka ran back to her barracks.

OCTOBER 10:

In the morning before work, we noticed standing at the gate of Camp I an unfamiliar officer with a bandaged hand. One of the old-timers said that this was Greischutz, the chief of the guards, who had returned from furlough. On the way to Germany he was wounded in an attack by our planes. His left hand was still not healed.

Tsibulsky proposed that when Franz ordered us to sing we should strike up the "March of the Fliers," and thus welcome Greischutz.

"Good," I said, "but all must join in."

And that's how it was. Oberscharführer Franz took a quick count of us, gave the command to march and ordered the Russians to start singing. Tsibulsky winked to us and began singing:

"We were born to make a fairy tale come true."

And just as we passed the gate all of us came in with:

"Always higher, and higher and higher
We strive to match the flight of our birds."

Greischutz apparently knew the Soviet fliers' song well. He felt it in his bones, so to speak. He was seething with rage. His eyes became bloodshot, his mouth twisted. He ran up to us and began to beat the singers over their heads with his whip. We turned our heads from the whip's range as far as possible and continued to walk and sing. Franz observed the scene and laughed. Then he walked over to Greischutz and tried to calm him with a smile. In the meantime the column continued on its way. Tsibulsky said quietly, "He caught it from our fliers more than we from him." We struck up a new song.

In the evening Shloime invited me to the smithy to listen to a record player which was brought from the guards for repair. Among the several inmates that were there was the kapo Brzecki. Someone had found among the things in Camp II several Soviet records. Now we played them. Naturally, if we were caught listening to records, we would be beaten mercilessly. But that was our life in camp, always on the edge of death. The blacksmith, Reiman, was baking pancakes made of flour and he sprinkled them with sugar.

"Where do you get sugar and flour?" Shloime asked.

"It all comes from Camp II. You always find some foodstuffs among the things sorted out after each transport. So we quietly take some for ourselves."

Brzecki made room for me so that I could sit next to him. "Eat," he said, pushing the plate of pancakes closer to me and Shloime.

"Thanks, but I can't eat it," Shloime said.

"And what do you think our usual meals are made of? The same things. The Germans are not going to spend money on food for us."

"The usual meal is something else. Then again, maybe you're right, but we're not used to it so we find it hard to take. Excuse us." And in order to put an end to this unpleasant conversation I began to tell them about the various records I had heard. Brzecki made several attempts at saying something but somehow failed to make himself understood. Finally he winked at the blacksmith, hinting that the record player be taken to the locksmith's shop which was in a nearby room. Reiman took the player and we all got up.

"Come, Sasha," Shloime said.

"He'll come along soon," Brzecki replied.

In the locksmith's shop I noticed someone standing by the window throughout the time and looking out into the yard. I thought to myself: So the kapo is also afraid.

"I would like to have a talk with you," Brzecki began. "You probably guess about what."

"What makes you think so?"

"And why are you so afraid that I may guess?"

"Unfortunately," I said, "I find it difficult to communicate with you because I understand neither Yiddish nor Polish."

"But with Luka you have no difficulty at all. So this is hardly an excuse. I understand Russian; I speak it badly, but if you want to, you'll understand me."

"Why shouldn't I want to, and why the caustic remarks?"

"I beg you not to interrupt me. Hear me out and then you can give me your reply. There is something stirring lately in Camp. The people are restless."

"They have good reason to be restless."

"Yes, but until you came it was not so noticeable. It is clear that you are getting ready for something. To put it to you plainly, you are preparing for an escape."

"It is easy to accuse. What proof have you?"

"You are doing it very carefully. You avoid gatherings. You don't carry on any big discussions. You spend the evenings with Luka. Luka is a good cover-up. I understand that several days ago you tossed out a remark in the barracks, 'No one will do our work for us.' It was repeated all over after that, and commented on. If I had wanted to I could have had you killed for these few words alone. But as you see I didn't do it. I know you have a very low opinion of me and I will not now try to defend myself. You need not tell me anything; I know it all. You yourself are not talking about it to anybody, but that little one, Shloime I believe his name is, that clever fellow, does all the talking for you. You are sleeping next to one another and you have the opportunity to talk things over. I know but I'm not informing on you and I don't intend to."

When Brzecki fell silent I said to him, "Continue, I'm listening."

"Sasha," he said, "I propose that you make me a partner in this undertaking. Together we'll carry it through much easier and more efficiently. We, the kapos, have the possibility, during worktime, to move about freely through all the camps except Camp III. We can talk with whomever we have to without arousing suspicion. Just think how useful we could be to you. You may ask why do I propose this to you? Very simple. Because I don't believe the Germans. Franz makes all kinds of rosy promises to us. We have privileges, but when the time comes to liquidate the camp we'll find ourselves standing next to you. They'll kill us too. That is clear."

"It is good that you understand this," I said, "but why approach me about it?"

"Because you are the leader. As you see, I already know this. So why waste time on unnecessary talk? We want to help you. We want to go with you."

"Who is the 'we'?"

"I and the kapo Genick."

"And Schmidt?"

"He could betray."

I had observed Brzecki more than once. His jacket wide open, his cap at a jaunty angle, his eyes squinting, he would strut about in the camp as though he owned it. The whip always in his hand, he didn't hesitate to use it on the inmates. If he had his eye on one of the girls, he pestered her until she yielded. Still, no one could say that he had ever informed on anyone to the Germans.

"Tell me," I asked unexpectedly, "could you kill a German?"

He hesitated a moment then said, "If it were vital to the plan, yes."

"And if it were not vital. I mean wantonly, just as they kill thousands of our brothers and sisters. Could you do it?"

He fell silent. "Hard to tell," he finally said, "I never gave it any thought."

"Well, time to go to sleep," I said. "Good night." Thus I ended the conversation and went back to my barracks.

It was clear that the kapos could be of much use to us. The question was: Could they be trusted? Brzecki became thoughtful when I asked him if he could kill a German. A traitor would have replied at once that he was ready to do anything. Beyond this, who the devil knew what he had in mind? It is difficult to fathom the human soul.

That night Shloime and I went to sleep very late. There was much to talk about.

OCTOBER 11:

In the morning we suddenly heard horrible screams and shooting from automatic rifles. Soon thereafter came a command that no one was to leave the workshops. The Camp I gates were shut. The number of guards was increased everywhere. The screaming and the shooting were heard more frequently.

"What do you think happened?" Shloime asked. "It seems to me that the shooting comes from the Nord-Camp. Maybe the fellows there couldn't control themselves and escaped."

"No, it's not from there. The shooting comes from closer by, somewhere in Camp II. I hear women screaming. A new transport has probably arrived. But why the shooting?"

It lasted for some time. Then it grew quiet. It was not until five in the evening that we learned what had happened. A new transport had arrived. When the people were already undressed, they realized where they were being taken and began to run, naked. But where was there to run? They were already in camp and fenced in on all sides. So they ran toward the barbed wire fence. There they were met by a hail of bullets from the

automatic rifles. Many fell dead on the spot. The rest were led away to
the gas chambers.

This time the fires crackled until late into the night. The flames shot
fiercely upward to the black fall sky. The terrifying blaze lighted up the
entire camp and cast its awesome reflection on the distant outlying areas.
Dumb with horror we looked at the fires where our tortured sisters' and
brothers' bodies burned.

OCTOBER 12:

I shall never forget that day. Eighteen of our camp inmates had been
sick for several days. In the morning a group of Germans, led by Franz,
barged into the barracks. Franz ordered the sick to rise at once. It was
clear they were being taken to their death. One of the eighteen was a
young man from Holland. He could hardly stand on his feet. His wife
found out where they were taking her husband.

She threw herself at the Germans, screaming, "Murderers! I know
where you're taking my husband. Take me with him. I will not, you hear,
I will not live without him. Murderers! Scum!" She took her husband's
arm, supporting him, and marched off with the others to her death.

At lunchtime I arranged with Shloime that we call a meeting with a
small group of people for nine o'clock that evening. The meeting was held
at the cabinetmakers' shop at which were present Baruch, Shloime, Janek,
the head of the cabinetmakers' brigade; Juzef, the head of the tailors; the
shoemaker, Jakub; Manny, myself, and two others.

In the yard and at the gate of Camp I lookouts were posted to warn
us in case we had to scatter.

First I gave a report of my talk with Brzecki and asked the comrades
to express themselves on whether he should be taken into our group. The
general opinion was that it could and should be done. Manny left and
returned soon with Brzecki.

"Brzecki," I said, "we have decided to invite you to our meeting. I
think you are aware of the responsibility you are taking upon yourself by
coming here. If we fail, you will be among the first to be killed."

"I understand," Brzecki replied. "You needn't worry."

"So, comrades," I said, "my plan is as follows: First we must do away
with the officer group that administers the camp. Naturally, one by one,
and without the slightest sound. But it has to be in a short time. I figure
in the course of one hour, not longer. In less time we won't manage to
do it, and if it takes longer there is the great danger that they might become aware that one of them is missing and sound the alarm. The task
of killing the German officers will be assigned to people selected from
our Soviet prisoners of war whom I know personally and on whom we

can depend. It is clear that such a task must be entrusted to people of courage and resolution, people who will be firm and unwavering. One moment of vacillation, one failure, and we're all done for.

"At half-past three in the afternoon the kapo Brzecki will, on some excuse, take three people whom I'll point out to him, to Camp II. These three will kill the four Hitlerites who are working there. Baruch must see to it that the officers come individually into the room where it will be possible to carry out the execution. Baruch must also make sure that from the moment the execution of the Hitlerites begins no one is allowed to leave the camp. If anyone should try to create a tumult, he must at once be silenced or killed. The operation in Camp II must be completed by four o'clock.

"At four o'clock people especially assigned for that task will cut the telephone wires connecting Camp II with the guard reserves. The wires must be cut at both ends and hidden in order to delay repairs.

"At that very moment the killing of the officers in our camp will commence. The officers should be invited individually to the workshops. In each shop there will be two people to carry out the execution. By half-past four it must be all over.

"At half-past four Brzecki and Genick will line up the inmates as though they were taking them to work and the column will be heading toward the exit. In the first row will be our Easterners. They will attack the weapons arsenal. The others will continue going and cover the attack. Those who will have seized weapons will catch up with the column, run beyond it, remove the guards at the gate, and attack the watchtower.

"It's quite possible that the guards will become aware of this before the anticipated time, cut off our path to the gate and open fire on us from the two machine guns they have there. In that case, if we have succeeded in arming ourselves, we'll engage them in battle. But just in case this doesn't come off, we must be ready with an alternate plan.

"Not far from the cabinetmakers' shop, very close to the wire fence, stands the officers' house. We must assume that even if the strip of field nearby is mined, it is mined with signal mines which are not dangerous. Right there, behind the officers' house, the wire fence must be hacked through. Those in the front lines will hurl stones as they advance. Where the stones fall, the mines will explode. Thus the way will be at least partially cleared of mines.

"This is the plan. Shloime and I have thought it through more than once. We see no other alternatives. Now let each of you consider carefully whether you'll be able to carry through the task assigned to you. Tomorrow evening we will meet again. And remember, comrades, not a word to anyone. Neither to wife, brother, nor friend may you utter a single word of what was here decided."

There were no discussions. We left the meeting one at a time.

I noticed that in the last several days the guards were given more than their usual amount of ammunition, five rounds apiece. Also, when they changed guards they passed on the ammunition to each other. From this one could conclude that the guards outside the watchtower carried no ammunition on them. I wanted to check this and so I arranged with Brzecki that tomorrow I be sent to the guards' barracks for some repairs.

On October 13, at ten in the morning, a request came to the cabinet-makers' shop that someone be sent to the guards' barracks to repair the doors. Janek picked me for the job.

First I walked through all the sections of the barracks and examined all the doors. I entered a room with no one in it, closed the door as though I were testing it, and quickly opened one of the closets. In the corner stood a rifle. I looked into its chamber. There was no ammunition. The ammunition-clip on the shelf was also empty. It was the same in a second closet.

When I returned to the cabinetmakers' shop, I went up to the attic. From there one had a good view of the area on the other side of the fence. To the left of the camp gates was the railroad, behind it the station and then the woods. To the right, about five hundred yards away, another woods. Wooden blocks lay scattered on the road. On the opposite side Poles were working, transporting wood. It was clear that the escape route would have to be to the right.

That evening we made a decision: Tomorrow, October 14, we escape.

October 14 was a clear, sunny day. The night before we distributed the knives that had been gathered and a number of hatchets which the blacksmith made to order for us, small enough to be hidden under a coat. Those who especially needed warm clothing received it. Only the leaders knew when and how we would escape.

I worked in a section of the cabinetmakers' shop. Through the windows one could see the entire yard of Camp I. In the nearby barracks worked Shloime and an especially selected group of twenty men. They had made the dugouts. It was arranged beforehand that at four o'clock Unter-scharführer Berg would come to the tailor shop for a fitting of his uniform which he had ordered. At a quarter after four the chief of the camp guards would come there for the same purpose. The chief of Camp III, Goettinger, and Oberscharführer Greischutz were to come at four o'clock to the shoemakers' shop. And Franz was to come to my barracks to look over the closets. At that very time Unterscharführer Friedrich

Haulstich was to examine Shloime's work. Baruch was responsible for getting four officers into Camp II. The rest were to be invited to workshops on one pretext or another.

All the men who had to carry out the assassinations worked with Shloime that day. He sent them individually to me and I gave each of them his assignment. Kalimali was the first to arrive. His real name, as I have already said, was Shubayev. In 1940 he graduated from the University of Rostov as a transport engineer. He was a tall, slender fellow of about twenty-five, with black, somewhat curly hair. Not very talkative, simple and strong—a good comrade.

"With you I don't have to waste any words," I said to him. "You and Benny will go to the tailor shop. Take along a plane, a chisel, and a hatchet. Remember, it has to be done in such a way that he shouldn't utter a sound."

"That's clear."

"Well, go. I wish you success."

We shook hands silently and he left. I asked him to send in Tsibulsky.

Tsibulsky hailed from Donbas. He was a drayman, a big strong man of about thirty-five, a good-natured, jolly fellow but somewhat of a blabbermouth. We had to keep many things from him, but whatever he undertook to do he carried through.

"Boris," I said to him, "you and I did time together in the cellar. I know you better than anyone else. You are getting the most difficult assignment. Benny and Michael will accompany you. Brzecki will come for you and take you to Camp II to Baruch. Take along the hatchets. Keep in mind, Boris, that yours will be the first blow. It'll have to give courage to all the others. If any of the other fellows going with you gets scared, put another one in his place. No one should be compelled to do this."

"You can be at ease, Sasha; all are awaiting the signal."

"And don't forget to remove the pistols from the dead ones. Go, do it right."

"It has to be done right."

At two o'clock Unterscharführer Walter Ryba came to Camp I, took Brzecki and three others and led them away. This upset us terribly. The Unterscharführer was armed with an automatic whereas ordinarily prisoners being taken to work were not guarded with automatics. What had happened?

We associated this with an episode that had taken place an hour earlier and it only heightened our apprehensions. In the morning Janek had put on his best suit, figuring that since he would not be able to take anything with him when he escaped he might as well try to salvage his most valuable possession. Franz had noticed him and said, "Is there going to be a wedding here? Why are you so dressed up?"

I ran immediately to the cabinetmakers' shop to see Janek. "I want you to find out at once where they took Brzecki," I said to him.

"How?"

"That's your business. You're the brigadier. You can move about more freely here than I can."

A whole hour passed in nerve-racking tension. We were stunned. At three o'clock the kapo, Genick, came to me and told me that Brzecki was taken to the Nord-Camp to pile up wood with the others. Since he was not accompanied by a guard, the Unterscharführer took along an automatic.

"Do you know," I asked, "that Brzecki was supposed to have taken several people into Camp II?"

"I know."

"Now you will take them."

"That is impossible. I have no right to get in there."

"You must. You'll say that Brzecki's not around and something has to be done there. Think up some excuse."

"We had better postpone it till tomorrow when Brzecki will be here."

It was clear, however, that the plan could not be delayed for even a single day. Although preparations were being made within a close group everyone sensed that something was about to happen soon. There was proof enough of this. During those days Yom Kippur came. Orthodox Jews prayed, pleaded with God. Some had said, "Don't plead with God, plead with Sasha . . . he'll help you sooner." The reply was: "We're pleading with God he should help Sasha." At every turn I was besieged with questions: "What's new? What will happen?" It wasn't easy to dodge them.

There was another reason why we had to hurry. Gomerski was about to return soon. For all his sadism Franz was an angel compared to Gomerski.

"No," I said to the kapo, categorically, "for what must happen today, tomorrow may be too late. We talked it over and you agreed. You can't back out of it now. You'll do as I tell you."

At twenty past three Genick entered Shloime's barracks and through the window I saw him, Tsibulsky, and two others leave for Camp II.

Unterscharführer Ernst Berg rode up to the tailors' shop, as was arranged beforehand, dismounted from his horse and left it standing there with its reins hanging down. From what I learned later this is what happened inside: When the Unterscharführer entered everybody rose as usual. Shubayev (Kalimali) walked over to the edge of the table. In the corner, near one of the table's legs, lay a hatchet wrapped in a shirt. The Unterscharführer removed his belt together with his holster and pistol and laid them on the table. Then he took off his jacket. Juzef, the tailor, immediately came over with the uniform and began to take the fitting. Senie moved up to the table to be able, if necessary, to grab the pistol. Juzef turned the German around with his back to Shubayev, explaining that he did so in order to get a better light on the uniform. At that moment Shubayev clouted the Hitlerite on the head with the flat side of the hatchet. He let out a frightful scream. Outside, the horse quivered and pricked up its ears. The second blow silenced the Hitlerite for good. The body was shoved under the bed and covered up. The bloodstains on the floor were also wiped away and covered.

Soon afterward Shubayev came running into my barracks. "Here, take it," he said, handing me the German's pistol.

"Now, even if anyone would want to turn back it would be impossible for him to do so. Thank you, Kalimali."

We embraced and kissed. He was in a hurry. Another "client" was to arrive soon in the shop.

"Run, run back," I said to him. "How did the others do?"

"Splendidly."

Shubayev hurried back. Ten minutes later the chief of the guards, Oberscharführer Erbert Helm, entered the tailor shop. He never came out again. He was waylaid by Senie as soon as he crossed the threshold.

At exactly four o'clock, as was arranged beforehand, Oberscharführer Goettinger, chief of Camp III, entered the shoemakers' shop. Arkady Vaispapir was repairing a stool. Grisha was standing near the door. The chief executioner was in a happy mood. "The sun is shining, it's warm, good," he babbled on. "Are my boots ready?"

"Here, please," Jakub said, handing him the boots, "try them on."

"Hey, you, Jakub," the Oberscharführer went on, "five days from now I'll be going to Germany. You must make a pair of slippers for my Frau. Remember that."

"I hope your Frau will be satisfied," Jakub replied.

At this moment Arkady brought the hatchet down on his head. The corpse was dragged away by his feet to a corner and covered with rags. The blood, too, was hurriedly covered with sand. Oberscharführer Greischutz was already on his way to the shop for the uniform he had ordered.

At a quarter to five Tsibulsky returned from Camp II. He was excited but not confused. "We finished off all four," he announced. "The telephone connection too is cut where it should be. No one is allowed to leave Camp II. Baruch is in charge there. He asks to be notified in time when to lead the people out."

"Where are the pistols?"

"Two remained there. One I have and one Michael has."

"Everything is in order. You, in the meantime, go into Shloime's barracks."

At four o'clock Luka arrived. I had called her out. "Luka," I said, "in half an hour from now we are escaping. Change into men's clothes. In the woods you'll be both cold and uncomfortable in a dress."

"Who's escaping? How? What are you talking about? Sasha!"

"Luka, dear, don't waste time on unnecessary questions. We've already killed nearly all of the camp's officers. To waver now is impossible."

"Yes, yes, I understand, Sasha, but I'm afraid. For such a long time only death was always before me. Don't listen to me. Do what has to be done."

"Luka, you see, we have already begun to pay them back. Wait till we get out of here. . . . Be brave, be strong, Luka. I beg you."

"Sasha, I'm afraid, I'm afraid. . . ." the girl muttered, as though in a fever. "No, don't look at me that way. . . . I'm afraid. Not for myself. I don't care anymore what happens to me. . . . But what will happen to you? Do you realize what these murderers will do to you if you should fail?" She threw her arms around me, pressed her face against my chest and burst into tears.

This was not the moment for gentleness. "Take yourself in hand at once," I said, with all the sternness at my command. "Aren't you ashamed of yourself? A daughter of a Communist! Go change your clothes. When you hear the signal, you'll come and take your place by my side. Don't you trust me, Luka?"

"Yes, Sasha, I trust you."

"So I am telling you: You must live. And what we are doing now is the only way to stay alive. You understand? We must live. We must not perish, because we must take revenge. Run quickly."

She ran off and returned soon, dressed in men's clothes. She held a broom in her hand.

"I took along the broom in case someone asks me what I'm doing here," she explained. Then she pulled a man's shirt out of her bosom and handed it to me.

"What's that?" I asked.

"Put it on."

"But I already have a shirt."

"Put it on."

"What for?"

"Sasha, I beg you, put it on. It will bring you luck."

"Luka, dear, I don't believe in old wives' tales. And I have no time."

"No. You'll put it on. You must put it on," she insisted, and with impatience began to remove my jacket. "If you don't want to do it for me," she said, "then do it for your daughter. You said yourself your daughter is dearer to you than anything else in the world. With this shirt on, you'll overcome all dangers. And if you overcome them, we will too." I quickly put on the shirt and ended the conversation. A smile of joy lighted up the girl's face. She kissed me on the lips and hastily ran off to her barracks.

A French Jew, who worked in my section, noticed this scene and came over to me. "Don't make fun of this shirt," he said earnestly. "Believe that it's lucky. Luka gave it to you."

At four thirty Brzecki and his group returned from the Nord-Camp. Just then Unterscharführer Haulstich appeared in the yard. Shloime ran up to him. "Unterscharführer," he said, "I don't know how to continue with the dugouts. I must have your instructions. The people are standing around, doing nothing."

The Unterscharführer started walking toward the barracks. The kapo, Schmidt, followed behind him. As soon as I noticed this I ran over to Brzecki. "Take Schmidt away from here. He must not enter the barracks."

Brzecki took Schmidt by the arm. "Don't go in there," he said to him.

"Why? What happened?"

"If you want to come out alive, don't mix into this. Nearly all the officers have already been killed. Every move of yours is being watched. Don't mix in, I'm telling you."

Schmidt was shocked by what he heard. His lips quivered. He was speechless.

In the meantime the Unterscharführer was taken care of inside. Shloime himself had finished him off. Skinny little Schloime clouted him once on the back of the neck with the sharp side of the hatchet and that was sufficient. He didn't have to do it again.

It was time to give the signal but Franz was still alive. He was in no hurry to come and inspect the closets which, according to prior arrangement, he was supposed to do. A while ago he was in the yard but did not come into the shop. The head of the camp administration was still intact.

Presently our tinsmiths arrived carrying tin pipes. In these pipes were concealed six rifles with cartridges. One girl brought cartridges for the pistols. She took them from the quarters of the killed officers. We heard that Engel, a locksmith from Lodz, had killed the Unterscharführer Walter Ryba in the garage where he was working that day. The German had entered the garage armed with an automatic. Engel was suspicious and finished him off right on the doorstep. It was clear that this incident at the garage would become known very soon. We couldn't wait any longer. But what about Franz?

"The devil take him," Shloime said. "Sooner or later he'll get the bullet he deserves. Time to get away from here. Every minute is precious."

We stood there listening for a moment. A deadly silence had descended on the camp. I ordered Brzecki to give the signal. The silence was shattered by a piercing whistle. Shloime dispatched someone to Camp II to inform them that we were marching out.

People came streaming from all sides.

Beforehand we had selected seventy men, nearly all of them Soviet prisoners of war, whose task it was to attack the arsenal. That was why they were in the forefront of the column. But all the others who had only suspected that something was being arranged but didn't know when and how, now found out at the last minute. They began to push and jostle forward, fearing they might be left behind. In this disorderly fashion we reached the gate of Camp I.

The commander of the watchtower, a German from Near-Volga, approached us. "Hey, you sons-of-bitches," he shouted, "didn't you hear the whistle? So why are you pushing like a bunch of cattle? Get in line, three in a row!"

As though in response to a command several hatchets suddenly appeared from under coats and came down on his head.

At that moment the column from Camp II was advancing toward us. Several women, shaken by the unexpected scene, began to scream. One prisoner was on the verge of fainting. Another began to run blindly, without any direction. It was clear that under these circumstances it would be impossible to line up the people in an orderly column.

"Comrades, forward!" I called out loud.

"Forward!" Someone on my right picked up the slogans.

"For our Fatherland, forward!"

The slogans reverberated like thunder in the death camp, and united Jews from Russia, Poland, Holland, France, Czechoslovakia, and Germany, six hundred pain-racked, tormented people, surged forward with a wild "hurrah" to life and freedom.

The attack on the arsenal did not succeed. A barrage of automatic fire cut us off. The majority of the people made a rush for the central exit. Trampling the guards, firing from the several rifles in their possession, hurling stones at the Fascists they met and blinding them with sand, they pushed through the gate and made for the woods.

One group bore left. I saw them hacking their way through the barbed wire. Farther on they had to pass a mine field about fifteen yards wide. There many most certainly perished. I and some others ran to the officers' house and made a passageway through the wire fence. My assumption that the field behind the officers' house was not mined was justified. Three were felled not far from the fence, but it is possible that they were killed, not by mines but by bullets, because we were shot at intermittently from all sides.

And there we were, on the other side of the fence! On the other side of the mine field! Already we had run a hundred yards! Another hundred! . . . And running faster, faster, through the barren strip of land, bodies so nakedly exposed to the eyes of the pursuers, so unprotected from bullets! Faster, faster, and into the woods, among the trees, under cover. And there I was—in their shadow.

I stopped a while to catch my breath and to glance back. Men and women, falling behind, continued running in a crouched position, getting closer to the woods. Where was Luka? Where was Shloime?

Later I saw in the papers several names of those who had escaped from Sobibor.

The carpenter Chaim Povroznik, from Chelm, a soldier in the Polish army who in 1939 was taken prisoner by the Germans and escaped from the camp with us gave the following account of the last moments of our escape: "We made a dash for the fence. We cut the barbed wire quickly, with whatever we had at hand. We managed to get through the pits without much difficulty, but the mines took many lives. . . . In the woods Sasha ordered us to divide up into small groups and find our way to the partisans."

The Dutch woman Zelma Weinberg relates: "When the revolt broke out I managed to escape. Two other girls escaped together with me. They were Katie Hokes from the city of Hach and Ursula Stern from Germany. Katie later joined a partisan detachment and there died of typhus. For some time Ursula also fought in a partisan band. Now she lives in Wlodowa. We had been together in Westerburg, in Ficht, and in jail. And together we escaped from Sobibor."

It is difficult to tell exactly how many people perished at the time of the breakthrough. The majority escaped from the camp, but many fell from bullets on the open field between the camp and the woods.

It was agreed upon that we would not stop in the woods but continue running further, breaking up into groups and fanning out in various directions. The Polish Jews went west, in the direction of Chelm. They were drawn there by a knowledge of the language and the population. We Soviet people went east. The Dutch, French, and German Jews felt especially helpless. In this vast area all around them there was no one they could communicate with.

For some time we continued to hear shots from rifles and automatics. This helped us orient ourselves. We knew that there, behind us, was the camp. The telephone connections had been cut, and Franz had not yet been able to call for reinforcements. Gradually the shooting became more distant until it died down altogether.

It was already dark when shooting broke out again from the right. It sounded distant and faint. It was clear that the pursuit for us was already on. The people noticed that I had stopped. Boris Tsibulsky and Arkady Vaispapir came over to me. "Where is Luka? Where is Shloime?"

No one knew.

I proposed that we continue going all through the night, and that we should go in a single file one behind the other. I would be in front. Behind me, Tsibulsky. Arkady would close the line. No smoking—no talking—no falling behind—no running ahead. If the man in front lies down all do the same. If a rocket flares up all lie down at once. There must be no panic no matter what happens.

Thus we continued. Every now and then someone would come over to me from one side or the other. I would ask each one whether he had seen Luka or Shloime. No one had seen them.

We were out of the woods. For about three kilometers we walked through an open field. Then our path was blocked by a canal about five to six yards wide. The canal was deep and it was impossible to wade through it, so we walked along the shore of the canal. Suddenly I noticed a group of people about fifty yards away. We all lay down at once. Arkady was given the task to investigate who they were.

At first he crawled on his belly; then he rose and ran up to the group. A few minutes later he returned. "Sasha, they're ours," he announced. "They found wooden stumps lying by the shore and are crossing over to the other side. Kalimali is with them." We all crossed over the canal on these wooden stumps.

Shubayev had no news about Luka, but he had seen Shloime. He said Shloime was wounded before he managed to get into the woods. He had continued to run for a distance of about three kilometers and then his strength gave out. He begged to be shot. The Polish ones said they would take him with them. They would not abandon him.

What horrible, painful news that was! To break out of the camp and on the way to freedom to remain lying helpless. We were like brothers. During the nights, lying next to each other, we talked about everything. His clarity of mind, his serenity, his courage, his loyalty, kept me going in the most difficult moments. We planned the revolt of the camp together. We consulted each other about the smallest detail as well as about the most important steps. What had happened to him? Would I ever hear from him again? And Luka—I was carrying her gift on my body. She trusted me so! What had happened to her?

By now our group numbered fifty-seven people. We covered another five kilometers and then heard the rumble of a passing train. Before us lay a broad open stretch of land, sparsely covered with short shrubs. We stopped. It was getting close to dawn, time to give some thought to the question where we should spend the day. It was clear that the Germans would be pursuing us during the day. The woods in these parts were not very thick and could be easily combed through in all directions.

I talked it over with Tsibulsky and Shubayev and it was decided that the best thing to do would be to scatter around the bushes, precisely because it was an open space, not far from a railway line. Therefore it wouldn't occur to anyone to look for us here. But we would have to camouflage ourselves well, lie motionless, and not utter a sound. Before we took to the bushes I sent out a few people to comb through them carefully for some distance on all sides.

Daybreak came. It was drizzling. Now, in the light, it was possible to have a good look around and see where we were. Arkady and Tsibulsky took one side, Shubayev and I the other. We covered about five hundred yards and came to a barren field. Beyond it, several kilometers away, there was a woods. We returned to our place and lay down to rest. A half hour later Tsibulsky and Arkady returned. They told us that the railway line was about a hundred yards from here and that to the right, about a kilometer away, was the station. A little closer to where we were Poles were working unguarded. That was all they saw.

We posted two well-camouflaged lookouts close to the station to observe all movements in that area and report back anything that might be of interest. The lookouts were changed every three hours. Throughout the day airplanes circled overhead, some quite low over the bushes where we lay. We heard the voices of the Poles who worked on the railway. Our people lay glued to the ground, covered with branches. No one moved until it grew dark. That's how the first day of our freedom passed. It was October 15, 1943.

Night fell. As we rose from our places we noticed two figures approaching us. They moved cautiously. We guessed at once that they were our people. It turned out they had already been as far as the Bug and were now returning from there.

"Why didn't you cross?" we asked.

They reported they had entered a hamlet not far from the river and were told that Germans had arrived at the shore during the night and that all crossings were heavily guarded. As with all escapees who joined us I asked them whether they had seen Luka anywhere. The unexpected reply was: Yes. They had met her in the woods. She was with the Polish Jews on the way to Chelm.

So she's alive and breathing the free air! Where was she now? I wondered. Who was her guide? On what paths was he leading her, and would he be leading her toward life?

We walked in single file, in the same order as yesterday: Tsibulsky and I were in front; Shubayev and Arkady were the last in line. After walking for about five kilometers we entered the woods and stopped.

It made no sense to continue together in so large a group. We would be too conspicuous. Also, it would be impossible to provide food for so many people. Therefore we divided ourselves into small groups, each going its own way.

My group consisted of nine people, including Shubayev, Boris Tsibulsky, Arkady Vaispapir, Michael Itzkowitch, Semion Mazurkiewitch. We headed east with the polar stars as our compass. The nights were starry. Our first aim was to cross the Bug. To do that we had to find the proper place and the proper time. In quiet, deserted hamlets we obtained food and received vital information and directions. We were warned which places to avoid and where it would be advisable to lay over because there had been a break in the camp, Sobibor, where people were being burned, and the Germans were combing through the entire area in search of the escapees.

We started out for the Stawki hamlets, about one and a half kilometers from the Bug. Throughout the day we remained in the woods. When it grew dark, three of us entered one of the hamlets. The others remained outside, ready to give the signal in case it was necessary to flee.

The room was lamplit. At the table stood a young man of about twenty-eight. He had long, light hair which fell over his forehead. He stood there, in his unbuttoned shirt and baggy peasant pants, cutting tobacco. By the stove sat an old man. In the far-off corner to the right a crib containing an infant hung from the ceiling; a young woman, her foot on a string, quietly rocked the crib, weaving at the same time.

"Good evening, may we come in?"

"Come in," the woman said in pure Russian.

Boris suggested to her that she cover the window.

"It could be done," she said, and rose to do it.

"Take a seat," the old man spoke up.

We sat down. The hosts were silent.

"Perhaps you can tell us where we could cross the Bug," Shubayev said.

"I don't know," the young man replied.

"You, Pop," I turned to the old man, "are living here long so you must know. They say that near Stawki there's a shallow spot where it is possible to cross."

"Well, if that's what they told you why don't you go there? We don't know. We don't go to the Bug and are not allowed to go there. Sit, rest a while. We're not chasing you out. But we don't know a thing."

We talkeɹ for about an hour. We told them we had escaped from imprisonment and were trying to get home, some to Donbas, some to Rostov, and that there was no reason for them to fear us.

"All right, fellows," the young man said, after a long silence, "I'll show you the place. I won't take you all the way to the river. You'll find the way. You must bear in mind, however, that the shore is heavily guarded. There was an escape from a camp not far from here where people were turned into soap. Now the Germans are searching every nook and cranny for the escapees. Go. If you make it, it's your good luck and I wish it to you from the bottom of my heart. If you fail, please don't destroy me."

"Friend, good man, don't worry. How can we express our gratitude to you? Words can say so little in this case. Let us go before the moon rises."

"Wait," the young woman said. "I want to give you some bread for your journey."

We thanked the woman and said goodby to the old man, who made the sign of the cross over us.

This happened on the night of October 19–20, 1943. Once again we were on Soviet soil. Although these parts were still occupied by the Germans, the air, it seemed to us, was different here; it was fresher. And the roads, the trees, the sky were more familiar, more friendly.

On October 22, in the area of Brest, we met up for the first time with the partisan unit called Voroshilov. My life and work with the partisans is an altogether different chapter about which I may perhaps tell on another occasion.

Editor's Postscript

Raul Hilberg, leading exponent of the theory of Jewish passivity, dismisses the heroic Sobibor revolt in three sentences, two of which are factually incorrect. The one correct sentence describes the date of the revolt. Hilberg writes: "The Sobibor revolt by about 150 inmates was an almost exact duplication of the Treblinka break. The date of the battle was October 14, 1943. The Germans lost an *Untersturmführer* in the fighting." (*The Destruction of the European Jews,* p. 586.)

What are the facts? Not 150, as Hilberg claims, but all 600 inmates made a break for freedom during the revolt. About 400 actually succeeded in breaking out of the camp, but about half fell as casualties to land mines. Some were killed by pursuing aircraft and by SS, police, and troops numbering in the thousands. More were murdered by Polish Fascists of the National Armed Forces and the Home Army. Still, some managed to elude their pursuers, and Pechersky's group of sixty men and women succeeded in making contact with Soviet partisans.

As a direct result of the Sobibor revolt Himmler ordered the total destruction of the camp on October 16, two days after the uprising. Thus, a death factory which had already claimed the lives of over 600,000 Jews, and would have continued to take the lives of thousands more, was once and for all put out of commission.

Hilberg tells us that all the Germans lost was one SS man. Actually the number of SS men killed by the rebels was ten, and one was wounded. As for Ukrainian guards, thirty-eight were either killed or wounded and forty escaped rather than face being called to account by their German masters.

Even more reprehensible than his ignorance of vital facts is a scholar's deliberate suppression of facts when they seem to be at variance with his preconceived premise. Hilberg, who relies mainly on German sources, does on occasion turn to Jewish sources as well. He did so in the case of the Treblinka and Sobibor revolts. As his Jewish source for the latter revolt he cites Tenenbaum's *Underground*, pp. 261–264 (generally considered a secondary source). The primary source on Sobibor is still Alexander Pechersky's *Revolt in Sobibor*.

But what does Tenenbaum actually say about that uprising? He says, "Sobibor had the distinction of being the scene of a rather successful Jewish revolt . . . the main organizers were Sasha [Alexander] Pechersky, a Russian Jew and former Red Army man, and Leon Felhendler [a Polish Jew]. . . . This time the Jewish prisoners paid back the murderers for the sufferings at their hands. . . ."

Tenenbaum then goes on to name the Germans killed by the rebels and describes how they met their death. "All in all," he writes, "13 Germans were killed by the blows of hatchets." (Our earlier figure of ten SS men killed and one wounded is based on more recent investigation and therefore seems to be correct.)

But even among German sources one finds a more factual account of the Sobibor revolt than the one Hilberg presents. Commenting on that revolt, former commandant of Auschwitz, Hoess, writes in his memoir: ". . . the Jews . . . were able by force to achieve a major breakout during which almost all the guard personnel were wiped out." *(Commandant of Auschwitz,* Weidenfeld and Nicolson edition, London: 1959, p. 143.)

*   *   *

In the spring of 1963 Sobibor figured in a courtroom trial in Kiev, capital of the Ukraine. The defendants were eleven Ukrainian traitors who had gone over to the German side during the war, and after a brief period of training were attached to the Sonderkommando SS as guards in Sobibor. Like their Nazi masters they participated in the murder of many Jews. At the trial it was brought out that there were two hundred such Ukrainian guards in Sobibor.

For twenty years these eleven had managed to elude the security organs of the Soviet Union, but in 1962 they were arrested and finally put to trial. The chief witness for the prosecution was Alexander Pechersky. Ten were sentenced to death and executed. The eleventh received a fifteen-year prison term.

* * *

In the fall of 1963 three Soviet Jews met in Rostov to commemorate the twentieth anniversary of the Sobibor revolt. They were: Alexander Pechersky, Arkady Vaispapir, and Semyon Rozenfeld. A fourth survivor, Yefim Litvinovski, was unable to attend. Present at that unique gathering was a writer from the Soviet-Yiddish publication *Sovetish Heimland,* who noted down their reminiscences. The following is drawn from this account.

Several days after he had joined a partisan detachment Alexander Pechersky already participated in the blowing up of an enemy troop train. ". . . Boris Tsibulsky and Alexander Shubayev died heroes' deaths. Pechersky and Vaispapir lived to see the day when they joined the Red Army and continued fighting. At the end of August Pechersky was severely wounded. Vaispapir advanced westward.

"During his four-months stay in the hospital, and later as a civilian, Pechersky continued to inquire about his friends who took part in the revolt. He also learned that on the very evening they had escaped from camp an urgent message was dispatched by railway-telegraph: 'Send military reenforcements at once to pursue rebels.' " A young woman telegrapher at the Chelm station, at the risk of her life, withheld the telegram from the German contact for over four hours.

On October 16, four days after the revolt, a special sappers commando arrived in Sobibor. All the buildings and watchtowers were dynamited. The barbed wire fence posts were pulled out of the ground. The excavators that dug the pits for the ashes of the burned, the transmitters still laden with dead bodies, the diesel motors that propelled the gas into the gas chambers, these were all piled up on platforms and removed. Even the geese and rabbits were killed on the spot.

"A strict and secret order came from Berlin: Destroy the rebels at all costs. Quite a number of the escapees were indeed caught. But many found their way to the partisans. Others were hiding out with Polish peasants.

"And what had happened with Semyon Rozenfeld? Three hours after the escape he became aware of a sharp pain in his right leg. He and two boys, the brothers Monek and Jusik, detached themselves from Baruch's group and headed south toward the Sawin forests. They had heard that a partisan detachment was operating there. For two weeks they wandered around in the forest until they came upon the charred remains of a camp fire near the village, Yanov. . . . About a hundred yards away they found a hideout where five Sobibor escapees lived. They had come here ten days earlier. With them were three Czech Jews (Schnabel, Kornischoner, and Zilbermann) who had escaped from another camp.

"Early in December the first snows fell. Apparently it was the snow tracks that led a band of armed Polish nationalists—A. K.'s—to the hideout. They shot five Jews (one managed to escape). Then the bandits threw in a hand-grenade and killed another Jew. They began to pull at the beams of the ceilings.

"Rozenfeld discovered three cartridges in his pocket. He quickly tied them together, put them down on the beams and placed a lighted candle beneath them. The cartridges exploded and set the bandits fleeing. The surviving four Jews hid out for nearly seven months with friendly peasants in villages between Lublin and Chelm.

"In the second half of July 1944 the Red Army liberated Chelm. Rozenfeld's wound was still seeping pus. Nevertheless he went to the Soviet commandant and demanded that he be sent to the front at once. He was a soldier near Lodz, a sergeant near Poznan. Again wounded in the right leg and the right hand. Back to Lodz—in a hospital—but this time not for long. When the Reichstag was enveloped in flames he was standing at one of its walls. . . . At the age of 23 his hair was silver-white, his brow deeply furrowed. With a splinter he carved out: 'Baranowicze—Sobibor—Berlin.' " (Misha Lev, "Almost a Legend," *Sovetish Heimland,* January-February, 1964, pp. 78–93.)

*   *   *

A recent book on Sobibor entitled *Return Undesirable,* by V. Tomin and A. Sinelnikov (Moscow: Molodaya Gvardia, 1965), described by its Russian authors as a documentary narrative, brings to light the following additional facts about the camp that were not mentioned in Pechersky's account. Early in August, 1943 a transport arrived in Sobibor, bringing five hundred prisoners from Treblinka. They were taken from the cattle cars straight to the gas chambers. The kapo, Czepik, in charge of the detail that cleaned out the cars, came upon a soiled jacket and, going through its pockets, found a small, leather-bound booklet in which the following was written:

I am from Treblinka, which is located about 80 kilometers from Warsaw. A few hundred of us worked in the camp; the others—perhaps a million more—perished in the gas chambers and crematoriums. We had organized an underground leadership of resistance numbering ten people. I am one of them. We did what we could. Our death is approaching. Maybe these jottings will be of some use to others. . . . Those working in the first sector decided to plan the destruction or crippling of the camp and make a dash for freedom. Within the camp's ammunition warehouse were located demolition explosives. But anyone approaching the depot closer than 20 paces was shot. We succeeded, however, in pouring some fine sand into one of the locks. The lock was removed for repairs and the locksmith made a mould of the key. The underground had organized three fighting groups, each consisting of twenty people. . . .

The prisoner goes on with a description of the Treblinka revolt which in its essentials substantiates Rajzman's account. From this we learn that the rounded-up escapees from Treblinka were sent to Sobibor.

*   *   *

Even before the Minsk transport with Pechersky and the others who later figured in the revolt arrived in Sobibor there existed in that camp an underground resistance group consisting of twenty Czech, German, French, and Polish Jews. The executive committee of five was made up of Polish Jews, who were in the majority. Pechersky with his small group of seven made contact with the existing group of twenty and together they planned and led the revolt.

*   *   *

At one point the Sobibor underground also considered setting the camp on fire, but the Treblinka experience alerted the German administration to greater security measures, especially in guarding the ammunition warehouse.

*   *   *

It is already known that the Germans saved everything that belonged to their victims: clothing, women's hair, gold fillings. But in this book we come upon yet another example of German efficiency: The victims' bones unconsumed by the crematorium ovens were pulverized with mallets and the powder stuffed into sacks and sent off to Germany where it was used as fertilizer.

*   *   *

In the midst of death, a flicker of life. One day, two members of the Sonderkommando (prisoners compelled to work around the crematoriums), a Czech and a Frenchman, came upon the body of a sixteen-year-old girl from Greece who was still breathing after she was carted out of the gas chamber. Her mother, before losing consciousness, had stuffed a wet rag into the girl's mouth, and this perhaps had saved her. Against the almost impossible odds that prevailed in the camp, the "death detail" set for itself the task of nursing the girl back to health.

They succeeded in hiding the girl for a week. Then an inmate betrayed her presence, and SS men took away the girl and the Czech. (The informer was hanged in the barracks by the other prisoners.) The Frenchman who managed to escape the fate of the Czech now planned with others to escape through a subterranean tunnel. After two weeks of digging, the underground passage was completed and diggers believed that its exit was safely past the mine field. One of the men climbed out for a final check—this was around the end of August, 1943—and stepped on a wire which set off a deafening explosion. This brought out the guards and reserves from a nearby village. There were wholesale executions of the old "death detail" and a new one was drafted from the prisoners.

Six weeks later Alexander Pechersky and his group led the successful revolt in Sobibor which put that death camp out of commission.

*   *   *

When the counselor of the District Court of Hagen (West Germany) announced to the press that September 6, 1965, was the date set for the trial of twelve SS men who had operated in Sobibor, he also stated that the number of Jews killed in that camp was 250,000 and that the armed revolt staged by several hundred Jewish prisoners was crushed.

Alexander Pechersky, organizer and leader of the revolt, in a public reply, characterized that statement as a "brazen lie." He pointed out that the number of Jews killed in Sobibor was over a half a million, a figure based on the prisoners' own tabulation of the number of transports that arrived in that camp. As for the revolt, said Pechersky, "It was not crushed. It was successful. Practically all of the prisoners had escaped. It was this that compelled the fascists to liquidate the camp." (Alexander Pechersky, "For Them There Shall Be No Forgiveness," *Sovetish Heimland,* April, 1966.)

It should be pointed out that the statement of the Hagen court cited above is not an isolated instance but reflects a general tendency of the West German courts where Nazis are put on trial for the murder of thousands of Jews. Frequently the presiding judge or the prosecutor is himself a former Nazi or Nazi sympathizer. In such courts the enormity of the crimes is minimized and the sentences handed out are so ridiculously low as to make a mockery of the machinery of justice.

*   *   *

The German writer Robert Neumann, in giving his reason why he chose exile rather than return to his native West Germany, stated: "Too many criminals are walking the streets free in the German Federal Republic. The average sentence for war crimes comes to ten minutes jail per murdered victim."

"Little Wanda with the Braids"

By Yuri Suhl

[EDITOR'S NOTE: *In his* Notes from the Warsaw Ghetto, *Emmanuel Ringelblum pays high tribute to the women couriers of the Warsaw Ghetto underground, who knew no fear and knew no rest. "Every day they are exposed to the greatest of hazards. . . . They take upon themselves the most dangerous missions and carry them out without a whimper or moment's hesitation." Niuta Teitelboim (Wanda) belongs to this category of brave women. Her story is drawn from sources listed at the end of this chapter.*]

———————◆———————

ONE DAY a young woman walked up to the German guards in front of a Gestapo building in Warsaw and, lowering her large blue eyes demurely, whispered the name of an important Gestapo officer and added, "I have to see him about a personal matter."

She was twenty-four, but her slight figure, her long, blonde braids, and the flowered kerchief she wore on her head gave her the appearance of a sixteen-year-old girl. She was very attractive. The guards smiled at her knowingly, ushered her into the building and gave her the officer's room number.

She entered and remained standing hesitantly at the door. A tall, elegant-looking German rose from behind his desk. He stared at the girl for a long moment and then called out in wonderment, "Gibt es bei euch auch Lorelei?" (Do you, here, also have a Lorelei?)

The girl did not reply. Instead, she quickly drew a revolver from her handbag and shot the German dead. Then she left the office and calmly walked toward the exit. As she passed the guards she smiled bashfully and lowered her eyes again. A moment later she was out of their sight.

51

That was Niuta Teitelboim, a Jewish girl from the Warsaw Ghetto, whose underground name was "Wanda." This was not the only death sentence she had carried out for the underground. On another day she surprised a Gestapo officer in his own house when he was still in bed. When the startled German saw the girl with a revolver in her hand, pointed directly at him, he ducked under the eiderdown quilt. Wanda shot him through the quilt, and disappeared.

Though she operated mainly in the Warsaw area, Wanda became a legendary name throughout Poland, a symbol of fearless resistance to the German occupation forces. In Gestapo circles she was known as "Die kleine Wanda mit die Zöpfen (Little Wanda with the braids) and she was high on the list of wanted "bandits," their term for underground fighters. They placed a price on her head of 150,000 zlotys.

Wanda was born in 1918, in Lodz, of a Hassidic family, but she did not follow in the footsteps of her Orthodox ancestry. She sought a place for herself in the secular world. She became a student in a Polish Gymnasium, joined the left-wing student movement, and soon became one of its most active members. Despite her excellent scholastic record, she was expelled from school for her radical activities.

But Wanda gained entrance into other institutions of learning, for in 1939 she was a major in history and psychology. That year Hitler's Wehrmacht marched into Poland. Wanda's studies came to an abrupt end. A year later she was one of half a million Polish Jews who were herded into the Warsaw Ghetto.

She joined the ghetto underground and became one of its most fearless members. An underground leader who worked closely with Wanda in those days remembers her telling him: "I am a Jew . . . my place is among the most active fighters against fascism, in the struggle for the honor of my people, for an independent Poland, and for the freedom of humanity." To the very last minute of her life she tried to live up to this credo.

In the ghetto she organized a woman's detachment which later produced heroic figures in the Warsaw Ghetto uprising. The underground was divided into cells of five, and Wanda was an instructor of one such cell in the use of weapons. One of her surviving students recalls: "Everyone who saw her giving instructions did not believe that until recently she had no knowledge of weapons. . . . Her innocent, jovial smile could fool the most suspicious German. . . . No one could lead Jews out of the Ghetto or smuggle hand grenades and weapons into the ghetto past the vigilant guards as did Niuta."

On July 22, 1942, when the Germans began the liquidation of the Warsaw Ghetto with mass deportations to Treblinka, the ghetto was completely cut off from the outside world. The Germans threw a heavy police cordon around the ghetto wall and cut the telephone wires linking the ghetto with the Aryan side of Warsaw. For the ghetto underground it was imperative to establish contact with the Peoples Guard [7] and apprise them of the new situation in the ghetto. Wanda volunteered to hazard the risk and sneak out of the ghetto. A few days later she returned with new instructions from the Peoples Guard.

At the request of the Peoples Guard, Wanda left the ghetto to become deputy commander of the special task force in Warsaw that carried out the most daring acts of sabotage against the Germans. On the nights of October 7 and 8, 1942, they blew up the railway lines at several points in Warsaw, paralyzing for many hours vital communication lines to the German eastern front.

The Germans reacted with bloody reprisals. On October 16 they publicly hanged fifty Poles, active members of the PPR (Polish Workers Party), let their bodies swing from the gallows all day long, and then ordered them buried in the Jewish cemetery. In addition, they imposed a levy of a million zlotys on the Warsaw population.

Eight days later came the reply from the Peoples Guard. One group of the special task force, with Wanda participating, bombed the exclusive Café-Club on Aleje Jerozolimskie, which was a gathering place for Wehrmacht and Gestapo elite. Simultaneously another group attacked the German coffee house in Warsaw's main railway station, and a third group tossed a few grenades into the editorial offices of the collaborationist *Nowy Kurier Warszawski* (New Warsaw Courier). It was estimated that about thirty German officers were killed in these attacks. Later the Peoples Guard distributed leaflets, informing the Warsaw population that with these acts they avenged the hanging of the fifty Poles.

On November 30, Wanda, together with other members of the special task force, staged a spectacular raid on the KKO, the Communal Bank, in broad daylight, and retrieved the million zlotys the Germans had confiscated from the people of Warsaw.

In the fall of 1943 Wanda was sent, at her own request, to the forest to join the partisans, but was later recalled to Warsaw to resume her duties with the special task force of the Peoples Guard.

In the early hours of April 19, 1943, the Germans marched into the Warsaw Ghetto to liquidate the last remnants of Warsaw Jewry. In the evening of that same day, in a secret room in Praga, a suburb of Warsaw, the leadership of the Peoples Guard met to discuss how best to express its solidarity with the embattled Warsaw Ghetto fighters. It was decided to attack a German artillery emplacement on Nowiniarska Street from which the Germans bombarded the ghetto. A special group was selected to carry out the attack. Wanda was one of the group.

Twenty-four hours after the decision was taken, around seven o'clock in the evening of April 20, the artillery gun was silenced, and the crew, consisting of two Germans and two Polish policemen, was killed.

The Gestapo intensified its hunt for "Little Wanda with the braids." Her comrades in the underground pleaded with her to cease her activities and go into hiding because the Gestapo was on her trail. Wanda did not heed their advice.

One day in July, 1943, Wanda came home and found Gestapo agents waiting in her room. She tried poisoning herself to avoid falling into their hands alive, but did not succeed. She was arrested and taken to the torture cellars of the Gestapo. Before she was killed she managed to smuggle out a note to her comrades in the underground, assuring them that she would not betray them.

In the spring of 1945, on the second anniversary of the Warsaw Ghetto uprising, the Polish Government posthumously awarded Niuta Teitelboim (Wanda) the Grunwald Cross, the highest battle decoration in Poland.

The story of "Wanda" was drawn from the following sources:

Ber Mark, *The Book of Heroes* (Lodz: 1947, I, 112–113).

Ber Mark, *The Uprising in the Warsaw Ghetto* (Warsaw: 1955, pp. 135, 137–138, 153).

Dos Neie Leben (Lodz: August 9, 1946).

Colonel G. Alef (Bolek), *Three Fighters for a Free Socialist Poland* (Warsaw: 1953, pp. 13–14).

Meilech Neustadt, *Destruction and Rising, the Epic of the Jews in Warsaw* (Tel Aviv: 1948, I, 37–38, II, 328).

The Herbert Baum Group
Jewish Resistance in Germany in the Years 1937-1942

By Ber Mark (1908-1966)

[EDITOR'S NOTE: *Perhaps the least-known chapter in the story of Jewish resistance is the one dealing with Jewish resistance in Hitler Germany. It has only recently come to light that in the very heart of the Nazi fortress, Berlin, there operated a Jewish underground group composed of young men and women of various political persuasions who found a common bond in their implacable hatred of the Nazi regime and in their dedication to combat it by whatever means were available.*

The story of the group's underground activities and its tragic end lay buried for a long time in the secret archives of the Gestapo. Professor Ber Mark, leading holocaust historian and, until his death, director of the Jewish Historical Institute of Warsaw, was a pioneer in the study of Jewish resistance in Hitler Germany. His comprehensive account of the Baum Group is based on first-hand examination of the original Gestapo files and other available materials.

The following is a somewhat condensed version of the monograph that appeared in the quarterly Bleter Far Geszichte, *Warsaw: Vol. XIV (Warsaw), 1961.*]

———◆———

THE YOUTHFUL Jewish resistance group known as the Baum Group conducted its underground activities in Berlin during the years 1937–1942. The first German writer to comment briefly on the Baum Group was Weisenborn.[8] Having been an active member of the resistance movement, he knew something about the Baum Group in the period of his own underground activity. He describes the Baum Group as "a strictly Jewish group in Berlin, consisting mainly of young people who, because of its specific Jewish fate, was isolated and came to a tragic end." He also tells us that this Jewish resistance group had contact with a German underground group in Berlin (in the Weissensee region), and that in 1942 it carried out a sabotage act against the anti-Soviet exhibit in the capital of the Third Reich. According to Weisenborn, this act was to have served as a signal to the German working class to protest against the Hitler regime. However, the act evoked no repercussions because it was completely ignored by the German press.

Weisenborn also informs us that there were differences of opinion within the group, that some members were against setting fire to the exhibit. Weisenborn believes the group fell into the hands of the Gestapo because they were informed on by an agent provocateur who most likely was himself later liquidated by the Gestapo.

For a more comprehensive picture of the origin and history of the Baum Group one must go to the interrogation transcript of the Gestapo, the trial record, and the prison documents, all of which are to be found now in the East Berlin archives. These documents provide the researcher with a key to the biographies, social composition, and ideology of the members of the Baum Group, as well as to their various activities. It must, however, be borne in mind that these official documents stem from the enemy camp and should be approached with reservations because of their one-sidedness.

Of special importance are the memoirs of two active members of the Baum Group, Charlotte and Richard Holtzer, who survived the war.[9] These deserve our fullest confidence.

For reasons both objective and subjective, the Jewish community of Germany from 1934 to 1943 did not develop a large-scale resistance movement. After nearly a century of emancipation and equality, the German Jews were suddenly struck by terror and discriminatory laws aimed especially at them. They could not count on the German population for any significant support, and the German resistance movement as a whole was too weak to come to their aid. Also, the German Jews lacked both a tradition of struggle and proper leadership. The Reichsvereinigung von Deutschen Judentum played the role of a Judenrat and thwarted the development of a resistance movement.

For these reasons the Jewish population of Germany, even before November, 1938 (prior to the Crystal Night),[10] was politically and morally disarmed, economically crippled, psychically broken, and in a state of resignation.

These moods of resignation, as well as the search for salvation through emigration (or in some instances through suicide), were characteristic not only of the majority of the German Jews—and first and foremost of those who regarded themselves as "Germans of the faith of Moses"—but also of the minority, which consisted mainly of first-generation immigrants from Eastern Europe. Out of a population of 575,000 German Jews there remained, in the beginning of 1942, 132,000.

But side by side with the ever-spreading mood of resignation, a movement of resistance emerged under the very conditions that drove the older generation, especially the middle class, into the abyss of despair. This turn toward resistance manifested itself within the ranks of the thinking youth and was an outgrowth of a certain development that had its origin in the last years of the Weimar Republic. It must be emphasized, however, that this was true of only part of the youth. That is why the resistance groups that came into being after Hitler had seized power were small. But they were a fact; and if one takes into account the state of the existing Jewish community, as well as that of the German resistance movement generally, they carried considerable weight.

It should be stated that within the Third Reich there existed, even before the war, both in and out of concentration camps, a number of illegal Jewish resistance groups in addition to the Baum Group, of which the following are known to us:

1) The Dresden Group led by Werner Witebski and Max Zimmering, and later by Hans Dankner; and the group that was active in the cigarette factory Iramas.

2) The group that operated in Munich.

3) The group that was active in the city of Wuppertal-Elberfeld under the leadership of Yitzchok Gersht.

4) The group in the concentration camp Dachau which was organized by Heinz Heshen and Hanz Litten.

5) The Buchenwald group under the leadership of Rudolf (Rudi) Arndt.

6) The group in the concentration camp Sachsenhausen at the head of which were Sala Lerner, Fried Gersht, and Lipschitz.

7) The women's group in the concentration camp Ravensbrück led by Olga Benario and Charlotte Eisenbletter.

The activities of these groups went beyond self-help and rescue work. They also organized active resistance of a political and sabotage nature, and even engaged in battles which might be described as active self-defense, as was the case in Sachsenhausen. They maintained contact with other German and international resistance groups or with committees in their own towns and camps. The combined membership of the groups numbered in the hundreds, and included German Jews, Jewish immigrants of the 1920's, and, in the camps, Jews from various countries. Their leadership came from a variety of anti-Fascist backgrounds: union leaders, Communists, Socialists, and Zionists of various shades and groupings. Many of them disappeared or were liquidated by the Gestapo. In the end only three groups remained in the active underground: Communists, Left-Poale Zionists, and a group called the Werkleute. The unity of these three divergent groups was forged by the tragic situation in which all Jews, without exception, found themselves; and by the object lesson of the anti-Hitler organizations, which were compelled to go underground because their efforts at uniting the weakened forces for the struggle against the common enemy had, unfortunately, come too late. The weakness of the latter had imposed significant limitations on the possibilities of the Jewish groups.

Unlike the resistance movements in occupied countries, the anti-Hitler resistance movement in Germany limited its activities to the maintenance of contacts; mutual aid; monitoring radio broadcasts from London and Moscow; distributing leaflets; and publishing illegal literature. The German resistance movement did not have any partisan units and did not carry out any sabotage acts. The several attempts at assassination were unsuccessful. The widespread agitational work and the small strikes organized by the Communist and Socialist parties during the early years of Hitler's reign had reached their zenith in 1936. From then on these activities gradually ceased. Nevertheless the German resistance movement could boast of a number of heroes whose conduct was not much different from that of other peoples' heroes. Between 1933 and 1944 the Hitler courts had issued 32,500 death sentences.

The German resistance groups were isolated from the rest of the population which branded them as national traitors. They were fully isolated during the war and their activities were scattered. These groups consisted of proletarian elements, intellectuals, students, Catholics, and the Protestant opposition. Being themselves isolated and terribly persecuted, the groups (they nearly all came to a tragic end) could be of little help to the even more isolated and more persecuted Jewish groups. Still, there are known facts of aid given to Jewish groups. This was especially true in the camps where the German anti-Fascists were well organized into very active groups.

The membership of the Baum Group, the most important Jewish resistance group in Germany from 1937 to 1942, consisted of very young people whose political consciousness developed and took shape under conditions of the Third Reich. When Hitler came to power, the age level of the majority of the leaders and members was from eleven to fourteen years. Of the thirty-two activitists, only four were nineteen years old in

1933—Herbert Baum and his wife Marianne, and Sala and Martin Kochmann. They were in the leadership of the group.

The ideological background of most of the leaders and members of the
Baum Group was Zionist but of various shadings. The two exceptions
were Sala Kochmann and Hilde Jadamowitz, both central figures in the
group, who were Communists. During the period of intensified activity
some non-political people also joined the Baum Group.

But even those who came from the Zionist camp did not form a unified
whole but could be classified into the following three categories: (a)
those who before the emergence of the Baum Group, that is before 1937,
or during the first period of the group's existence, had passed over from
Zionism to Communism and were in direct contact with the KPD (Kommunistische Partei Deutschlands); (b) those who even within the ranks
of the Baum Group remained left-wing Zionists; and (c) members of the
Werkleute.

As already stated, the Jewish resistance groups in Germany were
isolated. In the camps they were assigned to special barracks for Jews.
In the cities, especially after November, 1938 (Crystal Night), the Jewish
workers were concentrated in separate factory departments. In one Berlin
factory alone—the Siemens electrical motor plant—were about 700 young
Jews. (Among them were the majority of the organizers of the Baum
Group.) Beginning with September, 1941, they were compelled, like the
rest of the Jewish population, to wear on the left side of the chest the
yellow Star of David and the word *Jude,* stylized in the form of Hebrew
characters. On their way to work they were not allowed to sit in trolley
cars. Lunchtime they were taken to the factory kitchen under guard. Only
one Jewish worker was permitted to be the spokesman for all the others
before the German overseer in charge of the Jews. (Here, that one was
Herbert Baum.) The same was true of I. G. Farben in Berlin, the
Dresden, Leipzig, and Munich factories. This continued until the end
of 1942.

It was impossible to meet with members of the German underground
movement because a Jew who managed to slip out of the factory or leave
his home and remove the yellow badge was in danger of being followed
by a Gestapo agent, a neighbor, or any Aryan passerby. The attitude of
the German population to Jews, which in the main was poisoned by Hitler
propaganda, was generally hostile. There were some instances of expres-
sions of friendliness to Jews on the street. But these were rare. The
German underground cells therefore decided that their Jewish comrades
should not attend any of their meetings. The risk was too great.

The home of the Baum couple, on Stralanerstrasse 3, had been a meeting place for friends and acquaintances since 1937. In the beginning these

gatherings took on the form of musicals and social talks. They also went on outings together, but these had to be abandoned when Jews were compelled to wear yellow badges. The gatherings at home then became more frequent, and social conversation gave way to discussions on scientific themes and later on the political situation and the condition of the Jews in the Third Reich.

These discussions were guided by Herbert Baum who, with his wife, Marianne, and Sala and Martin Kochmann, in 1938 set up a secret cell whose aim was the organization of a Jewish resistance group. Herbert Baum and Martin Kochmann had been friends since their school days when they were classmates.

The recruiting of members at the Siemens plant was successful. There were at that time two sections of young Jewish workers, one numbering 700 people, the other 250. The group attracted scores of sympathizers. During the first period—1939–1940—emphasis was placed on two forms of activity: cultural work among the Jews, and raising the morale of those who were in psychic despair. Some in the group still had illusions about legality and the institutions of law in Hitler Germany. In the name of the Jewish workers, Baum and his comrades protested to the Arbeits-Front and the Arbeits-Gericht against the low wages and hard working conditions of the Jews. These interventions brought absolutely no results. They were soon rid of their illusions.

During the first part of 1941 the influence of the Baum Group grew considerably. Not only was the group well entrenched in the Siemens plant but it attracted Jewish youth from other factories as well. As the group moved gradually, under Herbert Baum's direction, from musicals and general discussions to the political scene, the membership was eager for political involvement and demanded some resistance activity. One day the members and sympathizers of the Baum Group learned something about a hero of the resistance movement who came from the ranks of the Berlin Jews.

Early in 1941 there appeared in one of Berlin's underground circles a German Social Democrat who had escaped from the Buchenwald concentration camp and reported on the activities of the Jewish resistance group headed by Rudi Arndt, a popular leader among the workers and the Berlin Jews. The Rudi Arndt Group, he related, which was one of the active groups in camp, engaged in vigorous political-educational activity, as well as self-help, and thwarted the SS plans at every opportunity. To all the political prisoners Arndt became a symbol of bravery and of human and national dignity. That is why, in the fall of 1940, he was murdered by the Sicherheits-Dienst (Security Service).

Elsa Stillman, a Jewish member of the Berlin underground group, reported the murder to Baum, who called a meeting in his own home of about fifty people, all his close political friends, to honor the memory of Rudi Arndt. Later he organized a memorial ceremony at the Jewish cemetery on the Weissensee for the murdered Arndt. Both these demonstrations were tremendously effective. They raised the prestige of the Baum-Group and heightened the yearning for resistance. Some Jewish underground leaders who were not in the Baum Group but who maintained contact with it thought that such large gatherings were too risky. Generally, the largest attendance of an underground cell in those days in Berlin was seven people.

Despite all of Baum's efforts and the membership's eagerness for resistance, they were far from translating their dreams into actual deeds. But the outbreak of the German-Soviet war had a tremendous effect on the Baum Group. From that moment on its activities were raised to a higher level. Its members and sympathizers were strengthened in their convictions that "the mighty coalition of the Soviet Union, England and the United States will fully destroy the eternal aggressor."

After June 22, 1941, the Baum Group entered the third phase of its activity, the phase of active resistance. The activity of the group developed in the following five directions:

1) Ideological and political schooling as well as educational actions.
2) Distribution of political literature and leaflets.
3) Mutual aid and the prevention of evacuations.
4) Seeking contact with German resistance groups.
5) Activity among the foreign slave laborers employed in the Siemens plant. Among those workers the Baum Group played a pioneering role in organizing resistance and self-help activities.

During the New Year holiday Heinz Birnbaum, active member of the Baum Group, obtained from the Jew Leon Hap, his contact-man with the German group, an eighteen-page pamphlet entitled "Organize the Revolutionary Mass Struggle Against the Fascist and Imperialist War." The membership of the Baum Group familiarized itself with the contents of the pamphlet and decided to distribute it among the population. For this purpose Joachim, another active member of the Baum Group, bought a hectograph.

The group now had at its disposal a large number of brochures and leaflets which they sent out to private homes, offices, distributed among the factory workers, and at night posted on the walls. Baum and his colleagues themselves wrote the leaflets, pointing out the pitiful food rations. In one of them, basing themselves on Goebbels' statements in the weekly *Das Reich,* they unmasked the leaders of the Third Reich. Scores of members of the Baum Group were involved in this activity. Two non-Jews, the German office worker Irene Walter, and the steno-typist of French origin Suzanne Wesse, collaborated with the group by typing stencils at their homes.

Going out with buckets of paint and brushes at night was a very risky business. Still, the young fighters went eagerly to post the leaflets and paint the slogans on the walls. The group considered such acts as a test of one's revolutionary ardor, and as the best way to strengthen the revolutionary daring and the spirit of self-sacrifice of the members. This activity was carried on from the summer of 1941 until May, 1942, without a single mishap.

In addition to collective actions, every member of the group had to carry out certain individual tasks, such as conducting educational work and raising the morale of the Jews in his immediate environment. A large part of Berlin Jewry was responsive to the Baum Group and gave it their support. Many who did not belong to the group gladly opened their homes to illegal gatherings. Thus the activities of the Baum Group took on the character of active resistance. It was an outspokenly political and militant anti-Fascist organization. This underlying principle of the group's activities must be underscored because simultaneously there existed in Berlin another illegal anti-Fascist group composed of elderly Jews, including some Communists, who maintained that their main task was to save Jews, which they regarded, in certain concrete circumstances, to be more important than political action. Their main activity was collecting money for the acquisition of forged passports and living quarters, and for help in escaping abroad.

This difference in orientation led to a conflict between the two groups. The money obtained by the Baum Group (from membership dues ranging from 50 pfennigs to 2 marks, or 20 percent of one's weekly earnings, as well as from other sources to be described later) was earmarked by Baum exclusively for resistance activities.

Herbert Baum was also concerned about the security of his comrades. As a precaution against forced deportations to the east, he procured forged Aryan documents. In the Siemens plant there were French, Belgian, and Dutch civilian workers who had been brought to Germany for slave labor. Baum made contact with them through the European Union, an organization to aid foreign workers, and thus obtained a certain number of French and Belgian documents for which members paid 150 reichsmarks each. Later, after the first arrests, these documents enabled some members to live on the outskirts of Berlin. Baum had even made plans that in case of a total deportation of Jews the entire group should escape to France.

The ever-increasing tempo of their illegal activities since the beginning of 1942, the procurement of forged documents which were costly, the continually decreasing food rations for Jews that compelled some to go without food—all these factors made it imperative for the group to obtain more money. And so the idea arose in the beginning of May, 1942, to carry out a series of "X's" (expropriations) from well-to-do families.

The first of these X's was carried out successfully on May 7 by the three leading members, Herbert Baum, Heinz Birnbaum, and the German anti-Fascist Werner Steinbrink. The latter two obtained documents from the finance department and, posing as members of the Criminal Police, entered the home of the Jewish family Freundlich, on Lizenburger Strasse, 43, and without any difficulty confiscated a rug, a typewriter, two cameras, a lorgnette, a watch, and a painting. Baum was standing guard outside. Freundlich's daughter Margaret then led the "policemen" to the home of the Jew Lubinshinski, where they confiscated a valuable painting. The procedure lasted half an hour. Some of the articles were sold to art dealers. The rest were hidden in Baum's cellar. The following day the newspapers wrote that three bandits had posed as members of the Kripo (Kriminal Polizei) and raided the home of the Jew Feliks Israel Freundlich.

The X was an attestation to the organizers' daring and vigilance. It was carried out in the heart of the lively Berlin section Charlottenburg. Only a few members knew of the act. The money from the sold articles (1,500 RM) was used for political propaganda activity, the acquisition of Aryan documents, and the purchase of food.

We now come to the most significant act of resistance carried out by the Baum Group, an act that highlights both the heroism of its members and the tragic finale of its activity. In the beginning of May, 1942, Goebbels organized in Berlin, in the Lustgarten, adjacent to the main street, Unter Den Linden, an anti-Soviet exhibit under the title Das Soviet Paradis (The Soviet Paradise). The exhibit was opened with great pomp.

In the opinion of the German anti-Fascist group, the purpose of the exhibit was to distract the population's attention from the defeat suffered by the German army at the Moscow front, the food shortages, and other difficulties resulting from the drawn-out war. The Berlin anti-Fascist circles considered taking some steps against the exhibit. The Schulze-

Beusen-Harnak group showed great initiative in this respect by issuing special leaflets and posting them on the walls at night. In these leaflets the group unmasked the real aim of the exhibit. The Baum Group also discussed ways and means of acting against the exhibit. It was decided to begin with the distribution of leaflets among the Berlin population and to start at the exhibit proper. Baum and Kochmann then went to the exhibit to study the possibilities of the leaflet distribution. They returned with a negative decision. Baum then proposed the plan to set the exhibit on fire. After an exchange of opinions in which Kochmann expressed certain reservations to the plan, it was adopted by all group sections. (In the end Kochmann also agreed.)

The plan was coordinated with the Franke Group, a German anti-Fascist group, through the intermediary Steinbrink. The collaboration of the Franke Group for the realization of the concrete plan was both welcome and necessary, because both Franke and Steinbrink worked in the Chemical Institute and were in a position to supply the needed explosives. On May 15 Steinbrink handed over to Baum explosive and inflammable substances. The date for the action was set for Sunday noon, May 17.

On the morning of the appointed day several activists of the group met at Kochman's home. A discussion developed about the plan. Practically all members of the group wanted to participate in the action, but for security and technical reasons the number of participants was limited. The group chosen to carry out the plan left for the Lustgarten, but because of the large number of viewers (it was on a Sunday) the plan could not be carried out and had to be postponed for the following day.

Monday evening, May 18, 1942, the group, consisting of Herbert and Marianne Baum, Hans Joachim, Sala Kochmann, Gerd Meyer, Suzanne Wesse, and Irene Walter, went to the exhibit and distributed the explosives and inflammable material in various places. In no time flames shot up. The group left without a mishap. Part of the exhibit was destroyed by the fire. Firemen called out by a fire alarm saved the rest. The act did not have any wide repercussions, because the newspapers, probably acting on orders from above, suppressed the entire affair.

The attack on the exhibit evoked recognition and enthusiasm in the underground circles, though there were some who expressed misgivings. One of the German Communist groups wrote: "Naturally, from a political standpoint the attack of the Baum Group was a mistake, because it could provide the Hitlerites with a pretext for increasing the wave of Gestapo terror against the Jews to a degree unheard of until now. Still, the attack should be regarded as an act of breaking through the isolation. The failure to evaluate the situation is also the result of this isolation."

The aim of the Baum Group, which acted on its own responsibility and had the approval only of the Franke Group, was to put on record the activity of the Jewish anti-Fascists. In this respect it achieved its goal. Four days later, on May 22, Herbert and Marianne Baum, Gerd Meyer, Heinz Rotholz, and Werner Steinbrink were arrested by the Gestapo. The following day Sala Kochmann, Suzanne Wesse, and Irene Walter were arrested. The seventh participant in the attack, Hans Joachim, managed to elude arrest until June 9. In the meantime others of the group were arrested.

These prompt arrests gave rise to the suspicion that a Gestapo agent might have infiltrated the Baum Group. This was the view of the writer Stephan Hermlin, who maintained that "The agent who had planted himself in the group had, in the following days (after the attack) handed over to the Gestapo practically all its members." Weisenborn also believed there was an agent in the group who was later liquidated by the Gestapo.

But there were some who disputed this view, among them Jewish witnesses, including Elsa Stillman, an active member of the underground, who had direct contact with the Baum Group. She maintains that despite the group's heroism and achievement it had little experience in underground work. The group was frequently unguarded in expressing its anti-Hitler opinions, a carelessness that made it easy for the Gestapo to spy on it.

The Gestapo was not satisfied with merely arresting the leaders of the Baum Group. Using the fire as a pretext, they arrested 500 Berlin Jews who were not involved in any political activity whatsoever, as well as a number of Jews suspected of political activity. For every five Jewish "terrorists" they claimed, they arrested 100 Jews. Two hundred and fifty of the arrested were shot on the Berlin SS airfield; the second half were sent to Sachsenhausen.

After the arrests the remaining members of the Baum Group did not panic. The leadership was taken over by Kochmann, Birnbaum, Heymann, and Holtzer. One of the first things they did was to remove from Baum's cellar the illegal literature, the hectograph, the articles that were expropriated from the Freundlich family during the X raid. Kochmann threw them all into the river. A box of literature that was hidden in the Jewish Children's Home was burned, and the membership was ordered to find lodgings with German families in resort areas in the Berlin suburbs, using the forged Belgian and French documents as identification. The leadership continued to monitor the London radio broadcasts. Thanks to the nurses in the Jewish hospital where Sala Kochmann was sent, the group was able to find out what the Gestapo was after during the interrogations, and to orient themselves in accordance with what the police already knew. The leadership had planned a mass escape of the members to France, but the large number of arrests thwarted the plan. Only the Holtzers managed to escape in the direction of Hungary.

The arrested were interned at the police headquarters at Alexander-platz where they were questioned by the Gestapo. Herbert Baum refused to make any statements. He was beaten to a bloody pulp and in that condition was taken through the Siemens plant and was asked to identify the accomplices to the conspiracy. That was the last time he was seen by the workers. Baum did not betray a single individual. On June 11, the Gestapo informed the prosecution that on that day Baum committed suicide. But there are witnesses' accounts which claim that he was tortured to death.

Sala Kochmann could not withstand the tortures and, fearing that she might break under the strain, threw herself out of a window. But she was not killed. She broke her spine and was taken to the Jewish hospital. Thus she avoided further interrogations. To the court trial and later to the place of execution she was brought on a stretcher.

The trial of the first group, which was directly involved in setting fire to the exhibit, was organized quickly. It took place in a "Sondergericht" (Special Court) and was carried out in strict secrecy. Baum was already dead, and Heinz Rotholz, who was arrested on May 22, was separated from this trial because he was not directly involved in the act of setting the fire. The rest of the accused were all sentenced to death and on August 18 were decapitated.

Little is known about the courtroom procedures of the trial. What is known is that the trial of the Franke Group took place simultaneously in another Sondergericht, and that Joachim Franke and Werner Steinbrink, accused of belonging to an illegal German Communist group (KPD), and of participating in the sabotage act, were condemned to death. They too were decapitated on August 18, together with Hilde Jadamowitz, who collaborated with the Baum Group.

The trial record of the second group reveals considerable information. The investigation began on May 22, 1942, and ended on August 29. They were indicted on October 21 and sentenced on December 10, 1942. At first the prisoners denied categorically all the accusations leveled against them, as well as their membership in an illegal group. But during the subsequent Gestapo interrogations, which lasted from July 8 to August 29, the accused suddenly changed their tactics and gave testimony in accordance with the actual facts.

Their reversal is probably due to the following two reasons: (1) The Gestapo, after failing to extract the vital information from the prisoners, began to use physical torture (there is documentary evidence in support of this assumption), (2) The accused had, in all probability, learned of Herbert Baum's murder on June 11, and thought that the Gestapo already knew everything anyway, so why prolong the tortures by continuing the denials?

In their confessions the accused did not accuse each other, although there were confrontations. Nor did any of them express regret or ask for mercy. Even the Gestapo records show that the confessions were made with dignity and pride. Heinz Rotholz, who on May 22 had denied everything, stated during the July 8 interrogation: "I wish to add that I knew about the preparations of the sabotage act against the exhibit 'Das Soviet Paradis.' Had the comrades not excluded me from the act because of my Jewish appearance I would have gone on Monday to the exhibit and taken part in the act."

And young Lotte Rotholz said at the interrogation: ". . . one must utilize every opportunity to fight against the present regime. I, personally, am not schooled in politics and I have not expressed any profound thought at these discussions. But one thing was clear to me: as a Jew I must not lag behind . . . my ties were and remain with Baum."

Throughout, the accused helped each other maintain their morale. On December 3, the prisoner Hilde Löwy tried to escape by lowering herself from a rope made out of a bedsheet. She was already on the other side of the window when she was spotted by the chief guard, and caught.

The prosecution did not allow the accused to be defended by attorneys of their own choice. All were sentenced to death on the charge of high treason, except Lotte Rotholz who received an eight-year prison term because she had not been active; Edith Fraenkel was sentenced to five years and Hella Hirsch to three, because of extenuating circumstances.

As soon as the verdict became known a struggle began to save the lives of the accused, but it was a struggle with very limited possibilities. The Jewish community was paralyzed, and the witnesses for the defense were not permitted to give their testimony. After sentence was pronounced the prisoners were transferred from police headquarters at Alexanderplatz to the Moabit Prison.

The execution took place on March 4, 1943. It was announced publicly on placards that were posted throughout Berlin. The names of the condemned were given in usual Nazi fashion. The men were referred to as Israel and the women as Sarah. Thus the Hitler regime sought to suggest to the German population that only Jews were resistance fighters. Similar trials and verdicts against German anti-Fascists were, as a rule, not announced.

In Berlin underground circles it was told that in their last minutes, when the doors of their prison cells were opened, the condemned took leave of each other and sang their favorite songs. Edith Fraenkel, Lotte

Rotholz, and Hella Hirsch, who received prison sentences, were sent to the concentration camps Theresienstadt and Auschwitz, where they perished in 1944. Other members and sympathizers of the Baum Group who were not put on trial also perished in the camps.

On June 14, 1943, the third and last trial against the members of the Baum Group took place. The previous convictions served as a basis for the prosecution. All were sentenced to death. The sentence was carried out in September, 1943. The number decapitated by Hitler's murderers was twenty-two. Eighteen were Jewish anti-Fascists, three German anti-Fascists, and one French woman. Nine Jewish activists of the Baum Group perished in concentration camps. The youngest of the condemned were at the time of their death between nineteen and twenty years old; the oldest (the Baums and Kochmanns), thirty years old.

The Baum Group occupies a unique position in the history of the German resistance movement. Its distinguishing characteristics were its youthful zeal and enthusiasm, and its capacity for self-sacrifice. The burning down of the Goebbels exhibit was a resistance act of the first magnitude. The heroism of this Jewish group takes on an added dimension when one considers the fact that as Jews its leaders and members were isolated not only from the general German population but also from the general resistance movement with which they had but slight contact.

The Jewish population in Germany, in contrast to Jewish communities in other occupied countries, was for a number of reasons not a very fertile soil for slogans and active resistance against the Hitler regime. The Baum Group had to overcome difficulties which no other Jewish community in occupied Europe faced. The Baum Group knew very little about the struggles of Jewish resistance fighters in the occupied countries. They had no knowledge of the song of Vilna partisans, *Zog nit keynmol az du geyst dem letstn veg*—Oh, never say that you have reached the very end. But their own healthy revolutionary instincts told them that even under the most horrible conditions there is always the path of struggle—a struggle to overcome evil and its origins.

The Story of Jewish Resistance in the Ghetto of Czestochowa

By Dr. William Glicksman
(For my son, Allen)

[EDITOR'S NOTE: *Czestochowa is an old, historic town in the southwestern part of Poland, about 150 miles from Warsaw. Before World War II its general population numbered about 130,000. Of these, 30,000 were Jews, of which only a handful survived the holocaust.*

Dr. Glicksman is one of those few survivors. He was arrested by the Gestapo and deported to Auschwitz and from there evacuated to Dachau, where he was liberated by the American Third Army on April 30, 1945. He came to this country in May, 1946, and resides with his family in Philadelphia.

Dr. Glicksman—teacher, lecturer, and historian—has written extensively on the holocaust theme. Among his important monographs are: Social Differentiations in the German Concentration Camps, The Function of the Jewish Police in the Ghetto of Czestochowa, *and* Aspects of the Economic and Social Life of the Jews in the Ghettos.

He is also the author of In the Mirror of Literature, *a portrayal of the economic life of the Jews in Poland as it is reflected in Yiddish literature (1914–1939). Currently Dr. Glicksman teaches at Dropsie University in Philadelphia and is a Fellow of the Diaspora Research Institute at the Tel-Aviv University.*

The account that follows was written especially for this anthology. It is based, in addition to the author's personal experiences in the Czestochowa Ghetto, on a variety of sources dealing with this subject, particularly the works of L. Brener, among them Resistance and Extermination in the Ghetto of Czestochowa *(Jewish Historical Institute of Warsaw).*]

———◆———

THE IDEA OF resistance movement was conceived in the very first months of the war when the leaders of various political parties, as well as politically non-affiliated young men and women, reorganized themselves into cells for the purpose of secretly continuing their activities. Their ultimate goal was the creation of a fighting organization. These groups met at cemeteries during funerals, in old-age homes, and in social welfare institutions, to work out plans for such illegal activities as education for the children, maintenance of a library, and the publication and distribution of periodicals.

In order to coordinate the illegal work of the various parties, intergroup conferences were held from time to time. At one such conference, in August, 1941, the question of organizing a unified resistance movement was brought up again. Unfortunately, differences of opinion among the members prevented its formation. But early in 1942 the combination of a number of factors made the creation of a fighting organization even more imperative than before. Hardships in the ghetto increased; contact with the ZOB (Jewish Fighting Organization) in Warsaw had lessened and only occasionally did couriers of the Polish underground in Warsaw bring information about life in other ghettos, and instructions. One such message brought the news about the mass deportations from the Warsaw Ghetto (summer, 1942) without the deportees having knowledge of what awaited them. This same note also contained the warning that Czestochowa would meet the same fate as other ghettos and must therefore prepare for open resistance.

A meeting was set for September 21, 1942 (Yom Kippur), with Jewish representatives of the PPR (Polish Workers Party), the Bund, the left wing of the Poale-Zion, the General Zionists and its youth movement, and of non-affiliated groups. A member of the Warsaw ZOB was to have participated in the deliberations. However, when the first two representatives, Brener and Rozyne, arrived at the meeting place in the offices of the TOZ (Society for the Protection of Health), they were detained and severely beaten by German police. They were later released, thanks to a deal between Jewish teamsters and the policemen for whom they worked, but as a result of this mishap the planned meeting did not take place.

The next day the Germans and their Polish Fascist helpers marched into the Ghetto and began the deportation round-ups. There was no resistance on the part of the Jews. The fighting organization which was about to become a reality had not come into being. Many of its potential members were deported to Treblinka and later perished in the uprising there in which they participated. Only a few of the original initiators remained and, together with other youth, continued to organize fighting groups which became active in the so-called Small Ghetto (which remained after the deportation from the Large Ghetto) until its liquidation, and later in the labor camp Hasag.

In October, 1942, during the height of the deportations, four members of the PPR made still another attempt at organizing the fighting groups. The meeting took place at the "Mobel-Lager" and was joined by members of other parties and of politically non-affiliated circles. H. Tencer, an active member of the anti-Fascist underground movement, headed the newly formed unit. Another meeting took place in November, 1942, when it was agreed upon to intensify the purchase of weapons, ammunition, and anything useful for defense and struggle in case of an "action" in the Small Ghetto. Two tinsmiths, Hersh Frayman and Yohimek, were to prepare wire cutters to snip the barbed wire fence surrounding the ghetto. It was also decided to acquire gasoline and store it in various parts of the ghetto to be able to set the ghetto on fire if it became necessary.

A youth group known as the Nadrzeczna 66, under the command of M. Ferleger, was very active in these preparations. Their main task was to procure weapons and ammunition. Lacking in financial means, these young men and women scrimped on their own meager food rations to save money. After a while they were able to buy two revolvers.

At the end of 1942 the various fighting groups were unified in one organization, also called ZOB, and divided into units of five. The commander of these "fifths" was Mordecai Zylberberg, and his deputy was S. Abramovitch. H. Peysack was liaison officer between the various groups. The elected command sought to establish contact with the anti-Fascist underground movement outside the ghetto. The number of ZOB members increased from 70 to 300, of which 120 formed a tight, well-trained fighting unit. They were further divided into smaller groups with each having its special assignments, such as appropriating money from the more wealthy Jews in the ghetto; stealing from the German warehouses valuables that the Germans had robbed from the Jews; obtaining German military uniforms; digging a tunnel that led to the outside of the ghetto; producing explosive materials and grenades. (The latter group was directed by an amateur chemist, Kaufman.) Some acted as liaison men between the ZOB of the Czestochowa Ghetto and the ZOB of the Warsaw Ghetto.

The first act of armed resistance took place on January 4, 1943. It was poorly organized. The German police captain Degenhart had ordered all Jews working in the ghetto that day to assemble on the square. Present were Mendel Fishelevitch, a staff member of the Fighting Organization, who had a revolver; his friend, Isadore Feyner, who had a knife; and some members of the group Nadrzeczna 66. The few pistols the Fighting Organization had were taken out that day by members who were on special assignments outside the ghetto. Armed with only one revolver and a knife, the fighters after long deliberation decided to assemble on the square. There an "action" was in progress. The old, women, and children were selected for deportation. The approaching members of the Fighting Organization and other young men and women were immediately surrounded by gendarmes and driven to the group slated for deportation. When the German officer Rohn resumed the selection, Fishelevitch attempted to shoot him, but his revolver jammed at first, and Rohn suffered only a slight arm wound. Fishelevitch then fought the attacking policemen with his bare fists until he was shot dead. Meanwhile Feyner attacked another officer, Soport, with his knife. Feyner was also mortally wounded. In reprisal the Germans picked twenty-five of the assembled Jews at random and executed them on the spot. About 300 men and women, among them some ZOB members, were taken to the Polish Police precinct. The ZOB command did everything possible to rescue their comrades. They succeeded in smuggling in to them files and other tools with which to cut the prison bars, but their rapid transfer to the nearby city Radomsko destroyed the hope of a prison break. They did, however, make use of the tools later when they were deported to extermination centers. They cut the bars on the cattle cars and together with other deportees leaped from the train. But most of them were shot down by the escorting gendarmes or caught on their way back to the ghetto. Only a few returned.

The acquisition of weapons was always a dangerous and costly undertaking. In December, 1942, M. Ferleger, commander of Nadrzeczna 66, was surprised by a German policemen as he was about to accept some weapons outside the ghetto. He knocked down the German and escaped but was later caught and taken to Gestapo headquarters where he was tortured and shot.

Zoska, the girl courier, suffered a similar fate. One day when she was bringing weapons from Warsaw she was followed by an informer who threatened to report her to the Czestochowa police. Zoska attacked him but was soon surrounded by a group of Germans. In the ensuing struggle she was shot.

On the outskirts of Czestochowa three ZOB members perished during a weapons-acquiring mission. German gendarmes and Gestapo agents surrounded them and opened fire. The three counterattacked and wounded several Germans (according to one version two Germans were killed).

Despite these setbacks the Fighting Organization continued with its work. Since the most urgent task was the acquisition of weapons, they set about to manufacture their own. They smuggled into the ghetto the various chemicals and other materials vital to the construction of grenades, set up a secret workshop, and produced the weapons themselves. They even managed to sneak out of the ghetto and test the first few on an open field away from town. The test was successful. A special detail was assigned to make grenades. The work was carried on at night. At dawn the workshops were dismantled and reassembled again each night. The digging of tunnels also proceeded well.

At the end of February, 1943, the ZOB explored the possibilities of sending some fighting units into the woods near Olshtin and Zloty-Potok to become partisans. They discovered that the time was not ripe for such action. A month later another try was made. This time some of the Jewish fighters succeeded in making contact with some detachments of the Gwardia Ludowa.[11] But after a while their stay in the woods was threatened by units of the Armia Krajowa [12] and they had to withdraw to Czestochowa, where they hid in a bunker. The Gestapo discovered the bunker, and six of the ZOB group were arrested, tortured, and then executed.

In the beginning of March three ZOB members returned from Warsaw with illegal literature and instructions from the ZOB High Command of the Warsaw Ghetto. Two had managed to pass through the gate; one was detained and taken into custody by the ghetto police for the night and was to be handed over to the German police the next day. But that very night five members of Nadrzeczna 66 freed him from prison and he escaped to Warsaw. As a result the Germans increased their vigilance and intensified their spying on the underground with the aid of Jewish traitors. The ZOB passed the death sentence on three such traitors and executed them.

In April, 1943, a group of ZOB members undertook the derailment of a vital military transport line near Czestochowa. They failed, and three paid with their lives. In reprisal the Germans executed twenty-five Jews who worked on the "Ostbahn" detail. Despite these severe setbacks the ZOB continued its struggle against the enemy.

In its search for new and effective methods of combating the Germans, the ZOB High Command grappled with the question of whether to send its members into the forests to fight as partisans, either as separate Jewish units or as part of other partisan groups, or whether to remain on their posts in the ghetto. In the end a compromise was reached. A small group of ZOB fighters was sent to the forests. The majority remained in the ghetto.

One day ZOB received a request for weapons from its fighters in the woods, and assigned several ZOB members to arrange for the transfer of weapons. One of them contacted a German truck driver who, for a large sum of money, agreed to take weapons and fighters to their destination. But the German betrayed the fighters, and on June 24, 1943, while they were on their way to the forest they were detained by heavily armed Gestapo men. The ZOB fighters opened fire and in the ensuing battle one fighter escaped, one was killed, and one seriously wounded. The wounded fighter was brought back to the ghetto and seated at a window of the Jewish Police Precinct. Gestapo then ordered the Ghetto inhabitants to pass by the open window and observe them torture the fighter as they tried to get him to name his associates. The fighter did not betray anyone and died on the way to the cemetery where he was being taken to be shot.

That same, supposedly trustworthy, German truck driver betrayed two other Jewish fighters to the Gestapo. They were arrested and broke down under torture, naming one of their comrades. He too was arrested and tortured but named no one. All three were executed.

On June 25, some ZOB members attached themselves to other work details outside the ghetto in order to smuggle into the ghetto any available materials for the production of grenades. The majority of the ZOB fighters, who had remained in the ghetto, were put on alert and took up their appointed positions in bunkers and tunnels. The largest number of this group gathered in tunnel 1 where the ZOB "armory" was located, containing some pistols, grenades, two rifles, Molotov cocktails, carbide lamps, and even some German military uniforms.

The roll call was taken by Marek Folman, member of the ZOB command in Warsaw. Everyone was aware of the tense situation and perhaps was conscious that these might be the last, decisive moments of their lives. Reports from the ghetto came every fifteen minutes. At 3 P.M. word came that the working groups were returning to the ghetto. Everything seemed normal. As a result the ZOB members were released from their positions.

It was quiet in the ghetto, and nobody suspected that this might be the calm before the storm. About an hour later, and in typical blitzkrieg style, German police raided the ghetto unexpectedly, occupied its streets and began shooting at homes, passersby, and at anything in sight. A particular target was several houses on Nadrzeczna Street, the center of the ZOB command. The fighters made every effort to reach the tunnels and the armory. Many were killed on the way. Those who reached their destination were felled by German grenades. Moytek, the commander, took his own life. The entire armory—30 grenades, 18 revolvers, and 2 rifles— was lost.

Only the ZOB fighters in tunnel 2 remained. This group reached the exit on Old Market 17, where they temporarily barricaded themselves, with the ultimate goal of escaping and joining their comrades in the woods. This had to be done in groups of three. While the first groups succeeded, the remaining two (six people) were surrounded by the Gestapo and police. With only two pistols and one grenade the six fought until death.

The Germans proceeded with the liquidation of the ghetto, killing scores on the spot and executing hundreds of men, women, and children at the Jewish cemetery.

The ZOB in Hasag and in the Woods

After the liquidation of the Small Ghetto the connections between the various remaining ZOB units were cut off. There were three groups in the woods around Konyetopol. Others were in the labor camps Hasag-Eisenhütte (Hasag steel mill in Rakov) and Hasag-Apparatenbau.

At this point contact with the underground movement in the Warsaw Ghetto was also temporarily disrupted. It was not until some weeks later that Wladka, a liaison officer of the Warsaw Coordinating Committee, came to Czestochowa, made contact with the groups in the woods, and through them was put in touch with some ZOB members in the two Hasag camps. Thanks to Wladka's frequent trips and those of two other girls, contact with the Warsaw Ghetto underground was established again.

In the meantime the surviving ZOB leaders successfully reorganized the inactive groups of five and prepared them for resistance in case of an "action." The advances of the Russian armies could lead to a rapid liquidation of the camps by the Germans and with it the further annihilation of Jewish lives. One had to be constantly on the alert to German dangers. Therefore wire cutters had been obtained to cut the barbed wire fence surrounding the camp and make escape possible. Various other tools were hidden away for use in fighting. Shock units were organized to attack the guards; sabotage was carried out in the production of ammunition and by delaying shipments.

Encouraged by the revived fighting spirit some members of the Warsaw ZOB favored an open revolt in both camps, promising to supply weapons. However, the Czestochowa ZOB was against the suggestion. The mounting terror and the frequent searches of Polish workers who would risk smuggling weapons into the Hasag camps militated against the idea. A plan to escape was also abandoned because it was practically impossible to reach the partisan groups in the woods. Moreover, the decree of collective responsibility as applied by the Germans restrained the ZOB command from sending out its members. The absence of one usually led to the execution of scores of others.

The fact that their number could not be enlarged limited the activities of the Jewish partisans in the woods to attacks on minor German posts and on Polish constables who collaborated with the Germans, and to obtaining food and ammunition. Lacking the necessary manpower and fighting equipment to undertake large-scale attacks against the Germans, the

Jewish partisans decided, therefore, to contact the Polish partisans and jointly fight the common enemy.

In the Konyetopol woods there operated at that time a group of the A. K. (Armia Krajowa) named Orzel (Eagle). Unaware of their political affiliation the Jews considered them as their natural allies and suggested common armed action. At the appointed day and place of the first meeting a group of Jews, under the command of Kuba Ripshtayn, waited for the representatives of Orzel. They came armed with machine guns and revolvers. Kuba and his comrades, without suspecting anything, greeted the approaching Orzel men with friendly gestures and, to prove their friendly feelings, did not even open their holsters. But when the distance between the two groups was narrowed, the men from Orzel fired on the Jews. Only one, the wounded Shidlovski, succeeded in escaping. The rest of the Jews were killed by the Polish Fascists. This was not the only treacherous act the Polish Fascists committed against the Jews in the Konyetopol woods. These Poles, together with Polish police, also massacred another Jewish partisan group.

The situation of the remaining Jewish partisans became more and more dangerous. They were forced to leave their fortified hiding places and live in the open woods. Fortunately, a Polish peasant named Romanow came to their aid, giving them a warm meal and bread at night. Another Jewish ZOB group joined a left-wing Polish partisan unit which operated in the Konyetopol area, under the leadership of the Pole Hanysh. The Hanysh unit received the Jews in a warm and friendly manner. With these progressive Poles the Jews could show their courage and share their fighting abilities.

Zofia Yamaika

By Esther Mark

[EDITOR'S NOTE: *Esther Mark, the widow of Ber Mark, was, until her departure from Poland in 1969, a research worker at the Polish Institute for the History of the Polish Working-Class Movement. She now resides in Israel where she works as historian, researcher, and archivist for the Society for Historical Research of Polish Jewry, founded by the Tel-Aviv University, Diaspora Research Institute, and the World Federation of Polish Jews.*

Mrs. Mark is the author of a number of documentary works on the Polish resistance movement and of a series of monographs on Jewish heroes of the anti-Nazi resistance movement in occupied Poland, 1939–44. She is currently gathering material for a memorial volume about the late Ber Mark, which will include his extensive correspondence, as well as a bibliography of his works.

The following chapter is a slightly abridged version of Mrs. Mark's account published in Pokolenia *(Generation), Warsaw: 1964, No. 1. It is translated from Ber Mark's Yiddish translation of the Polish.*]

ZOFIA YAMAIKA, daughter of a well-to-do and prominent Hassidic Warsaw family, was only fourteen when Hitler's Werhmacht marched into Poland in September, 1939. Her high-school studies came to an abrupt end, as did her activity in the radical student club Spartacus, to which she belonged. The club simply fell apart. But four months later, anti-Fascist posters and leaflets, printed in a toy printing shop, appeared on the streets of Warsaw under its imprint. Thanks largely to Zofia's initiative, the club was reorganized, and began an illegal existence which it maintained throughout the war.

In the fall of 1940, Zofia and her parents were part of nearly half a million Jews who were crowded into the Warsaw Ghetto. Despite the Nazi decree forbidding education, a network of illegal schools sprang up in the ghetto and Zofia not only resumed her studies but even managed to graduate. Every spare moment away from schoolbooks she devoted to Spartacus activities and when the club looked about for members to be sent for a special training course in leadership for fighters, Zofia was a logical candidate. Upon completing the course she became a leader of an underground group of five.

But armed struggle was still a thing of the future. The crying need of the moment was survival, sheer physical survival in the face of the Nazi-planned program of death by starvation. And so Zofia became a leader of a children's group in the House Committee of her father's house. [A House Committee was a voluntary organization set up to take care of the needs of the residents within a single courtyard. There were about 2,000 House Committees in the Warsaw Ghetto and they formed the largest self-help organization within the ghetto wall. The immediate impetus for their emergence was free soup kitchens for the destitute, but their range of activities soon broadened to include every need of the ghetto dweller. They even put on plays, arranged literary readings, and provided for the education of the children. Many of their activities were illegal.]

In addition to her work with the children Zofia helped organize a self-help apparatus for obtaining food for an illegal youth kitchen and stepped up her political activities.

After a while the Jewish youth realized that if Spartacus was to be effective and fulfill its role it must obtain help from its illegal Polish counterpart outside the ghetto. A member of the club was sent to the Aryan side to explore this possibility. She was unsuccessful and returned discouraged. Realizing that they would have to depend on themselves, the members now sought contact with other Jewish underground groups in the ghetto.

But not long afterward a Polish student named Kazik Denbiak arrived. He had put a Star of David band on his arm and, posing as a Jew, smuggled himself into the ghetto to contact Spartacus and other underground groups. It so happened that at the time the Spartacus courier was in Warsaw trying to make contact with Polish youth groups, Kazik had been away to the province organizing the first anti-Fascist partisan detachment composed of left-wing elements and escaped Russian prisoners of war. It then occurred to him that the ghetto might be a possible recruiting source for such a partisan movement. That was why he had come.

Zofia volunteered to join the partisans and was sent by her group to a special school (inside the ghetto) for two training courses: the use of weapons in combat and how to be a field nurse. But even as she prepared to go to the forest Zofia grappled with the agonizing dilemma of what to do about her parents. She simply could not bring herself to leave them, and one also had to take into account the law of collective responsibility which the Germans applied to the ghetto population—an entire family could be held responsible for the escape of a single member.

In the meantime these events occurred in the ghetto: In May, 1942, the leadership of the combat groups fell into the hands of the Gestapo and was executed. After that, members were not allowed to meet. Three months later, on July 22, the Germans initiated the largest deportation action in the ghetto, deporting over 300,000 Jews to the gas chambers of Treblinka, among them Zofia's parents. The action came so unexpectedly that even members of the fighting groups were caught in the round-up.

Now there was little time to lose. In August, 1942, at the height of the deportation action (it lasted until the middle of September), Zofia together with several fighting groups escaped to the forest to join the partisans.

The escape was a daring one and was accomplished with the aid of a group from Hashomer Hatzair (socialist-oriented Zionist youth) that worked as gardeners in the area between the ghetto and the cemetery. [The Warsaw Ghetto cemetery was located outside the ghetto limits.] The Hashomer group smuggled them into their work area and from there they made their way to the other side of the cemetery where Wiga, a staff officer of the Gwardia Ludowa, awaited them. Wiga's real name was Yankel Wishunski, and he too was a member of Hashomer Hatzair.

Their destination was a small town, Biala-Podliaska, where they were to contact a Polish underground courier who was to take them to the forest. While waiting for the courier there was only one place for them to go—the ghetto. Two days passed and there was no sign of the courier. In the meantime the Germans started a deportation action in this ghetto also, and what the young fighters escaped in Warsaw caught up with them in Biala-Podliaska.

They went into hiding. Some succeeded in evading the round-up; Zofia and her group did not. They were caught and herded into cattle cars headed for Treblinka.

Somewhere along the way, when the German guards opened the doors of the cars to remove the corpses of those who had died on the journey, Zofia jumped out of her car and made believe she was dead. After the train had pulled away, a peasant found her and took her to his home, where she stayed for several days. Then she set out on foot to Biala-Podliaska, where she reunited with her comrades who were still waiting for the Polish courier. He never showed up.

The groups split up and went their separate ways. Zofia returned to Warsaw. She was seventeen then. She had no one to turn to for shelter outside the ghetto and she did not want to go back to the ghetto. Her only valuable possession, a family ring, she had given to the underground fighters for the acquisition of weapons. Without identification papers, without any means of subsistence, she wandered the streets of Warsaw in a state of despair, not knowing where to turn.

It was during that period that she met the Polish underground worker

Eva Pewinska, whose home was a way station for Jews who escaped from the ghetto and were on their way to join the partisans. Eva obtained forged Aryan papers for Zofia on which her age was given as fifteen and her name was no longer Zofia Yamaika. She also taught her how to pray as a Catholic.

When she had thoroughly familiarized herself with her new name and the Catholic prayer she was assigned to the illegal printing press that published the *Gwardist,* official organ of the Gwardia Ludowa. She was allowed to live on the premises of the illegal press. Nothing about her manner or appearance suggested a hard-working member of the underground. Modest, reserved, frail, and often sad-looking, she surprised everyone with the zeal and dedication with which she worked.

On September 28 and 29, the Gestapo came upon the track of the illegal press, raided it, and found both Zofia and some illegal literature. Zofia was beaten and taken to Gestapo headquarters on Allee Szucha, for questioning. After giving her name and age, which corresponded to that on the forged papers, she told them that she was an illiterate orphan who had worked on a farm, had recently come to the city, and was hired as a cleaning girl at the place she was arrested. She insisted she knew nothing about the nature of the printing press and what was published there.

After questioning she was sent to the Pawiak prison where, to her great surprise, she found Eva. The Gestapo had left a plant at the printing press, and as soon as Eva arrived she too had been arrested.

At the end of 1942, after having been about three months in the Pawiak, she was set free. Before leaving the prison Eva had warned her not to get in touch with any of the underground workers because the Gestapo might use her as a ruse to entrap others.

And so once again Zofia found herself wandering around Warsaw without any friends or means. After a while her despair was so deep that she contemplated committing suicide.

It was at this point that she was recognized by an underground worker she knew, a Jewish girl who lived as a Pole in Warsaw. Always mindful of Eva's warning, the best she could hope for was for the girl to help her leave Warsaw. This she did. She arranged for her to leave with a Pole for the forest near Radom and there join the partisans. Both were provided with revolvers.

One day while walking on the streets of Warsaw they were approached by a German gendarme who demanded to see their papers. Not having any they shot the gendarme and escaped. They made several more attacks on police in order to obtain arms and then left for the forest.

On December 30, 1942, Zofia reached the partisan group Levi (Hebrew for lion), consisting of Jews and Poles but with a Jewish majority. The commander was a Jewish porter from Radom named Jonah Eisenman who now went under the Polish name Kaniewski.

Because of Zofia's knowledge of German she was assigned to reconnaissance and acted as liaison between various partisan units and the General Staff. She also organized a network of partisan reconnaissance while at the same time participating in other partisan activities, such as derailments of German troop trains.

On January 12, 1943, the Levi detachment captured the town of Gowarczow in the region of Konsk, Radom district, and held it for five hours while the partisans cut the telephone wires, destroyed the police station, the German headquarters, and the records listing the amount of provisions the peasants had to contribute to the Germans. They also seized the list of Nazi agents and collaborators. Zofia played a leading role in this episode.

She was assigned to a special task force that liquidated spies and agents, and became a kind of general trouble shooter among the partisans. She became a symbol of high morale in her detachment, and was decorated for bravery by the General Staff.

One day the Germans staged a raid in the area to round up Poles for slave labor. The Levi detachment combined with another Polish partisan unit to ward off the raid. They attacked the police, causing them to flee, thus giving the Poles a chance to escape.

On February 9, 1943, the Germans retaliated with a force of 300 men, determined to liquidate the partisans. At that time the number of the combined partisan units was no more than fifty. It would have been suicide to attempt a counterattack. They had to retreat in a hurry, and the retreat, if it was to be successful, had to be covered. Zofia and two Poles volunteered to cover the retreat.

Zofia manned the machine gun. She allowed the Germans to come within twenty meters of her position and then opened fire. Overwhelmed by the numerically superior force the three fell in battle, but they did assure the successful retreat of the partisans.

Even the Germans spoke of the heroism of these three partisans, and singled out the Jewish girl for special praise. They ordered the peasants to bury them. Later the partisans dug up her body and gave her a military burial. In April, 1963, on the twentieth anniversary of the Warsaw Ghetto uprising, the Polish government awarded her posthumously the Virtuti Militari, one of the highest military awards.

"Chief Physician Remba"

By Yuri Suhl

[EDITOR'S NOTE: *In their continuous struggle for survival, outwitting the enemy became a full-time occupation of the Jews in the ghettos and camps. The story of Nachum Remba, a communal worker turned "physician," is an unusual but by no means isolated instance of Jews matching wits with their German tormentors.*]

———◆———

UMSCHLAGPLATZ was a dread word among the ghetto Jews. It meant transfer point for deportation, usually located near a railroad siding. There was only one place to go from the *Umschlagplatz*—into the cattle cars. And when these were crowded to suffocation the train left for what the Germans called "Resettlement in the East." Though the Jews did not know yet that they were heading for an extermination camp, they were full of dark forebodings about their unknown destination.

But one Jew from the Warsaw Ghetto attempted the impossible and succeeded in rescuing hundreds of Jews already on the *Umschlagplatz,* hours and sometimes even minutes before they were pushed into cattle cars. His name was Nachum Remba. A modest, retiring man, described by those who knew him as a "saintly figure," he embarked on a rescue operation worthy of the most daring adventurer.

He set up a make-believe First Aid Station right next to *Umschlagplatz.* This "hospital" was staffed with trustworthy doctors and nurses. Then Remba donned a long white doctor's coat and entered the *Umschlagplatz* as head of the "hospital." (As an employee of the Jewish Council, Judenrat, Remba enjoyed a freedom of movement which most other Jews did not.) He then pointed out to the German officers Jews he claimed were too weak to make the journey east, and demanded that he be permitted to take them into the "hospital." And the Germans who, after a while, began to refer to him as *"Haupt-Artzt Remba"*—Chief Physician Remba—acceded to his requests.

The well-known Yiddish actor Jonas Turkow, whom Remba had saved in this manner, describes what the *Umschlagplatz* looked like in his memoir, *This Is How It Was:* [13] "Huge throngs of people are being pushed toward the barbed wires that divide the place in two. On the ground lie wounded men, women and children, valises, all kinds of possessions, bedding, prayer shawls, phylacteries, food packages and single shoes lost by some who were caught in the round-up. Police officers are running back and forth with orders from the little 'Napoleon' [chief of the ghetto police, Lejkin], and the convert Schmerling, who is Platz-Kommandant. . . . On the roofs are machine guns manned by SS-men and gendarmes. Bullets swish by your nose. Near me a woman falls, wounded. No one pays any attention to her. People pass by her, step over her, step on each other."

And in the midst of this nightmarish scene, writes Turkow, "Remba, dressed in his doctor's coat, went from one place to the next, from one German to the other, rescuing Jews, pulling them out of the *Umschlagplatz* and sending them back to the ghetto. Always calm, always smiling goodnaturedly . . . he would appear where no one dared set foot, where one could get shot for merely standing there. Fearlessly and with dignity he faced the German henchmen on the *Umschlagplatz* and demanded that they free this very sick one who is unable to make the 'difficult journey east.' "

In the "hospital" the rescued were ordered to lie on the beds. Some were "bandaged." As soon as the path was clear, they were taken by "ambulance" back to the ghetto. The nurses wore especially wide coats under which they were able to hide the rescued children. Frequently it was necessary to chloroform the little ones and put them to sleep to make their rescue possible.

How was Remba able to put it over on the Germans? "This is the irony of it," writes Turkow, "that even the Germans, with their refined system of punctuality, were capable of being fooled, at least for some time. And until they caught on to the 'Jewish trick' many a Jew was rescued." Who knows how many more Jews Remba might have saved had he not been betrayed by members of the Jewish police, who saw in him a dangerous rival because he rescued Jews for nothing while they demanded heavy bribes from the victims.

Born in Kolna, Poland, in 1910, into a prominent Zionist family, Remba spent most of his adult life as a communal worker. Prior to Hitler's invasion of Poland in 1939, Remba was secretary of the educational department of the Warsaw Kehilla, the official administrative body of the Jewish community of Warsaw. Although himself an employee of the Judenrat—a German-elected body regarded by most Jews of the ghetto as an instrument of the Germans— he did not hesitate to join a committee to combat corrupt Judenrat practices, and he secretly organized the Judenrat employees into an association of which he was chairman. Remba kept a diary of life in the Warsaw Ghetto, but it was lost. A few passages, however, are extant, thanks to the ghetto historian, Emmanuel Ringelblum, who quoted them in his sketch of the famed pedagogue and children's writer Janusz Korczak, who led the column of Warsaw Ghetto children deported to Treblinka.

"At night," Remba noted in his diary, "I imagined that I was hearing the thump of children's feet, marching in cadence under the leadership of their teacher. I heard the measured steps, tramping on and on without interruption to an unknown destination. And to this day I see that scene in my mind. I see clearly the figures, and I see the fists of hundreds of thousands that will come raining down on the heads of the henchman." [14]

In the spring of 1943, Remba was again on the *Umschlagplatz,* this time not in his white doctor's coat in the role of savior, but as victim. The Germans caught him during the Warsaw Ghetto uprising and deported him to the death camp, Maidanek. There, too, Remba did everything he could to alleviate the sufferings of his fellow prisoners. He was especially close to the children, telling them stories, taking them for walks, making them forget, if even for a while, their horrible surroundings. In the end, like their beloved writer, Korczak, he went to the gas chambers with them.

"Comrade Mordecai"

Mordecai Anielewicz—Commander of the Warsaw Ghetto Uprising

By Emmanuel Ringelblum

[EDITOR'S NOTE: *The two most famous names associated with the Warsaw Ghetto are Emmanuel Ringelblum and Mordecai Anielewicz. The one was the archivist of the Warsaw Ghetto; the other, the youthful commander of the Warsaw Ghetto uprising.*

Before his arrest, in March 1944, and subsequent execution by the Germans, Ringelblum was in hiding with his family and thirty-five other Jews in the cellar of a Polish worker in Warsaw, where he wrote, among other things, a number of biographical sketches of some of the leading personalities of the Warsaw Ghetto, including one of Mordecai Anielewicz. What follows is a somewhat abbreviated version of that portrait.]

———◆———

HE WAS a young fellow, about twenty-five, of medium height, with a narrow, pale, pointed face and a pleasant appearance. I met him for the first time at the beginning of the war, when he came to me, dressed casually, and asked me to lend him a book. From that day on he came to me frequently to borrow books on Jewish history, especially on economics, in which Comrade Mordecai was greatly interested.

Who could have known that this quiet, modest, and sympathetic fellow would emerge as the man who, three years later, would be mentioned with awe by some, with fear by others.

Soon after the outbreak of the war the Hashomer Hatzair, under the leadership of Comrade Mordecai, began to conduct educational and cultural circles embracing hundreds of young people of both sexes. This work was conducted in the refugee area at 23 Nalewki Street, where members from the outlying areas had found a haven. The Hashomer strove not only to provide their people with cultural nourishment but simultaneously with guidance for their educational advancement as well. Circles and seminars were created where young students received both a general and Jewish education. In the seminars for older comrades, leaders were prepared for the Hashomer circles. The Hashomer embraced with its activity not only Warsaw but the outlying areas as well. Hashomer instructors risked their lives traveling around the country on "left" (false) permits as Jews, and more frequently as Aryans, distributing the illegal publications of the movement and revitalizing legal organizations.

Seminars were set up in Warsaw to develop leaders for the groups in the outlying areas. These seminars were attended not only by the boys and girls from the *General Gubernie* (General Government—region administered by the Nazis in Poland) but by would-be students smuggled into Warsaw from the "Reich" (part of Poland incorporated directly into Hitler's Reich—Bendin, Sosnowice), some walking several weeks until they reached Warsaw. Only one who knew the dangers involved in moving about on trains in those days could appreciate the heroism of these young people thirsting for knowledge.

It so happened that several times I was a lecturer at the Hashomer seminars. When I peered into the glowing faces of the eager youth, I forgot that there was a war on in the world.

The seminars took place right opposite the German watch that guarded the ghetto gates. The Shomer bunch felt so at home in its own headquarters that more than once they would forget there was a war on. Now and then they would dance a hora, accompanied by Eretz Yisroel and revolutionary songs. Once the singing attracted a German guard, who came to ask what was going on. Upon learning that this was a gathering point for young scouts, the guard sat down to have a chat with the youngsters. At dawn he bade the Shomrim a hearty farewell and returned to his post.

Mordecai was exceptionally devoted to the people in Hashomer. Day and night they were the objects of his thoughts and concern. From various sources he procured provisions for the kitchen of the Shomer kibbutz— the main source of Hashomer's subsistence, however, was the earnings of its members, who worked at various slave labor jobs outside the ghetto and contributed their wages to the membership treasury.

One seldom finds in an organization or party Comrade Mordecai's exceptional devotion to his fellows. For a fellow member he was ready to leap into fire. As an illustration I should like to cite the following incident, which I witnessed myself. This happened to a member of Hashomer, Zandman, in Halman's shop on Nowolipki, where I lived after the first "resettlement action." This was in January, 1943. The Fighters' Organization had, at that time, carried out a number of reprisals against individuals guilty of crimes against the Jewish community of Warsaw. As punishment they were splashed with vitriol. At Halman's a former policeman was splashed. Fortunately the perpetrators escaped. But Zandman, who was connected with the carrying out of the verdict, was detained by the Werkschutz [factory guards] and splashed with vitriol. The German administration was also notified by the Werkschutz about Zandman's detention.

When Mordecai learned about this he came that very day to Halman's shop and, together with the leadership of the Fighters' Organization and myself, worked out the plan to rescue Zandman. Four o'clock at dawn, five masked strong men entered the Werkschutz headquarters and freed Zandman, taking with them at the same time all the Werkschutz papers and charts. This happened several hours before the beginning of the January action. Zandman was hauled off for the second time to the *Umschlagplatz,* where his comrades freed him.

The Zandman incident was not unique. Mordecai was ready to sacrifice himself for the comrades just as they were ready to risk their lives for him. Such an attachment of a leader to his comrades was rare even in the ghetto.

This was the kind of loyalty found in underground organizations where all thought of themselves as true brothers. Such mutual aid and devotion were then found only in workers' organizations, which organized mutual aid groups not only in the shops but even in the work camps of the SS.

Comrade Mordecai and the others of the top leadership had, from the beginning of the war, held to a clear, consistent political line, one that was brought out in all the seminars and in the publications in Polish and Hebrew. *Neged Hazerem* (Against the Stream) was the name of the Hebrew organ. One must admire the consistency and the steadfastness of character of the Shomrim who advanced, against the petty bourgeois spheres from which they hailed, their own political line, a line which was disliked by both the General Zionists and the Right-Poale Zionists (labor Zionists).

The orientation of Hashomer was a pro-Soviet one—faith in the victory of the Soviet Union and in its heroic army. The only party on the Jewish scene that had the same political orientation were the Left-Poale Zionists. In keeping with this line the Shomrim made preparations together with other partisan groups, established close relationships with the PPR, and were generally ready to do everything possible for the victory of the

Soviet Union. Hundreds of comrades of Hashomer have, indeed, in various parts of the country made contact with partisan groups. One should
bear in mind that this did not in the slightest diminish their positive
attitude to Eretz Yisroel and to Palestinism as a solution of the Jewish
question. The programs of the seminars and the illegal publications of
Hashomer Hatzair could attest to this.

Even before the war Comrade Mordecai had established good relationships with the Polish scout movement, the Polish Harcesz. This was
perhaps one of the rare instances in which a Jewish organization worked
together with a Polish one, and the Hashomer benefited greatly from those
contacts. In Vilna these contacts with the Polish Harcesz opened the way
for the Shomrim to the Polish clergy, which assisted in the illegal activities
of Hashomer. Thanks to this some individuals from Hashomer were
quartered with Polish families in the region of Vilna. Comrade Mordecai
related to me an interesting fact about the friendly relationships between
the Polish scouts and the Shomrim. One of the leaders of the Polish
Harcesz was, because of his German origin, mobilized as a doctor for
the eastern front. From Leningrad he sent greetings by field post to the
illegal gathering of Hashomer in Warsaw. Later this same doctor, while
on furlough in Warsaw, smuggled himself into the ghetto and spent
several days with the comrades of Hashomer. He recounted some interesting details of the severe catastrophe that the German army suffered
in the winter of 1941–1942.

The front, Comrade Mordecai told me, was then on the verge of
collapse. At that time Hitler personally visited the threatened front line
areas where the demoralization of the army took on a menacing character.
He addressed the soldiers and restored order and discipline. Hitler took
with him the generals who could not maintain order in their front line
areas, and it was reported among the soldiers that the generals were later
shot. Hitler also visited the area where our scout was, delivered speeches,
and restored order. When asked by a Jewish friend why he had not shot
Hitler since he had stood so close to him, the scout left the question
unanswered.

Once I saw the modest and quiet Mordecai in the role of Hashomer
commander. That was in the winter of 1941–1942. Mordecai one day
wanted to gather all the members of the movement together to strengthen
their consciousness of collectivism and demonstrate what a force this
represented for the Shomer movement. Despite the danger that this meeting entailed, I made available for a Shomer gathering the second floor of
the Judaic Institute at Tlomacki 5, headquarters of the communal department in charge of the House Committees. The evening was camouflaged
as a legal literary affair.

In the hall they gathered together the desks, arranged the chairs in rows, and set up a real stage. There came to the hall an audience of about 500 Shomrim and Shomrot, the latter dressed in white blouses. The culture program of the evening was carried through by their own members, young men and women. The caliber of the evening was high. After the program the entire *gan* (garden-youth group) marched around the room.

Simultaneously the graduation from one group into another took place, accompanied by a solemn declaration of dedication to the movement. A comrade of the Polish scout movement witnessed the ceremony.

This affair demonstrated to me with how much love, respect, and devotion the members of Hashomer surrounded the person of Comrade Mordecai. This same loyalty later was shown him when he was commander of the Fighters' Organization. This power, however, did not go to his head—he remained as modest as ever.

Once during an intermission between one lecture and the next at the seminar of Hashomer (I lectured there on the history of the Jewish resistance movement), the comrades Mordecai and Yosef Kaplan called me down to the courtyard of Nalewki 23, took me into a private room, and showed me two revolvers. These revolvers, the comrades of the top leadership explained, would be used to train the youth in the use of weapons. That was the first step taken by Hashomer, even before the creation of the Fighters' Organization.

Bad times were aproaching. From all over the country awful reports came streaming in, first about the terrible slaughter in Vilna and in other Lithuanian cities, brought by the Comrades Vilner of the Vilna Hashomer and Solomon of the Hanoar Hatzioni (Zionist Youth). Then came the accounts of the slaughter in Slonim and other cities in the east. Mordecai realized that the fate of the Polish Jews was sealed and that the Jews of all of Poland were doomed to destruction.

The young but quickly maturing Mordecai understood that at present there was but one question: What kind of death will the Polish Jews select for themselves? Will it be the death of sheep led to the slaughter without resistance, or of people with honor who want the enemy to pay for their death with his own blood? Mordecai wanted the slaughter of the Polish Jews not to come easy for the enemy; he must be made to bleed for it.

The moment Mordecai decided on struggle, no other questions existed for him. The scientific circles and the seminars came to an end; the manifold cultural and educational work was interrupted. Now he and his comrades concentrated only on the area of struggle.

When the National Committee of which Mordecai was a member

decided in February-March, 1943, to help re-settle the communal and cultural "active" over on the Aryan side, Comrade Mordecai remained very cool to this decision. He would certainly want the poet (Yitzhok) Katzenelson; the writer (Shia) Perle; the historian (Yitzhok) Szypper; the communal worker Bloch; the artist Tomberg; the painter Trembatch, and so on to survive the war and be saved by the Jewish people. But he and his comrades would not lend a hand to this.

The time came when all the important personages could be settled on the Aryan side, if there were only a little money. But Mordecai was against taking money from another fund with which he was connected. For him there existed now only one goal, and he was sacrificing all for that particular goal: the struggle with the enemy.

The Mordecai who had matured so rapidly and risen so quickly to the most responsible post as commander of the Fighters' Organization now greatly regretted that his fellows and he had wasted three war years on cultural and educational work. We have not understood that new side of Hitler that is emerging, Mordecai lamented. We should have trained the youth in the use of live and cold ammunition. We should have raised them in the spirit of revenge against the greatest enemy of the Jews, of all mankind, and of all times.

But our Mordecai committed here a second serious error which boomeranged on the history of the Warsaw and Polish Jews. Mordecai and his young companions of Hashomer and the workers' organizations had taken too much into consideration the opinions of the older generation, of the "wise," the "deliberating," who weighed and measured and who had up their sleeves a host of clever arguments against the struggle with the occupation forces. A paradoxical situation arose. The older generation, which had half a lifetime behind it, spoke, thought, and concerned itself about surviving the war, dreamt about life. The youth—the best, the most beautiful, the finest that the Jewish people possessed— spoke and thought only about an honorable death. They did not think about surviving the war. They did not procure for themselves Aryan papers. They had no dwellings on the other side. Their only concern was to discover the most dignified, most honorable death, as befits an ancient people with a history of several thousand years.

Our youth has studied too little of the history of the struggles for freedom, or they would have known that the idealists who cast their lives in the scale of events were young people, whose hands and feet were not bound by family ties. In such instances the older generation was confronted by accomplished facts, by situations that left only one way open— to join the fighters. Mordecai and his fellows of the young generation knew too little about the history of freedom struggles or they would have known that in these stormy times one had to give less consideration to resolutions of committees and administrations and depend more on oneself, on one's own healthy instincts.

Unfortunately our youth was too well disciplined, and this made it possible for the Germans to obtain 300,000 Jews at a ridiculously cheap price, not a single German killed. That truth was understood by the youth only when it was too late, when the majority of Warsaw Jews were already in Treblinka.

Mordecai threw himself into the defense activity with all his zeal. Together with other groups and parties the Fighters' Organization was created, at whose head the coordinating commission of the political organizations placed Comrade Mordecai. This is not the place to describe the history of the Fighters' Organization. Comrade Mordecai was the soul of the organization, one of its most devoted workers. He was not one of those leaders who sent others into the line of fire and themselves remained at a distance. In January, 1943, he participated actively in the fighting action. His revolver claimed German sacrifices.

Once he pressed his revolver to the head of a German guard. The revolver jammed and Comrade Mordecai was only saved from counterfire thanks to a comrade who rescued him from the danger. He was active in the April action. (The Warsaw Ghetto uprising began April 19, 1943.) Death found him several weeks after the beginning of the action, together with the best fighting comrades. He was in a hideout in the ghetto that had five entrances. Someone most likely betrayed the bunker of the valiant fighters who ordinarily went out from this place to attack the SS and Ukrainians. The "Juden-Sieger" (Jew conquerors)—as the SS were called by the Wehrmacht—entered through five sides of the hideout, but first they filled it with gas. Comrade Mordecai fell together with the best comrades of the Fighters' Organization.

The Warsaw Ghetto Uprising

By Ber Mark

[EDITOR'S NOTE: *The Warsaw Ghetto uprising has the distinction of having been the first major civilian revolt against the German forces in all of occupied Europe. It preceded the general Warsaw uprising in August, 1944, by one and a half years.*

Though much has been written about the Warsaw Ghetto uprising, which has become a universal symbol of the indomitableness of the human spirit, no chronicle of Jewish resistance to Nazism would be complete without an account of this historic revolt. The chapter that follows has the advantage of being drawn from Professor Ber Mark's fourth and latest book on the subject, The Warsaw Ghetto Uprising (*Warsaw: Verlag Yiddish Buch, 1963*). *It is the most comprehensive and up-to-date account of this event.*]

The Armed Forces of the German Goliath

THE GERMAN security forces knew that inside the ghetto there existed a Jewish underground. In January, February, and March, 1943, they had come face to face with the Jewish fighters in armed clashes. Himmler therefore decided to liquidate the Warsaw Ghetto as quickly as possible. On February 16, 1943, he ordered Higher SS and Police Leader of the "General Government" Friedrich-Wilhelm Krüger to wipe out the Warsaw Ghetto. The date for this action was set for April 19. The plan was to liquidate the ghetto in three days and to give the Führer a birthday present—his birthday was April 20—a *Judenrein* (clean of Jews) Warsaw.

But Himmler knew that the Jews would resist. And so he ordered that Police and SS Leader Von Sammern in Warsaw be assisted in this operation by the more expert police leader, the Waffen-SS General Jurgen von Stroop, who was familiar with the latest tactics in combating the Soviet partisan movement in the eastern Ukraine. On April 16, Himmler himself came to Warsaw for a series of secret conferences. He was accompanied by General Schnäbel, one of the top-ranking SS officers.

The Germans mobilized the following military forces for the liquidation of the ghetto:

Over 2,000 soldiers and officers of the Waffen-SS.
Three detachments of the Wehrmacht (artillery and mine-sappers). The artillery bombarded the houses; the sappers blew up the entire ghetto.
Two battalions of German police, numbering 234 soldiers and officers.
About 360 soldiers and officers of the Polish police.
A group of 35 members of the Security Police.
A battalion of the so-called Askari (Ukrainian and Lett Fascists, soldiers of the auxiliary formation of the SS), 337 enlisted men and officers.

Altogether the German forces numbered 2,842, plus an additional 7,000 SS men, police and gendarmes who were brought into Warsaw in case the ghetto revolt should spread to the Aryan side. Needless to say the German forces were fully equipped with the most modern weapons and led by trained military personnel.

The Forces of the Jewish Fighters

At the outbreak of the uprising the Jewish Fighting Organization consisted of about 600 organized fighters. The Jewish Military Association and the teamster groups combined numbered about 400. But the number of participants in the uprising was much larger. Thousands of Jews of various backgrounds spontaneously formed bunker groups, bought weapons, and offered active resistance. Others engaged in passive resistance by ignoring the orders of the Germans and their helpers to leave the bunkers and line up for the transports. There were instances where the so-called "wild groups" had more weapons than the organized fighting groups. But the initiative and the leadership of the uprising was in the hands of the organized groups.

The Jewish Fighting Organization concentrated its forces in three separate areas:

1) The central ghetto, mainly in the streets, Nalewki, Gensia, Zamenhofa, Mila and the adjacent streets.

2) The brushmakers' area Swientojerska-Walowa and part of the odd-number side of Franciszkanska Street.

3) The factory areas of Leszno, Nowolipie and Smoczo streets.

The groups of the Jewish Fighting Organization were armed with Molotov cocktails, hand grenades, bombs, rifles, and pistols. They had little ammunition. In several places they used mines. The Jewish Military Association had more weapons, more grenades, and some machine guns. One detachment alone of the Military Association, the largest, on Muranowska Street, had about 300 grenades, 8 automatic guns, 1 light and 2 heavy machine guns, and several thousand rounds of ammunition. A large number of the fighters were dressed in German uniforms, which they had acquired earlier. The Military Association took up its main position on Muranowska. Several of its groups, numbering from 15 to 40 men, operated in the central area of the ghetto.

Strategy of the Uprising

The leaders of the uprising carefully assessed the situation and realized that a face-to-face confrontation with the enemy would spell defeat for the Jews at the very outset. They therefore decided to attack the Germans from the houses situated on the crossings of the ghetto streets. Hiding behind windows, walls, and in attics the Jews would open the attack on the enemy as he marched into the ghetto and was exposed to the Jewish fire. Also, underground bunkers were prepared for hiding and entrenchment in case of bombardment; and tunnels were prepared for movement from one position to the next and for possible escape to the other side of the ghetto wall.

While these preparations were going on the civilian population was busily constructing bunkers and laying away provisions. Day and night the ghetto was preparing to meet the enemy with active and passive resistance. "We realized," writes the ghetto archivist Emmanuel Ringelblum, "that this was a struggle between a fly and an elephant. But their national dignity dictated that the Jews offer resistance and not allow themselves to be led to the wanton slaughter."

Mordecai Anielewicz, Commandant of the uprising, and others of the Jewish Fighting Organization, had foreseen the tragic end as a result of this uneven struggle and had hoped that the shooting in the ghetto would bring all of Warsaw to the aid of the Jewish fighters and that revolt would spill over to the other side of the ghetto wall. Indeed, this was the enemy's fear, and therefore he threw himself at the ghetto with all his might. Unfortunately, Anielevich's hope was not realized.

On Sunday, April 18, 1943, the chiefs of police and the SS leaders held a conference at which the plan for the ghetto attack was worked out in detail. It was to take place the following day at dawn. At 2 P.M. that day the SS and the German police received their mobilization orders. A similar order was received by the Polish police, who threw a heavy cordon around the entire ghetto at about 6 P.M. One hour later the chiefs of staff of the Jewish Fighting Organization and of the Jewish Military Association were informed of the enemy's preparations.

In the evening the group leaders of the central ghetto met at the High Command bunker on Mila 29, under the chairmanship of Mordecai Anielewicz. At the end of the meeting weapons were distributed. In addition, each group received grenades and ammunition. Molotov cocktails were put into baskets. There was also a distribution of food and ciankali (poison to be taken in case they fell into the hands of the Germans). The password was "Jan-Warszawa." It also served as a signal to be combat-ready.

The entrance gates of the houses, as well as the street paths, were barricaded with furniture. Sandbags and pillows were placed on the window sills for support and protection at the time of shooting. An all-night vigil was set up in the ghetto. This was also the night of the first Passover Seder and there were more people in the ghetto than usual because many Jews who were living on the Aryan side had sneaked into the ghetto to conduct the Seder among Jews.

At 2 A.M. the Polish police guard around the ghetto was supported by German police and Lett-Ukrainian SS Auxiliary formations. Every twenty-five feet there was a guard armed with a heavy machine gun. Groups of Lett Fascists and Polish police entered the ghetto in single file and marched in the direction of the *Umschlagplatz*. That night Gestapo chief Brandt himself inspected the ghetto streets in his black limousine.

Except for the Jewish fighters' reconnaissance groups not a single Jew was seen on the streets that night. But preparations were going on to meet the enemy. At certain conspicuous places banners were hung out: red, white-blue, and white-red. In one place a certain group hung out a white-blue flag with a five-pointed star in the middle. On the walls of the houses bordering on the Aryan side, such as Swientojerska Street, slogans were hung out calling the Polish population to act in solidarity with Jews.

According to the plan of SS and Police Chief Von Sammern the central ghetto was to be attacked first, on the assumption that when the Jews in shops and the brush factory saw how the resistance of the other part of the ghetto was crushed they would volunteer for the transports.

On Monday, April 19, Von Sammern led his armed forces into the central ghetto. The Germans were afraid to expose themselves to the fire of the Jewish fighters, and so they sent the Lett Fascists first. Behind them came the remainder of the Ordnungsdienst, the Jewish ghetto police. Those Jewish policemen who refused to participate in this action, or tried to escape, were shot at the Gestapo gathering point at 103 Zelazna Street.

Behind the Jewish police marched the German and Ukrainian columns. They were preceded by a squadron of motorcyclists, followed by heavy trucks, infantry, heavy machine guns, ambulances, a field kitchen, and field telephones. In addition the Germans brought into the ghetto 12 panzer vehicles. On the main streets they set up tables and benches. On the tables—telephones. It all looked like a major military operation.

Sammern's units did not advance very far. They were stopped in two places—on the Nalewki corner Gensia and on the Zamenhofa corner Mila. The Jewish fighters who were hidden behind windows, balconies, and attics were armed with Molotov cocktails, hand grenades, several pistols, and one light machine gun. When the German column, singing lustily, reached the cross section of Nalewki-Gensia-Franciszkanska it was met by a hail of Molotov cocktails, hand grenades, bombs, and bullets. The unexpected attack sent the Germans fleeing in panic, leaving behind them their dead and wounded. When after a while they tried to get near their dead and maimed, they had to withdraw again, so strong was the continued concentrated fire from the Jewish positions. The Jewish fighters then leaped out of their hiding places and opened fire at the Germans with pistols.

The fact that the enemy retreated in flight at the very first encounter naturally evoked great jubilation among the Jews. The lusty singing of the SS men turned into the wailing of their wounded. The fighter Tamara called out: "This time they paid dearly!"

The German officers soon restored order in their ranks. An alarm was sent out to Von Sammern's headquarters, and aid arrived quickly. The German reinforcements did not dare to move in open formation. They shot chaotically at the houses from which the Jews had attacked earlier. The battle was on again. This time, too, the Jews not only held their ground but forced the enemy to retreat a second time.

The first encounter on the corner of Nalewki and Gensia streets lasted two hours, from 6 to 8 A.M. Only the Germans suffered losses. Thanks to their secure positions the Jewish fighters did not lose a single man. When the German column had completely retreated, the Jewish fighters came out into the streets again, threw their arms around each other and wished each other mazeltov (good luck). Then they took the uniforms off the German corpses, as well as the helmets and weapons.

Describing their first encounter with the Jewish fighters, the high Nazi officers later admitted that, "The Jewish resistance was unexpected, unusually strong and a great surprise." The German forces were simply expelled from the ghetto, said SS General Jurgen von Stroop, who in his report to Krüger and Himmler wrote: "At our first penetration into the ghetto the Jews and the Polish bandits succeeded, with arms in hand, in repulsing our attacking forces, including the tanks and panzers."

A little later the second battle broke out somewhat to the north at the crossroad of Zamenhofa and Mila. Four groups of Jewish fighters lay in wait for the enemy. They allowed the advancing Jewish police to pass, and when the German and Ukrainian Fascists came into view they opened fire on them. According to a prearranged signal the confused enemy was met with a hail of grenades and bullets and Molotov cocktails. The Germans and Ukrainians offered no resistance but started running in all directions, looking for cover. They hid behind the gates and in devastated stores. The Jews then opened fire on their hiding places, and the ghetto street took on a bizarre appearance. The Hitlerites ran in panic. Their fleeing turned into a real rout as Germans, Ukrainians, and Letts tried to beat each other to the new hiding place. The Germans pushed the Ukrainians out of the gates, seeking a place for themselves. More than a quarter of an hour passed before the officers had the situation under control. The SS men were the first to run out of the holes and with whips in hand drove the Ukrainians back to their positions and to manning the guns. Tense and nervous, the officers began to regroup their scattered formations.

But the enemy could no longer cope with the situation because the Jews made a new concentrated attack. The Germans now brought in tanks. The frightened Hitlerites moved behind them. But as soon as the first tank appeared at the corner of Mila and Zamenhofa it was hit by several well-aimed Molotov cocktails and set on fire. In its report the Jewish Fighting Organization described this scene as follows: "The well-aimed bottles hit the tank. The flames spread quickly. The blast of the explosion is heard. The machine stands motionless. The crew is burned alive. The other two tanks turn around and withdraw. The Germans who took cover behind them withdraw in panic. We take leave of them with a few well-aimed shots and grenades."

After a brief pause a new tank appears. The Jewish fighters hurl a bomb at it. Once again a German tank is burning in the middle of the street. Now the fighters as well as the non-combatant Jews who have crawled out of their hiding places have reached the pinnacle of jubilation. They were like different people. According to one eyewitness account, "The faces who only yesterday reflected terror and despair now shone with an unusual joy which is difficult to describe. This was a joy free from all personal motives, a joy imbued with the pride that the ghetto was fighting."

Another eyewitness describes the confusion in the German ranks: "There runs a German soldier shrieking like an insane one, the helmet on his head on fire. Another one shouts madly, 'Juden . . . Waffen . . . Juden . . . Waffen! [Jews . . . weapons . . . Jews . . . weapons!]' " Among the wounded were two officers of the ghetto police, Captain Fleischman and deputy Fells. The former was hated even by the ghetto police (he had deported four Jewish policemen to Auschwitz). The latter died of his wounds.

The ignominious defeat suffered by the Von Sammern forces at Zamenhofa and Mila was underscored in Stroop's report to his chief: "The tank and the two armored cars which were used in the action were pelted with Molotov cocktails. The tank was twice set on fire. This attack caused the withdrawal of the units. The losses during the first attack were: 12 men (6 SS-men and 6 Trawniki-men)." Trawniki-men were the Ukrainian and Lettish fascists, Volksdeutsche, and other collaborators who "studied" in the SS school in the Trawniki camp.

The losses of the Jewish fighters in this battle were much smaller. One fighter, Yechiel, fell. The battle at Zamenhofa corner, Gensia, lasted half an hour.

"All Is Lost in the Ghetto"

The leader of the Nazi action, Oberst von Sammern, was stunned. He could never have dreamt that the Jewish *Untermenschen* (lower than human) were capable of such a strong reaction. Not knowing what to do next he came running around 7:30 in the morning to the Hotel Bristol where Himmler's emissary, General Stroop, had arrived a day earlier to supervise the liquidation of the ghetto. Stroop was in the midst of his toilette when Von Sammern stormed into his room and cried: "All is lost in the ghetto! We are not in the ghetto! We cannot get into the ghetto! We have wounded and dead!"

Von Sammern suggested that bombers be flown in from Cracow. Stroop dismissed the idea because it would humiliate and shame Germany before the whole world. He immediately removed the bumbling SS and Police Chief from his leading post in the ghetto action and took over the leadership himself. He was determined to penetrate the ghetto even at the cost of the greatest sacrifice. The task was a very difficult one as he later stated. "It was impossible to get into the streets of Mila, Zamenhofa, Muranowska and the Nalewki because they were under continuous fire."

The Second Battle at the Corner of Nalewki and Gensia

As soon as Stroop took over command he restored order in the ranks with iron discipline. He decided to change Von Sammern's tactic. Sammern's plan was to regard the attack on the ghetto as an ordinary action and embrace the entire area in one fell swoop. Stroop on the other hand, facing strong Jewish resistance at various points, concentrated the attack on one particular point at a time. His aim was to rout one Jewish position after another until the fighters were driven into a narrow area and caught in a trap. But he soon had to change his tactic because he had not reckoned with the stubbornness of the Jewish fighters.

At 12 noon Stroop began the second attempt at storming the positions of the fighters at the crossing of Nalewki and Gensia. Learning from the morning's bitter experience, he did not march his German detachments in parade fashion but ordered them to scatter like snipers and hug the buildings as they moved forward. The present attack took place—as on a regular battlefield—under cover of artillery fire. General Stroop, who had the experience of two wars—the First World War on the French front, and the Second World War on the Soviet front—placed light artillery guns on Muranow Place, which continually bombarded the Jewish position on the Nalewki.

The Jewish fighters defended themselves heroically with their grenades and bottles of explosives. But these light weapons were no match for an artillery bombardment. Besides, their supply was running out. Under these circumstances it was difficult for the Jewish fighters to maintain their positions very long. They changed positions by crossing over, through the attics, from one house to the next, while hurling grenades at the pursuing enemy.

In the end Stroop introduced airplanes into the battle. The Jews were now forced to vacate the bombed buildings. Covering their retreat with their remaining hand grenades and Molotov cocktails, the Jewish fighters withdrew to the small Rabbi Maisels Street, taking their dead with them.

Before their retreat the Jewish fighters set fire to the large German warehouse on Nalewki 31. The leadership of the Jewish Fighting Organization ordered that all valuables and warehouses be burned so as not to leave anything worthwhile for the enemy. This first major act of sabotage served as a signal for the burnings that followed. An observer of the Polish underground press noted: "The remaining Jews are dying with weapons in hand, destroying first the warehouses full of valuables and burning down the factories."

Enraged by the Jewish resistance Stroop's forces wreaked their vengeance on the sick. They bombarded and set fire to the ghetto hospital. The soldiers broke into the burning wards and carried out a horrible massacre. They tossed the sick into the flames. They seized infants and smashed their heads against the walls. In the maternity wards they ripped open the bellies of pregnant women with their bayonets. Most of the hospital personnel perished in the flames. The Ukrainian Fascists especially distinguished themselves with their sadism. But on that first day of the uprising there was yet another defeat in store for the Germans.

The Battle on Muranow Place

Around 4 in the afternoon a large contingent of SS and German police penetrated Muranow Place and opened fire on the Jewish houses. In the houses numbering 7-21 well-armed groups of the Jewish Military Association were entrenched. They opened a concentrated fire on the enemy. Their tactic was to attack from various points and then quickly to withdraw to other positions, thus confusing the Germans. The resistance of the Jews became ever more intense. In his report Stroop describes this battle as follows: "Around half past six we met with strong resistance from a certain housing complex where [the Jews] defended themselves with machine guns. A special combat group [of Germans] expelled the opponents and penetrated into the houses but could not seize them. The Jews and the criminals defended themselves, switched from one point to the next and finally disappeared through the attics and underground paths."

The defense of the Jewish position on Muranowska 7 was the strongest. On the roof of this house there was a heavy machine gun that spat fire at the Germans and kept the entire area in a state of high tension until eight o'clock in the evening. Stroop later admitted that this position had dominated the entire Muranow Place and that the Jewish fighters, both men and women, had moved over the roofs with unusual agility and hurled grenades at the Germans. The Jewish resistance fighters flew two banners from the roof of Muranowska 7. In the evening, when Stroop called a halt to the battle, the Jewish position on Muranowska was still intact.

On April 19, several smaller skirmishes took place in other parts of the ghetto. On the first day of the uprising the Jewish *Untermenschen* forced the arrogant *Uebermenschen* (superior people) to withdraw from the battlefield with humiliation.

The next morning, on April 20, General Governor Hans Frank dispatched an alarming letter to Reichsminister Dr. Lammers, Chief of Hitler's chancellery in Berlin, in which he said: "As of yesterday we have in Warsaw a well-organized uprising in the ghetto which we have to combat with artillery."

As night fell, Stroop withdrew his forces from the ghetto. At staff headquarters of the Jewish fighters the situation was evaluated and plans were made for the coming battles. Reconnaissance groups were sent out to observe the area and the German patrols. Everywhere the mood was one of pride and tension. On that fantastic Passover night Jews sat down in the bunkers to celebrate the traditional Seder. Thus passed the first day of the Warsaw Ghetto uprising.

The Second Day of the Warsaw Ghetto Uprising
April 20, 1943

The Germans began the second day of the action with an ultimatum to the resistance fighters, apparently through the intermediary of the Judenrat Presidium, which was under arrest. It was a categorical demand that the fighters lay down their arms at once and hand themselves over to the mercy of the *Uebermenschen;* otherwise the ghetto would be razed to the ground.

The leadership of the Jewish Fighting Organization rejected the ultimatum. Commandant Mordecai Anielewicz wrote about this in his letter of April 26 which was smuggled out through underground channels to Yitzchok Zuckerman on the Aryan side: "We rejected the German ultimatum which demanded our capitulation."

On Tuesday April 20, the geographic area of the uprising was widened. In addition to the central part of the ghetto the Germans were attacked for the first time in the brushmakers' area (Swientojerska, Wolowa) and in the factory area (Leszno, Smocza, Nowolipie). On the second day of the uprising the enemy brought up an artillery battery outside the ghetto wall.

Stroop's first aim was to crush the stubborn resistance on Muranowska Street where yesterday's battle was left unfinished. The two banners on the roof of house number 7—the white-red (Polish) and white-blue (Jewish)—though riddled with bullet holes, were still aflutter.

Early that morning tens of trucks filled with German police surrounded the block that included houses number 7 and 9 where the Jewish fighters were still well entrenched. They opened fire on the buildings and hurled hand grenades at the windows. But several minutes later house number 7 began to counterattack with two machine guns, sowing death in the German ranks. Several German policemen were killed or wounded; the others scattered in panic. The battle was interrupted for a half hour, after which the Germans brought up four small tanks equipped with anti-aircraft guns.

The Jewish fighters fired on the tanks from behind the windows and the attics. One tank was stopped by a grenade, but the others were placed in positions far from the range of the fighter's fire. The tank guns subjected the houses to a fierce bombardment. And the fighters, though hurling grenades at them, could not damage the tanks.

This uneven battle lasted a quarter of an hour. By now the houses were, to a large extent, destroyed and the resistance grew weaker. The Germans, armed with machine guns and grenades, now stormed the heavily damaged houses. A hand-to-hand battle ensued. One resistance group, after having shot the last round of ammunition, was taken prisoner. Jewish noncombatants observed this scene from their hiding places. One eyewitness, M. Berland, described it as follows: "The Germans rounded up on the street a group of captured Jewish fighters, numbering around 80 men, most of them young people. They were surrounded by a band of 300 Germans holding their grenades and guns at the ready. Many of the prisoners were bleeding to death. Many of them were wounded in the head and had feet and arms hanging, partly torn. Their clothing was ripped, but there was not a trace of fear in their faces, not a trace of despair."

In his report of Tuesday's events, Stroop underscored that battle on Muranowska Street, especially the fighting over the two banners, in which he lost a German officer of the SS cavalry division. In reprisal for the loss of the first German officer to fall at the hands of Jewish fighters, Stroop had several hundred Jews shot on the spot.

The Mine Explosion in the Area of the Brush Factory

In the area of the brush factory the tactic of the Jewish fighting groups was similar to the one they employed in the central part of the ghetto. The area of defense embraced ten houses numbering from 28-38 Swientojerska Street, directly opposite the Aryan side, and the several nearby houses on the small Wolowa Street. The Jews concealed a mine at the gate of Wolowa 6, and on the third floor of Wolowa 3 they had their observation post.

At 3 P.M., Tuesday, April 20, Stroop's unit began to storm the brush-makers' area. Stroop himself led the attack. He was ringed by a heavy security detail, and two SS men held long automatic guns over his head, ready to shoot. Three hundred German soldiers and officers stormed the area. The Jewish fighters let them advance up to the gate. Then they pressed the button, and the mine exploded instantly. Chunks of earth mingled with limbs from the SS men. The report of the Jewish Fighting Organization claimed that twenty-two Germans were killed on the spot. As they scattered in panic the Germans were pelted with bullets and grenades. "Ja, das haben die Juden gemacht" (Yes, that's the work of the Jews) some were heard shouting.

After a hurried conference with their High Command, the Germans interrupted the battle and sent out a well-protected group of stretcher bearers to pick up their dead and wounded. The interruption, which lasted an hour and a half, gave Marek Edelman, commandant of the resistance fighters in that area, the opportunity to strengthen his positions before the Germans resumed their attack.

Now the Germans advanced in loose formation, by twos, hugging the walls. The Jewish fighters greeted them with grenades, Molotov cocktails, and two heavy bombs. The Germans were compelled to withdraw again. But Stroop ordered a continuous concentrated fire. This time the reply of the Jews grew steadily weaker because their ammunition was giving out. They shot only at concentrated groups of Germans. They had to make every bullet count.

Suddenly something incredible happened. The Germans halted the shooting, and one of their group, wearing white cockades, began to advance toward the Jewish position. The observers of the besieged brush-factory area recognized the man who headed the group. He was the German factory director, Lautz. Lautz proposed to the Jews a truce lasting a quarter of an hour in order that the Germans collect their dead and the Jewish fighters leave their hiding places. The local leadership of the Jewish Fighting Organization rejected with contempt the enemy's proposal. One does not conduct negotiations with the practitioners of genocide. Especially when at the time the Germans were making their truce proposal other SS units were setting fire to some houses on the block.

Stroop's reply to the "arrogance" of the resistance fighters was a heavy artillery bombardment, which the Jewish fighters could not withstand.

Toward evening Stroop interrupted the action. The Jewish fighters held a brief conference and decided to move the battle to a new position—to nearby Franciszkanska Street. The night expedition was not an easy matter because the Germans lighted up the area with huge searchlights. The fighter Romanowitch took a well-aimed shot at one searchlight and smashed it.

While this was going on a brief skirmish was taking place on Berish Maisel Street (the Germans had renamed it Chicken Street) which the High Command of the Jewish Fighting Organization had not even included in the battle zone. Two participants in the encounter, Tuvia Borzykwski and Chaim Frumer, gave the following account of the battle: "Quite unexpectedly we found ourselves on Chicken Street and knowing that the Germans were pursuing us we set up an ambush and lay in wait for them. We caught the Germans in a cross-fire and they paid with several dead. We emerged without a loss and headed in the direction of Mila Street, where fighting has been going on for several days."

On the roof of Muranowska 7 the fighters had hoisted the white-red and the white-blue flags, and on one of the tall buildings of Mila, the street of the impoverished Jews and the Jewish proletariat, they flew the red flag. It was Stroop's ambition to capture it. After much effort he succeeded. The Jewish fighters were in complete control of Mila Street. The headquarters of their High Command was located there, as well as a large number of underground bunkers and ammunition storages. Though the Jewish fighters regarded Mila Street as their main battle area they were not concentrated here in a single position but rather in a series of resistance points, and fighting was scattered.

There was still another battle area in the ghetto, quite a distance removed from those already mentioned. It was on Leszno, Nowolipie, and Smocza streets where the slave labor factories of Toebbens and Schultz were located. These two German manufacturers had asked Stroop not to send any military units into their factories. They were under the illusion that they themselves would be able to persuade the Jews to go voluntarily to the *Umschlagplatz* for deportation. They counted on the support of the few Jewish traitors who were their business associates or occupied important administrative posts in their factories.

They had miscalculated. Not only did the Jews not respond to their pleas to volunteer for deportation, but on April 20, they took the offensive in attacking the Germans. At 6 A.M. that day a German military column, headed by a tank, marched through Leszno Street. An orchestra played and the soldiers sang a military song. They were marching to the battle area of the central part of the ghetto. As an expression of solidarity with their comrades in the other battle zones the Jewish fighters opened fire on the passing Germans with all the weapons at their disposal. Eight Germans fell wounded on the street.

Shortly thereafter fighting broke out on Smocza Street. Expecting another column of SS to pass through on the way to the central ghetto, the Jewish fighters mined the street. Unfortunately the mine failed to explode. The Jewish fighters then pelted the tank with Molotov cocktails. It burst into flames. The fighter Dora Goldkorn described the joy the Jews felt at the sight of the burning tank: "When we saw that that tank was burning we began to dance for joy. It was the happiest moment in our lives. Such jubilant moments did not return any more."

Stroop ordered a heavy attack on the Jewish positions. The resistance fighters were forced to abandon Leszno Street and withdraw to Nowolipie. The Germans' revenge took the form of destroying houses, exploding bunkers, driving the Jews out into the open and shooting them on the spot.

The Peoples Guard Comes to the Aid of the Jewish Fighters

As soon as the ghetto fighters had fired their first shots at the Germans on April 19, the Warsaw leadership of the left-wing Polish underground movement, the Peoples Guard, met secretly on Briska Street in the suburb of Praga and decided to express its solidarity with the Jewish fighters by staging an attack on German artillery emplacements on Nowajarska Street that were bombarding the Jewish positions in the brushmakers' area. With its small membership and limited supply of weapons it was all the Peoples Guard could undertake at the time.

The attack was carried out with complete success on April 20, at a quarter to seven in the evening. The entire artillery crew, consisting of two Germans and two Polish policemen was killed. The artillery gun was silenced and the guardists did not suffer a single loss.

That same day another group of the Peoples Guard, consisting of four Poles and its leader, Lerski (Lerner, a Jew), attacked a guard of SS men and Polish police on Gensia street, corner of Okopowa. This action was only partly successful.

Solidarity Action of A. K. (Land Army) Youth

At a meeting on April 19, not called especially for that purpose, Colonel "Monter," commander of the Warsaw region of A. K., who was close to democratic circles, ordered a solidarity action behind the ghetto walls. It was to take place that day at 7 in the evening. A fairly large A. K. group consisting of workers and students participated in the battle.

Their aim was to blast the wall facing Sapierzinska Street and thus give a number of Jews an opportunity to escape. Polish police spotted the A. K. soldiers and warned the Germans, who opened fire on them as they were carrying out their mission. The A. K. soldiers failed in their task, but in the ensuing battle two Germans and two Polish policemen were killed. The losses of the A.K. were two soldiers killed and several wounded.

The Ghetto in Flames

On the third day of the uprising Stroop, realizing that he was exposing his forces to grave losses, decided to avoid direct confrontations with the Jewish fighters as much as possible. To overcome both the active and passive resistance of the Jews he set the ghetto on fire. On April 22 a huge fire raged in the ghetto the likes of which history has not recorded since the day when Nero burned Rome. This gruesome change in the ghetto situation was described as follows in a communiqué issued by the Jewish Fighting Organization:

"Thursday was a day that saw large-scale fires that engulfed Swientojerska, Franciszkanska, Walowa, and Nalewki streets, and in the afternoon Zamenhofa Street also. The fires were started by the demolition and incendiary detachments of the German artillery. Columns of smoke are hanging over the ghetto and are growing larger by the hour. The force with which the fire is raging is indescribably fierce. The ghetto streets are enveloped in a thick, corroding smoke.

"Realizing that in armed combat they will not crush the resistance of the Jewish fighters, the Germans decided to destroy them by fire. Thousands of women and children are being burned alive in these houses. Horrible cries and calls for help are heard from the flaming buildings. People, enveloped in flames, leap from the windows like live torches."

On April 22, Mordecai Anielewicz sent the following cryptic letter to his comrades of the underground on the Aryan side:

"We are well. Have you sent food packages [weapons]? Don't forget the eggs [grenades] and candy [bullets] and that which is most important for Auntie [rifles]. You can't send salami [revolvers]. We are considering plans of how we could see you. Let T. [Tuvia Scheingut the courier] go to the cemetery and pray for the departed souls." The meaning of the last sentence is: Keep in touch through the cemetery.

On April 23, Himmler ordered Stroop through the High SS Police leader in Cracow, Krüger, to hasten the liquidation of the ghetto at all costs. Stroop set about to destroy every single house by fire and raze the ghetto to the ground. In his report to his superiors Stroop wrote on April 23: "The action will be completed this very day."

He was wrong. That very day there appeared on the streets of Warsaw, on the Aryan side, an illegal poster, a call from the Jewish Fighting Organization to the Polish population:

For Our and Your Freedom!
Poles, Citizens, Soldiers of Liberty!

Amidst the booming of guns with which the Germans bombarded our houses, the homes of our mothers, women and children; amidst the rattle of machine guns which we have captured from the gendarmes and SS-men; amidst the smoke and fire and blood of the Warsaw Ghetto we appeal to you, we, the prisoners of the ghetto and we send you our brotherly greetings. We know that you are following with anguish and tears, with admiration and anxiety the outcome of the struggle we have been waging for the past several days with the invader.

You have seen and will see that every doorstep in the ghetto is and will continue to be a fortress. We may all perish in the struggle but we shall not surrender. Like you, we are seething with the passionate desire to avenge all the crimes committed by our common enemy.

It is a struggle for our and your freedom.
For our and your human, social and national honor!
We shall avenge Auschwitz, Treblinka, Belzec and Maidanek.
Long live the brotherhood of weapons and blood of fighting Poland!
Long live Freedom!
Death to the murderous and criminal occupants!
Long live the life-and-death struggle against the German occupant!

THE JEWISH FIGHTING ORGANIZATION

On Saturday, April 24, the fires in the ghetto continued to rage. Wehrmacht sappers went through the streets in groups, and with dynamite blew up one house after the other, while overhead airplanes circled, dropping incendiary bombs. The Jewish fighters retaliated by setting fire to and destroying military factories and warehouses. In their communiqué they said: "The fighting is fierce. The Jewish resistance fighters are hurting the enemy. They are setting fire to the factories and warehouses of the German war industry."

In some parts of the ghetto that day a large segment of the civilian non-combatant population, faced with the prospect of perishing in the flames of the burning houses, emerged from their bunkers and reported for the transport. But the fighting groups continued to offer resistance. They managed to reach the roofs of the burning buildings and from there shot at the enemy, running from corner to corner and hopping from roof to roof until the German machine gun fire compelled them to vanish.

The changed situation, the systematic burning down of the ghetto by the enemy, compelled the High Command of the uprising to change the tactics of the struggle. It was decided to pass over from the method of open confrontation with the enemy to the underground guerrilla warfare of surprise and attack. In his letter of April 23, to Antek (Yitzchok Zuckerman), his representative on the Aryan side, Mordecai Anielewicz wrote about this change:

Shalom, Yitzchok!
I don't know what to write you about. Permit me a few personal moments. I wish to express my own feelings and the feelings of my comrades. What we have lived through here is beyond description. All we know is that what has happened has surpassed our most daring expectations. Twice the Germans fled from the ghetto. One of our groups held onto its position for 40 minutes; another fighting group for six hours. The mine we laid in the brushmakers' area exploded. Our losses of people are very small. This is also a victory. Yechiel met a hero's death, a soldier killed at his machine gun. I have a feeling that great things are happening, that what we have undertaken is of tremendous significance.

As for the general situation:
Beginning with tonight we are adopting the tactic of partisan warfare. Tonight three fighting units will go out into the combat area. They will have two tasks: armed reconnaissance and the capture of weapons. Bear in mind that small arms have absolutely no value for us today. We rarely use them. What we are terribly in need of are: grenades, rifles, machine guns and explosives.

It is impossible to describe the conditions under which the Jews in the ghetto are living today. Only a few will survive. All others will perish sooner or later. Their fate is sealed. In practically all the bunkers where thousands of Jews are hiding it is impossible to light a candle for the lack of air!

The news that reached us yesterday that the comrades of the

P.P.R. [Polish Workers Party] have attacked the Germans, and the very fine broadcast of radio "Swit" [Polish underground radio] about our struggle, which we picked up on our receiving set, gave us much satisfaction. The fact that we are remembered on the other side of the ghetto wall encourages us in our struggle.

Be well, dear friend. Maybe we will see each other some day. The main thing: the dream of my life was realized. The Jewish Self-Defense in the Warsaw ghetto became a fact. The armed Jewish struggle and the revenge became a reality. I am a witness to this grand, heroic battle of the Jewish fighters.

M [MORDECAI]

The switching over to partisan warfare took on the following form: Jewish fighters would go out at night in groups of ten. Most of them would wear German uniforms and helmets which they had captured from the Germans, in order to confuse the enemy. They would tie rags around their feet to muffle the sound of their steps. They would reconnoiter for weapons and food, ambush the enemy, and attack his patrols from behind.

Anielewicz sent out the first partisan group on the night of April 23–24.

On April 24 it was learned that the Germans shot four members of the Judenrat Presidium whom they had taken as hostages when they commenced the liquidation of the ghetto. Soon thereafter the remnants of the Jewish ghetto police were also liquidated.

On April 25, the Jewish Fighting Organization suffered a serious loss. It sent out for the first time, to the Aryan side, a reconnaissance group to explore the possibilities of organizing a rescue action for the ghetto fighters. In its effort to reach the Aryan side the group had first contacted several Polish firemen stationed at the burning ghetto. (They were forbidden to extinguish the fires. Their job was to prevent the fires from spreading beyond the ghetto.)

On the way to meet the firemen, as was arranged beforehand, the group ran into a German patrol. A battle ensued in which all but one of the Jewish fighters was killed. Seriously wounded, the sole survivor managed to reach the headquarters bunker and report the mishap.

Despite this severe blow the Jews continued to fight. The next day, the 26th, marked a week since the uprising had begun, and still the ghetto had not been conquered. On that day Stroop was forced to admit in his report that everywhere his units ran into stubborn resistance.

On that day, too, Commandant Mordecai Anielewicz sent out his last letter to the representatives of the Jewish Fighting Organization on the Aryan side. What follows is a slightly abbreviated version of the letter:

This is the 8th day of our life-and-death struggle. The Germans suffered tremendous losses. In the first two days they were forced to withdraw. Then they brought in reinforcements in the form of tanks, panzer artillery, even airplanes, and began a systematic siege. . . .

Our losses, that is, the victims of the executions and fires in which men, women and children were burned, were terribly high. We are nearing our last days, but so long as we have weapons in our hands we shall continue to fight and resist. . . .

Sensing the end, we demand this from you: Remember how we were betrayed. There will come a time of reckoning for our spilled, innocent blood. Send help to those who, in the last hour, may elude the enemy—in order that the fight may continue.

On the night of April 27–28, the leadership of the Jewish Fighting Organization held a meeting in a bunker on Leszno Street. It was decided that owing to the extremely difficult situation and the ever-narrowing battle zone every possible effort should be made to leave the ghetto and join the partisans. The very courageous and agile courier Regina Fudin (Lilith) was given the task of gathering the scattered fighting groups in the factory area and preparing them for departure.

Before entering the sewers the fighters set fire to a German warehouse on Leszno 72. A most painful moment for them was the taking leave of their severely-wounded comrades who could not move. The fighter Lea Korn remained behind to guard them. It was hoped that the wounded would follow later, but this turned out to be an illusion because within a matter of a few days the Germans discovered the bunker with the Fighting Organization's "hospital" and killed all the wounded together with Lea Korn.

The exodus from the ghetto through the sewers was organized by the representatives of the Jewish Fighting Organization on the Aryan side, in collaboration with the Peoples Guard. On April 28, at 11 at night, forty Jewish fighters entered the sewer at Leszno 56, holding their weapons in their hands. The expedition was led by the fearless Regina Fudin. On the night of the next day, April 29, the group emerged from the sewers on the Aryan side on the corner of Agrodows and Zelazna Streets. The ghetto fighters found a temporary haven in the attic of the Polish worker Riszard Trifon, who undertook to shelter them.

On Friday, April 30, the Pole Gajek, of the Peoples Guard, and Tuvia Scheingut, courier man for the Jewish underground, took the entire group in a truck to the forest in Lomianka, about seven kilometers from Warsaw. The journey was made in broad daylight and without a mishap.

Another attempt by a group of Jewish fighters to escape through the sewers on April 29 ended in tragedy. While the group had waited for the signal to emerge the Germans had, in the meantime, learned about the successful exodus of the previous group and surrounded the manhole and the entire area. When they emerged the exhausted fighters found themselves face to face with the armed enemy. A brief but stubborn battle ensued during which all the fighters perished.

Friday, April 30, marked the twelfth day since the fighting began. Observers on the Aryan side, even those friendly to the Jewish cause, doubted whether the Jewish fighters could hold out much longer. One such observer, Ludvik Landau, noted in his secret diary on April 30: "It seems that the heroic struggle is nearing its end. The fires continue to rage and the armed resistance grows weaker owing to exhaustion and the enemy's superior forces."

But on that same Friday new fighting broke out in the ghetto. Jewish fighting groups suddenly appeared in places where nothing had happened before. On Priejard Street a group arrived consisting of remnants of the Jewish Military Association and set fire to a Wehrmacht warehouse. The area resounded with the thunder of shooting.

As the uprising continued the enemy became restive and panic broke out in the ranks of the Polish police, who suffered increasing losses at the hands of the Jewish avengers. There are official documents attesting to the fact that many Polish policemen either refused outright or used various subterfuges to avoid doing duty in the ghetto area.

With regard to the Jews the role of the Polish police was generally a shameful one. It was particularly so during the uprising. Polish police hunted down Jews who were hiding on the Aryan side, blackmailed them, squeezed large sums of money from their victims and then handed them over to the Gestapo. They robbed and tortured Jewish food smugglers at the ghetto gates. They belonged to the "evil spirits" about whom Ringelblum wrote in his well-known work *Polish-Jewish Relationships During the Second World War.*

Side by side with the Polish police, bands of civilian blackmailers, the so-called *szmalcovniki,* exploited the Jewish tragedy. They lay in wait at the ghetto gates and pounced on the despairing escapees from the conflagration and the German bullets. They pursued them, robbed them, and drove them back into the burning ghetto. They raped them, informed on them, and then handed them over to the Gestapo. Squeezing money out of Jews, putting fear into their hearts, giving them no rest, driving them out of their hiding places, collaborating with the Nazis in their hatred of the Jews, all this became a new source of income, a kind of sport for these elements, who consisted of all kinds of scoundrels—the "golden" youth, hypocritical fanatics, a part of the middle class that was eager to take over the commercial establishments left by the annihilated Jews, and even professionals. But at the head of them all was the Polish police with its arrogance and greed.

But when their own safety was at stake; when they became the target of Jewish bullets and grenades, they revealed their true cowardice and avoided the dangerous areas around the ghetto.

Only the proletarian and democratic elements in the Polish underground combated both the Polish police and all other manifestations of blackmail and rabid anti-Semitism. There were instances when they carried out death sentences. The right-wing elements took their orientation from the Provisional Government in London, the dominant influence in the Polish underground. Despite the urging from Premier Sikorski they did little to combat anti-Jewish blackmail and the collaboration of the extreme anti-Semitic elements with the Germans in their persecution of Jews.

Amidst the thunder of guns and the raging fires the Jewish fighters decided to celebrate May 1, the day of international solidarity. They gathered in their bunkers to listen to speeches and sing songs, then they sent out special groups to seek out the enemy and engage him in battle. "Our struggle," said one May 1 speaker, "will undoubtedly be of historic significance not only for the Jewish people but also for the resistance movement of all of Europe that is fighting against Hitlerism."

At dawn, on May 1, a fighting group emerged from the bunker on Mila 18, the headquarters of the Jewish Fighting Organization. The Jewish fighters wore German helmets. This confused the enemy, and three Germans were killed. The Jews escaped without any losss.

On May 8, Germans came upon the headquarters of the Jewish Fighting Organization, a large bunker on Mila 18. It was the hiding place for 300 civilian non-combatants and 80 fighters. Mordecai Anielewicz was one of them. Here strategy was planned and contact with the outside world was maintained. It was the nerve center of the uprising. How the Germans discovered the bunker is not known to this day. They surrounded the area and the bunker's five entrances. The civilian population of the bunker emerged and surrendered, but the fighters offered resistance. The Germans blew up the entrances with hand grenades and when the fighters still refused to come out the Germans let gas into the bunker. The fighters began to choke and decided to commit suicide. Before their death they each sang the hymn of their party or group. Then they died either by gas or suicide, including Anielewicz.

Only a small group that happened to be standing near the exits and therefore was not as affected by the gas as were the others fell unconscious. They were later discovered by the fighters Zivia Lubetkin, Kanal, and Frimmer and taken to the Aryan side in an exodus arranged with the Peoples Guard. About fifty fighters were pushing forward in the filthy, stinking water of the sewers, their weapons tied around their necks. On their stooped backs they carried their rescued comrades from Mila 18. The march through this sewage-gehennah lasted thirty hours.

On May 10, at 8 in the morning, they heard what seemed to them a tremendous explosion. The manhole was pried open. Outside a truck was waiting for them. They reached the Lomianki forest in a matter of half an hour. The new arrivals, among whom was Marek Edelman, commandant of the Bund fighting group, were now united with their comrades of the previous exodus.

But not all of the fifty had managed to emerge from the sewer in quick time. After thirty-four had been loaded into the truck there was the fear that Germans might arrive any minute. The rest of the fighters were left in the sewer to await the truck's return. In the meantime police, SS and Lettish Fascists arrived, mined the exit, and surrounded the area. The Peoples Guard made several attempts at breaking through but was unsuccessful. The fighters in the sewer were unaware of this. When their patience wore out they emerged and found themselves face to face with the enemy. A tragic uneven battle took place. The Germans and their helpers hurled grenades at the remaining Jewish skeletons. They were all killed.

On that very day two Jewish couriers were to have received from the Peoples Guard a supply of weapons for the fighting ghetto. They ran into a police ambush and were shot. That is how the first twenty-two days of the uprising ended. The fighting now entered a new and final phase.

On Saturday, May 13, the twenty-fifth day of the uprising, when the ghetto had been razed to the ground and the Fighting Organization no longer had a High Command, SS General Stroop was compelled to note in his report that new fighting had flared up with fierce stubbornness.

On the night of May 13–14, Soviet aviation, in response to a radio-telegram sent by the Polish Workers Party, attacked German military objects in Warsaw as an act of reprisal for the liquidation of the ghetto. The Soviet bombers were guided to their targets by the fires of the still burning ghetto. The attack lasted from midnight to 2 A.M. Several Jewish fighting groups, taking advantage of the confusion the bombardment caused among the German guards, tried at three different points to break out of the ghetto. They were only partly successful.

On May 16, after four weeks of continuous fighting, the ghetto, burned out and bled white, had still not capitulated. Nevertheless Stroop sent an official report to his superiors claiming that, "The former Jewish residential district [a German euphemism for ghetto] in Warsaw no longer exists."

To celebrate this "great historic victory" as a symbol of the destruction of Warsaw Jewry, Himmler ordered that the big synagogue on Tlomacka 5 be blown up. It was a magnificent structure built in 1877 by the Italian architect Leonardo Marconi, in the style of German neo-renaissance. The explosion was so powerful that the detonation reverberated throughout Warsaw. On that very day new Jewish fighting groups appeared on Mila Street. They were young and tall. They wore German uniforms and were armed with pistols and hand grenades.

On May 31, Hans Frank, governor general of occupied Poland, held a conference at his Cracow headquarters at which General Krüger, minister of security, reported that "he was informed by the security police in Warsaw that the Jews were continuing their attacks and assassinations." Krüger continued, saying that crushing the Jewish resistance and liquidating the Warsaw ghetto were most difficult tasks for the police, but that they must carry out what the Führer ordered.

There are eyewitness accounts and reports of clashes between Jews and Germans in June and as late as July. On the nights of September 23 and 26 some Jewish fighters, their weapons in their hands, managed to slip past the enemy guards to the Aryan side, leaving behind them a desert wrapped in deadly silence. But from time to time this silence would be broken by shots that rang out in the ghetto when armed Jewish remnants, compelled to emerge from the hiding places in search of food, shot it out with the Germans.

The Germans brought in several hundred Jewish prisoners from Auschwitz to clean up the ghetto debris. They were housed in a newly-erected SS camp on Gensia Street. A survivor of this slave labor detail recounts that one day, in October, when he and some fellow prisoners entered a bunker they found on the table the fresh remains of an unfinished meal and an open volume of Sholem Aleichem's stories. The occupants of the bunker had just fled to another hiding place.

The last recorded report of a Jewish fighting group wandering through the ruins of the ghetto is dated June 1944. The Polish underground publication, *Eastern and National Information,* wrote on July 7, 1944, that in June of that year a Jewish group attacked a detachment of gendarmes that happened to pass the ghetto area in broad daylight, killing three Germans. The Germans immediately ordered a round-up. They caught and shot twenty-five Jews.

Individual Jews, hiding in ghetto caves, survived until the very end, until the Polish uprising in August, 1944. Jewish fighters and leaders of the Warsaw Ghetto uprising, who had managed to escape earlier through the sewers or by other means, later joined in the Polish uprising in Warsaw in August, 1944. Some fell in that battle. One of them was Hersh Berlinski, Commandant of the Jewish Military Association.

Editor's Postscript

"The most important engagement was fought in the Warsaw ghetto (16 dead and 85 wounded on the German side, including collaborators)." (Raul Hilberg, *The Destruction of the European Jews*, p. 663.)

As his source for this low estimate of German casualties Hilberg cites Jurgen Stroop's report, which he accepts uncritically. Here are some other versions of the number of casualties suffered by the Germans: *Glos Warszawy,* organ of the Peoples Guard, reported that "the German casualties during the first week of the struggle were about 360 dead and over 1,000 wounded." (*Documents and Materials About the Warsaw Ghetto Uprising,* compiled by Ber Mark, Warsaw: 1953, p. 185.)

"For nine days now has the Warsaw Ghetto been valiantly fighting. . . . The Germans have lost about 1,000 dead and wounded." (From a telegram dated April 28, 1943, sent to Dr. I. Schwartzbart, representative of Polish Jewry with the Polish Provisional Government in London by the leaders of the Jewish underground in Warsaw, signed by M. Feiner and A. Berman. (See Yad Washem Bulletin No. 13, p. 20; see further reference to this telegram later on in the Editor's Postscript.)

Describing the events of her own fighting group on the very first day of the uprising, Zivia Lubetkin writes: "We allowed the Germans to pass our hidden positions until they reached the mined spot. Then we pushed the electric buttons and soon we saw the torn limbs of hundreds of Germans flying in the air. This was our first reward."

*   *   *

In his review of Professor Mark's latest book, *The Warsaw Ghetto Uprising,* from which the preceding chapter was drawn, Reuben Ainsztein, well-known writer on the holocaust period, returns again to the question of weapons, which the Jewish Fighting Organization repeatedly raised and which the Polish Home Army Command repeatedly ignored. Ainsztein cites one of the documents in Professor Mark's book, a radiogram sent by General Grot-Rowecki, then Commander of the Home Army, to the Polish Provisional Government in London on January 2, 1943:

Now, when it is too late, Jews from various little Communist groups are asking us for weapons, as though we had stores full of them.

As a test I have given them a few pistols. I have no certitude that they will use them. I will not give any more arms, for, as you know, we ourselves have not got them. I am waiting for supplies from you. Let me know what means of contact our Jews have in London.

"The ill-will and dishonesty of the radiogram," writes Ainsztein, "cries out in its very first sentence. For the Jews who asked the Home Army Commander for arms did not belong to 'various little Communist groups' but to the Jewish Fighting Organization, in which the Communists formed only four fighting units as compared with fourteen Zionist and four Bundist ones. As for the ten pistols General Grot-Rowecki agreed to give the Jews, they 'were in a very poor condition and only in part usable.' " This quotation comes from another document in Mark's book.

As for General Grot-Rowecki's crying poor about the Home Army's meager supply of weapons Ainzstein exposes this hypocrisy by quoting from the Home Army's own official history, published by the General Sikorski Institute in London in 1950. Of the seven territorial commands into which the Home Army was organized, the Warsaw Home Army Command alone had the following supply of weapons hidden since September 1939:

131 heavy machine-guns with 16,900 rounds; 190 light machine-guns with 54,000 rounds; 6,045 rifles with 749,000 rounds; 1,070 pistols with 8,708 rounds; 7,561 grenades; seven small anti-tank guns with 2,174 rounds.

This, Ainzstein points out, does not take into account "the arms obtained from airdrops, purchased from Germans, Italians or Hungarians, or manufactured in its own secret workshops . . ." (See "New Documents on the History of the Ghetto Uprising" by Reuben Ainzstein, *The Jewish Quarterly,* Autumn 1964, pp. 33–36.)

And in his review of *Fighting Warsaw: The Story of the Polish Underground State, 1939–1945,* by Stefan Korbonski, chief of the Directorate of Civil Resistance during the war, Ainzstein comes to the conclusion that ". . . the attitude of the Polish Home Army command was to avoid at all costs military action against the Germans to help the Jews." (See Wiener Library *Bulletin,* Nos. 1, 2, 1958.)

*   *   *

On March 13, 1943, only five weeks before the uprising, Mordecai Anielewicz, commander of the Jewish Fighters Organization, found it necessary to write to the high command of the Home Army complaining that "of the 49 weapons [pistols] you gave us, only 36 are usable, because of a lack of ammunition. . . . The fact that we were given weapons without ammunition strikes us as a cynical mockery of our fate and confirms the hypothesis that the poison of anti-Semitism continues to corrode Poland's ruling circles despite the cruel and tragic experience of the past three years." And on the very eve of the uprising Anielewicz cried out: "If only we could get the weapons and ammunition we need. . . ." (From Anielewicz's letter to the leadership of the Home Army dated March 13, 1943 in the archives of The Jewish Historical Institute of Warsaw. See Ber Mark, *Uprising in the Warsaw Ghetto;* Part II Documents, New York, Schocken Books, 1975.)

*   *   *

On April 28, 1943, the ninth day of the uprising, the beleaguered Warsaw Ghetto fighters wrote an urgent message addressed to Dr. I. Schwartzbart, member of the National Council of the Polish Republic in London, which contained, in part, the following cry for help:

> On behalf of the millions of Jews burnt and murdered and burned alive, on behalf of those fighting back and all of us condemned to die we call on the whole world: It is imperative that the powerful retaliation of the Allies shall fall upon the bloodthirsty enemy immediately and not in some distant future, so that it will be quite clear what the retaliation is for. Our closest Allies must at last understand the degree of responsibility which arises from such apathy in the face of an unparalleled crime committed by the Nazis against a whole nation, the tragic epilogue of which is now being enacted. The heroic rising, without precedent in history, of the doomed sons of the ghetto should at last awaken the world to deeds commensurate with the gravity of the hour.

The message was delivered on May 21 by Pawel Siudak, director of the Department for Social Affairs. Dr. Schwartzbart made the following entry in his diary: "Friday, May 21, 1943. Siudak gave me two telegrams from the Jewish National Committee and the Jewish Labor Organization Warsaw. One of them is dated April 28. I can't understand why it was held back so long. Siudak blames the forwarding system. I have my doubts. I immediately forwarded both messages to Tel Aviv and to America."

In the meantime Szmul Zygelboim, representative of the Jewish Bund with the London Polish Government, despairing over the world's indifference to the plight of Polish Jewry, committed suicide on May 11, 1943, hoping by this act to arouse the world to some action. In a farewell letter to his friends he wrote: ". . . Maybe my death will achieve that which I did not succeed in achieving during my life, the starting of a definite action to rescue at least the less than three hundred thousand Jews who are the only survivors in Poland of the former population of three and a half million. Now is the last minute for such an action. . . ."

On May 22, 1943, one day after Dr. Schwartzbart had received the two messages from Poland, he began forwarding them to the United States Ambassador in London, to the Allied governments-in-exile in London, to the British Government, as well as to various Jewish organizations and leading British personalities. The following is the full reply sent by Anthony Eden, then Minister of Foreign Affairs, through his secretary: "I write on Mr. Eden's behalf to thank you for your letter of the 24th of May in which you enclosed two messages addressed to the late S. Zygelboim and yourself by the Central Committee in Poland describing Jewish resistance to the Germans in the ghetto of Warsaw." (See Philip Friedman, *Martyrs and Fighters: The Epic of the Warsaw Ghetto*, New York: Frederick A. Praeger, 1954. pp. 269–277.)

* * *

Six months after that event, when most of the fighters in the Warsaw Ghetto uprising, including their Commander, Mordecai Anielwicz, lay buried under a heap of charred rubble, and "the less than three hundred thousand Jews" for whom Zygelboim expressed concern in his farewell letter, had already been cut down by the Nazi extermination machine to half that number, Antek (Yitzchok Zuckerman), who was then Commander of the Jewish Fighting Organization, made yet another plea for help. In November, 1943, Antek sent a memorandum to General Komorowski (Bor), Commander of the Home Army, in which he listed the previous calls for help made by the Jewish Fighting Organization since November, 1942, and concluded the memorandum with the following plea:

To our regret the support given us by the armed forces has been exceedingly restricted, as shown by the facts stated above. Today, when the conqueror is murdering the last of Polish Jewry, the Jews still surviving in the ghettos and camps are crying out for arms and the possibility of establishing a partisan movement.

Sir and Commander, during the last hours of Polish Jewry we appeal to you in the name of 150,000 Jews who are still alive. Help us to die fighting the enemy. We need arms for the camps at Czestochowa and Piotrkow, for the remaining Jews at Radom and in the

Kielce region, and also for the camps in the Cracow district. Our own resources alone do not enable us to establish the necessary contacts with the Lodz Ghetto. Help us to transfer the arms, support our efforts to organize Jewish partisan units. Give us the opportunity to organize, with joint forces, armed assistance for those of the Jewish forces that are ready to engage in the struggle.

Time presses on. In a few weeks it may possibly be too late. By that time all our work and the cooperation between us may quite possibly be entirely useless.

On behalf of the Command of the Jewish Fighters' Organization.

THE COMMANDER (ANTEK)

General Bor through his representative, promised some action and a written reply. In their introduction to the memorandum the editors noted, "No written reply was ever received, so this was actually the last attempt to induce those with arms to come to the aid of the surviving Jews in their desperate struggle." (See "The J.F.O. [Jewish Fighters' Organization] and the Polish Underground," in *Extermination and Resistance, Historical Records and Source Material,* Israel: Ghetto Fighters' House, 1958, I, 14–19.)

*   *   *

In his assessment of the Warsaw Ghetto Uprising the Polish military historian and former member of the Home Army's General Staff, Major-General Jerzy Kirchmayer, put the meaning of that event in its proper historic perspective when he wrote:

The Warsaw Ghetto fell after a heroic fight, but the idea of armed struggle, in the name of which the insurgents had died, reached beyond the walls, survived and endured until victory. It was carried abroad by the few Jews who reached the forests and fought there as an element of singular determination. It was spread by Poles who in Warsaw saw Nazis unsuccessfully endeavouring to break the resistance of the few and almost weaponless ZOB groups.

Thus the military importance of the Warsaw Ghetto Uprising is, above all, in its repercussions among the Polish people, in the fact that being an uncompromising armed deed it undermined the idea of "enduring" and "waiting," and thus contributed in a capital manner to the rise of an active struggle against the invader. The momentary successes of the insurgents toppled the Germans from their pedestal of omnipotence and proved to the Poles the effectiveness of armed resistance. Thus the blood of the ghetto defenders was not shed in vain. It gave birth to the intensified struggle against the fascist invader and from this struggle there came victory. (Quoted by Reuben Ainsztein in his "Thirty Years After: A Reassessment of the Warsaw Ghetto Uprising in 1943," *The Jewish Quarterly, 1953–1973*, p. 29, from Kirchmayer's as yet unpublished "Wojskowe znacznie Powstania Kwietniowego" ["The Military Importance of the April Uprising"], Archives of the Institute of Party History in Warsaw).

* * *

In his reflections "Twenty Years After the Ghetto Revolts" Dr. Nahum Goldmann, President of the World Zionist Agency and of the World Jewish Congress, writes:

The sum total of the behavior of the democratic powers in Europe and the United States in the period of the Holocaust does not reflect glory on their peoples or on modern democracy. . . . I do not know whether the Allied Powers could have prevented the murder of millions of Jews during the War, but I do not doubt (and I was then closely acquainted with our struggle and with day-to-day events) that thousands and tens of thousands of Jews could have been saved by more active and vigorous reaction on the part of the democratic governments.

Looking back at those day-to-day events Dr. Goldmann points out that the Jewish leaders in the Western democracies, himself included, also did not act with the necessary vigor and understanding demanded by the times:

. . . because we did not go beyond routine petitions and requests, and because the Jewish communities did not have the courage and the daring to exert pressure on the democratic governments by drastic means and to force them to take drastic measures.

"I will never forget the day when I received a cable from the Warsaw Ghetto, addressed to Rabbi Stephen Wise and myself, asking us why the Jewish leaders in the United States had not resolved to hold a day-and-night vigil on the steps of the White House until the President decided to give the order to bomb the extermination camps or the death trains [elsewhere quoted more correctly as the railway line leading to the camps]. We refrained from doing this because most of the Jewish leadership was then of the opinion that we must not disturb the war effort of the free world against Nazism by stormy protests. (Nahum Goldmann, "Jewish Heroism in Siege,"

In the Dispersion, Jerusalem: World Zionist Organization, Winter 1963–1964, p. 7.)

* * *

Commenting on the relatively small number of suicides in the Warsaw Ghetto, Ringelblum had this to say in his diary entry of December, 1942 [three months after the deportation of over 300,000 Jews to Treblinka]: "One cannot but marvel at the fact that the number of suicides was not large; that of over 300,000 victims there were only several hundred suicides. The large masses of people, as well as the overwhelming majority of the intelligentsia, did not permit themselves to break down, and resisted passively as long as it was possible. As for the question why did the Jews not defend themselves? the answer is: They offered a strong and effective psychic resistance. No other people in the world could have endured psychically as long as the Jews."

Even to this phenomenon, the German reaction was typically racist. Having subjected the Jews to so much humiliation and suffering, they expected them to commit suicide *en masse.* But when they saw so few suicides in the Warsaw Ghetto, they allegedly complained the Jews lacked a sense of honor.

* * *

Cultural Life in the Ghetto

In his memoir *This Is How It Was,* Jonas Turkow describes the cultural life in the Warsaw Ghetto. The Germans granted permits for entertainment in the ghetto in the form of plays, reviews, and vocal and symphonic concerts, provided the material used by the performing artists satisfied the censor and was not of Aryan authorship. Despite these restrictions, sharp satire mocking the enemy was frequently introduced into scripts under the guise of allegory, and plays by non-Jewish authors were at times performed. For example, Molière's *The Miser* was presented as the work of its Yiddish translator, A. Einhorn, and the comedy *Freud's Theory of Dreams,* written by a non-Jew, Antoni Cwoidzinski, was credited to the Jewish author Sigmund Freud.

There were five regular theatres in the Warsaw Ghetto, two of which performed in Yiddish and three in Polish. In addition, there were several professional as well as amateur choruses, an outdoor orchestra that played in courtyards, and a puppet theatre. In one year alone, between September, 1940, and September, 1941 inclusive, there were 1,814 stage presentations of various kinds, including eight symphonic concerts.

Other forms of cultural expression were forbidden and had to be conducted illegally. This was the work of the underground Jewish Cultural Organization known as YKOR, which Turkow says, "organized a network of schools and a People's University, and operated a large library. It also arranged lectures on both literary and scientific topics. . . . Its large staff of speakers, writers, scientists, and artists penetrated the remotest areas of the ghetto and with their program of education and enlightenment helped dispel the apathy and indifference of the despairing masses and infused them with a sense of life and hope."

To protect the speakers from unexpected visitors, permits were obtained in their behalf as for dramatic artists. When a German did show up—as frequently happened—the lecture hall was at once transformed into a concert hall, and the lecturer into an actor.

"YKOR," writes Turkow, "organized youth branches in every House Committee. Through the educational work it conducted in the ghetto, especially in the House Committees, it helped, to a large extent, to prepare the ground for the Jewish resistance movement."

*   *   *

In an entry dated February, 1941, in his diary, *Notes from the Warsaw Ghetto,* Emmanuel Ringelblum writes: "There are several illegal mobile libraries that bring books to the home of the reader. There is a Hebrew School of 700 pupils where rabbis are the teachers."

*   *   *

There was a vital literary creativity in the Warsaw Ghetto as well as in other ghettos. Jewish writers depicted the life around them in poems, short stories, and plays and frequently recited their works to eager audiences. Though the life from which they drew their themes was one of unimaginable suffering, despair was not their dominant note.

The Yiddish poet Kalman Liss, who was in the ghetto of Otwock about twenty miles from Warsaw, wrote in a poem entitled "I Sing the Song of the Blossoming Faith":

> The autumn is menacing with rain
> angry winds and icy gales,
> but my song leaps like a brown antelope
> over the path,
> bearing a promise of freedom to the world.

And the Polish Jewish poet Leon Staf, who was in the Warsaw Ghetto, said: "Even more than bread we now need poetry in a time when it seems that it is not needed at all."

The Ringelblum Archives

Not the least of the miracles achieved by the Warsaw Ghetto underground was the setting up and the preservation of the Ringelblum Archives, the most authentic source of information we have today about life in the Warsaw Ghetto, as well as about several hundred other Jewish communities in wartime Poland.

Founder, organizer, and moving spirit of this historical project throughout its existence was Emmanuel Ringelblum (born 1900), well-known historian of Polish Jewry and a leading cultural and communal figure. In the fall of 1939, when Hitler invaded Poland, Jewish refugees from various Polish cities began streaming into Warsaw, their number growing steadily to a high of 150,000. Ringelblum, who was one of the leaders of the Jewish Social Self-Help organization that aided these refugees, found himself in a rapidly changing swirl of events unique in contemporary history. At the end of each day, he made hurried entries of these events in his diary, which became the genesis of the future archives.

A year later, when already in the ghetto, Ringeblum gathered around him a number of historians, teachers, and communal leaders and formed a secret organization which became known as Oneg Shabbat (the pleasures of the Sabbath) because they met on Saturdays. At these Sabbath meetings they would discuss assignments for sociological studies that would embrace every aspect of ghetto life, such as: "The Jewish Police . . . communal life, the school system, the life and creativity of the Jewish cultural collective during the war, Jewish-Polish relationships, smuggling . . . youth, women." Even sanitation, corruption, and demoralization in the ghetto were subjects for study.

"The aim of Oneg Shabbat," Ringelblum wrote later, "was to present a comprehensive picture of Jewish life in time of war. . . . We tried to have the same event, as for instance, an account of a community, described by both an adult and a youth, a religious Jew who thinks at every turn about the rabbi, the synagogue, the cemetery and other religious institutions, and by a secular-minded Jew who, in his description, would stress other, but equally important, elements. . . . The main principle in our work was comprehensiveness. Another principle that guided us was objectivity. Our aim was to present the whole truth, no matter how harsh it might be. . . . On the first order of our work were the atrocities the Germans committed against the Jewish population."

Papers submitted by members of Oneg Shabbat were thoroughly discussed and, in some instances, rewritten, in order to assure the maximum objectivity. But these works form only part of the archives. By various clandestine methods the Oneg Shabbat group would obtain from the

Judenrat files documents of anti-Jewish edicts issued by the Germans. Scenes of ghetto life were photographed to have a visual record of the actual results of these edicts. Copies of the underground press in Yiddish, Hebrew, and Polish were collected, as well as diaries, poems, and short stories. They all became part of the archives. Thus was the collective record of Polish Jewry under German domination in World War II written and compiled for future generations.

Refugees from other towns now in the Warsaw Ghetto became a vital source of information about events in their own communities prior to their escape. But Oneg Shabbat was an illegal organization and pains were taken to assure its safety. "Before contacting a person," Ringelblum writes, "we learned something about his character, his social and political past, etc. It was only after obtaining this information that we sat down to talk with him. Few people knew the real reason for these talks." In this manner the archive was enriched with monographs about hundreds of towns.

Work for Oneg Shabbat was carried on under extremely difficult conditions. In addition to the strain of constant vigilance against informers there were the overcrowded quarters unheated in the winter, the ravages of hunger and disease, the threat of deportation. "Typhus and the deportation," writes Ringelblum, "were the deadly enemies of Oneg Shabbat, and claimed the greatest number of victims."

And Hirsh Wasser, the secretary of Oneg Shabbat (he survived the war and now resides in Israel), writes, "Death was the constant companion of its workers. . . . Day and night every member was threatened with the greatest dangers, of which death was the most comfortable."

Ringelblum concludes his account of the history and methods of Oneg Shabbat with these words: "Oneg Shabbat was a brotherhood, a fraternity of brothers on whose banner was inscribed: self-sacrifice, devotion to one another, and service to humanity."

In August of 1942, at the height of the mass deportation during which the Germans dragged over 300,000 Jews out of the Warsaw Ghetto and sent them to the gas chambers of Treblinka, the preservation of the Ringelblum Archives became a matter of great urgency. The materials were placed part in tin boxes, that were then sealed hermetically, and part in iron milk cans, and buried in the ghetto grounds.

The first part of the Archives was discovered in September, 1946. It was buried beneath a building of a former Jewish school on Nowolipka Street 38. The second part was found in December, 1950, beneath the same building. A third part, which was to have been buried in the cellar of Swientajerska Street 36, is still missing.

Ringelblum, a leading figure in the Left-Poale Zionist movement, was an active member in the Warsaw Ghetto underground. He headed the underground's propaganda department and edited its illegal publication *Wiadomosci* (News).

After the Warsaw Ghetto uprising, Ringelblum was deported by the Germans to the SS camp Trawniki, near Lublin. (His wife and son had already managed to escape to the Aryan side.) The underground arranged for his rescue by two underground workers, an eighteen-year-old Jewish girl and a Polish railway man, and he was reunited with his wife and son, who were sheltered by a Pole in a bunker on the Aryan side, together with thirty-four other Jews.

There Ringelblum continued his work on the Archives and during the last months of 1943 wrote two important works: *Polish-Jewish Relationships During the Second World War,* and a series of biographical sketches of ghetto personalities, including writers, actors, and painters, as well as communal and underground leaders. (The Jewish Historical Institute of Warsaw came into possession of both manuscripts in 1957.)

Early in March, 1944, the Gestapo discovered the bunker and arrested all the Jews in it along with the Pole who sheltered them and they were taken to the Pawiak prison. Once again the underground tried to rescue Ringelblum, but this time it did not succeed. He was taken to Gestapo headquarters on Allee Szucha. Although he was subjected to terrible tortures he refused to divulge any underground secrets. He was later returned to the Pawiak prison and some time in the middle of March (some set the date as March 14), he and the other Jews arrested were taken to the ghetto ruins and there executed by the Germans.

(See "Oneg Shabbat" in Ringelblum's *Notes from the Warsaw Ghetto,* 1963, Yiddish Buch, pp. 76–102, also Aaron Eisenbach's introduction to Vol. I; "The Ghetto Archives Established by Dr. Ringelblum" by Hirsh Wasser, in *Extermination and Resistance, Historical Records and Source Material,* Israel: Ghetto Fighters' House, 1958, pp. 40–45; "The Last Chronicler of the Warsaw Ghetto" by Ber Mark, *Folks-Shtimme,* Warsaw: April, 1963; "Dr. Emmanuel Ringelblum" by Adolf Berman, *Yiddishe Kultur,* May, 1954, pp. 2–4.)

*   *   *

Gallows Humor

They also laughed in the ghetto. The Jews laughed at their enemies and were not averse to laughing at themselves, but the humor was rooted in the bitterness of their existence and may properly be called gallows humor.

It was never just a form of entertainment. It served the far more vital function of providing emotional release from the oppressiveness of ghetto life; it was another weapon in the struggle for survival.

Jokes

The following anecdotes that circulated among Jews are culled from Emmanuel Ringelblum's diary, *Notes from the Warsaw Ghetto:*

"We have obeyed the Ten Commandments. The reason we're in trouble now is because we have neglected the 11th."
"What's the 11th?"
"Thou shalt choose for thyself the proper grandparents."

Hitler came to Heaven and saw Jesus in Paradise.
"What is this Jew doing here without an armband?" he demanded.
"Let him be," said St. Peter, "he's the boss's son."

A woman in labor was unable to give birth and all efforts to induce delivery failed. But as soon as everyone had left the room an infant-boy emerged and said: "Mommy, is it safe to come out? No round-ups?"

Around New Year's [1942] there were many anecdotes connected with that event. One of them went like this: The year 1942 will henceforth be known as 1941A because Hitler promised his people to end the war in 1941.

Churchill invited the Rabbi of Ger to consult him on how to defeat Germany.
"There are two ways," the rabbi said, "the natural way and the supernatural way. The natural way would be for a million angels with flaming swords to attack Germany and destroy her. The supernatural way would be for a million Englishmen to make a landing in Germany and annihilate her."

God sent an angel down to Earth to investigate what was happening. Upon his return the angel reported: In Germany, Italy, and Japan everyone is in uniform and talking peace. In England everyone is in civilian clothes and talking war. In Poland everyone is barefoot and confident of victory. (The Jews in Poland say: Better days are coming.)

Why should the Germans fly to bomb London, and the English fly to bomb Berlin? It's a waste of gas. Better let the Germans bomb Berlin and the English London.

A Jew prayed badly on Rosh Hashanah [the Jewish New Year]. When asked why, he replied: "The prayer fits the year."
A Jew both laughs and yells in his sleep. His wife wakes him. He's mad at her for that. "I was dreaming I saw slogans on the walls that said: Beat the Jews! Down with ritual slaughter!"

"So what's there to rejoice about?"

"Don't you see? It means that ours [the Poles] are back in power again."

A police officer came into a Jewish home and wanted to confiscate the possessions. The woman cried, pleading that she was a widow and had a child to support. The officer agreed not to take the things, on one condition: That she guess which of his eyes was the artificial one.

"The left one," the woman guessed.

"How did you know?"

"Because that one has the human look."

*   *   *

The Warsaw Ghetto Monument

On the very spot where, on the night of April 18–19, 1943, the Jewish Fighting Organization gave the signal to commence the uprising, there now stands the Warsaw Ghetto Monument of bronze and granite. About thirty feet high, it is a towering symbol of martyrdom and human courage.

In addition to what it symbolizes, it has a history of its own worth telling. When Hitler unleashed World War II with the invasion of Poland in September, 1939, he was so confident of eventual victory that at the very outset of the war he bought from the Swedish quarries some of the finest granite for three victory monuments to be erected in three capitals of conquered European countries, one of them presumably in Warsaw. He had also engaged a Nazi sculptor for this ambitious project.

When the Allied powers smashed Hitler's grandiose dream of world conquest the Swedish masons stopped working on the "victory" monuments.

At the end of the war, when the Jewish Committee in charge of Jewish life in Poland conceived the idea of a Warsaw Ghetto monument, based on a design submitted by the Polish-born Jewish sculptor Nathan Rappaport, the Swedish Jews acquired the granite Hitler had bought and offered it as a gift to to the Polish Jews.

But Poland in those postwar days had neither the equipment nor the necessary conditions for the construction of such a monument. And so the granite was shipped to Paris, where sculptor Rappaport worked on it, and it had its first exhibit there to the acclaim of leading art critics.

In April, 1948, five years after the Warsaw Ghetto uprising, the monument was unveiled on the ghetto grounds in the presence of the entire Polish government and Jewish delegations from all over the world. It is now Poland's most famous monument.

Uprising in Treblinka

By Samuel Rajzman

[EDITOR'S NOTE: *Until World War II Treblinka was a small, practically unknown, railroad station near the town of Sokolow, about fifty miles northeast of Warsaw. When the Germans occupied Poland they chose that spot for a penal and slave labor camp for Jews and Christians whom they charged with criminal acts and minor acts of sabotage. In May, 1942, they began turning it into an extermination camp exclusively for Jews.*

Between July and September, 1942, over 300,000 Jews from the Warsaw Ghetto were forcibly sent off to Treblinka in sealed cattle cars. Other transports arrived from Germany, Austria, Macedonia, Greece, Yugoslavia, Slovakia, Czechoslovakia, occupied Soviet territory, especially Byelorussia, and, of course, from various points in Poland. In terms of the number of victims killed, Treblinka was the second largest extermination camp after Auschwitz. Eight hundred thousand Jews perished there. The ghetto historian Emmanuel Ringelblum described it as "the slaughterhouse of European Jewry."

Samuel Rajzman was a participant in the Treblinka uprising and one of its few survivors. After his escape, he made his way, together with several other fighters, to the forests of Wengrov, Rajzman's birthplace, and there hid out for an entire year. Edward Galasz, Rajzman's boyhood friend, a Pole, who later became a judge in Warsaw, risked his own life and that of his family by bringing the Treblinka escapees food and other necessities to their hideout.

During his hiding he recorded his experiences in Treblinka in order to inform the world of the German crimes in that camp. His account was smuggled out of Poland, and on March 25–26, 1945, while the war was still going on, was incorporated in the Hearings before the House Committee on Foreign Affairs on punishment of war criminals (79th Cong., 1st Sess., on H.J. Res. 93). In 1946 Rajzman also appeared as a witness at the Nuremberg trials at the request of the Polish representative.

The following is an abbreviated version of the account that was entered in the Hearings before the House Committee on Foreign Affairs.]

The Camp

THE TRAIN went up on a sidetrack. It was surrounded by barbed wire entanglements on all sides. We were led out of the train to a nearby square enclosed by a high fence made of pine and fir branches. The passengers could not see what went on behind the fence.

On the square the whole transport was divided. The women were directed to the barracks on the left, the men to the one on the right. Everyone was ordered to undress completely and to deposit all valuables and money in a special place; these were to be returned after the bath. While undressing I saw Engineer Galewski of Warsaw, a friend of mine, among the workers. Galewski asked one of the Elite Guards to assign me to the workers' brigade. I was told to dress and was placed in a group employed in carrying bundles of clothing from this square to the storehouses. I never saw my traveling companions again. After a few minutes I understood everything. I felt resentment against Galewski, due to whose intervention I was still alive. Carrying extremely heavy bundles, we had to run the gauntlet between lined-up overseers who beat anyone they could lay their hands on with heavy sticks. All those who carried bundles had swollen faces. By noon no one who knew me would have recognized me, for my face had become a bluish mass, my eyes were bloodshot. During the pause for lunch I complained to my friend and reproached him for having saved me. His answer was unexpected: "I did not save you to keep you alive," he whispered, "but to sell your life at a higher price. You are now a member of a secret organization that is planning an uprising, and you must live."

The camp of Treblinka occupied a clearing one mile square, surrounded by woods and situated about a mile and a half from the railway station of Treblinka, on the line Malkinia-Siedlece. Beginning in May, 1942, every day, with only brief interruptions, trains bringing Jews to Treblinka arrived from all over Poland, Russia, Czechoslovakia, Germany, Bulgaria, and Greece. On the average, three to four trains of sixty cars arrived every day; each car containing eighty to one hundred and fifty people. The trains traveled along a siding to the entrance gate, where the train escort got off and a camp escort received the deportees. Soldiers from outside were forbidden to cross the camp grounds. Precautions to insure secrecy went so far that an electric siren was placed on the main observation tower to signal any German plane that approached to change its course. No plane ever flew over the camp. The whole station was camouflaged in the most cunning fashion. Thus, the large barracks adjoining the platform which served as the main storehouse for the stolen clothes was covered with timetables of trains that allegedly came to Treblinka Station (some months later, when Treblinka had become famous, the name of the station was changed to Ober-Majdan). Then one saw a huge signpost bearing the inscription: "To Bialystok and Baranowicze": such signs as "Tickets" and "Stationmaster," and finally an enormous painted arrow with the words: "Change for east-bound trains." There was also a large station clock.

Inside these barracks there was nothing but clothes, shoes, and rags, but incoming people had the impression that they were really at a junction where they would change to another train going still further east. Near the platform there was a stout fence about nine feet high with a gate through which the newly arrived were driven in to a huge square. Their disappointment and surprise were overwhelming: Instead of a junction, they were in a huge concentration camp. On both sides of the square there were barracks and enormous piles of clothing and shoes, sometimes nine feet high. One could hear the rattle of excavators, and the air was permeated with the odor of corpses. On the square men were at once separated from women and told to undress and deposit their papers and valuables. The most heart-rending scenes took place in the winter when women were compelled to strip their children at tempera-tures of 20–30° below zero in the yard or in open barracks whose walls were of thin plywood. The unfortunate creatures had nervous shocks, cried and laughed alternately, then wept desperately while standing on line in the cold, their babies pressed close to their breasts. The hangman lashed their naked bodies to force them into silence.

The naked women were then taken care of by "barbers." Every woman was shaved to the skin with a clipper, then sent to the bath establishment, which consisted of ten cabins with room for seven hundred to eight hun-dred persons each. In these cabins there were even towels and rules posted. Once the people were inside, the cabins were hermetically sealed, and the air pumped out with a machine (poison gas was used later). Thus the victims were suffocated to death. Before the corpses were burned a group of dentists verified whether they had any gold teeth. These were torn out of the mouths.

The workers in the camp were divided as follows:

Group   I—Classifying the new arrivals, carrying clothes and bag-gage to the storerooms.

         II—Sorting stolen clothes and loading them on cars going to Germany.

     III—Sorting, packing, and counting money, foreign ex-change, gold, and valuables.

IV—Crafts, such as shoemakers, tailors, carpenters, masons, locksmiths, etc., and those who worked in shops.

V—Barbers.

VI—Dentists.

VII—Porters to carry the corpses to the ovens.

Groups I to V were strictly separated from groups VI and VII. Even the slightest communication was made very difficult in order to prevent the crews that did not work directly in the cabins from learning how the mass murder was being carried out.

The Uprising

Among the first six groups there was a conspiratorial committee whose task was to avenge at least to some extent the millions of innocent people executed. They dreamed of setting fire to the whole camp and exterminating at least the cruelest engines at the price of their own lives. The work of organization was difficult, because the Germans had several stool pigeons among the workers, and all our moves had to be most carefully guarded.

Finally it was decided that the only practical plan was to get ammunition and arms from the camp's arsenal. Luck favored us, for a few days after this resolution was taken one of the Jewish locksmiths was sent to repair the lock of the armored door of the arsenal, which was out of order. The locksmith took an imprint of the key, and after four months' work another key was ready. Three combat units were then organized, and our leader, Dr. Julian Chorazyski, a former captain in the Polish Army, worked out a detailed plan of action. The coup was to take place on April 21, 1943. Unfortunately, on April 19, Dr. Chorazyski failed to give a proper salute to Untersturmführer Franz, who struck him in the face with his riding crop. In his excitement Dr. Chorazyski reached for his knife and was about to strike. Franz jumped out of the window shouting that Chorazyski must be taken alive. He was foiled in this design; the doctor had time to take poison. After Chorazyski's death our plan had to be postponed for several months because we had no qualified leader, and none of us wanted to take the moral responsibility for an unsuccessful coup.

On May 1, 1943, Dr. Leichert, a physician from Wengrov, came to our camp. He was also a former Polish officer, and after a few days in camp he agreed to take the leadership of our group. We waited for an opportune moment to get into the arsenal.

On August 2, 1943, while a large group of masons were working nearby, we finally managed to open it. Thus we were able to get one of our comrades into the building and lock him up there. One of the Unterscharführers lived in a room adjoining the arsenal, and at that moment he happened to be in his quarters. The slightest rustle in the stacks of weapons could have betrayed us. For that reason we delegated Engineer Sudowicz of Czestochowa to go to this Unterscharführer, with whom he had good relations, and under some pretext lure him out of his room. At the same time we cut a pane out of a window opposite the door in a spot that was unguarded.

Outside the arsenal there was a pile of debris and bricks. A cart driven by a member of our group drove up to the building ostensibly to remove the debris. Under it twenty hand grenades, twenty rifles, and several revolvers with cartridges were loaded. They were all taken to the ditch where lime and gravel were kept for construction work, and divided among the combat units.

The disinfector of the camp belonged to one of these units. His work in the camp consisted in walking around with a sprinkler full of disinfectant. We had gotten some gasoline from trucks and tanks in the garage through one of our comrades, a mechanic from Czestochowa. On the day of the coup the gasoline was poured into his apparatus instead of disinfectant, and he sprinkled it liberally according to our leader's instructions. Curiously enough, the "disinfection" of one of our objectives took place in the presence of one of the Unterscharführers, who did not notice anything.

At 3:45 P.M. we heard the signal—a rifle shot near the gates of the Jewish barracks. This was followed by the detonations of hand grenades hurled at previously "disinfected" objects. An enormous fire broke out in the whole camp. The arsenal exploded and everything was burned, except the "bath" cabins, because it proved absolutely impossible to get near them.

The victim of the first shot was Oberscharführer Kittner, the chief of the guards and the leading camp spy. The flames devoured all the storerooms for clothes and shoes. Of the 700 workers on the camp grounds, only 150 to 200 succeeded in escaping; the others perished in the camp as well as more than 20 Germans. Of the 150 to 200 who managed to escape, only 12 are still alive; the others were later murdered by the German hangmen.

Editor's Postscript

"The Jews of Western Europe do not know what Treblinka means. They think it is a labor colony and ask at the railroad station how far it is to the "Treblinka Industrial Works.' If they knew that they were going to their death they would certainly offer resistance." See Emmanuel Ringelblum, *Notes from the Warsaw Ghetto* (Warsaw: Verlag Yiddish Buch, 1963), vol. II, p. 22, in Yiddish.

The Warsaw Ghetto uprising was an inspiration and a signal to Jewish undergrounds in other ghettos and concentration camps to stage revolts. That this was also true of Treblinka is substantiated by survivor Stanislaw Kon, who writes: "At first the uprising was set for April 1943, when Dr. Chorazyski was still alive. At that time there arrived in Treblinka the last transports of Jews from the Warsaw Ghetto. It was from them that we learned about the ghetto uprising. . . . Unlike the men, women and children of previous transports these were not broken and defeated. Instead of tears in their eyes they brought grenades and other explosives in their pockets. From them we received some weapons. The leadership thought that this was the proper moment to begin the revolt." ("The Revolt in the Death-Camp, Treblinka," *Dos Neie Leben,* Lodz: May 10, 1945, pp. 3, 8.)

Another survivor, Yankel Wiernick, whose pamphlet *A Year in Treblinka,* smuggled out of Poland and published in this country a year before the war ended, is regarded as the fullest account to date of the horrors of Treblinka, gives this description of the uprising: "In camp II we began to organize ourselves into groups of five. Each group had to fulfill its separate tasks: kill the German and Ukrainian personnel, set fire to the buildings, clear the path for the escapees, etc.

"Everything was prepared for this goal: blunt weapons to kill with, wood for bridges, buckets of gasoline for setting fire. . . . As I mentioned earlier, there were watchtowers on all sides manned by armed guards. At every turn there was either an armed Ukrainian or an armed German. . . . Everyone who was in our path was killed. . . . Immediately after the signal the guard at the well was killed and his weapon taken away. . . . In a matter of minutes everything was burning. We carried out our sacred mission in an exemplary manner. I armed myself and hacked away at all around me, right and left. When I saw that everything was burning and the path was clear I grabbed an ax and a file and escaped." With that ax he later killed his Ukrainian pursuer. (See *"A Year in Treblinka,"* Undzer Tzeit, New York: 1944, pp. 47, 51, 61.)

*   *   *

From all the aforesaid it is clear that the Treblinka revolt—considering the conditions under which it was organized and carried through— belongs to the most heroic feats of Jewish resistance to Nazism. But

Raul Hilberg, the leading spokesman for the theory of Jewish passivity, although he cites Rajzman and Wiernick as authorities for his information, manages to reduce the heroic Treblinka revolt to an insignificant event. He achieves this reportorial sleight of hand by simply ignoring those facts in his cited sources that negate his theory of Jewish non-resistance. He writes: "The breakout plan was very simple. A locksmith made a duplicate key to the arsenal, and a former captain of the Polish Army, Dr. Julian Chorazyski, worked out the escape plan. He was killed just before the coup was to take place, but his place was taken by a new inmate, the physician Dr. Leichert, also a former officer. On August 2, 1943, 20 hand grenades, 20 rifles and several revolvers were secretly removed from the arsenal. At 3:45 P.M. the guards were rushed. Of 700 inmates, 150 to 200 got out. The escapees were hunted down one by one. About 12 survived." (See *The Destruction of the European Jews,* p. 586.)

Hilberg makes no mention of either the fire or the German casualties. But from significant passages in his own cited source, which Hilberg chose to omit, it is clear that one of the main objectives of the leaders of the revolt was to destroy the killing center, Treblinka, by fire, and they planned their strategy accordingly. That was why they filled the disinfector with gasoline and sprayed everything in sight. "An enormous fire broke out in the whole camp," writes Rajzman. That this aim was uppermost in the minds of the organizers of the revolt is underlined by Rajzman in another article on this subject: "The difference between the uprising in the Warsaw Ghetto and the revolt in Treblinka is one of technical possibilities. In the Warsaw Ghetto it was still possible to hope to receive weapons and get some kind of support from the outside. But we, in Treblinka, had to depend entirely upon ourselves. That was why our plan of action was worked out entirely in the direction of destroying the camp. . . . We realized our aim fully and in martyrdom. Treblinka was wiped out. A fortress of horrible Nazism was erased from the face of the earth." (See *Wengrov, a Monument to the Perished,* Tel Aviv: 1961, pp. 221–223.)

*   *   *

In various accounts of the Treblinka uprising Rudolf Massarek is singled out for bravery and for having manned a machine gun at the time of the revolt. But in all of these accounts he is erroneously described as a relative of the late Czechoslovakian president, Thomas G. Masaryk, who chose to accompany his Jewish wife to Treblinka rather than be separated from her. Even in Gideon Hausner's recently published *Justice in Jerusalem* the error is repeated (see p. 187). The similarity of the sound in the two names (though the spelling is different) is no doubt partly responsible for the error. But once started it continues to perpetuate itself.

The true Rudolf Massarek, a leading member of the Treblinka underground, was a half-Jew from Prague. Under German occupation he had the status of a *Mischling,* the offspring of a mixed marriage. As such he could have escaped the fate of being deported to a death camp were it not for the fact that in October, 1942, he married a Jewish girl, which automatically put him in the category of a full-Jew.

Of the entire transport that brought Rudolf Massarek to Treblinka the Germans selected only six men for the camp's working complement and led away the rest, including his young wife, her mother and thirteen-year-old sister, to the gas chambers. (One of the six, a man named Goldschmidt, who happened to be on a work detail outside the camp during the uprising and was able to escape now lives in Czechoslovakia.)

Rudolf Massarek is survived by his mother and two sisters. One of the sisters lives in Israel. Among the 77,000 names inscribed on the walls of the Pinkas synagogue in Prague, a memorial to the Czechoslovakian Jews killed by the Nazis, are the names of Rudolf Massarek and his wife. These names are from the official records of the Jewish community with whom the Jews were registered.

This account, it is hoped, will correct a factual error so that the identity and the heroism of the real Rudolf Massarek will henceforth not be ascribed to another person.

The Bialystok Ghetto Revolt

By Reuben Ainsztein

[EDITOR'S NOTE: *The following account of the Bialystok Ghetto Revolt first appeared in the spring issue of* The Jewish Quarterly *(London), 1956. It was somewhat revised by the author for its publication in this anthology.*

Reuben Ainsztein was born in Vilna on November 30, 1917. He left Poland in 1936 to study medicine at Brussels University. A few weeks before the Germans invaded Belgium in May, 1940, he obtained permission to join the British R.A.F., but he was unable to reach England because the boat, which he had boarded at Boulogne with soldiers of the British Expeditionary Force, was sunk by German bombers. After the fall of France he went back to Brussels, where he lived for a year under the Germans. He crossed France in October, 1941, and made his way by himself over the Pyrenees, intending to reach Portugal and, ultimately, Britain. Caught by the Spanish police near Gerona, he spent fourteen months in Spanish prisons and the Miranda de Ebro Concentration Camp. Released in the spring of 1943, he finally reached England and flew as an air gunner with an R.A.F. bomber squadron until January, 1945, when he was wounded parachuting from his shot-up Lancaster over Belgium.

Mr. Ainsztein, who resides in England, has written for the Wiener Library Bulletin, Times Literary Supplement, Twentieth Century, Midstream, Jewish Social Studies, Jewish Observer *and* Middle East Review, Jewish Quarterly, *and the B.B.C. Third Programme. Mr. Ainsztein's most recent work,* Jewish Resistance in Nazi-Occupied Eastern Europe, *with a historical survey of the Jew as fighter and soldier in the Diaspora, was published in England and the United States in 1974. He is currently writing a history of the destruction of Polish Jewry, a work commissioned by The Royal Institute of International Affairs in London.*]

The last fighting engagements in the Warsaw Ghetto took place in July, 1943. A month later, from the 16th to the 20th of August, Jewish men and women defended the honor of their people and the dignity of man in a few miserable alleys of Bialystok.

Five days after Hitler's attack on the Soviet Union, Bialystok fell to the pincer movement of Guderian's and Hoth's panzer divisions. The Germans entered the city at six in the morning of June 27, 1941, and two hours later began the first massacre of the Jews and of all left-wingers who after the end of the Polish campaign of 1939 had found refuge in Bialystok. Some 2,000 Jews were murdered on that Friday by the Reichswehr acting in pursuance of Hitler's orders that east of the Bug no laws of war applied to Jews and Bolsheviks. Hundreds were crammed into the largest synagogue and burned alive. (A few were saved by a Polish cobbler, Winicki, who managed to make an opening into the burning building from outside.) On July 3, 200 Jews caught in the streets were taken outside the city to Pietrasza and machine-gunned. On July 12, some 5,000 more were taken to the same field and shot. On July 30, thousands of Jews were driven through the streets to the accompaniment of the Polish anti-Semites' howling: "Judeo-Communists." Forced to dress in their best clothes, the large crowd of Jewish men and women were driven to the Jewish cemetery and there compelled to behead busts of Marx, Engels, Lenin, and Stalin and then to bury them. The spectacle was staged by the Germans to mark the end of the "Judeo-Commune" in the city. Four days later came the order creating a ghetto for the remaining 50,000 Jews. Hardly had they settled within its walls when on September 16, the Judenrat was ordered to find 4,000 victims for "resettlement" at Pruzany. But after that Bialystok began to enjoy a special kind of immunity, for even in November, 1941, when the 200,000 Jews in the towns and villages of the Bialystok province were exterminated, the ghetto remained untouched. Two factors intervened which made its position unique.

Firstly, Bialystok was incorporated into East Prussia instead of forming part of the General Government or the *Ostgebiet*. This opened the city, the second largest textile center in prewar Poland, to the grabbing hands of German entrepreneurs. Secondly, because of its position, Bialystok became one of the most important supply centers for the northern Nazi army group operating from Smolensk to Leningrad. To run the city's industries without Jews would have been impossible, for they formed a large proportion of Bialystok's mill hands and a predominant part of its skilled workers, artisans, and specialists. Military necessity combined with the Prussian businessmen's rapacity for easy gain held back for a time the inexorable march of Hitler's policy of total extermination from engulfing the 50,000 Bialystok Jews and resulted in the creation of a "show ghetto," which to the surviving Jews of Vilna or Warsaw appeared to be a place of peace.

Under these conditions the policy of collaboration and ignominy represented by the ghetto Judenrats assumed a particularly effective form in Bialystok. Its main champion and executor was Ephraim Barasz, an engineer by profession, who unlike so many other Judenrat presidents was neither a crook nor a coward. He ended, however, like all other collaborators, a man without honor and an enemy of his people.

His main policy was to prove to the Nazis that the Jews of Bialystok represented a first-rate economic asset worthy of preservation. To convince them of their usefulness, he did not spare his efforts to re-start all the existing mills and factories in the city and to open new workshops. His policy seemed to be on the right lines, for unlike Warsaw and Lodz, which to all intents and purposes were concentration camps, the Bialystok Ghetto was not hermetically sealed from the Aryan world. Many of its prisoners worked in the factories and mills situated in the Aryan part of the city. Moreover, as "productive" Jews, the inhabitants of the Bialystok Ghetto did not suffer to the same extent from hunger as the Jews of Warsaw and Lodz and many other closed ghettos, especially as they were able to smuggle considerable quantities of food into the ghetto.

Barasz's position became even stronger when the surviving members of the Hashomer Hatzair kibbutz in Vilna were "evacuated" to Bialystok to carry on preparing themselves for their future life in Israel in the security of the "show ghetto," and when their example was followed by the surviving members of the Hekhalutz organizations in Vilna, Slonim and Grodno.

It is when seen against this background that the greatness of the men who created the resistance movement in the Bialystok Ghetto can be fully appreciated.

Its first organizers were the surviving Jewish Communists, who had suffered particularly in the June and July massacres. The first actions of the resistance movement were to spread leaflets and posters warning the mass of the ghetto Jews against Barasz's policies, and to help people who were even worse off than the Jews: the Soviet prisoners of war in the camps outside the city. Clothes, food, and medicaments were collected and smuggled into the camps.

As in Warsaw, the initiative for the creation of a common anti-Nazi front and a joint defense organization came from Hashomer Hatzair. In April, 1942, Hashomer Hatzair established a common platform of action with the Communist-led United Anti-Fascist Bloc, and then proceeded to build a bridge between the Communists and the parties united in the so-called Second Bloc: the Hekhalutz, the organization Dror, the left wing of the Bund, and a small number of Beitar and Hanoar Hatzioni members. The attempt to bring the two camps together was undertaken by

Elijah Boraks, one of the Hashomer Hatzair leaders; it failed in the first place because the Communists refused to co-operate with any body supporting or represented on the Judenrat, while Dror, led by Zvi Mersik, refused to admit that the 50,000 Bialystok Jews must inevitably share the fate of all other Jewish settlements in Poland.

It was mostly due to the work and remarkable personality of Mordechai Tenenboim-Tamarof, who took over the leadership of Dror after Mersik's death from typhus, that the two blocs finally merged into the Anti-Fascist Fighting Bloc. But this happened in July, 1943, only a month before the liquidation of the Bialystok Ghetto.

Bialystok lies surrounded by immense forests, which stretch east as far as Smolensk, while its countryside is mostly Byelorussian. These two factors were responsible for the rise of a vast Soviet partisan movement, which in the final stages of the war practically controlled the whole area. Only west of Bialystok, in the Lomza area, did the London-controlled Polish Home Army preserve an operational basis, which meant that no Jew was safe there, for instead of fighting the Germans, the well-armed Poles spent most of their time murdering Jews and escaped Soviet prisoners of war seeking refuge in the forests, or exterminating all left-wing Poles the Nazis had not dealt with. Thus, unlike the fighters of the Warsaw Ghetto, surrounded by a mostly hostile city and a countryside devoid of forests and inhabited by unfriendly Polish peasants, the fighters of Bialystok had to some extent the choice of deciding where they would strike against the Nazis.

One faction, led by Judith Nowogrodzka, was for abandoning the ghetto to its inescapable end and saving as many of the young and fit as was possible by taking them to the forests, where they would be able to carry on an effective fight against the Nazis. Nowogrodzka's views were opposed by the Communists Daniel Moszkowicz and Hela Mendelson, and the left-wing Zionist Mordechai Tenenboim. Tenenboim opposed with particular vehemence the "forest" faction, regarding all partisans as no better than marauders. All the three—Tenenboim, Moszkowicz and Hela Mendelson—shared the conviction that the duty of the ghetto resistance organization was to fight inside the ghetto.

A third faction, represented by the Communists Joseph Kawe and Rebecca Wojskowska, held the view that the Jewish resistance should be active both inside the ghetto and in the forests, the purpose of the Jewish partisans being to come to the aid of the ghetto in its greatest hour of need. It was their view that won the day.

The first armed group of Jewish partisans left the ghetto in December, 1942, and three months later, in March, 1943, the first Jewish partisan detachment in the Bialystok forests, which called itself *Forois* ("Fore-ward"), became a reality.

The fighting organization set up by the Anti-Fascist Fighting Bloc was commanded by Tenenboim and Moszkowicz. Its main problem was how to acquire weapons. The Polish left-wing underground was willing to help but was itself insufficiently armed to be able to supply more than a token quantity of revolvers and ammunition. To all the demands for arms addressed by Tenenboim to the representatives of the London-controlled Home Army, he received polite replies assuring him that the Home Army was willing to help, but that although its commanders were quite certain that the Jews shared their own views on the Germans, what was the Jewish attitude to the Soviet Union? To Tenenboim's letters asking that Jews should be allowed to join the Home Army detachments, he received no reply.

Thus the ghetto fighters were left completely to their own devices in their quest for arms. They obtained their weapons mainly by stealing them from German barracks, or by buying them from Polish and Byelorussian peasants, who had hidden some of the immense quantities of arms left scattered over the countryside following the battles of 1939 and 1941. They also obtained some of their weapons from anti-Nazi Germans, and even succeeded in buying some from ordinary Nazis. They also manufactured inside the ghetto a small quantity of rather inefficient hand grenades and Molotov cocktails. Bottles filled with vitriol formed an important part of their fighting equipment. The dangerous task of smuggling the weapons into the ghetto was almost exclusively carried out by Jewish women and girls, some of them mere children.

Yet when the terrible day of total liquidation came upon the ghetto, all the military organization of the Anti-Fascist Fighting Bloc could muster in the way of arms were twenty-five German rifles, about a hundred revolvers and pistols, a few tommy guns, a small number of hand grenades, and one heavy machine gun. They also had a few sticks of dynamite, bottles filled with vitriol, and an unspecified number of axes, scythes, knives, and bayonets. The few tommy guns, which could have proved very useful in street fighting, went out of order after a few rounds had been fired.

The total liquidation of the Bialystok Ghetto came at a time when the defeat of Nazi Germany became certain. "Never before had the mood of the ghetto been so good as in the last days before its liquidation. This was the time after Stalingrad, after El Alamein, after the victorious con-clusion of the North African campaign and after the Sicilian landing. The Eastern Front was on the move. On August 5th, 1943, the guns of Moscow for the first time roared a salute to mark the liberation of Orel and Belgorod. Their roar reverberated with echoes in the hearts of the ghetto inhabitants." [15]

But Hitler and Himmler were fully aware of the hopes that the Allied victories had awakened in the surviving Jews of Byelorussia and Poland. Whatever the economic value of the Bialystok Ghetto to the Wehrmacht, it was more than outweighed in the minds of the Nazi leaders by the possibility that its inhabitants, if left alone, might live long enough to see the arrival of the Red Army. Consequently, despite the attempts of German businessmen and Wehrmacht authorities to delay the total annihilation of the ghetto, or limit its extent, Barasz was called to the Gestapo headquarters on August 15, 1943, and informed that all the Jews of the ghetto, now reduced to some 40,000, would be "evacuated" the next day to Lublin, where they could be more "productively" employed.

Barasz returned to the ghetto and did not warn the Jews of their impending doom. Next day he set an example of submissiveness, being among the first to turn up with rucksack and suitcase, all ready for the journey.

The liquidation of the Bialystok Ghetto was entrusted to SS Major General Odilo Globocnik, head of Action Reinhardt, the Nazi code name for the greatest organized mass murder in history: the extermination of Poland's 3,000,000 Jews. His plan of action was to prevent at all costs a repetition of the Warsaw uprising. He brought with him one German battalion of special troops trained in partisan warfare and two battalions of Galician Ukrainians, the most brutal thugs and murderers the last war had seen. He could further count on the local German police, gendarmery. Wehrmacht and auxiliary police composed mostly of prewar Polish policemen. After having thrown a cordon round the ghetto fence, armed with machine guns and light artillery, he marched in the early hours of August 16 his gangs of trained murderers into the ghetto and, having achieved tactical surprise thanks to Barasz's treachery and cowardice, deprived the ghetto fighters of their operational base even before the fighting began.

Guided by the Jewish police, the Nazis drove the mass of the 40,000 Jews into six narrow streets lying close to the ghetto fence. These six narrow streets, or rather alleys, were no longer part of the city. Unpaved and lined with single-story wooden houses, they could not provide the shelter and cover the tall tenement blocks of Warsaw afforded to the fighters of the Warsaw Ghetto.

Having lost their operational base at the very outset, 500 men and women of the fighting organization led by Tenenboim and Moszkowicz decided to storm the ghetto fence, and after breaching it, to launch the thousands of crowded Jews into the countryside to make for the near forests, where *Forois* was waiting to receive them. They expected that thousands would be mown down by the Nazis' machine guns, but that thousands would also get through.

But deprived of sufficient firearms and space for maneuvers, they failed in their repeated attempts to br~ach the ghetto fence, while the partisans of *Forois* were blockaded in the forest by strong German forces. Nevertheless, they carried on the fight for four days. Inspired by their example, old folk and children advanced against Ukrainian tommy guns and bayonets singing the *Hatikvah* and the *Internationale,* while the workers refused to surrender their factories and mills without a fight and set fire to them when all was lost. Globocnik had to use three light tanks, a number of armored cars and even call in the Luftwaffe to liquidate all resistance in six miserable alleys crowded with 40,000 living and dead Jews.

Both Tenenboim and Moszkowicz refused to flee to the forest when all armed resistance had broken down on August 20, and saying good-bye to each other, shot themselves when the Nazis encircled their headquarters.

Of the spirit in which the members of the Anti-Fascist Fighting Bloc fought and died tells the proclamation which they stuck on the walls of the ghetto only a few hours after Globocnik's murderers had invaded it. It told the 40,000 Jews of Bialystok:

Five million European Jews have already been murdered by Hitler and his executioners. Of Polish Jewry no more than a tenth remains. Over three million Polish Jews have been tortured to death at Chelmno and Belzec, at Oswiecim and Treblinka, at Sobibor and other death camps.

You must know that all Jews driven away are led to their deaths. Do not believe the Gestapo propaganda about letters allegedly written by people who have been taken away. This is nothing but a cynical lie. The road followed by those who are driven away leads to gigantic crematoria and common graves in the depths of Polish forests. Each of us is under sentence of death.

We have nothing to lose!

We are being driven to Treblinka!

Like mangy beasts we shall be poisoned with gas, then burnt in crematoria. Let us not behave like sheep going to their slaughter!

Even if we are too weak to defend our lives, we are strong enough to defend our Jewish honor and human dignity, and thus prove to the world that we are captive but not defeated.

Do not go freely to your death! Fight for your life until your last breath! With tooth and nail, with axe and knife, with vitriol and iron greet your executioners. Make your enemy pay with blood for blood, with death for death!

Will you hide in rat-holes while your dearest are being driven away to be desecrated and murdered? Will you sell your wives, your children, your parents, your very souls for a few more weeks of a slave's existence?

Let us attack the enemy from ambushes. Let us kill him, get hold of his weapons, fall like heroes and thus, in our death, defy death!

Do not sell cheaply your life! Take revenge for the exterminated communities and obliterated settlements! When forced to abandon your home, set it on fire. Set on fire and demolish the factories! The executioners must inherit nothing from us!

Jewish youth! Hitler will lose the war, the axis of slavery and cannibalism will be wiped off the earth and the world will become a clean and sunny place again. Because of the bright future awaiting mankind you must not die a dog's death. Make your way to the forest, to the partisans!

Do not run away from the ghetto. You will perish without weapons. After doing your national duty here, make your way to the forest armed with the weapons of the Germans you have killed in the ghetto.

Had they only had a hundredth part of the arms possessed by the London-controlled Home Army, had only one load in ten of the arms brought by R.A.F. aircraft for the Polish underground reached them, the fighters of the Bialystok Ghetto would have made their murderers pay a fairer price for the 40,000 lives they attempted to defend.

Those who managed to escape to the forests carried on the battle against the Nazis as partisans and later in the ranks of the Red Army. Of those who survived to see the end of the war, many fought later in Israel's War of Liberation.

The Evidence

By Yuri Suhl

NO DETAIL was overlooked by the Nazis and their collaborators when it concerned the tracking down of Jews. In his *Polish-Jewish Relationships During the Second World War* [16] Ringelblum writes: "Jews dyed their characteristically dark hair. But this too was of little help because the agents would inspect the hair-roots. . . . Jewish eyes, experts maintain, could be recognized by their sadness, their thoughtfulness. There is concentrated in them all the sorrow of the ghetto, the sufferings of the last years, the loss of the nearest kin. . . . An acquaintance of mine found a way out. When he was about to leave the ghetto for the Aryan side his face assumed a severe look and his eyes, he said, darted angry glances. . . .

"There are some who have an excellent Aryan appearance but whose knowledge of Polish is very poor. They cannot even pronounce their own Aryan name right. But one finds a remedy for this too. One makes believe he is a deaf-mute and wears an armband saying, 'Deaf-mute.'"

With such ingenuity or other advantages, some Jews did manage to escape from the ghetto and live on the Aryan side. It is estimated that in Warsaw alone there were 25,000 such Jews. They used forged papers; they needed a substantial amount of money and a lot of nerve. With it all, life for these Jews was a daily contest of wits with the Germans and their Polish collaborators. The slightest misstep could lead to disaster. Some could not endure the strain and slipped back into the ghetto.

In this precarious existence the female had an advantage over the male. If ever she got into a tight spot she could insist on her Aryan status, provided, of course, that her papers and accent were in order and she did not lose her nerve. The male, however, started out with a handicap which was beyond his control—his circumcision, and even if he met all the other requirements for living on the Aryan side to perfection, this one "flaw" could spell his doom.

Ringelblum writes:

The agents and the police made great progress in the detection of

Jews. With regard to men the matter is not a difficult one; you drop your pants and the evidence is right there. And the pants are ordered dropped at every opportunity. . . . For this, too, a solution was sought. Some were of the opinion that surgery could make the sexual organ of a Jew resemble that of a non-Jew. Because of the sexual complications connected with this costly operation the idea was generally abandoned.

In certain instances doctors would get an official order to examine the genitals of people suspected of being Jewish. If the doctor happens to be a decent human being his diagnosis will be—phimosis, that is, the loss of the foreskin due to venereal disease. Such medical diagnoses have saved the life of many a Jew. Quite a number of Jewish "Aryans" are carrying with them papers certifying that they had lived through a phimosis.

In their quest for security some Jews were more daring than others. Not only were they *living* on the Aryan side, they even *made a living* in the Aryan world. For many it meant striking out into new areas of employment; others continued in their old professions. It was, of course, easier for the woman than the man, who at every step had to take into account the telltale evidence of his circumcision. This led him at times into situations that might have been hilariously funny were it not for the fact that his very life was at stake. Ringelblum describes one such situation:

> The tragedy of Jews on the Aryan side is not lacking in comical moments. I heard about a Jewish engineer who worked on the railway for a certain construction firm. He had the necessary papers and traveled around the country representing the firm. In Chelmno he ran into a railway inspector who boasted that he could detect a Jew no matter what his disguise. For sociable reasons our engineer had to accompany his colleagues to the bath. He had to resort to all kinds of means to cover up his genitals. He lathered up the unmentionable spot and turned and twisted in all directions to avoid detection. The demands of sociability were met and the engineer's "Jewishness" was not discovered.[17]

When a Jew living on the Aryan side was in danger of being exposed, he had to abandon his residence at once. If he had nowhere to go, one way out of his dilemma was to volunteer for a slave labor job in Germany. There were hundreds of such Jewish volunteers, but most of them were women. Applicants had to pass a medical examination and that automatically ruled out Jewish males. Still, some managed to get around this obstacle. They would either purchase the certificate from a Pole who had passed the physical examination, or would send a Pole to substitute for them.

But even if he succeeded and was already on the job in Germany, the danger of exposure-by-genitals was always present. The story of Simcha Poliakiewicz is a case in point.[18]

Simcha was a slave laborer in Treblinka. He knew his fate in advance. When he would have no strength left for work, he would be sent to the gas chamber. One hot summer day he and other prisoners were loading the freight cars with clothing of victims already gassed for shipment to Germany. The prisoners were naked and the Ukrainian auxiliary police kept beating them with their truncheons as they staggered under the heavy bundles of garments.

At the end of the day, when the loading was finished and the others leaped, exhausted, from the cars, Simcha remained behind, hiding beneath a heap of clothes. He held his breath as he heard the door of his car clang shut. Soon the train began to move. Hours later, and many kilometers away from camp, he pried open the door and leaped from the train. As he rolled down the steep embankment and was enveloped by the chill of the night he realized that he was still naked. A while ago he could have had all the suits he wished, but he lacked the presence of mind to dress. Now his nakedness was an added hazard.

He made his way across the field to a nearby forest and remained there overnight. The next day a peasant woman who happened to pass by gave him her apron and a drink of milk. With the aid of friendly Poles, who gave him clothing and temporary shelter, he obtained forged papers that recorded his new genealogy. He was no longer Simcha Poliakiewicz, a Polish Jew, but Stanislaw Frubel, a Pole of German descent. His grandfather was a *Volksdeutsche* who had settled in the Poznan area.

Armed with the proper papers he schemed his way into Germany and was sent to work in the Westphalian coal mines together with hundreds of other Poles.

"But as soon as I began working in the coal pits," Poliakiewicz writes in his memoir, *Days Without Light,*[19] "I faced the difficult problem of the daily bath right after work. . . . As I was looking for a way out of this danger I discovered that cold water shrunk my body somewhat and minimized the obvious differentness of my genitals as compared to those of other Poles. From then on, as soon as I removed my clothes I would rinse off the layer of coal dust with some warm water, lather up my body and go immediately under the cold shower. The others looked at me with astonishment. The curious I told that the cold water refreshed my tired body. They accepted the explanation. Many tried to follow my example but only a few were able to take the numbing, ice-cold shower." One day Simcha had a inflammation of the throat and ran a temperature. Shivering and in terrible pain, he still had to go under the icy shower.

The problem of the daily baths was solved, but the basic threat remained and could appear at any moment from the most unexpected quarter. Some enterprising German overseer had set up a brothel near the camp for the benefit of the miners. Soon thereafter there were cases of venereal infection among the workers. One day a sign appeared in the dining hall bearing the following announcement: "Every camp dweller, without exception, must report tomorrow between 10 A.M. and 4 P.M. for a medical examination. Those who fail to show up will be deported to a concentration camp."

Simcha had not even been near the brothel, but he knew that if he wanted to live he had to stay away from the medical examination and have a legitimate reason for doing so. "At dawn," he recalls, "when the watchman woke us for the morning shift, I had been awake for a long time scheming how to avoid death."

By the time he descended into the coal pit he already had a plan. Shortly before the shift ended the foreman called out, "Sauber machen!" (Clean up.) There was no delaying any longer. "I grabbed the hammer by its wooden handle, and with all my might, brought it down on a finger of my right hand. My cries for help brought Albert running. He tried to stop the bleeding with the bandage in my jacket. He ran down for another bandage and it too was quickly soaked through with blood. . . . At the First Aid station the medical assistant thought that the bone was fractured and that the first part of my finger would have to be amputated. He bandaged my hand and sent me to the hospital to see the surgeon."

Simcha deliberately took his time walking to the hospital. When he got there it was three o'clock. The doctor did not find a bone fracture and prescribed light work for a week. In the meantime another hour had passed. The plan had worked!

"When I returned to the barracks the medical commission had already completed its work. The barracks was alive with talk as my neighbors recalled the scenes of how the doctors examined some of them with their pants down. Wacek and Bolek were sorry for me because I missed it all. Had I seen it with my own eyes, they said, I, too, would be laughing now."

The Resistance Movement in the Vilna Ghetto

By Abraham H. Foxman

[EDITOR'S NOTE: *Because Vilna, capital of Lithuania, had a large Jewish population and was a vital center of Jewish culture and creativity (both were destroyed by the Nazis), the story of the Vilna Ghetto is well-documented both in Yiddish and Hebrew. The chronicle that follows is by a student of the holocaust who made the Vilna Ghetto his research specialty. He is perhaps the youngest writer on this subject.*

Born in Baranowicze, Poland, in 1940, Abraham H. Foxman (son of Joseph M. Foxman, who is represented elsewhere in this book) was an infant when the Germans invaded Vilna. He was hidden on the Aryan side throughout the war years. In 1950 he emigrated with his parents to America. He is the holder of a B.A. from the City College of New York, and a J.D. from New York University Law School. He is a contributor to various English and Hebrew periodicals. At present he serves as Director of National Leadership for the Anti-Defamation League of B'nai Brith. In April, 1966, Mr. Foxman received the Annual Essay Award given by the Jewish Scientific Institute, for his essay "The Jewish People Concept in International Law."]

———◆———

PRIOR to the holocaust Vilna, the capital of Lithuania, was a city of piety, scholarship, and art and was properly called by Jews the "Jerusalem of Lithuania."

On June 24, 1941, when the German Army marched into Vilna the Jewish population of the city was over 80,000. On the fifth day of the occupation the Germans arrested eighty Jews and took them to the Lukiszki Prison as hostages. The arrest was explained as a step to insure peace and security and to prevent acts of resistance and sabotage.

In the ensuing weeks the persecution of the Jews was stepped up with the issuance of a series of anti-Jewish decrees, and on July 17, 1941,

German and Lithuanian soldiers surrounded the Novogrod section of Vilna and took away 800 Jews to Ponary, a wooded area, fifteen kilometers from Vilna, which became the extermination site of the Vilna Jews. On August 31, 1941, German soldiers together with Lithuanian police staged another round-up, this time on a much larger scale, and during the next few days 10,000 Jews were led to their death in Ponary. By September 6, 1941, the day of the creation of the ghetto, the number of Jews killed reached 35,000.

Actually there were two ghettos in Vilna. The bulk of the Jews were crowded into Ghetto Number One. The remainder, about 10,000-11,000, were pushed into Zydowska and Jatkowa Streets, that area forming the temporary Ghetto Number Two. Once they were in the ghetto, the gates were locked and exit for Jews was forbidden without special permits issued by the *Gebiettskommissar.* The Jews left the ghetto only in labor columns, as forced laborers, employed by the Germans in war-effort industries. Outside the ghetto the Germans hung up signs saying: "Attention! Jewish Quarter. Danger of Epidemics. Entry to Non-Jews Forbidden!"

The greater part of resistance was of a passive nature. Attempting to stay alive was passive resistance. Escaping, hiding, or giving birth to a child in the ghetto was resistance. Praying in congregation, singing, or studying the Bible was resistance.

In spite of the many dangers, including death, the cultural dedication of the Jews of Vilna remained creative in all its aspects. Schools were organized, theatre groups performed, concerts were given, a series of adult education courses were set up, and a library and museum were in operation. The "Jerusalem of Lithuania" became the "Jerusalem of the Ghettos."

The first resistance acts in the ghetto were passive. At the liquidation of Ghetto Number Two, in 1941, hundreds of Jews refused to go to Ponary and lay down on the ground. During the "actions" of the "Yellow Certificates" [20] in the main ghetto many Jews refused to leave the ghetto and were shot on the spot.

Before any organized resistance movement came into existence, the Jews sought ways and means of causing damage to the German war effort. They performed various acts of sabotage while working in German installations. Workers would remove vital parts of machines, destroy documents, and produce defective products.

At the outbreak of the war in 1939, a Joint Coordinating Committee of the Hechalutz and other Zionist youth movements was formed under the leadership of Mordechai Tenenboim. This committee formed the nucleus of the resistance in Vilna during the early days of the occupation. With the creation of the ghetto it served as the center of the ghetto's organized underground activities. It conducted various activities during the first few weeks of the ghetto. It dispatched messengers to the ghettos of Warsaw, Bialystok, Grodno, and other Jewish centers, to find out what was happening in other ghettos and to inform the Jews of the other Jewish communities of the true meaning of "transports" and "work camps." The committee also attempted to call the Jews to action and revolt.

On January 1, 1942, the Hechalutz Movement held a memorial meeting in memory of those Jews killed in Ponary. There the first call for resistance was made:

> Jewish youth, do not believe those that are trying to deceive you. Out of 80,000 Jews of Vilna, only 12,000 are left. . . . Where are our own brethren from the other ghettos? Those who are taken out through the gate of the ghetto will never return. All the Gestapo's roads lead to Ponary and Ponary means death. Let us not be led like sheep to the slaughter. True, we are weak and helpless, but the only response to the murderer is self-defense. Brethren, it is better to die fighting, like free fighting men, than to live at the mercy of the murderers: To defend oneself to the last breath. Take Courage!

After the January 1 memorial meeting, the various political organizations held meetings to discuss the creation of an armed resistance movement in the ghetto, and on January 23, 1942, laid the groundwork for the formation of a unified fighting organization, called in Yiddish by its initials, FPO *(Fareinikte Partisaner Organizatzie).*

FPO—United Partisan Organization

The FPO was formed by most of the Zionist groups and the communists with the exception of the Bund. At its first meeting a staff of operations was chosen. The commanding staff was composed of the following three people: Isaac Witenberg (Communist), under the code name "Leon," who served as commander; Abba Kovner (Hashomer Hatzair), known as "Uri"; and Joseph Glazman (Revisionist), who took the pseudonym "Abram."

From the beginning the FPO was faced with a dilemma which agitated other ghettos as well. The problem was whether to fight in the ghetto or join the partisans in the forests. Some members were of the opinion that they should lead the fight in the ghetto itself in order to show the world and posterity that the Jews revolted against their German oppressors and died an honorable death. The proponents of this view were well aware that they could not count on the support of the non-Jewish population. In no country was the Jewish underground treated on an equal footing with the recognized national independence organizations. Jewish requests for weapons were refused outright in Vilna. They realized it would be a struggle without hope, a struggle for honor and history, and not life.

The opposing opinion argued that the purpose of the resistance movement was to combine and participate in the general struggle against the German enemy. Those who held this view felt that it was necessary to smuggle out to the forests as many fighters as possible so that they might join in the over-all struggle against the Germans.

In the end the position of fighting within the ghetto walls prevailed. The plan was to await the decisive hour when there would be sufficient ammunition to arm the masses, and then to begin the uprising.

The goals of the FPO were three: (1) To prepare for an armed revolt in the ghetto and to defend the lives and honor of the ghetto Jews, (2) To carry out acts of sabotage in the German installations and institutions, (3) To make contact with the partisan movement in the forests.

The organization was structured upon military principles. Each unit consisted of three members, all belonging to one political party. Every political party was responsible to the central command for its units. Later, as the organization grew, the units were expanded into groups of five, no longer made up of one political orientation. Each unit of five fighters had a group leader, and four such units made up one military section, with a section commander. Five sections made up a battalion, headed by a battalion commander who was a member of the central FPO command. Special units for communication, sabotage, mine layers, and intelligence were added to the organization.

The signal for mobilization was *"Lize Ruft"* (Liza Calls). Liza Magun was a member of the FPO. She was caught by the Germans on one of her missions outside the ghetto and was tortured to death without betraying the resistance movement.

The first revolver was smuggled into the ghetto in January, 1942. By the middle of 1943, the Vilna Ghetto possessed an arsenal of all kinds of weapons—fifty machine guns, fifty grenades, thirty revolvers, a few rifles, and a few thousand bullets. Most of the arms were smuggled in by Jewish workers employed in the German ammunition factory and depot in Burbiszki.

At one of the meetings of the FPO command, Isaac Kowalski, a member of the underground, suggested that a secret press be organized, and that this press publish a newspaper for the non-Jewish population of Vilna. The suggestion was accepted, but in order to minimize the danger to the ghetto, it was decided to set up the press outside the ghetto walls. Kowalski secured a job at the German Press *Auara* and managed to steal type. The newspaper, published in Polish and called *Sztandar Wolnosci* (Flag of Freedom), was the propaganda organ of the underground. It continually attacked the German regime and publicized news that the German-controlled newspapers did not print.

An important job of the underground press was the printing of forged documents. In order to raise money for the FPO, the secret press printed food cards and sold them. In addition, the FPO issued a daily bulletin, handwritten in Yiddish, which was distributed to its members in order to keep them informed of the news from the "front," as received from the underground wireless. The FPO also issued a bulletin of news written in Russian which was distributed to the Russian prisoners of war.

In his memoir, *Vilna Ghetto,* Abraham Sutzkever gives this account of an anti-Nazi sabotage act carried out by the ghetto underground.

On a May night, 1942, Vitka Kempner,* Icke Mackiewitz, and Moshe Brauze sneaked out of the ghetto before the ten o'clock curfew. With the Star of David removed from their clothing, they were indistinguishable from Aryans on the street.

The three then headed for the woods where they arrived at 2 A.M. While Moshe was standing guard Icke and Vitka were digging an emplacement for a mine under a railway track. Soon thereafter a German troop train passing over the mined rail was blown up. The peasants whom the Germans had ordered the next day to clear the debris counted 200 dead troops, in addition to the many maimed and wounded. There was also a lot of damaged military equipment.

The peasants hid some guns and ammunition, and a year and a half later, when the Vilna Ghetto partisans broke out of the ghetto and came to the forest they claimed some of these hidden weapons with which they continued fighting the Germans.

Fighting Group Jechiel

Besides the FPO group, another organization arose under the leadership of Jechiel Sheinbaum. This resistance group consisted of several partisan-oriented groups united in the desire to leave the ghetto and fight in the forests.

The fighting group Jechiel joined forces with the FPO, and the ghetto resistance movement became unified. The problem of whether to fight

* Vitka Kempner, wife of Aba Kovner, now residing in Israel.

Alexander Pechersky, organizer and leader of the Sobibor revolt.

Niuta Teitelboim (Wanda), underground fighter in Poland.

Photomontage of Baum Group in relation to its underground activities in Berlin. Single photo, top left, is of the leader of the group, Herbert Baum. The mass scene, below, is of a Nazi celebration marking the opening of the anti-Soviet exhibit that the Baum Group attempted to destroy. The poster below is a public announcement of death sentences passed by the Nazis on members of the Baum Group. Photographs to the right are members of the Baum Group. This photomontage, courtesy of the Centre de Documentation Juive Contemporaine in Paris, is part of the permanent exhibit there on Jewish resistance to Nazism.

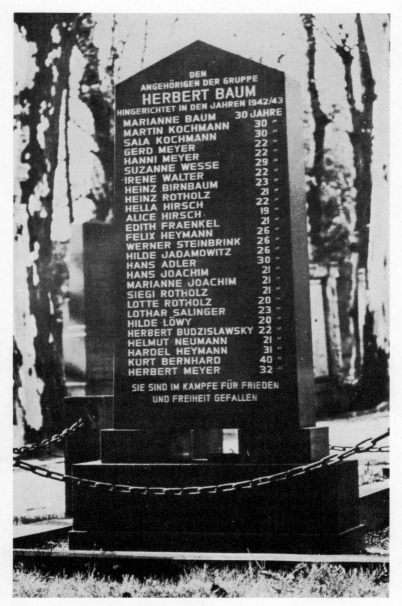

DEN
ANGEHÖRIGEN DER GRUPPE
HERBERT BAUM
HINGERICHTET IN DEN JAHREN 1942/43

MARIANNE BAUM	30 JAHRE
MARTIN KOCHMANN	30 "
SALA KOCHMANN	22 "
GERD MEYER	22 "
HANNI MEYER	29 "
SUZANNE WESSE	22 "
IRENE WALTER	23 "
HEINZ BIRNBAUM	21 "
HEINZ ROTHOLZ	22 "
HELLA HIRSCH	19 "
ALICE HIRSCH	21 "
EDITH FRAENKEL	26 "
FELIX HEYMANN	26 "
WERNER STEINBRINK	26 "
HILDE JADAMOWITZ	26 "
HANS ADLER	30 "
HANS JOACHIM	21 "
MARIANNE JOACHIM	21 "
SIEGI ROTHOLZ	21 "
LOTTE ROTHOLZ	20 "
LOTHAR SALINGER	23 "
HILDE LÖWY	20 "
HERBERT BUDZISLAWSKY	22 "
HELMUT NEUMANN	21 "
HARDEL HEYMANN	31 "
KURT BERNHARD	40 "
HERBERT MEYER	32 "

SIE SIND IM KAMPFE FÜR FRIEDEN
UND FREIHEIT GEFALLEN

Monument to the Baum Group in the Weissensee Cemetery in East Berlin.

Zofia Yamaika, underground fighter in Poland.

Nachum Remba, a communal worker in the Warsaw Ghetto who outwitted the Nazis to save Jewish lives.

Mordecai Anielewicz, commander of the Warsaw Ghetto Uprising.

Emmanuel Ringelblum, founder of the Warsaw Ghetto Archives.

Monument to the heroes of the Warsaw Ghetto by the sculptor Nathan Rappaport, erected in April, 1948.

Isaac Witenberg, commandant of the United Partisan Organization of the Vilna Ghetto.

Emil F. Knieža, Slovak resistance leader.

The "Runner" Mala Zimetbaum, Auschwitz heroine.

The plaque on the house where Mala Zimetbaum had lived.

A group of naked women on the way to the gas chamber in Birkenau (Auschwitz II). The picture was taken by the prisoner David Szmulewski, a member of the underground, from the roof of a building in the crematorium compound.

Corpses of victims gassed in the Birkenau (Auschwitz II) gas chambers are being dragged to open pits for burning. These pictures were also taken by the prisoner David Szmulewski.

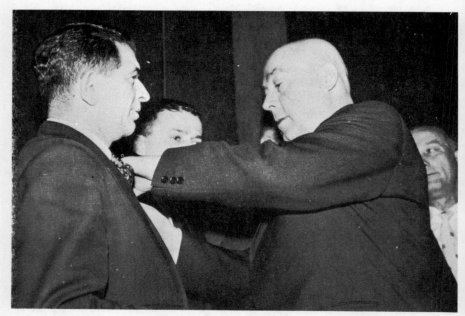

David Szmulewski, leader of the Auschwitz underground, being decorated by Jozef Cyrankiewicz, Premier of Poland, in January, 1960.

Erich Kulka, member of the Au-schwitz underground.

Rosa Robota, Auschwitz heroine.

Joshua Wermuth, Jewish partisan fighter.

From right to left: Isak Parda, Bulgarian Jewish partisan; Abba Kovner, last commandant of the United Partisan Organization of the Vilna Ghetto; Hersh Smolar, leader of the Minsk Ghetto underground; Colonel Senk-Malecki of the Peoples Guard (Warsaw Division); Alexander Levi, Yugoslavian Jewish partisan.

From left to right: Partisans Oswald (Shmuel) Rufeisen (Father Daniel); and Jacob Greenstein.

Dr. Yehezkel Atlas, partisan commander.

Misha Gildenman (Diadia Misha) partisan commander.

Abraham Lissner, leading member of the Jewish Partisan Unit of Paris.

Jacob Gutfreind, commandant of the first Jewish Partisan groups in Belgium.

in the ghetto or in the forests was resolved by the tragic events that shaped a synthesis of both objectives. The synthesis was expressed in the following order:

> We will leave for the forests after the struggle. After we fulfill our obligations we will take with us many, and as a part of the partisan army, we will continue our fight with the murderers.

After a great deal of negotiations and meetings the Bund also joined the FPO. With the inclusion of the Bund, the FPO was a representative resistance organization of all the political views in the ghetto.

The Glazman Affair

Joseph Glazman, a member of the Command Staff of the FPO, was also a member of the Ghetto Administration, first serving as assistant chief of the Ghetto police and later as chief of the housing department. When the Vilna Ghetto police was sent to set up various small ghettos, Jacob Gens, Chief of the Ghetto Administration, wanted Glazman to go to Swienciany and make "housing arrangements" there. Glazman refused and at a meeting of the Ghetto police he chastised the police and the authorities for collaborating and not joining in the plans for revolt. Gens arrested Glazman after his speech and refusal to obey orders. The FPO command sent a delegation headed by its commander Witenberg and requested Glazman's release. Gens refused to bow to the request, and Glazman was chained and led to the gate to be taken to the work camp Sorok-Tatar, fifteen kilometers outside of Vilna. A group of FPO fighters freed Glazman on his way to the gate. The Jewish ghetto authorities requested that Glazman leave the ghetto of his own free will so that the prestige of the Ghetto Administration should not suffer. It was agreed by the command that Glazman go to the work camp Resza.

Glazman was brought back a few weeks later and interrogated by the Ghetto police about the underground movement and released. Thus the first attempt by the Ghetto Administration and police to weaken and disrupt the organization of the underground movement failed.

The Witenberg Day

The Vittenberg episode in the Vilna Ghetto, better known as Witenberg Day, which occurred on July 16, 1943, is regarded as one of the most tragic chapters in the annals of the holocaust.

On July 9, 1943, two of the leaders of the Communist City Committee of Vilna were arrested by the Germans. They were tortured, and it is believed that one of them revealed to the Gestapo their contact with Witenberg and the underground in the ghetto. Details of what followed afterward vary with the sources. One version is that Kittel, an officer of the Gestapo, asked for Witenberg and was told that he was dead. Another version is that Gens ordered Witenberg to surrender and when he refused he was arrested by the Ghetto police and handed over to the Lithuanians. A third version is that Witenberg was asked to come to a meeting of the Judenrat, and when the two Gestapo officers walked in on the meeting, Salek Dessler, the Ghetto police commissioner, pointed to Witenberg, saying, "This is the Commander of the underground, arrest him!"

While Witenberg was being led out of the ghetto the fighters of the underground attacked the guard and freed him. The leaders of the resistance knew that there would be a price to pay for this act of defiance and ordered mobilization of all the fighting units. It was clear that the critical moment had arrived.

The Ghetto Administration headed by Gens assembled the populace and told them that Witenberg was endangering the life of the ghetto. Gens said that he had been given this ultimatum by the Germans:

If by 6 A.M. the next morning the ghetto does not hand over Witenberg to the Germans, they will come with tanks and airplanes and wipe out the ghetto.

Gens and Dessler organized the Ghetto police and members of the "underworld" to look for Witenberg. Panic overtook the ghetto and the population demanded that Witenberg surrender. There was no mistaking the temper of the ghetto; it was Witenberg or bloodshed.

In his *The Jerusalem of Lithuania in Struggle and Destruction,* a memoir which has become an important source book on life in the Vilna Ghetto, Dr. Mark Dworzecki gives the following account of Witenberg Day as it was told to him by Nisel Resnik, a member of the FPO Command:

In the morning the FPO Command was of the opinion that Witenberg should not surrender, and they began to arm the FPO members with weapons from its arsenal in preparation for combat and defense. Jacob Gens sent intermediaries. . . . The leaders of the Communist groups, Chiena Borowski, Berl Shershniewski, Sonia Madaiska deliberated among themselves and came to the conclusion that the ghetto must not be placed in jeopardy because of Witenberg's life. They informed the Command of their thinking and influenced it to accept their view.

Sonia Madaiska and Nisel Resnik came to Witenberg on Straszun Street 15, where he was hiding, and Sonia, his party comrade, told him of the FPO position. Witenberg disagreed and disappeared from Straszun Street 15. (According to the late Philip Friedman, Witenberg was supposed to have said: It has never yet happened that an organization should by its own will surrender its commander. An organization that does that is doomed to failure.) The FPO Command began a search for him but couldn't locate him; it lost contact with him. The leadership of the FPO was in a highly agitated state.

What was to be done? Surrender the Commandant of the FPO, or resist and lead to an eventual entrance of the Germans into the Ghetto and its destruction? Had the time come to begin the final battle?

Chvonik proposed that they go out into the street and commit suicide with their revolvers.

In the meantime the Ghetto Police caught Isaac Witenberg, disguised as a woman. He tore himself free from their hands, firing his revolver, and ran into Deutsche Street 21.

The FPO Command held a long and tragic deliberation with the participation of Joseph Glazman, Abba Kovner, Chvonik, Sonia Madaiska, Nisel Resnik. It was agreed that they inform Witenberg of their decision—that he must surrender.

Sonia Madaiska, Abba Kovner, and Joseph Glazman went to tell him of the decision. He refused to accept it, saying: The ghetto is anyway on the verge of liquidation. The Gestapo wants to liquidate first the resistance leaders and then the entire ghetto.

The FPO Command members told him: The ghetto population does not believe that all is already lost, that the last hour has struck. The ghetto population does not wish to hasten the hour of liquidation. The people do not want the struggle now.

Anatol Fried, Trafida, Minna Svirska, and Dr. Milkanowitzki also came to discuss with him and persuade him to surrender. They also told him of Gens's assurance that he would do everything to rescue him from Gestapo hands.

Dessler kept telephoning and sending emissaries to say that any minute now the Gestapo will march into the ghetto with tanks.

Finally, Isaac Witenberg accepted the decision of the FPO Command. He said: "If that is your wish I'll go." And he left.

A Gestapo auto was waiting in front of the gate. Isaac Witenberg walked silently to the gate. Behind him followed Ghetto Police with drawn revolvers to give the Gestapo the impression that they had caught the criminal. . . . The auto took him away to the Gestapo cellars.

Rumors circulated that Dressler had given him [Witenberg] a poisoned drink before he went to the gate.

The next day Isaac Witenberg was dead. It is not known whether he was tortured to death during the interrogation, or whether he committed suicide with the cyankali [a vial of poison] he had with him.

As a result of these events the FPO became disorganized. The ghetto population was opposed to its existence and activities, owing to fear of extermination.

The FPO Command decided to change its tactics:

> As a result of the events of July 16, we are forced to evacuate and transfer our activities to the forest.

The first detail of Jewish partisans left the ghetto on July 25, 1943, headed by Joseph Glazman. On the road, they were joined by others from surrounding work camps, who were seeking an opportunity to fight as partisans. They were successful in reaching the forests, but there they were ambushed and most of them perished. Only fourteen of the group reached the forests of Narocz, where they formed the nucleus of the Jewish partisan units "The Vengeance," whose contingent grew to four hundred fighters.

On July 26, Neugebauer, an officer of the Gestapo, came to the ghetto and demanded the surrender of the families of all those who had gone to the forests. He also wanted the brigadiers of the work groups that the partisans had belonged to. Eighty Jews were taken to Ponary and shot. The work camps Nowa Wileika and Bezdany were completely destroyed in reprisal for the flight of the partisans there.

On August 1, 1943, the following article appeared in the official organ of the Jewish ghetto administration *Geto Yediot #50 (Ghetto News):*

> According to the order of the German Security Police and S.S., a number of Jews, and among them brigadiers, were arrested.
>
> We want to remind the ghetto of the words and warning of the Ghetto Representative, that as of the latest order received from the German authorities, all Jews are collectively responsible.
>
> It is your duty to yourself and to the ghetto to inform on any activity which might endanger the existence of the ghetto.

The remaining ghetto fighters were again faced with a dilemma. If they left the ghetto to go to the forests they endangered the lives of their families. The Germans also introduced the wearing of metal dog tags to facilitate identification. They now were able to bring back identification tags of the murdered partisans for public exhibition.

Anton Schmidt, a *Feldwebel* in the German Army stationed in Vilna, was anti-Nazi and aided the Jewish underground. He transferred Jews from Vilna to Bialystok in trucks. He often hid Jews in his house. There are no definite facts about how he was arrested and killed. It is believed that he was arrested and sentenced by a German Military Court Martial to be shot for aiding Jews.

On September 1, 1943, the ghetto was sealed off. The Germans, with the aid of Lithuanian and Estonian troops as well as Ukrainian volunteers, surrounded the ghetto. Neugebauer issued the following order: "As of today, no one is permitted to leave the ghetto."

The FPO was mobilized at once. Some wanted to fight immediately, but Abba Kovner, the new Commander, ordered them to wait until the situation became clear. In the morning the Germans, Lithuanians, Estonians, and Ukrainians entered the ghetto, and the first chance for effective action was missed.

The FPO fighters took up their positions. They set up barricades in two places, one at #6 Szpitalna Street and the second at #12 Straszuna Street. The first position at #6 Szpitalna Street was surrounded by the enemy, and because of a lack of ammunition most of the fighters were captured. Those that escaped went to #12 Straszuna Street. The Germans proceeded to surround the second position. As they approached the barricade, Jechiel Sheinbaum, who was in command, began to fire. The Germans opened with a barrage and blew up the house. Sheinbaum and several other fighters lost their lives defending their position.

Gens and Dessler petitioned that the Germans, Estonians, Lithuanians, and Ukrainians leave the ghetto. They feared that a battle between the enemy and the fighters would bring immediate destruction to the ghetto. The Germans accepted the petition and withdrew from the ghetto. It was then that the FPO decided to evacuate, and during the days of September 8-11, 1943, two hundred fighters left to join the partisans in the forests.

The assembling of Jews for deportation to Estonia lasted four days, from September 1-4, 1943. During those four days, 8,000 Jews were deported to labor camps in Estonia. After this deportation, Neugebauer and Kittel came to the ghetto and announced that the deportations would stop and that the remaining Jews would be given work in the ghetto.

On September 14, 1943, Gens was summoned to Gestapo headquarters. He was accused of having helped the partisans and was shot on the spot by Neugebauer. Salek Dessler was appointed Ghetto Representative in his place. On September 15, the ghetto was again surrounded by soldiers, and seven trucks of soldiers entered the ghetto. The remaining FPO fighters were again mobilized. The Germans had come with the intention of taking the rest of the Jews for deportation, but when they learned that the ghetto fighters were mobilized to fight they withdrew.

On September 23, 1943, Kittel arrived and ordered the Jews to be ready for deportation by 12 A.M. The ghetto was then officially to be closed and all Jews sent to Estonia.

The Gestapo officer Franz Murer, when captured by the Russians, gave the following version of the ghetto liquidation:

The liquidation of the ghetto was postponed for a few weeks in order to hunt for the partisans in the forests. But Kittel wanted to be promoted, so he asked for two hundred Ukrainian soldiers to aid him in liquidating the ghetto. He received permission, and on September 23, 1943, he began the liquidation.

On that day the FPO evacuated the last of its fighters through the underground sewers. Some were captured while escaping and resisted with arms. They were later publicly hanged. On the following day, the Ukrainians and Germans entered the ghetto and carried off the last remaining Jews.

Although the Vilna Ghetto was liquidated, the spirit of its resistance was carried on. The fighters who succeeded in reaching the forests gathered at two bases, in Rudnitska and Narocz forests, where they continued their battle against the Germans. The fighters of Vilna who were deported to the concentration camps of Estonia carried on by organizing an underground movement and communicating with the partisans.

Bibliography

Mark Dworzecki, *The Jerusalem of Lithuania in Struggle and Destruction* (Tel-Aviv: Mapai Press, 1951) (Hebrew).

Shoshana Kahn, *In Fire and Flames* (Buenos Aires: Union Central Israelita Polaca en la Argentina, 1949) (Yiddish).

Shmerke Katsherginski, *The Destruction of Vilna* (New York: Ciko Farlag, 1947) (Yiddish).

Shmerke Katsherginski, *Partisans On the March* (Buenos Aires: Union Central Israelita Polaca en la Argentina, 1947) (Yiddish).

Rayzl Korchak, *Flames in Ash* (Israel: Sifriat Poalim, 1965) (Hebrew).

Isaac Kowalski, *The Secret Press of the Jewish Underground Movement* (New York: 1953) (Yiddish).

Herman Kruk, *Diary of the Vilna Ghetto,* edited by M. V. Bernstein (New York: Yivo Institute for Jewish Research, 1961).

Chaim Lazar, *Destruction and Revolt* (Tel-Aviv: M'Shot, 1950).

Leizer Ran, *Ashes From the Jerusalem of Lithuania* (New York: Vilner Farlag, 1959) (Yiddish).

J. Robinson and P. Friedman, *Guide to Jewish History Under Nazi Impact* (New York: Yad Washem-YIVO, 1960).

Abraham Sutzkever, *Vilna Ghetto: 1941–1944* (Buenos Aires, Ikuf Press, 1947) (Yiddish).

Joseph Tenenbaum, *Underground* (New York: Philosophical Library, 1952).

The Revolt of the Jews of Marcinkonis

By Leyb Koniuchowski

[EDITOR'S NOTE: *Right after the liberation of Lithuania, survivor Leyb Koniuchowski dedicated himself to the compilation of an authentic collective record of the martyrdom and resistance of the Jewish communities in Lithuania, before time dimmed the memories and distorted the perspectives of survivors who had experienced those events.*

To that end he traveled extensively, first in Lithuania and later through the DP camps in Germany, tracking down survivors of ghettos and partisan units and recording their accounts.

This labor of love and high dedication which lasted for nearly five years yielded 1,683 handwritten pages, folio size. Each account was checked and rechecked by taking down the stories of several different survivors who had had the same experience to assure as much factual accuracy as possible under the circumstances. The result is an amazing document of the holocaust period. What follows is an abbreviated version of part of that document, which was published in the YIVO Annual of Jewish Social Science, *New York: 1953, VIII, 205-223.*

Mr. Koniuchowski, a civil engineer, now resides in New York.]

DURING the night of Sunday, November 1, 1942, the Jewish ghetto police noticed that the ghetto was being surrounded by a heavy and strongly armed guard. They immediately notified the Judenrat and all the Jews in their homes. Many Jews had returned late that evening from work and had gone to bed very tired, but no one slept that night. Everyone anxiously waited for the coming of dawn. Marcinkonis at that time had already been severed from White Russia and joined to the Third Reich. On Monday, November 2, at 6 A.M. the Jews gathered at the gate to go out to their work in the town. But they were not allowed to leave the confines of the ghetto. The members of the Judenrat came to the ghetto gate. The Commissar of the Town Office, accompanied by armed police, told

160

the Judenrat that the Jews would no longer go to work and ordered everyone to pack up their belongings and make ready to leave the ghetto for "work" in another place. Freight cars stood in readiness a small distance from the ghetto. The commissar told the Jews to make haste and that all must be at the station with their families by 8 o'clock, lined up six in a row.

A few had managed to steal out of the ghetto at night. A few left the ghetto in the morning and stole through the armed ring. Only a few score Jews came to the place before 8 o'clock. The Germans began to feel nervous. The military commander of the White Russian town of Sobakince had come to help in the successful liquidation of the ghetto. He was a notorious butcher who had experience in several acts of annihilation of Jews in ghettos in White Russia. This time he failed. He sensed that something was going on which he had not been accustomed to seeing in the destruction of Jews. The Jews did not even dream of carrying out his order to line up.

A group of bold Jews, among them Bentsiyon Kobrovsky, seventeen years old, Fayvl Rapoport, and others, were preparing to attack the assassin with the "red boots" (this is what the Jews called the commander of Sobakince) and to take away his automatic pistol.

The members of the Judenrat approached him as if to make a request. But he would not allow them to come near. Ahron Kobrovsky, president of the Judenrat, then cried out: "Jews, whoever wants to live, let him run where he can! The play is with the devil!"

The Jews began to run toward the ghetto fence. The commandant with the "red boots" began shooting his pistol in all directions. His subordinates did likewise. Cries of women and children were heard and the groans and rattling sounds of the wounded and the dying. Everybody ran from the ghetto. The fence was broken down. The panic and pandemonium in the ghetto were indescribable. There were not a few cases of Jewish men beating the armed murderers with their bare fists and trampling them underfoot. The shooting on every side became intensified. Many dead and wounded fell. Groans and wails filled the air. The Germans did not succeed in catching alive one single Jew, man, woman, or child, to throw into the freight car. One hundred and five Jews remained lying dead in the ghetto and outside the enclosure. The plan to transfer the Jews of Marcinkonis to Kelbasin near Grodno and thence to the crematoriums in Poland was frustrated by the Jews of Marcinkonis, who paid for their effort with blood. Like wild beasts the Germans set upon the abandoned Jewish houses looking for hidden Jews. But even there they failed to capture any Jew alive.

The president of the Judenrat, Ahron Kobrovsky, his brother Bentsiyon, Yossl Gilinsky, and Berl Aizenshtat had managed to hide in a bunker underneath a house. The Germans discovered the bunker and ordered the Jews to come out. Revolver shots came out of the bunker in reply. The Germans threw two hand grenades into the bunker and put an end to the lives of the four Jews. A number of women and children had gone into the underground hideouts previously prepared under their homes. Apart from the hideout of Ahron Kobrovsky, not one such place was discovered by the Germans. Christians, however, who came in search of loot, stumbled upon some of them and reported them to the Germans and their collaborators.

Several days after the liquidation of the ghetto some twenty Jews, men, women, and children, gathered in the forest. These Jews "settled" in tents, covered with branches and foliage, three kilometers from the village of Musteika.

After a few days the Jews established contact with the Lithuanian peasant Jonas Balevicius, in Musteika. He was one of the truly fine peasants who fully sympathized with the plight of the Jews and did all he could to help them. He was a good friend of the Kobrovskys. Jonas would get money from the Jews and buy them food, traveling many miles to make purchases and to bring provisions to the forest. A few days after they settled in the forest he sold them three rifles and ninety bullets, for which the Jews paid him twenty-five rubles in gold. The possession of firearms made the Jews feel more secure.

On November 2, when the ghetto of Marcinkonis was liquidated, the ghettos in the neighboring towns and in Grodno were also liquidated. Some Jews who escaped from the Grodno ghetto, including the three Kobrovsky brothers, also managed with the aid of friendly peasants to reach the forest. With the help of these peasants the Jews increased their supply of weapons.

When the Jews in the forests received reports that a well-armed German detachment was getting ready to carry out raids against the partisans, they did not remain idle. They sent out scouts to every trustworthy friend in the villages to obtain more information about the impending blockade, and they prepared to change their quarters and move into more remote parts of the woods.

In the autumn of 1943 a great battle took place between the Germans and Kapustin's Red partisans about one and a half kilometers from Kobrovsky's Jewish group. The Germans used heavy artillery, tanks, and airplanes. Kapustin's Red partisans were also fairly well equipped and had artillery. They could not stand up, however, against the regular German army units and they were surrounded on all sides. The supply convoy with a substantial portion of the Red partisans, including Kapustin and his staff, broke through the ring and penetrated into the forest. A short distance from the Kobrovsky group the supply convoy bogged down in the swamps. The Germans stopped at the edge of the forest, fearing to go into the dense interior. Kapustin and his aides visited the Kobrovsky group and held a friendly conversation with its members. He listened attentively and with interest to their experiences, and told them of his own struggles with the Germans during the past few days and about the losses inflicted on them by his brave soldiers. Khayim Kobrovsky, Efrayim Pilevsky, and a few others of the group led Kapustin's staff out to the edge of the forest near the village of Kotre. At Kapustin's request the Jews, in the company of a few of their soldiers, brought to him the forester Shilka, a confidant of the Jews. The forester showed Kapustin and his staff the trails of the vast woodland and took him nearer to its eastern part. A number of the partisans remained in the forest with the wounded. The whole supply convoy, with produce, horses, and dogs, remained bogged down in the mire not far from Kobrovsky's group. The Jews transported the largest part of the supplies further into the interior of the forest, where they hid it and camouflaged the hiding place. The Jews now had enough food for several months. The rest of the supplies fell to pilfering peasants from the surrounding villages.

Late in the fall of 1943 a company of Red soldiers took up its quarters in the Russian forest, commanded by Davidov and known as the "Davidov company." It engaged in sabotage and intelligence activities. They were all first-class fighters and well equipped with modern weapons, which were parachuted to them from planes. This company which arrived from the east took over command of all Red companies in the forest. Among the soldiers in the Davidov company were many Jews from White Russia who escaped the massacres of the spring and summer of 1942, including Lipe Skolsky, a good friend of the Kobrovskys, who had survived the massacre at Aran. Lipe spoke with enthusiasm and admiration of the virtues of Commander Davidov and of his help to the Jews. Davidov himself was a Jew. Lipe took Yitzkhok, Leybe, and Shloyme Peretz and a few others of the Jewish group to Commander Davidov for a consultation. Davidov received the Jewish representatives very cordially and listened with interest to their experiences. He expressed his sympathy, comforted them, and promised to do all in his power to help their family group.

The next day Davidov paid a visit to the Marcinkonis Jews. He chatted amiably with everyone and played with the children and kissed them. They all lined up before him and Davidov promised to provide everyone with automatic pistols and food supplies. He appointed Yitzkhok Kobrovsky as commander of the Jewish family company and asked that he be obeyed. All other partisan companies were forbidden to molest the Jewish unit. No one could now deprive the Jews of their weapons. The Jews in the new family company were now infused with a new spirit of hope and confidence. Firmly resolved to be loyal to their new "father," Davidov, and to the newly appointed commander Yitzkhok Kobrovsky, the brave Jews of Marcinkonis now began the life of true partisans.

The Marcinkonis Jews together with the fighters in Davidov's company set out to work in earnest. A joint group of both companies derailed a military train, and the locomotive was blown to pieces and three cars were damaged. The fighters of Yitzkhok's company once adopted a resolution at a conference to ask Davidov to let a group consisting only of their men blow up a military railway convoy. Davidov agreed. Khayim, Leybl, Shloyme Peretz, and Khayim Weinberg, led by Yitzkhok Kobrovsky, blew up a military train on the road between Grodno and Vilna, nine kilometers from Marcinkonis. Twelve cars of ammunition and the locomotive were damaged and several hundred meters of railway tracks were destroyed. The great success of this undertaking meant that the Jewish unit had stood its first test of sabotage action. It now became endeared to Commander Davidov and to his company. The success of this act of sabotage was all the more amazing since it was carried out in broad daylight. For several days the railway connection between Vilna and Grodno was paralyzed. Davidov and his fighting men congratulated the Jews on their success.

After this event all acts of sabotage were undertaken with the participation of the Jewish unit. The Marcinkonis Jews enthusiastically carried out such tasks and returned happy with their execution, fired by a desire to avenge the extermination of the Jews of Europe. Dozens of military trains never reached the front. Those that did arrive were badly damaged and behind schedule. Other Red partisan groups hammered away at the German military machine. The trains that managed to get through without damage at one place were harassed at other points.

Davidov's company destroyed not only military trains but also many bridges. There too the Marcinkonis Jews displayed their courage and daring. Following every successful act of sabotage the fighters were given testimonials. The Jewish family company acquired a very large number of such testimonials. Many Jews of other companies were taken by Davidov into his own lines. The four Jews who had joined Stankevich's company also went into Davidov's unit. The Jews, thoroughly familiar with the whole region, successfully carried out acts of espionage with the assistance of their friends in the villages. Many German spies were thus liquidated by Davidov's group during that winter.

Revolt in Lachwa

By Aaron Schworin, Chaim Shkliar, Abraham Feinberg, Chaim Michali

[EDITOR'S NOTE: *The surviving Jews of Lachwa, a small town in the southwestern part of Byelorussia, proudly claim that theirs was the first ghetto to revolt when the Germans and their Ukrainian helpers came to liquidate it. The story of their revolt, presented here, is a montage of different eyewitness accounts by four survivors. Each account contained some pertinent facts which the others did not mention. The reason for the montage was to gather all these facts into one account and present as full a picture of this historic event as possible.*] [21]

LACHWA HAD a community of 2,000 Jews. With the outbreak of World War II, on September 1, 1939, the Jewish population of Lachwa increased by 40 percent. Jewish refugees from the German-occupied areas fled to Lachwa, which was already in the Soviet zone. The native Jews lived side by side with the new arrivals. In the summer of 1941, when the German-Soviet war broke out, only a small percentage of the population saved itself by fleeing deeper inland. The majority, however, remained and fell into the hands of the Germans.

The Germans occupied Lachwa on July 8, 1941, and the persecution of the Jews began at once. For this the Germans found devoted helpers among the native Byelorussians, who joined the police force, put on white armbands, and strutted arrogantly through the streets with rubber truncheons in their hands shouting, "Your time has come, Jews!"

On the eve of Passover, April 1, 1942, the Jews were herded into a ghetto which consisted of two small streets. It was terribly crowded. The ghetto was surrounded by a barbed wire fence and guarded by local police and patrols of the German Wehrmacht.

A large section of the native population viewed with satisfaction the misfortune of the Jews and looked forward to their annihilation so that they could satisfy their lust for looting. But there were also some elderly peasants who took in the Jewish possessions for safekeeping and later returned them to the surviving Jews.

The ghetto did not exist long. Together with other ghettos in nearby towns the Lachwa Ghetto was to be liquidated in 1942. But in Lachwa it happened differently.

All the towns in the vicinity of Lachwa had already been made Judenrein. The Jews of Lachwa felt that their days, too, were numbered. The youth began to organize itself for resistance, but despite all efforts it was impossible to obtain weapons. Still the ghetto was determined not to allow itself to be driven to the slaughter like sheep. At the head of the resistance group was Yitzchok Rochtchin. Preparations were made to meet the murderers with axes, hammers—with anything that could deliver a deathblow.

On August 2, 1942, the Germans ordered peasants to dig a pit at the outskirts of the town, fifty meters long and four meters wide. On the night of August 3, the lookouts posted by the ghetto committee noticed an increase in the number of native police that surrounded the ghetto on all sides. The news was quickly spread throughout the ghetto, and the people began to gather near the gate that led to the square.

Shooting was heard continuously from the direction of Nohorodek, a town six kilometers from Lachwa, where the Germans were liquidating the last survivors of the ghetto. In this tragic moment a heated discussion arose among the assembled Jews on how to resist the criminals. The proposal of the youth was that the entire mass attack the Germans at once, storm the gates and the barbed wire fence, and escape to the swamps of the Pripet. But the idea was abandoned because of the concern for the old, women, and children who would not have enough strength to flee from their pursuers. Family sentiment conquered logic. The nightmarish prospect of abandoning one's dearest relatives to the Nazis made one relinquish the luring possibility of one's own survival.

At eight in the morning, while the excited populace was still debating, five truckloads of SS men arrived. They were the same liquidation commandos that carried out the annihilation of tens of thousands of Jews in Polesia. They leisurely sat down to eat. They had not had a bite of food in six hours because they were busy liquidating the Jews of Nohorodek and Luniniece.

When several members of the ghetto committee, the Judenrat, approached the Germans and asked why they had come here, they replied calmly that they came to liquidate the Jews of the Lachwa Ghetto, and added, "But we decided to let thirty of you live, including the members of

the Committee and about three to four people of every useful trade. . . .
And now 'be so kind' and ask the gathering to go back home and wait
there until we call for them. . . ."

At this, Dov Lopatin, president of the ghetto committee, cried out,
"You will not murder us piecemeal! Either we all live, or we all die!"

At this moment the SS men entered the ghetto and ordered everyone
to line up. Instead, the Jews ran to their houses and set them on fire.
Dov Lopatin was the first to apply the torch to the headquarters of the
Judenrat. Soon all the others followed his example. Smoke and flames
shot up in the air. A panic arose among the SS. They fired into the
crowd. The first victims fell. They were Abraham Slutzki and Israel
Drepski.

Yitzchok Rochtchin attacked the SS chief with an ax. The SS officer
fell to the ground, covered with blood. Having no way out Rochtchin
jumped into the nearby river. He was struck down by a bullet. At the
same time another SS man was felled at the gate by Chaim Cheiffetz and
the brothers Asher and Moshe-Leib Cheiffetz. Still another German fell
at the hands of Moshe Klopnitzki.

Now the crowd was aroused and stormed the ghetto gate. Those who
were able to run did, leaving behind a flaming ghetto. They were pursued
and shot at. Many fell. The town was littered with corpses. People ran
with their last ounce of strength to the forests near the river Pripet, hoping
to find a haven there. Of the 2,000 Jews, about 600 managed to reach
their destination. But the police and the Byelorussians of that region, who
pursued them, murdered most of them brutally. The forester Polin with
his own hands shot about 200 Jews.

The Germans succeeded in leading to the grave only a few, because
young and old alike ran. They would rather die from a bullet while
running than be led to the grave.

Several days later 120 Lachwa Jews gathered in the Chobot forest,
about twenty kilometers from town, and joined the partisans, fighting side
by side with them, and later with the Red Army, thus taking revenge for
their beloved ones.[22]

The Revolt in the Tuczyn Ghetto

By Mendel Mann

[EDITOR'S NOTE: *The little-known town Tuczyn found a painstaking chronicler of its remarkable revolt in the writer Mendel Mann. Though not an actual participant, he pieced together the story of the revolt from the eyewitness accounts of a handful of Jewish survivors and native non-Jews, when he entered the town upon its liberation with the advancing Red Army.*

A native of Warsaw, Mendel Mann participated in the defense of that beleaguered city in 1939 prior to its fall to the German invaders. He later escaped to Soviet territory and from 1940 to June 1941 lived in Tuczyn where he was employed as a teacher.

When the Germans overran Tuczyn he escaped as far as the Volga, where he was mobilized into the Soviet Army. It was on his return to Tuczyn in February, 1944, as one of its liberators that he recorded the story of its revolt. It is condensed, edited, and translated from Fun Letzten Churbon (From the Last Extermination), *Munich: September, 1948, No. 9, pp. 59–66.*

Mr. Mann has written extensively on the holocaust, both fiction and non-fiction. His trilogy, At the Gates of Moscow, The Fall of Berlin, *and* At the Vistula, *was translated from Yiddish into many languages, including French, English, Spanish, Italian, and Hebrew. He makes his home in Paris.*]

TUCZYN, A SMALL town in Volhynia, Ukraine, twenty-seven kilometers east of Rovno, was invaded by the Germans on June 30, 1941. That very same day the Germans dragged the Torah Scrolls out of a synagogue into the street and compelled several elderly women to dance on the parchment. Later these same women were forced to tear the Scrolls into shreds and burn them in the middle of the street.

This and other facts about Jewish life in Tuczyn under German occupation was related to me by a group of Jews who had managed to hide in the forests, and by the Ukrainian teacher Jegor Krirzanowski, who had worked for the Germans as an interpreter, when I visited that town after its liberation.

Before the Germans had taken full command of the administration of Tuczyn native Ukrainians pogromized the Jewish community, leaving seventy dead and a large number of wounded, including women and children. When a delegation of Jews went to Rovno to plead for protection against the Ukrainians the Gestapo chief said to them: "The killing of Jews is *our* right. We shall look into the matter."

In July, 1941 the Germans set up a Judenrat in Tuczyn, headed by Getzl Schwartzman, and in the latter part of that year they posted a decree forbidding the peasants to trade with the Jews or to have any dealings with them. Although a small number of peasants ignored the decree and smuggled some food and firewood into the ghetto, the order created a state of hunger in the Jewish community.

Besides not having enough food for themselves, the Tuczyn Jews had to share their meager rations with Jewish refugees from the neighboring towns of Kostopol, Ludvipol, Berezne, Rovno, Koszcz, and Aleksandria. The refugees brought horrifying reports of "actions" during which young and old were shot for no reason at all. The German crimes, they said, had no parallel in history. Particularly painful were the stories of atrocities committed by Ukrainians against their Jewish neighbors who had lived for centuries on that soil.

What saved the Tuczyn Jews from a similar fate, for the time being at least, was the presence of two factories, a tannery and a cotton mill, that had been in town for years before the war. Thanks to the initiative of a group of Tuczyn Jews and a refugee from Lodz, engineer Gross, the two factories were activated soon after the Germans occupied the town and began to produce quality leather and cloth which were needed badly. And so while there were hardly any Jews left in the entire region of Rovno, and all the neighboring towns were practically Judenrein, many Tuczyn Jews were employed at the factories. Each employee received a working certificate which in those days was equivalent to a life certificate.

But even the Tuczyn Jews were not entirely spared from "actions." They were subjected to several small "actions" during which hundreds of Jews were rounded up, taken to the brickyard wall and shot by the Ukrainian police. To those who in 1942 were still working in the two factories it became clear that their days were numbered. Indeed they were. By the end of the summer the Germans issued a decree ordering all Jews, including those employed at the factories, to move into a ghetto.

About 3,000 were crowded into a few narrow streets and were compelled to build their own ghetto wall with the wood of the abandoned houses. As soon as the gate was locked the ghetto was surrounded by armed Germans and Ukrainians.

On September 23, 1942, a Gestapo officer appeared in the ghetto and ordered all Jews to assemble at the gate. He also announced that all young people, as well as others who were physically fit, would be taken elsewhere to work.

Tuvia Tchubak, a former *chalutz* and son of a blacksmith, and another Jew named Taflik began to exhort the people not to obey the German command but to gather in the synagogue instead. When the synagogue was filled one Jew leaped to the platform and called out: "Resist! Do not go voluntarily like sheep!" Another jumped on a bench and cried out: "Jews! You should know that the pits have already been dug at the Katowski forest!" The young people were in a fighting mood. One of them shouted: "Let's set the ghetto on fire! Burn it down!" "Burn everything!"

From somewhere barrels of kerosene were rolled out. Jews fetched ladles, pots, jugs, and other kitchen utensils and filled them with kerosene. Even children came running with pots. The few orthodox Jews did not participate. They gathered in the large synagogue and read the Psalms.

When night fell the Jews put the torch to the kerosene-soaked houses. Flames shot up in the air. Soon the whole ghetto was in flames. The Germans and Ukrainians, taken unawares, were stunned and confused, and the Jews utilized their confusion to their advantage.

"Smash the fence!" Someone cried out. The youths attacked the Germans and Ukrainians with hatchets. From some houses shots rang out and grenades were thrown. Jews stormed the wall and began to run in the direction of the forest, leaving behind them a burning ghetto. The flames were visible for miles around. The Ukrainian teacher told me that he had seen two wagonloads of Ukrainian and German corpses taken out of the ghetto. About 2,000 of the fleeing Jews reached the forest, though they fled under continuous German fire, and were frequently attacked on the way by Ukrainians who lay in wait in their scattered huts.

Soon after the revolt the Germans posted announcements that Jews would be allowed to live in Tuczyn and would not be persecuted. Those who were caught on the roads in those days were not shot but were brought back to town and settled in a number of houses selected from the ones that had not burned down.

Plagued by hunger and deluded by the hope that this time, perhaps, the Germans would keep their promise, about 400 Jews returned to Tuczyn. They were rounded up one night and shot near the cemetery.

Still a large number of Jews continued to hide out in the forest, risking their lives each time they searched for food. A small number of Jewish tailors and shoemakers worked for Ukrainian peasants in their huts, attics, and woodsheds.

In November, 1943 the Germans succeeded in luring another 150 Jews into town. They too were shot. The rest were determined to remain in the forest even at the risk of death.

In the early hours of January 17, 1944, the Red Army entered Tuczyn, but all that was left of the Jewish community was rubble and debris, overgrown with weeds and covered with snow. The handful of surviving Jews was transferred to Rovno where a larger number of Jewish survivors from the neighboring towns now lived.

The flames of the Tuczyn ghetto revolt illuminated not only the towns of Volhynia; they were also a bright moment in the martyrdom of Eastern European Jewry.

The Escape from Koldyczewo Camp

By Joseph M. Foxman

[EDITOR'S NOTE: *"The Escape from Koldyczewo Camp"* belongs to the *many lesser-known episodes of Jewish resistance.*
Joseph M. Foxman was born in Baranowicze, Poland, and spent the war years in the Vilna Ghetto and the concentration camp Gunskirchen (Austria). Prior to the war he was an editor of a Zionist publication and a contributor to various Yiddish periodicals. After the war he served as an Associate with the Jewish Documentation Center, War Criminals Division, in Austria. He emigrated to the United States in 1950 and is presently a research associate with Joint Documentary Projects of Yad Vashem (Israel) and the Jewish Scientific Institute—YIVO (USA). He is the editor of Baranowicze in Martyrdom and Resistance, *a compilation of memoirs and documents (New York, 1964).*
The account that follows was written especially for this anthology.]

AT THE END of 1942 when the Germans began the decisive liquidation of the ghettos in the parts of Byelorussia that once belonged to Poland, the younger people, especially the skilled craftsmen, were deported to Camp Koldyczewo in the region of Baranowicze. A former estate, this camp had gone through several transformations. In the beginning of the war it was turned into *Stalag 337* for Russian prisoners of war. Later it became a slave labor camp for prisoners of various nationalities, except Jews. Now its stables were converted into a camp for Jews—a reservoir of shoemakers, tailors, locksmiths, blacksmiths, tanners, electrotechnicians, watchmakers, and other skilled workers, The non-skilled were used as peat diggers in the woods.

They were brought from the ghettos of Baranowicze, Nowogrodek, Slonim, Molczadz, Stolpce, Swierzen, Horodyszcze, Zdzieciol, Horodziej, and other ghettos. When forty-five Jews of a Baranowicze labor camp escaped to the forests to join the partisans, the remaining eighty Jews were deported to Koldyczewo.

Camp Koldyczewo was also a training school for Byelorussian police, and the school utilized the Jewish prisoners both as servants and guinea pigs for the trainees. The latest achievements of Nazi "science" in the field of torture and murder were demonstrated on the Jewish prisoners.

Camp Koldyczewo was widely known as a place of horror, suffering, and death. It was the only camp in Byelorussia that had a crematorium. The prisoners were forced to stand six Appells (roll calls) daily, and hardly a day passed without some prisoners being hanged on the pretext that they planned to escape. Because of starvation rations (50 grams of bread and some water per person daily) and the lack of warm clothing in freezing winter weather, many prisoners suffered from frostbite and tuberculosis and were removed to the camp "hospital," under the supervision of Dr. Zelig Levinbuk of Baranowicze. Dr. Levinbuk did all he could for the prisoners, saving many of them from certain death. At the risk of his life he would issue sick certificates to the Hassidim and their rabbi, Shloime Weinberg, to free them from having to work on the Sabbath.

When reports of German defeats on the Russian front became known in the camp the Germans and the Byelorussian police avenged themselves on the Jewish prisoners, increasing the selections from once a week to once a day. The last selection took place on November 4, 1943, leaving only ninety-five Jews in the camp.

Among the victims who perished in Koldyczewo were the saintly Dr. Vladimir Lukaszenia and his wife, both Byelorussians from Baranowicze. They were deported to this camp for giving medical supplies to the ghetto pharmacy in Baranowicze, for aiding the ghetto Jews, and for furnishing medical supplies to the partisans.

Despite the terror that reigned in Koldyczewo the Jewish prisoners managed to set up an underground organization headed by Leibel Zeger and Kusznier. Thanks to a Byelorussian policeman who acted as courier for the partisans the underground's arms cache was enriched by several pistols and hand grenades.

The leaders of the underground worked out the following plan of escape, which would take the ninety-five Jews to the forest to join the partisans. The carpenters Berkowski, Koren, and Rawicki were ordered to drill holes beneath the barracks wall adjoining the tannery. The holes were then well camouflaged. The electrified barbed wire fence, only five meters away from the tannery, was cut by the locksmith Erlichman and the blacksmith Peissach. The tools for this purpose were acquired by the locksmiths Norman, Szenicki, and Romek. Before the wire was cut the Jewish electro-technician of the camp made a short circuit.

The escape was set for the night of March 22, 1944, when all the Germans and Byelorussian overseers of the camp were amusing themselves at a ball. (On that night there occurred a snow storm and freezing weather.) Every Jew received a small bottle of poison extracted from the chemical materials in the tannery. Lookouts were posted. Those who were armed went first.

Of the ninety-five Jews ninety-three squeezed through the holes beneath the barracks wall, entered the tannery, and from there headed straight for the cut barbed wire fence. When all were on the other side of the fence Berkowski and Romek slipped back into the camp to close the barracks doors in order not to arouse any suspicion on the part of the Germans. They mined the doors with dynamite so that the next morning when the guards would come to wake the Jews for the Appells they would be met by an explosion. And that was precisely what happened. The next morning ten Germans were killed and the entire barracks burned down.

One Jew, a tailor, who had slept through the escape and whom the others in their haste had forgotten to awaken, perished in the fire. Another Jew, also a tailor, was under arrest at the time, on the charge that he had planned to acquire arms. Arrested on the same charge and tortured to death was the underground fighter Borowski, a chimney sweep from Baranowicze. He died two days before the escape without revealing a single word of the underground's secrets.

Despite the fact that one side of the camp bordered on a tributary of the Niemen River, and that on either side of the barbed wire fence there were tents for the guards and a police department numbering 120 mounted police, the escape was successful.

Of the ninety-three Jews who escaped from Koldyczewo Camp about seventy split up into smaller groups and fanned out in various directions. After many wanderings and much hardship they reached the forest. There they faced new problems—finding food, eluding the enemy's reconnaissance, making contact with the partisans.

Some made their way to the forest of Polesia, the swamps of Pinsk, and the clearings of Naliboka. The majority reached the Naliboka forests, where they joined the partisan brigade headed by the Jewish partisan leader Tuvie Bielski. Other partisan detachments accepted into their ranks only the young and those who possessed weapons. Tuvie Bielski made no exceptions. He admitted the old and the young, men and women, people with and without weapons.

The new partisans adjusted themselves quickly to their new life. They participated actively in all tasks such as attacking police patrols, mining railway lines, derailing German troop trains, blowing up bridges and electric stations, cutting telephone and telegraph communications, ambushing German soldiers. They also took part in punitive expeditions to villages that collaborated with the Germans. Bielski's partisans became famous for their daring attacks on the enemy. Many were later decorated by the Soviet government for heroism.

The Resistance of the Slovak Jews

By Emil F. Knieža

[EDITOR'S NOTE: *During the occupation of Slovakia, Emil Knieža served in the 4th Battalion of the Slovak Labor Brigade, which consisted of Jews and Gypsies. After it was disbanded, he went underground and later participated in the uprising as commander of a scouting unit. At the end of the war he was decorated with the highest Slovak order: The Order of the Slovak National Rising First Class, and other medals.*

Mr. Knieza, who lives in Slovakia, is a professional writer. His account was written especially for this anthology.]

———◆———

LESS THAN a week after Britain's Chamberlain and France's Daladier traveled to Munich to capitulate to Hitler, the Fascist and violently anti-Semitic Hlinka's Slovak People's Party tore off Slovakia from the Czechoslovak Republic with the help of its Hlinka Guard, fashioned on the model of the German SS and SA. Within a year after coming to power, this Fascist government, headed by the Catholic priest Monsignor Jozef Tiso, began to pass anti-Jewish laws which robbed the Slovak Jews of their small properties and savings and made them prisoners in their own homes. Finally, in September, 1941, a comprehensive anti-Jewish set of laws, the so-called Codex Judeorum based on the Nuremberg laws, was passed almost unanimously by the Slovak parliament. Only Count Janos Eszterhazy voted against it, calling it a shameful act. On the basis of this "codex" they began to drive the Jews out of their homes and deport them to concentration camps in Poland and Germany, paying the Nazis 500 reichsmark per person for the job of murdering them. At that time the number of Jews living in Slovakia was approximately 90,000. Between March and October, 1942, 58,150 Jews were deported, of which only a few dozen survived. Then followed a temporary halt in deportations caused by the Nazi debacle at Volgograd (then Stalingrad). They were resumed only toward the end of 1944 when the Slovak National Rising broke out. After we had recovered from the first shock of the Fascist takeover, everybody looked for a way to save his own life. At that time escape was still possible and in the period between the Fascist takeover in March, 1939, and the beginning of 1942, when the deportations began, 7,116 Jews managed to leave Slovakia—3,777 of them for Palestine. Various Zionist groups helped in this. There were other ways, too, by which many Jews tried to avoid deportation; the easiest seemed to be conversion to Christianity. But as it turned out, of the 8,945 who converted, only 2,082 persons—those who were baptized before March, 1939, when the Fascists came to power—were saved from deportation. All the other converts were treated by the clerical-Fascist government as Jews. Many Jews tried to save themselves from deportation by acquiring false documents, such as baptismal certificates. Some moved to towns where they were unknown and managed to find a way of making a living.

I myself lived throughout that period in Slovakia and was active in the anti-Fascist movement and finally had a chance to face the Germans in armed battle. I know of hundreds more who did likewise. Some of them died heroes' deaths. Many still live here or have since emigrated to other countries.

As soon as the Slovak authorities started calling up young men of sixteen upward for a kind of physical checkup prior to being sent to work in Poland, the Hashomer Hatzair and Makabi (general Zionist sport movement) organizations began to plan the escape of young people to Hungary. Hundreds managed to escape deportation in this manner, while hundreds more remained in Slovakia and managed to get along on false documents. In the meantime, the first partisan groups came into existence in eastern Slovakia, in the forests between Michalovce and Humenne. They were centered in the village of Vinné and headed by Pavel Boroš, a communist small holder from that village. Of the twenty-five members of his group, eighteen were Jews. Seven came from Michalovce: Šalamon Landau, thirty-six; Rozalia Markovicova, twenty-eight; Albert Abiš Katz, twenty; Martin Katz, thirty-five; Izak Brandt-Präger, thirty; Ernest Lipkovič, thirty-four; and Martin Mayer Landau, twenty-six, now living here under the name of Rudolf Bugan. The members who came from Humenne were: Izidor Ickovic, thirty; Jakub Haber, twenty; Anton Winkler, twenty-eight; Emanuel Mandel, thirty-six; Ladislav Deutsch, eighteen; Simon Winkler, seventeen; František Winkler, twenty; Samuel Farkaš, thirty-four; and Ferdinand Klein, twenty-six. Two came from Vinné: Frida Feldmanová, twenty-two; and Vojtěch Klein, twenty-seven. They were all tradesmen or farmers, except Ferdinand Klein who was a teacher. Of the twenty-five in the group, ten were Communists, and the only one who had battle experience was Ernest Lipkovič who fought in the Spanish Civil War. Their weapons were: two army rifles, one hunting rifle, three pistols, and a few hand grenades. Naturally, they could not consider offensive action under those circumstances. Under favorable conditions, if the attacking force was not too big, they might at best defend themselves. They lived on what they got from nearby villages. Because a villager informed the security organs at Vinné of their whereabouts, less than a month after the unit was formed they were attacked by a police force. In the fight which ensued, they shot dead Andrej Pazický, a police officer from Vinné, but were soon overpowered and all but their commander Pavel Boroš were taken prisoner. They spent some months in Michalovce prison awaiting trial, but shortly before their trial was due to begin, their escape was arranged with the help of the communist underground organization. They lived on false documents up to the outbreak of the Slovak Rising. Most of them survived the fighting. Pavel Boroš died in battle.

In the same period at least two similar groups existed which were led by Communists and had Jewish fighters in their ranks. One of them, led by Ladislav Exnár and Jozef Büchler, operated in the forest around the town of Banska Stiavnice. This group as well was soon broken up, although some of its members, including Büchler, a peace-time army officer, saved themselves.

In the forests of the Little Carpathians in western Slovakia, a partisan group was organized and led by a young teacher named Alexander Markus, a well-known figure among the young communist intellectuals before the war. Markus came from a poor Jewish family. He was taken prisoner and perished at Mauthausen concentration camp shortly before the end of the war.

The exploits of four young Jews from my native eastern Slovakia caused a great stir in my circle of acquaintances. They managed to escape from Poland, after witnessing the massacre of Slovak Jews at Lukow, near Lublin. Among the escapees was a former classmate of mine, Zoltan Ehrenreich, a tailor from Michalovce, who later joined a partisan unit under the name of Sykora. He now lives in New York. His friend, Elias Fuchs, a farmer from Nacina Ves, near Michalovce, also survived the occupation, and after the war emigrated to the United States. Moving only at night, it took them more than three weeks to get to the Slovak border, where they came across brave, anti-Fascist Slovak folks who took good care of them.

Even the cruelest reprisals could not dampen the growing spirit of resistance in the crucial year of 1942. Over 1,000 Jews between the ages of twenty-two and twenty-three served at that time in the VI Regiment of the Slovak Army Labor Corps. Probably every one of them maintained contact with anti-Fascist elements among the population, in the event that they would need temporary refuge and to prepare for life in the forests if and when orders should be issued for them to be dismissed from service and deported. I have heard of dozens of people who managed to escape by hiding in freight cars which carried timber to Switzerland. From my own regiment, three persons and their families escaped in this manner: Samuel Trenk, Alexander Schwarz, and Simon Ruder. After an exhausting fortnight's journey hidden under the shipment of boards, together with their parents, they got to Switzerland and finally ended up with the Czechoslovak allied force fighting at Dunkirk. One of them now lives in California, the other in South America, probably Bolivia, and the third is either in the United States or Israel.

Many of those living on false documents helped to undermine the Fascist regime and its armed forces. My friend, Vojtěch Rosenbaum from Trebišov, under the name of Michal Kasimir, occupied a little room at Bratislava, together with his wife. In his little room, many underground communist functionaries found refuge, including the above-mentioned partisan commander Alexander Markus. Together with his wife, he prepared pamphlets and news bulletins which found their way into military barracks. He wore a plumber's outfit for disguise. I met him later, toward the end of 1944, during the Rising. He was then a member of a scouting unit, together with Turis Turteltaub, another Jewish boy.

In the spring of 1944, when the Red Army was nearing the Czechoslovak frontier, we, the remnants of Slovak Jewry, together with the majority of the Slovak working people, began to hope anew that the hour of reckoning with the Fascist regime of Monsignor Tiso was at hand.

According to the statistics of the Fascist Interior Ministry, 19,021 Jews lived in Slovakia at that time. Of them, 15,253 lived in the larger towns as economically vital persons or enjoyed preferential treatment for other reasons. Three thousand seven hundred and sixty-eight persons worked in labor units. This figure ought to be extended by about one thousand persons who lived on false documents or were in hiding or in prisons. In the early summer of 1944 the deportation of Hungarian Jews began, with the result that the majority of those Slovak Jews who had previously escaped to Hungary now began to come back, increasing the number of Jews in Slovakia by about 3,000 to a total of 23,000. There were cases of young Hungarian Jews, passing in cattle cars en route to Auschwitz, who jumped from the moving trains onto Slovak territory. I met two such boys from Budapest, Jeno Eckstein and Rudi Feiles, both twenty years old. They cut the barbed wire over the train window and jumped out in the vicinity of the town of Žilina. Although they spoke no Slovakian and the people who found them were well aware that they were escapees and should be reported to the police, they treated them kindly and brought them to the forest where they could join a budding partisan group. They finally became members of the battalion where I commanded the scouting unit.

In those days, we in the labor units lived in feverish expectation of the armed fight which was approaching and did everything we could to prepare ourselves for it. Preparations went on among the 1,644 people stationed at Novaky, the 1,127 stationed at Sered, and among those stationed at Devinska Nova Ves, Kostolna near Trencin, and Kralovany.

Members of the underground communist organization at Novaky planned the struggle together with members of Hashomer Hatzair and Makabi. They had long waited and hoped for it, having acquired their first weapons as far back as 1943 and smuggled them into the labor camp where they hid them well. By August, 1944, when the Slovak National Rising broke out, they had accumulated enough weapons to support 161 fighters. Their joint cooperation at the camp continued for a full two years. It was headed by the experienced old Communist Julius Schönfeld; and young Šimon Porges from Topolčianky, now Čermak; Dr. Hela Volanska, the author; Juraj Spitzer, now one of the prominent literary critics in Slovakia; Karol Friedman; and others. This group maintained contact with the communist cell at Horná Nitra.

When, in August, 1944, at the request of Monsignor Tiso, Nazi divisions invaded Slovakia to put down the National Rising, Jewish boys and girls, their weapons in hand, enthusiastically marched to meet the enemy. Wherever fighting went on, in eastern Slovakia in the Capajev brigade, in central Slovakia around Banska Bystrica, and Martin, as well as in western Slovakia in the forest of the Little Carpathians and Javornik, Jewish fighters were in the front lines. Long before August, 1944, when the actual Rising broke out and the majority of the Slovak army units turned against the Fascist regime, the partisans of the Capajev brigade became famous for their bravery in destroying the railway crossing at Hanu Sovice and attacking German troop trains. Those daring actions were planned and executed by Stefan Friedman (now Kubik). Many of my friends fought in this brigade, among them Ludovit Zulc, now head of the Journalists Institute in Prague; Dezider Karniol, disabled in battle, now employed at the City Educational Institute of Bratislava; Ladislav Schwarz (now Cerny), junior professor of medicine, and others. Many of my friends died heroes' deaths. To name but a few—Sano Schein from Nova Zamky, Alexander Markovic from Vinné, Viliam Lefkovic and Elisa Schwarz from Michalovce.

Of the total number of 60,000 soldiers and partisans, about 2,500 were Jews. Unfortunately a considerable part of western Slovakia remained outside the revolutionary territory, and as it happened this was the area where many Jews lived, about one half of the total number. They were loaded onto trucks and deported.

Of the 161-man Jewish unit from Novaky, thirty-five were killed in action, twenty-two were wounded, most of them seriously, and twenty were taken prisoner. Most Jewish fighters, however, fought in mixed units together with Slovaks, Czechs, Soviets, and Hungarians. In many instances they held commander's posts. For example, Edita Katzova was commandant of the third battalion of the Jan Zizka brigade which operated in the region of Banovce and Bebravou. By her heroism she saved the entire battalion from disaster. On September 26, 1944, the Nazis, supported by Slovak Fascists and informers, suddenly attacked. Edita Katzova continued to hold the position in spite of heavy odds. When the second gunner was killed, she took his place, stemming the advance of the enemy and covering the retreat of her unit, which escapd without further loss. When the first gunner was killed, she took over his post until all the ammunition was gone. When the Nazis finally advanced toward her, she threw hand grenades at them. The Nazis, afraid to come near, continued to fire at her long after she was dead.

The advancing Nazi divisions finally forced us to retreat into the mountains. As winter came on, the number of fighters decreased to about 15,000, of which about 2,000 were Jews. As the commander of a scouting unit, I passed through the whole territory held by our forces, and everywhere I met Jewish boys and girls among the fighters. For example, in the Omastina Valley near Banovice I met a Jewish girl of fifteen named Alica Schwarzova (her married name is Fodorova), whose rifle was almost as big as herself. She is an architect now and a happy mother. Her friend, fourteen-year-old Anicka Weissova fell into the hands of the Germans and died tragically. In the partisan brigade at Inovce, one of the deputy commanders of a battalion was a bearded Jew, in charge of supplies, named Julius Ascher (now Taborsky) from Zlate Moravce. There I saw a Jewish boy of fourteen named Miki Broder. He was an orphan and under the special care of Mr. Ascher. There were about fifteen Jewish fighters in this unit, including two brothers, as well as Rosenbaum (now Rosina), Pavel Weiss, Emil Mandel, and others. Not far from them was a unit commanded by a Jew named Alexander Bachnar, now on the staff of the Slovak Trade Union daily *Praca* in Bratislava (Pressburg).

This is but a short account of the heroic effort of my Jewish brothers and sisters in Slovakia in that darkest period of our history.

Translated from the Czech by Jakub Markovic

The Escape and Death of the "Runner" Mala Zimetbaum

By Giza Weisblum

[EDITOR'S NOTE: *To thousands of women prisoners in Auschwitz, Mala Zimetbaum was a legendary name, a symbol of hope and human solidarity. This is the first authentic account of her story. Giza Weisblum, a relative of Mala Zimetbaum, was born in Tarnow, Poland, in 1916 and emigrated to Belgium with her family in 1937. In World War II she was a member of the Belgian underground until 1943 when she was arrested by the Gestapo and deported to Auschwitz. She now lives in Israel and is working on a play about Auschwitz with Mala as the central character. The following account was written especially for this anthology.*]

———◆———

THOSE OF US who knew of Mala's escape awaited the *Appell* with pounding hearts. We hoped that by the time her disappearance was discovered she would be far away from camp.

It was five in the evening. The orchestra played as the exhausted prisoners, guarded by SS men and their dogs, returned from work. The prisoners were counted but the count did not add up to the expected number. Another count was taken and yet another with the same result. The *Appell* dragged on. The SS men now realized that the missing prisoner—number 19880—was none other than the "runner" Mala. This caused a flurry of excitement.

Frau Drecksler, the head overseer, was beside herself. The "runner" Mala? Impossible! We've treated her so well. Maybe she has fainted and is lying somewhere. She had been ill lately with a spell of malaria.

The whole camp was searched. Frau Drecksler herself was running around, looking into every nook and cranny. No Mala. She informed the guard house: One missing. The sirens were sounded. An SS man on motorcycle was dispatched to Auschwitz I to alarm the camp. Frau Mandel, camp commander of Birkenau, Auschwitz II, sharply reprimanded Frau Drecksler for having given Mala too many privileges, too much freedom. Mala knew all the secrets of the camp. She could reveal much.

She had to be caught at all costs. All Gestapo departments and police stations were alerted by telephone.

A feeling of elation swept through the prisoners. They all knew Mala and were convinced that she would arouse the world. The siren continued to scream without a letup because it was discovered that in the men's camp there was also one prisoner missing—Edek Galinski.

Mala's friends, the three "runners," Lea, Sala, and Herta, were accused of having helped in her escape. They were taken to the Political Department for questioning but they insisted they knew nothing. They were stripped of their privileged functions as "runners" and sent to a punitive Kommando.

Time passed. The prisoners, caught in their daily struggle for survival, gradually forgot about the joy Mala's escape had evoked in them. But we, a small group of her close friends, talked about it frequently and continued to hope that by now Mala was far away, perhaps even beyond the Polish border. (As her relative, I was one of the very few who knew of her plan to escape.)

Mala was born in Brzesko, Poland, in 1920. When she was eight years old the Zimetbaum family emigrated to Belgium and settled in Antwerp where Mala, one of five children, went to school. She was a member of Hanoar Hatzioni, a Zionist youth group, among whom she was very popular. Her education was interrupted when her father became blind and Mala had to assume the burden of supporting the family.

When World War II broke out and the Germans occupied Belgium they would stage round-ups to catch Jews, presumably for labor. Actually they were sent to the collecting center, Malines. When the Germans had rounded up about 2,000 Jews they would make up a transport to Auschwitz. In 1942 Mala was caught in one such round-up. She had made detailed plans to escape from Malines but the transport left much sooner than was expected.

I remember the postcard Mala sent us from Auschwitz. It read: "I am well. I work and am in good health." The text was the same on all postcards which the Germans compelled their victims to write home in order to deceive the people. Mala dared to add: "All the others are with our sister, Etush." Mala's sister, Etush, had died before the war. But Mala's warning eluded us. We thought that the work was hard, the conditions bad; that the old and the weak would probably not survive, but that young people like Mala would manage to hang on to life.

In 1943, when I was a member of the Belgian underground movement, I too was arrested and sent to the same camp where Mala had been. Shortly afterward we were herded into cattle cars and after a three-day journey under horrible conditions we arrived in Auschwitz. As soon as we got out of the cars the men were separated from the women and we had our first selection. The young and the healthy were marched away; the old, the weak, the women, and the children were ordered into trucks, presumably to "follow the others."

In camp we were forced to undress; our heads were shaved and our arms tattood with numbers. We discovered where we were and where the people on the trucks had been taken to. It was then that I understood the message on Mala's card. "All the others are with out sister, Etush."

But what about Mala herself? Was she still alive? And if so where could she be in this Gehenna?

I found her. Or, rather, she found me. Mala, at that time, was already a "runner" and interpreter. She was picked by the SS for this work because she spoke several languages. As a "runner," or *Lauferin,* as it was called in German, she could move about freely from one part of the camp to another, which was strictly forbidden to ordinary prisoners. She utilized this privilege to help establish contact between members of separated families, and frequently risked her life by carrying messages and medicine. She displayed similar courage in assisting the underground movement, which was then beginning to be organized.

As soon as Mala learned that a new transport had arrived from Belgium, she hurried to seek out acquaintances, to inquire about the situation in the outside world, to warn the already spiritually broken of the horrible reality they faced, and to console them. That was how we found each other.

One of Mala's functions was to assign the sick released from the hospital to various work details. She always tried to send the women still weak from their illness to the lightest type of work. And she always warned the patients of the coming selections, urging them to leave the hospital as quickly as possible. In this way she saved the lives of many women.

Mala spoke gently to the prisoners and urged other prisoner-functionaries, especially the kapos, who shouted at the prisoners, to behave humanly. "We're all in the same boat here," she would remind them. "We're all prisoners and the same fate is awaiting all of us."

Mala had infinite patience. Someone was always asking her for help, and she did everything she could, regardless of nationality or political affiliation. She was a human being in the fullest sense of the word.

And to be a human being in Auschwitz was no easy thing. Upon your arrival in camp the Germans informed you with a devilish little laugh that "From here one leaves only through the chimney." The human being was transformed into a number and nothing remained but the instinct to live, to live one more day, one more hour.

May, 1944. Day and night the transports kept coming from Hungary. Ninety-five percent of the new arrivals were sent directly from the cattle cars to the gas chambers. The crematoriums blazed away without a stop, their chimneys belching flames. The camp was enveloped in a thick black smoke. The stench of the burning bodies was suffocating. "Operation Hoess" (Hoess was the commandant of Auschwitz) had reached its peak. The crematoriums could no longer accommodate the accelerated tempo of the transports. The victims were standing around for hours, waiting their "turn" for the "bath." We were not allowed to get near them. We could not cry out to them that they were being deceived, that they were going to their death. And even if we could what good would it have done? They were surrounded by SS men, armed to the teeth.

Mala's barracks was located very close to the barbed wire fence where the nearby path led to the crematoriums. Through the walls she could hear the conversations of the waiting victims, the wailing of the children, the shouting of the SS and their barking dogs, the screams of the beaten and, frequently, the shooting. She could endure it no longer. She decided to escape and alarm the world—tell the world what was happening. We believed that if only the world knew . . .

Escape? But how? Some Poles had tried, those who came from the region, who had friends and relatives there. And they did not succeed. How would a Jew? And even if she succeeded in escaping, where would she go? Who would help her? But the thought gave her no rest.

One day Mala told me of the escape plan of a Pole named Edek Galinski. He had been in camp since 1940. He came with the first transport and had worked on the construction of the camp. His number was 531. He was familiar with every part of the giant complex Auschwitz-Birkenau. As a mechanic he came into contact with civilians who did various jobs in camp that the Germans did not entrust to prisoners for fear of sabotage. It was through them that he got in touch with people in the outside world. His work frequently took him to the women's camp and that was how he got to know Mala.

This was Edek's plan: He would get an SS uniform and, disguised as an SS officer, would lead a friend, a fellow prisoner, out of the camp, presumably for outside work. For this he needed a Passierschein (a special permit). Mala was in a position to steal such a permit from the guardhouse to which she had access. She agreed to do it and proposed to Edek that he take her along. Edek's friend was against it. He was afraid to escape with a woman, especially a Jewish woman. Edek then decided to escape with Mala. He too wanted to arouse the world.

They decided to leave on a Saturday. Saturday noon some of the SS men went off duty and the guard was somewhat lighter than usual. Mala was to wear a man's uniform. As a prisoner-functionary she was allowed to let her hair grow. That was an advantage on the outside. But disguised as a man she would have to tuck her hair well under her cap and carry a washbowl on her head to hide her face.

In addition to myself, Mala confided her plan to her closest friends, the three "runners" with whom she worked and who lived in the same barracks. They promised to help.

Everything was ready for the appointed date—June 24, 1944. On that day Mala put on an abdominal belt in which was hidden a stripeless dress. (On the backs of all prisoners' clothing a thick stripe or cross was painted in red, a telltale mark that made escape difficult.)

We said goodby to each other. Mala was calm. We all marveled at her and envied her courage.

The camp was ringed with two *Posten-Kette* (chains of guard posts). The first was an electrified wire fence that surrounded all parts of the camp, with a watchtower at every fifty meters manned by SS with machine guns. If Edek and Mala succeeded in getting past the guardhouse they would find themselves in the second *Posten-Kette*, which ringed all the camps of the Auschwitz-Birkenau complex, in the middle of armed SS and the dogs that guarded the prisoners working outside the camp.

As Mala approached the gate of Camp A her three friends, the "runners," were already standing at the *Blockfuhrerstube* (the guardhouse). They were always there ready to carry out the commands of the SS, but this time they were there as lookouts to warn Mala if anyone unexpected or one of the SS overseers wandering around camp should suddenly appear.

It was noontime. The SS guard, now off duty, emerged from the guardhouse and rode away on his motorcycle. Mala and one of the "runners" entered the guardhouse. Only one woman SS overseer was there. They knew her well. She liked to drink. Mala had a present for her, a bottle of vodka. The overseer thanked her and poured herself a drink. The "runner" engaged her in conversation while Mala left the room and went to the washroom where Edek had hidden the uniform and the washbowl.

From a distance I could see Mala leaving the guardhouse, bent under the weight of the washbowl on her head, her face almost completely hidden by it. Outside, Edek was waiting. He had concealed himself in a potato bunker (a kind of cellar) not far from the guardhouse and, at a sign from his friends, emerged from the bunker unnoticed.

Edek let Mala go first and followed a few paces behind her. This was the procedure for an SS man leading a prisoner and Edek was well acquainted with the rules. This was how he himself was frequently led to work outside the camp.

Now they were both heading in the direction of Camp Budy. They knew that on the way they would probably run into some sentries, but they took comfort in the fact that these were new arrivals from the front "for a furlough in Auschwitz," who were not yet familiar with the guard personnel of the camp, numbering around 3,000 SS men.

The plan was that if Edek and Mala passed Camp Budy without a mishap Mala would discard the heavy washbowl somewhere in a cornfield and take off her uniform. Edek would remain dressed in his and give the appearance of an SS man out for a good time with his girlfriend.

One day a rumor spread throughout the camp that Mala and Edek had been caught—that they were already in Auschwitz I, in Block 11, where prisoners were tortured to death during interrogations and shot by the hundreds at the Black Wall.

Mala and Edek in the Bunker? We could not believe it. We did not want to believe it. After two weeks? How was it possible? But the rumor turned out to be true. Mala managed to send us a message, smuggled out from her Bunker: "I know what is awaiting me. I am prepared for the worst. Be brave and remember everything."

Various fantastic versions of their capture were circulated in camp but nobody knew exactly how they were caught. In the men's camp a barber working for the SS said he had heard that Mala and Edek were caught in a restaurant for SS men. Edek was still in his uniform and he was recognized by an Auschwitz guard. The girls working in the Political Department had another version: The two were caught at the border as they were about to cross into Czechoslovakia.

Boger himself conducted the interrogation.[23] Known as "the devil of Auschwitz," he would extract all the information he wanted from his victims with his horrible tortures. In this case he wanted to know who had helped Mala and Edek to escape. Despite the tortures Mala and Edek maintained their silence throughout. Weeks passed and no one else was called to the Political Department; no one else was interrogated.

It was the evening of August 22, nearly two months since her attempted escape. Once again the orchestra played as the slaves returned from work. This time nobody was missing at the *Appell*. All were accounted for. Even Mala was there, standing at the gate. Why had they brought her to Birkenau? What was the verdict? There were no gallows in sight so we consoled ourselves with the thought that she would probably be flogged publicly and then sent to a punitive Kommando.

After the *Appell* a command was shouted: "All Jews must gather in camp B." When we got there I remained standing in the first row. We wanted Mala to see us and we wanted her to know that we wanted to see her. We wondered what would happen next.

Mala came walking proudly, head high. Behind her walked Riters, head of work details. He ordered her to stop a few paces away from us. Mala stared at us but I had the feeling that she did not see us. Her glance was vague and distant. The camp commander, Frau Mandel, appeared. She read something from a paper but I did not hear a word. I kept looking at Mala. She was smoothing down her hair. Suddenly Mala began to cut her wrist with a razor. We were petrified with horror. We bit our lips to keep from screaming and remained glued to the spot.

Riters probably noticed the expression on our faces and suspected that something was happening. He looked at Mala—then grabbed her arm. Mala slapped his face with her bloody hand. Riters pulled her arms behind her and shouted: "You want to be a heroine! You want to kill yourself! That's what we are here for. That's our job!"

"Murderers!" Mala cried out. "You will soon pay for our sufferings! Don't be afraid, girls! Their end is near. I am certain of this. I know. I was free!"

Riters struck Mala on the head with his revolver and pushed her in the direction of the hospital. The camp kapo blew her whistle and ordered the prisoners to disband and return to the barracks. Two nurses came running out of the hospital carrying a stretcher, but Frau Mandel shouted: "No! Take it back! This one belongs to the crematorium. This one must be burned alive!" She ordered that a handcart be brought.

Meanwhile Mala was dragged into hospital barracks Number 4. There they tied her arm tightly so that she would not bleed to death and beat her. The girls returned with the handcart and put Mala into it. She noticed the tears in their eyes. "Do not cry," she pleaded in a weak voice. "The day of reckoning is near. You hear me? Remember everything they did to us."

"Shut your mouth, you pig!" an SS man shouted.

"For two years I had to keep silent. Now I can say what I please," Mala said, with all the strength she could muster.

The SS man taped her mouth with adhesive. "Now she'll be quiet," he said to Frau Mandel. He accompanied the cart to the crematorium compound.

The city government of Antwerp put up a plaque on the house where Mala had lived. It reads:

> To Mala Zimetbaum
> Symbol of Solidarity
> Murdered by the Nazis
> In Auschwitz
> August 22, 1944

Underground Assignment in Auschwitz

By Yuri Suhl

[EDITOR'S NOTE: *In January, 1960, all of Poland marked the fifteenth anniversary of the liberation of Auschwitz with special ceremonies, first on the Auschwitz grounds and later in Cracow where Jozef Cyrankiewicz, Premier of Poland and himself a former Auschwitz prisoner, decorated a number of Polish citizens for their outstanding bravery during the German occupation of Poland. One of them was David Szmulewski.*

I was privileged to attend these ceremonies as an American writer and to speak with the Premier about his Auschwitz experience. Later I had a lengthy interview with David Szmulewski in his Warsaw home. "Underground Assignment in Auschwitz" is the result of that interview. In 1969 Mr. Szmulewski emigrated to France where he now lives.]

———◆———

DAVID SZMULEWSKI is a Polish Jew in his early fifties now residing in Warsaw. As a survivor of the Auschwitz inferno he is living with memories a thousand years could not erase. But the memory most deeply etched in his mind is of the time he carried out his most dangerous assignment for the Auschwitz underground of which he was a member— photographing operations inside the crematorium compound. The man who gave him this assignment was Jozef Cyrankiewicz, prisoner No. 62933, a top leader of the camp's underground. Today he is the Premier of Poland.

Why, one might ask, would people living daily in the shadow of the crematorium want to photograph it? Cyrankiewicz himself answered this question when, in the winter of 1960, I asked him what was his most difficult task as a leader of the underground. He thought a moment and said, "To convince the outside world that what we said was happening in Auschwitz was really true." The crimes committed by the Germans in Auschwitz were too staggering for the human mind to comprehend, and so it fell to the victims themselves to supply the visual proof of the process of their extermination.

Szmulewski could lay no claim to any special talents as a photographer.

Why, then, was he picked for the assignment and how did he carry it out?

One evening that same winter we sat with Szmulewski in the living room of his modern apartment facing Constitution Place, a lively square in the heart of Warsaw. Seated next to him was his attractive young wife who had spent the war years as a slave laborer in Germany. In another room slept their five-year-old son. Though it was very cold out the room was pleasantly warm, and we were sipping tea from glasses— Polish style. In this peaceful family setting it seemed a crime to ask this man to lift the memory-curtain on his Auschwitz nightmare. But Szmulewski himself was eager to talk. As an active member of the International Auschwitz Committee he has dedicated himself to sharing the truth about Auschwitz with as many people as would care to listen.

He arrived in Auschwitz in March, 1942, when the camp was still being built and expanded to accommodate the unending flow of new prisoners. One evening, soon after his arrival, an SS man came storming into his barracks looking for roofers. "I'm a roofer," Szmulewski volunteered, though he had never been one. "You better be good," the SS man warned him, as he scrutinized him from head to foot. Szmulewski's nerve did not desert him and he somehow bluffed himself into a roofer's classification.

The first and most important benefit of his new occupation was life itself. As a prisoner with special skills needed by the administration he was no longer among the immediately expendable. There were other advantages as well. He now had a *Passierschein* (permit) which enabled him to move about the camp unguarded, including Auschwitz II (Birkenau), where the gas chambers and crematoriums were located. He was thus a valuable link between the various underground groups scattered in the vast Auschwitz complex. His skill as a roofer and his mobility made him the ideal man for carrying out the photography assignment.

Obtaining a camera was the least of the problems. With the daily transports that Eichmann dispatched to Auschwitz from all parts of Europe came whatever valuables the victims were able to salvage and take with them. Some brought cameras too. As soon as the new arrivals stepped out of their freight cars their possessions were taken away and carted off to the *Effectenkammer* for sorting, storaging, and eventual shipping to Germany. There were thirty-five warehouses in Auschwitz bulging with these confiscated articles, all destined for the Third Reich. The underground had its people in every branch of camp activity, including the *Effectenkammer*. With a little skill and caution it was not too difficult to filch a small, concealable article like a camera. The *real* problem was how to get it into the crematorium compound.

This dread enclosure, whose smoke-belching chimneys were visible to thousands of prisoners in the Birkenau barracks, was under the separate administration of Oberscharführer Moll, a one-eyed sadist who boasted that his Nazi membership card numbered below 1,000. The several hundred Jewish prisoners compelled to operate the crematoriums, who were called the Sonderkommando, had to live on the premises, and every two or three months they were themselves marched off to the gas chambers and replaced by a new Sonderkommando. This was, after all, the scene of the Nazis' most heinous crime and so its witnesses had to be disposed of.

But the brotherly hand of the underground extended even into the ranks of the Sonderkommando. Though cut off from the rest of the prisoners and condemned by the Nazis to spend the last months of their agonized lives burning the bodies of fellow Jews, the underground kept alive within them the spirit of revenge and revolt. When the underground high command decided on the photography assignment, strategy for carrying it out was planned together with members of the Sonderkommando underground. It was decided that one of them should damage the roof of a crematorium chamber. This would provide the necessary pretext for bringing a roofer into the compound. Szmulewski would be that roofer. But it was clear that the camera had to precede him. The rigid inspection the guards would subject him to at the entrance could lead to the discovery of the camera, doom the plan, and cost Szmulewski his life.

The scheme for smuggling in the camera was an elaborate one. The crematorium compound was not equipped with kitchen facilities. The Sonderkommandos were fed from the central camp kitchen. To prevent their contact with other prisoners even during mealtime the black ersatz coffee and the thin, tasteless liquid that passed for soup were brought into the compound in huge kettles. It was decided that the camera should be transported in one of these kettles.

The underground tinsmiths immediately set to work making a false bottom for one of the kettles. When it was completed it was kept for twenty-five hours filled with water to see if the bottom was leakproof. The test was successful. The camera was then slipped into the false bottom and the kettle taken to the kitchen (the underground had its people in the kitchen too). The next time the Sonderkommando detail came to the kitchen for its rations there was a quick exchange of kettles. The one containing the camera was filled with the liquid and taken into the compound.

It was now Szmulewski's turn to enter the compound. Having been officially requested to do the roof repairs he showed the guards his tools and tar and was passed without difficulty. Once inside the compound he had to report to Oberscharführer Moll.

"*Du verfluchte Judensau,*" Moll growled at him. "Do you know where you are?"

"*Jawohl,* Herr Kommandant."

"I want you to stay at your job like a dog chained to his post. If you move away from there for one minute you will not come out of here alive. You hear me, you *Schweinhund*?"

"*Jawohl,* Herr Kommandant."

Moll left the compound several times a day to meet the new transports that arrived at the special railway siding in Birkenau. Szmulewski was waiting for that moment. As soon as Moll had gone one of the Sonderkommando men slipped him the camera. He enlarged the middle button of his prisoner's jacket wide enough to push through the lens while keeping the rest of the camera concealed beneath the jacket. Then he climbed to the top of the roof and set to work.

He was able to snap three shots unobserved. One was of a group of naked women on the way to the gas chamber. The other two were of gassed bodies being burned in the open pits within the enclosure.[24] The four crematoriums working around the clock could not accommodate the ever-growing number of bodies to be burned during the stepped-up executions. And so the Nazis hit upon the scheme of supplementing the crematoriums with open pits, reaching a combined high of more than 20,000 bodies daily.

As soon as he had finished taking the pictures Szmulewski removed the film from the camera, wrapped it in a piece of rag and stuck it into the tar he had brought for the roof repair. The camera, already an unnecessary hazard, was quickly buried in the compound grounds. The roof repaired, Szmulewski left the compound with the film safely hidden in the remaining tar. He then passed on the film to Cyrankiewicz, who in turn passed it on by secret courier to the Cracow underground for developing.

The underground has thus provided the outside world with the first photographs of Nazi atrocities inside Auschwitz, giving visual support to the word-picture painted by Cyrankiewicz in his secret report to the P.P.S. (Polish Socialist Party) in which he wrote:

A terrible massacre of Hungarian Jews has started now which has no parallel in history, not even in the history of previous Hitlerist atrocities. It is vast in scope and bestial in execution. The Hitlerists behave like wild beasts, if it is not an insult to wild beasts to compare them with these murderers. They have lost all sense of responsibility. They are mad with blood lust. They are working quickly, without respite, to complete their horrible task before any report of it can reach Hungary and the outside world.

Transports of Hungarian Jews have been arriving here in quick succession since the middle of May, 1944, eight transports a night and five a day, night after night and day after day, each train of forty-eight to fifty cars, with a hundred people in each car. These transports bring "colonists" for settlement on special allocated areas of land, or to be "exchanged" for German war prisoners through the Red Cross. An old German game, to fool people by using the cover of the recognized international institutions for their most inhuman activities.

Each train of "colonists" has attached two cars of wood, which they must unload themselves, carry to the appointed places, for fuel for their own burning. . . .

Both gas chambers are working without interruption, yet they cannot catch up. Only enough time is allowed between the gassing of one group and the admission of another, to air the room. On the other side of the room, where those who enter cannot see them, lie piles of dead bodies, which the ovens are not able to burn quickly enough. . . . The four crematoriums smoke incessantly and so do the pyres under the open sky.

On the afternoon of October 7, 1944, an explosion rocked the crematorium compound. The Sonderkommando staged their long-planned revolt. It was to include the destruction of all the crematorium installations, but something had gone wrong and only crematorium III was blown up and its chimney enveloped in flames. (See the Rosa Robota chapter for a detailed description of the revolt.)

By the end of 1944, with the Red Army steadily advancing in the direction of Auschwitz, the Nazis themselves ordered the dismantling of the remaining crematoriums to remove the evidence of the mass murders. They did not wholly succeed. When the Red Army liberated Auschwitz on January 25, 1945, the remains of a partly demolished crematorium were still there. They are now part of the Auschwitz Museum.

In January, 1960, when all of Poland observed the fifteenth anniversary of the liberation of Auschwitz, David Szmulewski was awarded the Virtuti Militari, Poland's highest military decoration. The medal was pinned on him by Premier Jozef Cyrankiewicz, Szmulewski's former comrade in the Auschwitz underground.

In his *Wiederstand in Auschwitz* (VVN-Verlag, Berlin-Potsdam, 1949, p. 32), Bruno Baum makes the following significant observation about the underground's activities: "Our most important task was to inform [the outside world], by letters or reports, what was happening in Auschwitz. The enormous gassings, as well as this form of killing, generally, were not believed even by those who, for many years, had fought in illegal movements against Hitler and were familiar with the endless cruelties of the Nazis."

* * *

Editor's Postscript

Rudolph Vrba in his excellent Auschwitz memoir, *I Cannot Forgive* (New York: Grove Press, 1964), tells of his first contact "with an element in camp I never knew existed: a powerful underground movement, without whose help I could never have escaped" (p. 154). Vrba had contracted spotted typhus and was already a candidate for the crematorium when Josef Farber, a member of the underground who had fought in the International Brigade in Spain, gave him the life-saving injection. And when he was about to be transferred to Birkenau, Farber gave him the names of two members of the underground in that part of Auschwitz. One of them was David Szmulewski.

Vrba writes: "Szmulewski I knew, too, by reputation. He was a man who had fought for his ideals all over Europe and was still fighting. In Poland he had known persecution because he was a Jew. He had resisted until he managed to escape and make his way to Palestine, an illegal immigrant. There he was harried by the British and harried back until another call came, this time from Spain. He linked up with the International Brigade against Franco, and, when that war was lost, he crossed into France where he was interned. There the Germans found him and his road to Auschwitz began, a road that was to take him through Dachau and Sachsenhausen.

"Yet still he was only thirty, tall, dark haired, strong and remarkably unscarred for a man who had been at war all his life" (p. 172).

It was through the underground that Vrba obtained the strategic post of Registrar. ". . . I reported everything I knew to Szmulewski, who, I had learned by this stage, was the leader of the Birkenau underground" (p. 181).

Prior to his contact with the underground and the post of Registrar it secured for him, Vrba had worked on many slave-labor details, including the ramp. What he has to say about that experience sheds additional light on the question of resistance:

"The ramp . . . to which transports rolled from all parts of Europe,

bringing Jews who still believed in labor camps. . . . There I worked
for eight months. There I saw three hundred transports arrive and
helped to unload their bewildered cargoes. There I saw in action the
greatest confidence trick the world has ever known. . . . The system
behind the Great Swindle was very simple and very effective. As soon
as a transport arrived, it was surrounded by S.S. men with sub-
machine guns, rifles or heavy bamboo canes. As the dazed victims
tumbled out, they were forbidden to speak and about twenty to
thirty S.S. men were detailed to ensure that this rule was observed.
They ran up and down the ragged, shuffling lines, bellowing: 'Silence, everybody!' . . . Invariably the order was obeyed, for these
were people who were thoroughly confused and already a little de-
moralized by the fetid squalor of their journey. They wanted no
trouble, particularly because they had their families with them and
partly because they saw how quickly any of the few rebels were
clubbed down by the S.S.

"So simple, as I say, and so effective. Without speech, without a
whisper to fan spirit into flame, there can be no rebellion. Those
who had doubts kept them to themselves and felt a little easier in
their hearts when they saw an ambulance with a big Red Cross go by,
though they would not have been quite so comforted had they
known that it was filled with the chemicals which were to kill them
in the gas chambers half an hour later" (pp. 147–8).

*   *   *

And what has become of Herr Walter Dejaco, the man who built the
Auschwitz crematorium? Mr. Vrba tells us:

"Auschwitz survivors who, like myself, were the slave laborers who
worked to build it may be interested to learn, incidentally, that
Herr Dejaco still practices his craft in Reutte, a town in the Austrian Tyrol. In 1963 he won warm praise from Bishop Rusk of
Innsbruck for the fine new Presbytery he had built for Reutte's
parish priest" (p. 16).

Five Escapes from Auschwitz

By Erich Kulka

[EDITOR'S NOTE: *Erich Kulka, holocaust historian, writer, research worker, and, by early training, a lumber expert, was born in Vsetin, Czechoslovakia, on February 18, 1911. In June, 1939, he was arrested by the Gestapo for anti-Fascist activities and kept in various prisons. In 1940 he was deported to Dachau, in 1941 to Neuen-Gamme, and in October, 1942, to Auschwitz-Birkenau, where he was a member of the underground.*

In January, 1945, during the evacuation of the camp he escaped with his twelve-year-old son, and with the aid of civilian workers made his way to Prague where he now resides. He has written extensively on the holocaust and is the author of The Dead Accuse, The Death Factory *(together with Ota Kraus), and* Night and Fog *(together with Ota Kraus).*

In "Five Escapes from Auschwitz," written especially for this anthology, Mr. Kulka combines a first-hand knowledge of the subject with scrupulous research done both in his native Czechoslovakia and in Yad Washem, the documentation center in Jerusalem. In 1968 Mr. Kulka emigrated to Israel, where he is now working at the Institute of Contemporary Jewry at the Hebrew University in Jerusalem. His most recent work, The Participation of the Czechoslovak Jews in the CSR Fighting Units *("Svoboda Army"), is to be published in both Hebrew and Czech.*]

IN THE YEAR 1943 reports of Nazi extermination camps in occupied countries in the East began to increase in the international press and radio. Goebbels was looking for a cogent refutation to weaken and disprove the unwelcome wave of hostile atrocity reports, particularly because the "final solution" of the Jewish question was very far from finished.

According to entries at that time in Goebbels's diary, the most troublesome phase of the "Final Solution" would confront the Nazis in Hungary. In this situation it was necessary to do something that would quiet the intended victims in the satellite states and at the same time prevent international intervention.

The R.S.H.A. (Reichssicherheitshauptamt, or Reich Central Security Office), Division for the Solution of the Jewish Question VI B, developed

196

the plan of utilizing the good reputation of the "privileged ghetto" of Theresienstadt, and it was decided to transfer part of it into the center of the extermination camp of Auschwitz. On September 6, 1943, in Theresienstadt, two "Eastern transports" were made ready, designated in the deportation lists with the code letters DL and DM: total number 5,007 men, women, and children. The following day the cargo arrived at the railroad station of Auschwitz.

The old Auschwitz prisoners stared in amazement. SS men, who usually robbed and tortured new prisoners, had become transformed into gentlemen. They were polite, helped children carry things, supported old people, and saw to it that luggage remained intact. For the first time in the history of the camp, there was no selection of victims for the gas chambers on the ramp and all the deportees were taken to thirty horse stables of the new camp of Auschwitz II, Birkenau B-II-b, a previously uninhabited part. This was the only one of the thirty-nine Auschwitz camps in which families could live together, and the Nazis even left them some of the privileges they had enjoyed in the Theresienstadt Ghetto. They were strictly isolated from the rest of the Auschwitz inmates and were not permitted to meet the other prisoners. They had their own administration, with the single exception that applied to all the other camps: the function of camp elder (chief of the camp prisoners) was entrusted to the German professional criminal Arno Boehm. To the old Auschwitz inmates the setting up of this privileged camp was an inexplicable mystery.

The Theresienstadt prisoners considered the family camp a continuation of their ghetto. They had various advantages which strengthened them in the belief that they occupied a special position in contrast to the other Auschwitz prisoners. This is seen from a previously unpublished document that makes known the setting up of the camp. It is a letter on the "Unification of the Jews of Germany" sent by Dr. Leo Janowitz, a member of the Theresienstadt "Council of Elders," to Dr. Riegner, representative of the World Jewish Congress in Geneva. From this document, dating from Dr. Janowitz's early days at the camp, we learn that under his leadership a new Jewish settlement, called "Work-Camp Birkenau," is to be set up. Janowitz hopes that he will be able to use the experience he has acquired in the building of Theresienstadt and requests that the International Red Cross continue to send food and medicines to Birkenau. There is mention of the sending of these food parcels to Birkenau in the correspondence of the Slovakian Red Cross with the German Red Cross.

One of the privileges referred to, but which was also an obligation, was that the prisoners in the family camp write to their relatives and friends in Theresienstadt and also to their former homes. Although the Theresienstadt family camp was less than two miles from the main camp at

Auschwitz and a scarce few hundred yards from the gas chambers of the crematorium, the recipients of the censored post cards learned that those deported to the east were alive and building a new, hitherto unknown "Work-Camp Birkenau near New Berun."

On the 16th and on the 20th of December, 1944, another 4,964 men, women, and children arrived from Theresienstadt and were likewise put up without previous selection in the Theresienstadt family camp. The number of prisoners grew to 10,000 and the capacity of the camp was reached. These latter prisoners also wrote post cards. A quantity of food parcels from Bohemia and Moravia and from the International Red Cross arrived at Birkenau. At the end of February a commission from Berlin visited the family camp at Birkenau. Among its members was the chief of Division IV B in the R.S.H.A., Adolf Eichmann, and the head of the foreign division of the German Red Cross, Niehaus. The commission showed great interest in the life of the people in the family camp. It stayed longest in the "school," which was set up in a wooden horse stable in block 31. The school was headed by Fredy Hirsch, one of the intellectual leaders of the camp. Eichmann praised the unique development of a center of spiritual life in this milieu.

On March 5, the commandant of Birkenau, SS First Lieutenant Hans Schwarzhuber, came to the camp and ordered the Jewish leadership to prepare the prisoners who had arrived in September for transfer to the new camp, Heydebreck. A small group from Theresienstadt was informed by prisoners in the underground movement of the neighboring camp that the transfer to Heydebreck meant extermination in the gas chambers. However, the attempt at organizing resistance was undermined by a whole series of carefully planned deceptive measures. Not until they were in the basement disrobing room did the Theresienstadt prisoners realize that they had been deceived. They resisted, attacking the guards with their bare hands, but the SS men were prepared. Rifle butts and flame throwers completed the work of annihilation. With heads smashed and bleeding from their wounds they crossed the threshold of the gas chamber.

According to the statement of a surviving member of the so-called "special detachment," Filip Müller, they died in the gas chambers singing the national anthem, "Kde domov muj" ("Where Is My Home"), and the Hebrew song "Hatikvah." Fredy Hirsch, who at the last moment refused to resist, anticipating an inhuman massacre of the children, poisoned himself before entering the crematorium. On March 3, four days before their "resettlement" to Heydebreck, the condemned had to write post cards postdated March 25, 1944 (that is, after their "special treatment"), explaining that the cards had been mailed late because of censorship.

The vacated space in the family camp was filled after two months by a new shipment from the Theresienstadt Ghetto and it became clear that what was taking place was a large-scale hoax based on periodic deportations from Theresienstadt and liquidation in Auschwitz. Every group of deportees, during the time it lived in the privileged family camp, had to perform the task for which this new camp had been built: To disprove the reports of extermination in Auschwitz and to make smooth the process of deportation from the ghettos.

The background of this operation, the purpose of which the prisoners only suspected at that time and which was not even clarified at the Eichmann trial, is revealed by hitherto unpublished documents from the correspondence of the foreign department of the German Red Cross, whose microfilms are in the Yad Washem archive. Most important are all the letters between the German Red Cross and Eichmann's division in the R.S.H.A. and between the German Red Cross and the International Red Cross in Geneva dealing with the answers to questions on the fate of the deportees. Most vital for us are those communications that tell of a visit to Theresienstadt and a "Jewish work-camp" and those letters in which this Jewish work camp is identified with the "Work-Camp Birkenau."

One of the key documents that makes it possible for the first time to clear up the circumstances under which the September arrivals were liquidated is Niehaus's letter of April 14, 1944, to the R.S.H.A., the week after the mass execution of the prisoners from Theresienstadt. In this communication the chief of the foreign division of the German Red Cross makes reference to a conversation with the commandant of the Prag "Central Emigration Office," Hans Günther, of March 6, 1944, and a conversation a few days earlier with Eichmann concerning the visit to Theresienstadt and Birkenau. Niehaus points out the importance of having food parcels and especially medicines sent to the prisoners by the International Red Cross and that representatives of the Geneva International Red Cross have the opportunity of observing the truth of this by a personal visit. In conclusion Niehaus emphasizes the urgency of the purpose of visiting these camps: "Considering the increasing questions from abroad concerning the various Jewish camps, the expediency of these planned visits is quite clear."

It is obvious that the purpose of the extermination of the prisoners ordered by Eichmann several days after the conversation referred to, was to make room for more deportees from Theresienstadt. The ghetto was overfilled at that time and the overcrowded barracks prevented the success of the "cover-up job," whose purpose it was to prepare the privileged settlement for the visit of the International Red Cross. The "resettlement" of the people from Theresienstadt was to permit a simultaneous check by the commission of those prisoners being sent to the east together with the notorious "East Transports."

After further correspondence the visit was permitted in a letter from Himmler to Niehaus dated May 11, 1944: "The Reichsführer SS has agreed to an inspection of the ghetto of Theresienstadt and a Jewish work-camp by you and a representative of the International Committee of the Red Cross. . . . The time of this inspection is to be the beginning of June, 1944. . . ." The words a *Jewish work-camp* and *a representative of the International Committee* are underlined and a handwritten note in the margin adds that permission to visit this camp had been communicated by telephone to Dr. Martin of the Swiss delegation at 6 P.M. on May 19, 1944. The visit to Theresienstadt took place on June 23, 1944.

Niehaus wrote to Hertmann, the representative of the German Red Cross in Switzerland, about the result in a communication of June 27, 1944: "The inspection in Theresienstadt went off satisfactorily in all respects. I am convinced that the foreign representatives will make a favorable report on it. . . ." The reports of the favorable course of the visit are well known and, as was to be expected from such a successful operation, it was the opinion of the German representatives that the requirements of the International Commission had been fully met and that therefore the existence of the Jewish "work-camp Birkenau" no longer had a purpose. Several days later its liquidation was carried out, this time, however, by the well-tried Auschwitz practice—by selection.

A group of Jewish prisoners who had been in the underground movement and who had tried and failed to convince the people from Theresienstadt in Camp B-II-b of their danger and of the need for resistance drew the logical conclusion from the fate of the September transport. It was obvious that the Nazis were preparing an uninterrupted continuation of their policy of extermination, the center of which was to be Auschwitz after the loss of the lands to the east. This conclusion was reinforced also by the increasing length of the trains and the construction by around-the-clock labor of a branching three-track concrete ramp in the immediate vicinity of the crematorium.

This being the case, the prisoners felt that the only effective possibility of halting this last phase of the annihilation of European Jewry was to unmask the fraudulent nature of the deportations to Birkenau in a way that would convince and stir up world opinion to take decisive counteraction. It is true that reports sent from the main camp of Auschwitz to the Polish resistance movement did arrive abroad, but it seems that they were not sufficiently convincing and brought no help. The prisoners who thought through the situation thoroughly were convinced that only the

personal testimony of a well-informed eyewitness who had fled from
Auschwitz could break through the wall of indifference and doubt.
The organization of a flight from Auschwitz was extraordinarily difficult. The camps of the industrial and extermination combine were surrounded by tall fences of high-tension barbed wire, supplemented by a
system of deep ditches and a chain of watchtowers and packs of trained
dogs. The so-called "company territory" extended all around to a radius
of forty kilometers. From here the civilian population had been removed.
The space in which the camps were located, the Nazi industrial installations, and the buildings in which the prisoners lived and worked, were
declared a "prohibited area." After every reported attempt at flight the
watchtowers of the "big chain of posts" were manned continuously for
three days and nights.

Nevertheless, during the existence of Auschwitz, 230 attempts at escape
were noted and about eighty prisoners succeeded in accomplishing this
daring feat. Five of them, who fled immediately after the first liquidation
of the family camp, had a higher goal than the saving of their own lives.
They consisted of three completely independent actions, which can be
considered the culmination of the efforts of the resistance movement to
inform the world of what was happening.

The first was an escape from the Theresienstadt family camp, which
had been kept most strictly isolated under circumstances that had no
equal in Auschwitz. On April 5, 1944, the prisoner Siegfried Lederer fled
in an SS uniform together with one of the guards of the family camp,
SS corporal Viktor Pestek. Pestek, who was originally a Rumanian German, had fallen in love with a beautiful Jewish girl, Renée Neumann,
who was from the Theresienstadt camp. He wanted to save her from
extermination, which was to take place in June. But Renée refused to
leave her mother. Therefore Pestek sought a secure hiding place for himself and the two women where they could await the end of the war.
Lederer saw an opportunity to carry out his plan and offered Pestek the
help of his friends in Bohemia.

Lederer gives the following account of his courageous accomplishment:

> On the agreed-upon day a red light blinked three times in the
> window of the SS guard-house in front of the gate of the family
> camp. At that moment I opened the door of the washroom and
> stepped out in the uniform of an SS staff sergeant, complete with
> the silver cord of the "Special Service." I mounted the bicycle that
> was waiting for me and with a "Heil Hitler" and my right arm
> raised rode through the gate of the family camp. The gate was
> opened for me by my fellow SS corporal Viktor Pestek, who was on

duty at the time. He informed the man taking his place on night guard duty that he was going on leave. Together with Pestek I walked past a cordon of guards and the password "Inkwell" opened all barriers to us. Pestek and I reached the nearby railroad station of Auschwitz at eight thirty P.M., just in time to jump into an already moving express train. We had reason to fear the strict check of personal papers at the border station of Bohumín, since the soldier's pay book that had been furnished me by Pestek would not be sufficient. We made our way up front to the mail car. Pestek threw open the door and shouted, "Heil Hitler! Baggage check!" Two surprised railroad men merely looked on as we confiscated suspicious packages, and not even the customs officers, who looked into the car, saw anything suspicious in our official zeal. Early in the morning, as we were riding in the Prague express, the sirens in Birkenau were whining and the SS was setting trained dogs to pick up my trail. The order for my arrest was telegraphed by the office of the Auschwitz Gestapo to Berlin, Oranienburg, and the commandants of the police stations at the border crossing points. We succeeded in getting to Pilsen and there found our first hiding place and got help from my friends of the Weidmann group of the resistance movement.

My first job after my successful flight was to warn the people in Theresienstadt. With the aid of a friend, Vaclav Veselák of Travčic, who was a barber to the military police in the barracks of Theresienstadt. I got by a secret way into the ghetto from which I had been deported to Auschwitz. I told of the extermination of the September deportees and explained the whole system of murder at Auschwitz to a small circle of my friends, among them the chief of the fire brigade Leo Holzer, Jirka Petschauer of the ghetto guard, and Otto Schliesser, member of the Council of Elders. My friends believed me but the majority in Theresienstadt were skeptical of my reports. The postal cards of those who had perished in the gas chambers, which had arrived in Theresienstadt after their death, was convincing proof to them.

Twice more I went into the ghetto. I brought my friends letters, arms, and radio parts. On my last visit I brought out information on the Theresienstadt ghetto and on the secret archives of the Nazis, which had been transferred to the Theresienstadt barracks after a bombardment of Berlin. Using the papers of a machine engineer, I got to the southwest German-Swiss border at the city of Constance. With the help of a boatman I smuggled the information about Theresienstadt and Auschwitz to the International Red Cross in Geneva.

However, the time for the extermination of the December group of the Theresienstadt family camp was approaching and Renée Neumann was in the greatest danger. Pestek pressed for the execution of the second part of the plan. In June we boarded an express train in Prague dressed in the uniforms of SS-men. The plan was simple: a masterfully forged document with the letterhead of the Berlin R.S.H.A. and with the seal of the Prague Gestapo empowered Second Lieutenant Hauser, Pestek, and First Lieutenant Welker—me— to remove two women from the family camp of Birkenau for interrogation purposes.

As our train approached Auschwitz, Pestek decided to continue on to Myslovic, which was not far away, where he wanted to pick up the valuables he had accumulated from deportees and which he had given for safe keeping to a former Polish girl friend. I got out at Auschwitz to see whether I could arrange for a car for taking the two women prisoners to nearby Katowitz from the Auschwitz military car pool. The next day I waited for my companion at the Auschwitz station about noon, the agreed-upon hour. Shortly before the arrival of the train, an SS flying squad on motorcycles surrounded the station buildings. They cleared the station platform and when the train from Myslovic pulled in, surrounded it from all sides. Pestek was leaning out of the window of the car. The commander of the flying squad recognized Pestek, jumped onto the stairs of the car and the shooting began. Pestek resisted. A hand grenade exploded among the SS-men on the platform. I took advantage of the general confusion, jumped out of the window of the waiting room, grabbed the nearest motorcycle from a line of them and rode in the direction of Bohumín. In two hours I was sitting in the Ostrava-Prague express. I found a secure hiding place among my friends in the Theresienstadt ghetto. I stayed with them and helped a small group prepare for resistance against the expected extermination of the ghetto.

The reports which had in the meantime reached the International Red Cross had their effect. As a result of the constant request of international humane organizations and as a result of the pressure of reports of the extermination of the Jews, the Nazis agreed to an inspection of the ghetto. Theresienstadt prepared for the important visit from abroad. The fraud not only fooled the members of the international commission but confused the majority of the Theresienstadt prisoners. To my forcible warning under no conditions to believe the Nazis, even well-informed officials of the ghetto answered, "Now, when the Nazis have lost the war and will need us for an alibi? To revolt, when the International Red Cross is concerning itself with us? Any attempt at revolt is suicide!" Even my most steadfast friends in Holzer's fire brigade refused. Rumors circulated that a partisan had appeared in the ghetto who was bringing in weapons. I was threatened with betrayal. I left the ghetto and joined the partisans in Slovakia. When the Slovakian national revolt collapsed, I returned to the partisans in Zbraslav and up until the liberation of Prague took part in acts of sabotage against the SS."

This testimony of Lederer's has been confirmed in all details by the record of his activity in Partisan Detachment 28 "Plzeňák" in Zbraslav from the time of his arrest in 1940 to May, 1945, as well as the supplementary testimony of living witnesses, such as Leo Holzer of Prague, the former chief of the prison fire brigade, of the former members of the Weidmann sabotage group who are still alive today in Pilsen, among whom Lederer hid during the war, and especially of his former fellow prisoner of Theresienstadt and Auschwitz, Mirek Zeimer of Prague. These depositions prove that he received a government citation after the liberation.

There is no doubt that Lederer's courageous return even before the beginning of the large-scale deportations in September and October, 1944, had the result that preparations were carried out in the ghetto for resistance in case of an attempt at extermination or of a mass deportation. These actions of the prisoners were thwarted, particularly by a series of tricky acts by the Germans, such as the fraud of the visit of the International Red Cross, films, and the enticing of capable forces to the so-called "work transports" into Germany, who ended up in Auschwitz.

According to testimony of the last president of the Council of Elders, Murmelstein, at the trial of the chief of the Theresienstadt Ghetto, Karl Rahm, the arrest and execution of his predecessor, Dr. Paul Epstein, in September, 1944, was connected with the suppression of the resistance in preparation. According to Rahm's own statement, his task at that time was to make sure that there would be no following of the example of the Warsaw Ghetto uprising. According to information from Lederer on the fate of those deported to Auschwitz, preparations for revolt had already been started in Theresienstadt.

Until now it has been impossible to obtain definite reports on the second part of Lederer's mission: the delivery of his message to the International Red Cross in Switzerland. But there can be no doubt about the success of his attempt, considering the proof of his trip to Constance in May, 1944.

What Lederer apparently did not succeed in accomplishing, or at any rate of which we have no real proof, was achieved with complete success by two other Jewish prisoners from Auschwitz who fled to Slovakia. In contrast to Lederer's flight to Bohemia, from which the whole Jewish population had already been deported, there was organized in Slovakia at this time a Jewish community that maintained contact with the free world. Thanks to these conditions, their reports were quickly and reliably transmitted to the outside world. We are much better informed of the repercussions of these activities.

Two days after the escape of Lederer, the sirens in Birkenau announced the flight of two more Jewish prisoners. After an unsuccessful pursuit through the prohibited area and company territory of Auschwitz, the local division of the Gestapo sent out the following telegram, No. 2334/2344:

> To R.S.H.A., Berlin, WC2, to the SS Administrative Office D, Oranienburg, to all commanders Eastern Gestapo criminal investigation police and border commands in reference to: Jews in preventive arrest 1. Rosenberg, Walter Israel, born Sept. 11, 1924, at Topolčany, arrived June 30, 1942, from R.S.H.A. 2. Wetzler, Alfred Israel, born May 10, 1918, at Trnava, arrived April 13, 1942, from R.S.H.A.: Rosenberg and Wetzler escaped April 7, 1944, from concentration camp AU II, sections II A and II D. Immediate search unsuccessful. Request from you further search and in case of capture full report to concentration camp Auschwitz. Additional to R.S.H.A.: request from you transcripts on Rosenberg and Wetzler from official search ledger. Additional to SS headquarters: information forwarded to the Reichsführer. Further report follows. Fault of any guard so far not determined. Concentration camp AU, Division II/44070/4/8/44 D4 (signed) Hartenstein, SS major.

Walter Rosenberg was a clerk in the prisoner block of the quarantine camp, room 7 of the Section B-II-a. Alfred Wetzler had the same job in the main camp of Birkenau in section B-II-d. This relatively special position permitted them a comparatively greater freedom of movement into all parts of the camp and allowed them to collect exact information on the course of deportations, selection, and the extermination of prisoners in Auschwitz. With the help of prisoners from the construction battalion they constructed a bunker in section B-III—an excavated pit well hidden by boards and pieces of wood from the barracks. They protected themselves against police dogs by scattering gasoline-soaked tobacco around the bunker. They waited for three days and nights in their hiding place until on the evening of April 10 they heard the anxiously-awaited command, "Vacate guard posts!" Only then did they leave their hiding place, which was hardly 500 meters distant from the block commander's office, and crawled behind the circle of empty watchtowers of the outside chain. After a ten-day-long flight that was full of dramatic experiences, Wetzler and Rosenberg crossed the German-Slovakian border. They rested for three days and nursed their injured feet in the house of a farmer named Cánský in the Slovak community of Skalite. Then they went to the town of Cadca and from there to the provincial city of Žilina. The fugitives had no inkling and are perhaps to this day ignorant of the fact that the help they got was probably the first organized aid of Jewish organizations in Slovakia. According to testimony of a member of the illegal activity group of the committee for aid, Dr. Karmil-Krasňanský, of Bratislava, this organization was able by means of money from abroad to get the peasants to furnish help to Jewish fugitives. First contact with the fugitives was made by a member of the executive committee of the Jewish community in Žilina, Ernst Steiner, who immediately telephoned the Jewish central committee in Bratislava of their arrival.

Dr. Karmil-Krasňanský immediately went to Žilina and states he spoke with the fugitives for three days. After their return to Bratislava he wrote up the information they furnished in a twenty-six-page-long statement on the extermination camp of Auschwitz-Birkenau, to which he added the following introduction:

Two young Slovakian Jews—whose names must for the time being be kept secret for reasons of security—who were deported in 1942 and spent two full years in the concentration camps of Auschwitz-Birkenau and Lublin-Maidanek, miraculously succeeded in escaping. One of them was taken directly from the assembly camp of Sered on April 13, 1942, to Auschwitz and from there to Birkenau. The other was taken from the camp at Nowaky on June 14, 1942, to Lublin, then after a short stay to Auschwitz and finally to Birkenau.

The following report does not contain everything that they experienced during their period of imprisonment. Only that has been written down which one or both experienced, saw, witnessed, or had knowledge of directly. No individual impressions are given, and nothing that they knew only on the basis of information supplied by third persons. The report tells first of the experiences of the young Jew who was transported from Sered, beginning with the time when the second was also brought to Birkenau, and based on the statements of both. Then follows the report of the second Jew, who was taken from Nowaky to Lublin and from there transferred to Auschwitz.

The statements coincide with the reports, undoubtedly only fragmentary yet reliable, that had been received up until then, and the information supplied on the individual transports agrees exactly with the official listings. Hence the statements are to be considered as completly authentic.

From information supplied by Rosenberg and Wetzler, Dr. Karmil-Krasňanský, an engineer, had an architect prepare professional sketches of the building plans of both main camps at Auschwitz with clear indications of the areas to be destroyed and the railroad network. To this he added a supplement in which he urged the governments of the allied powers to destroy the Auschwitz crematoriums and approaching roads. Dr. Karmil-Krasňanský tells what was done with the report.

Of course, our working group considered how the report was to be utilized. We decided to forward the report to the following places: to the liaison committee in Istanbul, to Mr. Nathan Schwalb in Geneva; a copy was given to the Papal nuncio (Borzic) in Bratislava to be forwarded to the Vatican. In addition, a copy of the report was sent to Dr. Kastner, to give to the Reich Administrator Horthy and to Prince Primasz Seredy. At the request of Dr. Kastner, I myself translated the report into Hungarian, so that it could be read by the Hungarians who did not understand German. Rabbi Weissmandel had a copy prepared in Yiddish and sent it to his contacts, the Orthodox community in Switzerland; likewise to Istanbul and London. In the working group participants in the discussion were Mrs. Gisi Fleischmann, Leo Rosenthal, Dr. Tibor Kovacz, Dr. Oscar Neumann, Rabbi Frieder, Rabbi Weissmandel, the architect Steiner, the director Fuerst, and perhaps still others.

Nathan Schwalb, to whom the report had been sent to Switzerland, was a delegate from the Jewish Agency or the Histadrut ha Ovdim. Our connection with him was by secret messengers, who transferred our information very reliably.

After the escapes of April, 1944, conditions in Birkenau became much worse. The SS men vented their rage on the Jewish prisoners, tricked and punished them for every insignificant infraction. Schwarzhuber deprived them of all responsible jobs and sent them out on the worst work details. This directive applied also to the leader of the Jewish block, Arnošt Rosin in Camp BB-II-d, where Alfred Wetzler had been clerk. Rosin was called in for questioning and tortured. He was accused of complicity in Wetzler's escape and as punishment was given hard labor in the gravel pit. There he made the acquaintance of another Jewish prisoner, Mordowicz, who had been punished by transfer from clerk to the same detail. During their work the prisoners discovered in the wall of the gravel pit a short, narrow passageway—a bunker—that had been filled in with broken stones after the escape of other prisoners. From time to time during their work, when they were not being watched, they took turns in getting the bunker ready and waited for a suitable opportunity.

In Auschwitz in the meantime there was no indication that the April escape was as successful as had been hoped. The deportations continued in increased measure. Beginning May 15, with the punctuality of a diabolical timetable, a large number of transports from Hungary and Hungarian-occupied areas of Slovakia and Carpathorussia began to arrive at the new, enlarged death station at Birkenau. By day and night lines of unsuspecting victims filed past the SS doctors, who with a wave of the hand sent them to the "baths and disinfection room." Tall flames leaped out of the chimneys of the crematorium, and because the ovens could not meet the capacity of the gas chambers, corpses were burned in pits in the open. The "Special Detail," enlarged to 800 prisoners, operated the gas chambers continuously in alternating shifts. The production of the extermination machines climbed higher and higher and reached a record at that time: The conveyor belt of Auschwitz consumed in twenty-four hours nearly 20,000 men, women, and children, who disappeared without a trace, transformed into smoke and ashes.

On May 27, 1944, the sirens in Auschwitz-Birkenau announced the escape of two more Jewish prisoners: Arnošt Rosin of Snina in Slovakia and Czezlaw Mordowicz of Mlawa of Poland. When three days later, after unsuccessful searches in the area, the commander recalled the SS guards from the towers of the "big line of sentries," Rosin and Mordowicz left their hiding place in the underground bunker in the gravel pit which was near the water supply of the guard headquarters. In the darkness they crawled through the space between the watchtowers, swam across the Sola River, and fled toward Cracow, where Mordowicz hoped to find contacts. But in the neighborhood of the town of Chelmek they ran into a "lapanka"—a round-up of Polish workers for slave labor in Germany.

They changed the direction of their flight, at a small railroad station, climbing onto the roof of an overfilled passenger train that was going in the direction of the Polish resort town of Zakopane. In the heavily forested region before the town of Novy Targ they jumped off the train and waded across the Černý Dunajec River. They went along the river bank through the forest, and when Rosin found a matchbox with the label *Slovenké žapalky* (Slovakian matches), he realized that they were home. In the nearest village of Nedeca they entered an inn. It was noon of June 6, 1944, and the radio was announcing at that very time that American armed forces were landing on the coast of France. Rosin felt so secure in his native Slovakia that he neglected to be careful. Excited by the news of the invasion, the guests in the inn ordered beer for the fugitives and as they were getting ready to drink to the success of the invasion gun barrels of the Slovakian military police appeared in the doorway. The escapees were fettered and taken away to prison in Stará Spisská Ves. In vain they tried to explain that they had fled from forced labor in Germany. The military police wanted to send them back. "You'll turn us over only as corpses," said Rosin, and asked for permission to speak with an official of the local Jewish community. A Mr. Mangel appeared. In the presence of the sergeant he spoke with the fugitives and then went to take counsel. Soon he returned and through the bars of the cell window he gave each one of them a dollar bill. They were accused of smuggling. The court in Liptovský Mikuláš handed down its verdict: eight days in prison and a fine of 5,000 crowns. The representatives of the Jewish community paid the fine and the liberated smugglers were given a place to stay in the Jewish home for the aged in Liptovský Mikuláš, which at that time seemed the safest place.

Dr. Karmil-Krasňanský's testimony shows the methods used by the Slovakian Jews to help escapees across the border with the aid of the local peasants, and saving those who were caught when crossing over by bribing the security forces. Rosin and Mordowicz met their comrades Rosenberg and Wetzler for the first time in the Jewish home for the aged.

As he had done at the end of April in Žilina, Dr. Karmil-Krasňanský now wrote reports during the first half of June with the new escapees. Their conferences took place in the home of Mr. Boby Reich, a member of the Jewish community of Liptovský Mikuláš. What needed to be done was merely to add a supplement of about five pages of material that had not been contained in the reports of the first escapees in April. This supplement furnished principally new and important facts on the course of the deportations and the mass extermination of Hungarian Jews in Auschwitz, to the extent that Rosin and Mordowicz had witnessed them up to the time of their flight.

Early in the second half of June the chief Slovakian enemy of the Jews, the minister for home affairs, Sano Mach, was expected. In anticipation of his visit special security measures were taken in Liptovský Mikuláš and all four escapees supplied with false papers went to Bratislava, where they were given aid by the illegal Jewish organization ÚŽ. Dr. Karmil-Krasňanský procured perfectly forged personal documents for the escapees. Their new names were entered in the rolls of the proper municipalities and were similar to the names prevalent there. One of the escapees said, "Our papers were so good that we could register and study at the University of Bratislava." Neither the original nor the new names of the escapees were mentioned in the report. Dr. Karmil-Krasňanský says they were the following: Walter Rosenberg became Rudolf Vrba (he kept this name permanently), Alfred Wetzler became Josef Láník (he uses this name now as a literary pseudonym), Czezlaw Mordowicz became Petr Podulka, and Arnošt Rosin became Jan Roháč.

The first sign that the reports had arrived at their destination came when Mikuláš Sternfeld of Bratislava made direct contact with the papal nuncio Borzic in Slovakia. Dr. Karmil-Krasňanský gives us the following information in his testimony:

I have received information from Mr. Mikuláš Sternfeld that a legate or courier would like to see the escapees from Auschwitz and speak to them. He asked me to bring two of the men who had escaped and to meet with the courier in the Piarist monastery in Svatý Júr. Rosenberg and Mordowicz went with me [according to testimony by Rosenberg-Vrba, this was about June 20, 1944] to Savatý Júr. . . . There we met Monsignor Mario, the rest of whose name I cannot now remember. . . . I had the impression that he had seen my report and knew it well. He was reserved and quite detached. He asked questions which the escapees answered. He took brief notes. We were there until about nine o'clock in the evening, about six hours. He gave us wine and Camel cigarettes (which we had never seen before), and photographed the numbers tattooed on the arms of the prisoners. Later he asked questions, particularly about what had happened to the Catholic clergymen imprisoned in Auschwitz and about whom nothing had been said in the report. At the end of our talk I requested him to report what he had heard to the proper people, particularly directly to the Pope. I also requested that he perhaps intercede with President Tiso on behalf of the 20,000 Jews still remaining in Slovakia, to improve their conditions and if possible to render them aid. He promised to do all I asked. Monsignor Mario said nothing about the Nazi crimes; he only asked questions and wrote down the answers.

This objective description of the dispassionate meeting between the papal diplomat and the escapees from Auschwitz puts what we had formerly known about the reports on Auschwitz in a somewhat different light. Contrary to the testimony of the men from Auschwitz, they met in the monastery of Svatý Júr not with the papal nuncio Borzic but with the papal courier Mario, who had been sent to establish the credibility of the reports. Thus, it was not the latter's first contact with information about Auschwitz but a confirmation that the documents had reached the Vatican. At least in this respect the Papal Curia had not been passive. But both statements agree that the papal legate was interested in the fate of the priests in Auschwitz and that he had promised to carry out all the requests made of him.

Previously published information has proved that the reports about Auschwitz had reached not only the Vatican but wherever they had been sent from Bratislava by the Jewish organization. They first reached Hungary where the danger was most immediate. At about the same time they arrived in Switzerland by various detours and from there, in the beginning of June, 1944, through the mediation of the consular representative of San Salvador, G. Mantella, they were given to the British Foreign Minister Anthony Eden and to President Roosevelt.

A little while later, and by other routes via Istanbul and Palestine, the reports reached the British Ministry of Foreign Affairs in London accompanied by a personal letter from Weizmann containing a pressing request for the immediate bombing of the Auschwitz crematoriums. The reports contained also the first authentic information on the fate of the Jews deported from Theresienstadt. One part, beginning on page 14 with the numbers series 148,000–152,000 that were tattooed on those from Theresienstadt, states:

During the week of September 7, 1943, trains arrived from Theresienstadt bringing Jewish families. For us it was entirely incomprehensible why these new arrivals enjoyed a very special position. The families were not separated, not a single one of them was treated in the usual way: to be gassed. In fact, they were not even given haircuts but were taken just as they arrived, men, women, and children, to a separate section of the camp, and they were even permitted to keep their luggage. The men did not have to work, and for the children there was even a school allowed, headed by Fredy Hirsch (of the Maccabees of Prague), and they were even permitted to write at will. The only thing they suffered from was the extreme chicanery of their "camp elder," a German professional criminal by the name of Arno Boehm, prisoner number 8, one of the biggest bandits in the camp. Our amazement increased when we later saw the official designation of this group, which read, "SB Transport, Czech Jews, 6 Months Quarantine." We knew very well what SB meant (Sonderbehandlung, special treatment), but we could not figure out what this special treatment was and especially why there was such a long period of quarantine, since by our limited experience there had never been a quarantine longer than three weeks. We were puzzled. But as the six-month quarantine period approached its end, we became more and more convinced that these Jews would meet their end in the gas chamber, too.

We found opportunities to come into contact with members of this group. We explained to them what the situation was and what they had to expect. Several of them, especially Fredy Hirsch, who apparently had the confidence of his fellow prisoners, informed us that if our fears should prove correct they would organize resistance. Those in the "special detachments" promised us that if the Czech Jews resisted, they would join them. Some believed it possible in this way to bring about a general revolt. On March 6, 1944, we learned that the crematoriums were being prepared to receive the Czech Jews. I hurried to Fredy Hirsch to give him this information and urged him to act, since there was now nothing to be lost. He told me that he knew what his duty was. Before evening I crawled over to the Czech camp. There I learned that Fredy Hirsch was dying. He had poisoned himself.

The next day, March 7, 1944, still in a state of unconsciousness, he was taken by truck, together with the 3,791 others who had come to Birkenau on September 7, 1943, to the crematoriums and gassed to death. The young people rode to their death singing. To our greatest disappointment, there was no resistance. The men of the "special detachments," who had resolved to cooperate, waited in vain. About five hundred elderly people died during the quarantine period. Of the whole Jewish group only eleven pairs of twins were permitted to remain alive. Various medical experiments were performed on these children in Auschwitz. When we left Birkenau they were still alive. Among those gassed was the Slovakian Prince Rozsi of Sered.

A week before they were gassed, that is, on the first of March, 1944, all the camp inmates had to write to their relatives about how well they were doing. The letters had to be post-dated March 25–27, 1944. They were to request that packages be sent them by their relatives abroad.

The second statement about the Theresienstadt prisoners is continued on page 16 and begins with the numbers series 165,000–168,000, tattooed on the forearms of the group brought from the ghetto in December:

> On December 20, 1943, 5,000 more Jews came from There-
> sienstadt. The transport list carries the same heading as did that of
> the September group: "SB Transport, Czech Jews, 6 Months' Quar-
> antine." Upon their arrival they were lodged in the same section of
> the camp as the September group, men, women, and children. They
> enjoyed the same favorable treatment as their predecessors. Twenty-
> four hours before the gassing of the first group they were transferred
> to the neighboring quarters, now happening to be vacant, and in this
> way separated from the others. They are still in this section now.
> Since after the gassing of the first group there can be no doubt about
> what is in store for them, they are even now planning resistance.
> The organizing of the resistance is being done by Ruzenka Lauf-
> schner and Hugo Langsfeld, both of Prague. They are slowly col-
> lecting combustible material and, if it should become necessary,
> intend to set fire to the blocks of their section. Their quarantine
> period will be over on June 20, 1944.

This extremely important section of the report telling of the annihilation of the Czech family camp and at the same time revealing its fraudulent character moved the diplomat Dr. Kopecký, who was representing
the London Government-in-Exile in Geneva, to take action. As a result
of the transmission of the report to Dr. Kopecký, an important document
has survived, written on June 23, 1944, by R. Lichtheim, representative
of the Jewish Organization in Geneva:

> 1. The enclosed reports and letters were transmitted to Dr.
> Kopecký from Bratislava about June 10. . . .
> 2. Dr. Kopecký called in Ullmann, his official adviser in Jewish
> matters, and gave him the material for examination and translation.
> At the same time he tried to reach Schwalb, who was away, however,
> and did not see Dr. Kopecký until a few days later.
> 3. On the basis of the reports concerning the deportation and
> murder of the first group of Czech Jews from Theresienstadt, Dr.
> Kopecký wired London via the London embassy, in order to prevent
> the murder of the second group that had been deported in the
> meantime. It was due to this that the BBC broadcast communica-
> tions and warnings between June 15 and 20.
> 4. Dr. Kopecký then conferred with Dr. Ullman and Dr. Riegner
> on further steps to be taken. Copies of the reports were given to
> Mr. McClelland, who intends to have English translations sent to

America. The whole report was excerpted and given to Dr. Kopecký in English, who is going to wire the summary to London. There was a further conference of Dr. Kopecký, Dr. Ullman, Dr. Riegner, and McClelland, and another meeting in the office of Dr. Schwarzenberg, attended by Dr. Kopecký, Dr. Ullmann, and Dr. Riegner, since in the meantime the Red Cross had received an inquiry from London asking what was known about the situation in Auschwitz-Birkenau.

The following further actions were considered:

Intervention by the Pope.

A demand for reprisals, especially the bombing of the camps, and in particular of the crematoriums, as well as of the railroad sections used for the transportation of Jews from Theresienstadt and Hungary.

These proposals will be telegraphed by Dr. Kopecký to his government.

A five-page English extract of the twenty-six-page report of the Auschwitz escapees sent from Bratislava to Geneva, was sent by Dr. Kopecký to the Czechoslovak government in London with the request to transmit it to the British Prime Minister, and proposing the following [These six proposals are in English in the original Prague document]:

1. The Allied governments should issue a warning to the Germans and the Hungarians that they will use reprisals against the Germans living in the Allied countries.

2. The camps of Auschwitz and Birkenau and especially the buildings containing the gas chambers and crematoriums recognizable by the high chimneys as well as the sentries around the railways and the watch towers and the industrial installations should be bombed from the air.

3. The following main railway lines which are used for the daily transports should also be bombed.

4. Without mentioning where this report comes from, the foregoing report should be given widest publicity by radio and newspapers so that the Germans may know that the outside world is fully informed about their activities.

5. The public warnings of the Allied nations over the radio and at other occasions should be constantly repeated.

6. The Holy See should be asked to issue a strong condemnation of these crimes.

Similar action and others firmer and more far reaching were undertaken by representatives of various sections of the World Jewish Congress, who made direct contact with the general staffs of the Western powers, with the Soviet embassy, and with representatives of the Polish and Czechoslovak governments-in-exile in London.

At the same time, information from the whole report, if only in an insufficiently organized way, was spread among the Jewish population that was immediately threatened with danger. In Hungary copies of the report were at first secretly made; later they were distributed in wider circles, but nowhere were they supported by representative organs of the Jewish institutions. In Slovakia, too, those who had information thought it their main task, according to Dr. Karmil-Krasňanský, to get the facts known and to help those who had escaped from Poland.

To judge the historic significance of the reports from Auschwitz and the possibility of utilizing them to prevent the final phase of the catastrophe being prepared by the Nazis in the spring of 1944, it is necessary to investigate the reaction of the various officials who had direct knowledge of the information supplied by those who had escaped from Auschwitz.

After confirmation in the monastery of Svatý Júr of the veracity of the reports of those who had fled from Auschwitz, the Vatican began various efforts through the organization of the church in Hungary to halt the deportations to Auschwitz. These efforts were climaxed by the direct intervention of Pope Pius XII through his personal communication to the Hungarian regent Horthy on June 25, 1944. But this move too was disregarded and remained unknown to the world at large. In this desperate situation there was only one effective course of action left open: Public disclosure by the head of the Catholic Church, who had been recognized by both sides in the war as having general authority and whose influence on the populations involved was undeniable. But the Pope decided against so firm an act and so this last and perhaps most effective possibility—the publishing of information about extermination of the Jews and others at Auschwitz—was lost. But the information was made public by the British Broadcasting Corporation. However, it was easy to call such broadcasts sent by a belligerent in a war mere propaganda meant to incite feeling against the enemy. On the other hand, as a belligerent Great Britain had a much more effective way of using the exact reports and detailed descriptions it had received. In spite of all strong and repeated requests of the representatives of Jewish organizations, this military operation was never carried out during the whole course of World War II because of "technical difficulties."

The reports of the men who had escaped from Auschwitz were published in Washington by the War Refugee Board, and on the basis of these President Roosevelt through the Swiss legation urged the government of Hungary to halt the deportations. At the expiration of the period of ultimatum set by President Roosevelt American squadrons carried out a bombing mission at the beginning of July. But this action conformed entirely to the usual type of that time and on July 5 there was another air attack against the civilian population of Budapest. It is true that deportations from Hungary stopped immediately, but the operation of the Auschwitz extermination camps proceeded unhindered until the beginning of November, 1944. Even on August 14, 1944, when the last inhabitants of the Lodz Ghetto were being liquidated and the extermination of the Jews from the last ghetto of Theresienstadt was being prepared, the United States Assistant Secretary of War, John J. McCloy, gave the following answer to the appeal of the World Jewish Congress to bomb the extermination camps and their railroad lines in Auschwitz [This quotation is in English in the original Prague document]:

. . . After a study it became apparent such an operation could be executed only by the diversion of considerable air support essential to the success of our forces now engaged in decisive operations elsewhere and would in any case [need to?] be of such full efficiency that it would not warrant the use of our resources. There has been considerable opinion that such an effort, even if practicable, might provoke even more vindictive [acts] by the Germans.

Nevertheless, there was a partial attempt made to halt the extermination in Auschwitz. What to the war strategists of the Allied powers seemed impossible of accomplishment was proved possible by a desperate attempt on the part of a small group of prisoners in the Auschwitz "special detail." They were armed with weapons of their own making. The gunpowder was supplied by four courageous Jewish girls who were working for the Weichsel Metal-Union munitions company making explosive charges. On Saturday, October 7, 1944, the prisoners who worked in the crematoriums and gas chamber, only some of whom had arms, started an uprising. They killed several SS men and set fire to the building of crematorium number 3. Although the revolt was barbarously suppressed by the superiority of the SS armed to the teeth, one of the four Birkenau crematoriums was destroyed and it was never put into operation again.

Thus, the only success in the struggle against mass extermination in Auschwitz was indeed the action carried out by the Auschwitz prisoners themselves. Their escape broke the barrier of the "secret matter of state," revealed its fraudulent nature, and gave the world the possibility of effective action. The uprising of the Auschwitz "special detachments" was the first and only purposeful action; it destroyed a fourth of the capacity of the extermination camps while the death factory was going at full blast by a planned operation. At this time the approaching Soviet army was still far from Auschwitz.

There only remains, therefore, the often heatedly discussed question of whether it was possible to have made better use of the reports from Auschwitz to stop the mass murders. Was it possible, by utilizing the information furnished by the Auschwitz escapees, to warn the broad masses of the Jewish population who were destined for deportation and annihilation, and thus lessen or prevent the catastrophe? Perhaps it is possible to doubt that more intensive efforts to make use of the information of the escaped prisoners would have led to greater success in Theresienstadt, Slovakia, and Hungary. But it is not possible to avoid the truth that the responsible Jewish leadership in these centers of Jewry at the time of the Nazi occupation did not do everything that it was in their power to do.

The men who had escaped from Auschwitz were in a state that was neutral at that time. Through the connections that the Jewish organizations had it was certainly not impossible to get them to Turkey or another country and to arrange an international press conference with the eyewitnesses that could perhaps have been decisive in halting the Auschwitz murders.

It will be both useful and interesting to mention here what was said recently by two men who were directly connected with the Auschwitz reports twenty years ago. On the occasion of the trial in Frankfurt of the former SS guards in Auschwitz a Paris newspaper published a comprehensive article by Dr. Rudolf Vrba, who had been a prisoner in Auschwitz and had escaped. The former diplomat, Mr. Georges Mantello, in correspondence with Dr. Vrba, wrote on May 18, 1964:

> I read your article in *France Dimanche* . . . with great interest. I must tell you in addition, that during the war I was First Secretary of the General Consulate of El Salvador in Geneva and cooperated in the rescue attempts. In May of 1944 I asked one of our couriers to bring me information from Budapest and on June 19, 1944, we got two reports, one of which was based on information supplied by two young Czechs, who had escaped from Auschwitz. The second concerned deportations from Hungary. I see now that they were you and your comrade.

These reports, however, were short and arrived in Switzerland rather late. They were sent to me from Budapest by Mr. Nicolas-Krauss [Mikos], head of the Palestine office in Budapest. If we had received your complete report about six or seven weeks earlier, say about the same time that you had sent it to Budapest, perhaps we could have put a stop to the deportations, since we would have started a big press campaign in Switzerland and abroad.

The various means of contact, the couriers who carried the reports, the exact times of sending out and delivering information, their repercussions and effect, and the reactions of those who had contact with them and had the opportunity to act, all this has by no means been adequately explored and ascertained. Several aspects, particularly those dealing with the Papal Curia and hitherto unpublished diplomatic documents of the governments that received the reports, will certainly not be available to the public for a long time. It is also true that many parts of the statements of witnesses quoted here are unexplained and contradict one another in many details. Nevertheless, it is already possible on the basis of all the available material to characterize these five escapes and the three independent attempts to awaken the conscience of the world and the resistance of the Jewish prisoners in the crematoriums as the high point of the Auschwitz resistance movement.

Translated from the German
by Harold Kirshner, Ph.D.

Rosa Robota—Heroine of the Auschwitz Underground

By Yuri Suhl

[EDITOR'S NOTE: *"The truth about Auschwitz? There is no person who could tell the whole truth about Auschwitz." These words were spoken by Jozef Cyrankiewicz, Premier of Poland, who was one of the top leaders of the Auschwitz underground.*

With each new memoir about that camp a little more of the truth is brought to light, as in the case of Rosa Robota who helped make possible the only revolt there. Yet it was only recently that her role in this uprising became known in many of its details.]

———◆———

ON SATURDAY, October 7, 1944, a tremendous explosion shook the barracks of Birkenau (Auschwitz II), and its thousands of startled prisoners beheld a sight they could hardly believe. One of the four crematoriums [25] was in flames! They were happy to see at least part of the German killing-apparatus destroyed; but none was happier than young Rosa Robota, who was directly involved in the explosion. For months she had been passing on small pieces of dynamite to certain people in the Sonderkommando. Daily she had risked her life to make this moment possible. Now the flames lighting up the Auschwitz sky proclaimed to the whole world that even the most isolated of Auschwitz prisoners, the Sonderkommando Jews, would rise up in revolt when given leadership and arms.

Rosa was eighteen when the Germans occupied her hometown, Ciechanow, in September, 1939, three days after they had invaded Poland. She was a member of Hashomer Hatzair and, together with other members, was deeply interested in the organization of an underground resistance movement in the ghetto.

In November, 1942, the Germans liquidated the ghetto of Ciechanow, deporting some Jews to Treblinka and some to Auschwitz. Rosa and her family were in the Auschwitz transport. Most of the arrivals were sent straight to the gas chambers from the railway platform. Some of the younger people, Rosa among them, were marched off in another direction and later assigned to various work details. Rosa was sent to work in the *Bekleidungstelle* (clothing supply section). Some Ciechanow girls were sent to the munitions factory, "Union," one of the Krupp slave-labor plants in Auschwitz, which operated round the clock on a three-shift basis. Rosa, as well as all the women who worked in the munitions factory, lived in the Birkenau barracks.

One day Rosa had a visitor—a townsman named Noah Zabladowicz who was a member of the Jewish section of the Auschwitz underground.[26] As soon as they managed to be alone he told her the purpose of his visit. The underground was planning a general uprising in camp, which included the blowing up of the gas chamber and crematorium installations. For this it was necessary to have explosives and explosive charges. Israel Gutman and Joshua Leifer, two members of the underground who worked on the day shift in "Union," had been given the task of establishing contact with the Jewish girls in the *Pulver-Pavilion,* the explosives section of "Union." But all their efforts were in vain because the girls were under constant surveillance and any contact between them and other workers, especially men, was strictly forbidden. It was decided, therefore, to try to contact them through some intermediary in Birkenau. Since several of the girls who worked in the *Pulver-Pavilion* came from Ciechanow and Rosa knew them and was in touch with them, she seemed to be the ideal person to act as intermediary between them and the underground.

Rosa was only too glad to accept the assignment. Ever since that day of November, 1942, when she saw her own family, together with the rest of the Ciechanow Jews, taken to the gas chambers, the strongest emotion that suffused her being was a burning hatred of the Nazis, coupled with a deep yearning to avenge the murder of her people. Now the underground gave her the opportunity to express these feelings in the form of concrete deeds.

Rosa set to work and in a short time twenty girls were smuggling dynamite and explosive charges out of the munitions factory for the underground. They carried out the little wheels of dynamite, which looked like buttons, in small matchboxes which they hid in their bosoms or in special pockets they had sewn into the hems of their dresses. These "buttons" would then pass from hand to hand through an elaborate underground transmission belt that led to the Russian prisoner Borodin, an expert at constructing bombs. For bomb casings he used empty sardine cans. The finished bombs then started moving again on the transmission belt to various strategic hiding places in the sprawling camp. The Sonder-kommando had its cache close to the crematorium compound.

Israel Gutman and Joshua Leifer concealed their "buttons" in the false bottom of a canister which they had made especially for that purpose. They always made sure to have some tea or leftover soup in the canister at the time of the SS inspection after work. Since it was customary for prisoners to save a little of their food rations for later, a canister containing some liquid would usually get no more than a perfunctory glance from the inspecting SS man.

One day after work as they were standing in line during the SS inspection, Leifer whispered to Gutman: "I had no time to hide the stuff in the canister. I have it in a matchbox in my pocket." Gutman grew pale and began to shake all over. The SS had been known to look into matchboxes also. He could not stop thinking that they were at the brink of disaster, and the more he thought of it the more nervous he became. So much so that the SS man became suspicious and gave him a very close and thorough inspection. Behind him stood Leifer, appearing very calm. Frustrated at having spent so much time on Gutman and finding nothing, the SS man gave Leifer a superficial inspection and passed on to the next man. This was one time, Gutman writes in his account of the incident, when nervousness paid off well.[27]

Moishe Kulka, another member, recalls that "the entire work was carried on during the night-shift when control was not so strict. In the morning, when the night-shift left the plant, I waited around. A Hungarian Jew I knew handed me half a loaf of bread. Concealed in the bread was a small package of explosives. I kept it near my workbench and later passed it on to a German Jew who worked on the railway." [28]

Rosa was the direct link with the Sonderkommando. The explosives she received were hidden in the handcarts on which the corpses of those who had died overnight in the barracks were taken to the crematorium.

The Sonderkommando, which according to plan was supposed to synchronize its revolt with the general uprising, one day learned through underground sources that it was about to be liquidated. For them it was a matter of acting now or never. Not having any other choice they acted. They blew up Crematorium III, tossed a sadistic German overseer into the oven, killed four SS men, and wounded a number of others. Then they cut the barbed wire fence and about six hundred escaped. They were hunted down by a large contingent of pursuing SS men and shot.[29] (As it turned out the general uprising never took place and the Sonderkommando action was the only armed revolt in Auschwitz.)

The political arm of the SS immediately launched a thorough investigation of the revolt. They wanted to know where the explosives came from and how they got into the hands of the Sonderkommando. With the aid of planted agents, the SS in a matter of two weeks came upon the trail of the explosives. They arrested several girls from the munitions factory, and after two days of interrogation and torture released them. The investigation continued and soon other arrests were made. Four girls were taken to the dread Block 11 for questioning. Three were from "Union"; the fourth was Rosa Robota.

Gutman, Leifer, Noah, and others whom Rosa knew now expected to be arrested at any moment. They had full faith in her trustworthiness, but they also knew something about the torture methods the SS employed in Block 11. At one point they considered suicide. They feared that what might happen to Rosa under questioning could happen to them too.

In the meantime they watched from a distance how Rosa was being led daily to Block 11 for questioning. Her hair was matted, her face puffed up and bruised beyond recognition, her clothes torn. She could not walk and had to be dragged by two women attendants.

One day the underground decided on a daring step. Moishe Kulka was acquainted with Jacob, the Jewish kapo of Block 11. He asked him if he would be willing to let someone see Rosa Robota in her death cell. Jacob agreed and asked that the visitor bring along a bottle of whiskey and a salami. Her townsman Noah was chosen to see her. The kapo introduced him to the SS guard as a friend of his. The two plied the SS man with drinks until he fell to the floor unconscious. Then Jacob quickly removed the keys from the guard and motioned to Noah to follow him. Noah describes the incident as follows:

I had the privilege to see Rosa for the last time several days before her execution. At night, when all the prisoners were asleep and all movement in Camp was forbidden, I descended into a bunker of Block 11 and saw the cells and the dark corridors. I heard the moaning of the condemned and was shaken to the core of my being. Jacob led me through the stairs to Rosa's cell. He opened the door and let me in. Then he closed the door behind me and disappeared.

When I became accustomed to the dark I noticed a figure, wrapped in torn clothing, lying on the cold cement floor. She turned her head toward me. I hardly recognized her. After several minutes of silence she began to speak. She told me of the sadistic methods the Germans employ during interrogations. It is impossible for a human being to endure them. She told me that she took all the blame upon herself and that she would be the last to go. She had betrayed no one.

I tried to console her but she would not listen. I know what I have done, and what I am to expect, she said. She asked that the comrades continue with their work. It is easier to die when one knows that the work is being carried on.

I heard the door squeak. Jacob ordered me to come out. We took leave of each other. It was the last time that I saw her.[30]

Before Noah left Rosa's death cell, she scribbled a farewell message to her underground comrades. She assured them that the only name she mentioned during the interrogations was that of a man in the Sonderkommando who she knew was dead. He, she had told the interrogators, was her only contact with the underground. She concluded her message with the Hebrew greeting of Hashomer Hatzair, "Khazak V' Hamatz"— Be strong and brave.

Several days later all the Jewish prisoners were ordered to the Appel-Platz to witness the hanging of the four young women—Esther, Ella, Regina, and Rosa.

Editor's Postscript

Despite the risks involved and in constant view of the crematorium compound, there existed in Auschwitz a well-organized underground movement that penetrated every aspect of camp life. Indeed, so remarkably well-functioning was this underground that one of its top leaders, Jozef Cyrankiewicz, was also directing the underground activities in Cracow while being imprisoned in Auschwitz. From time to time couriers from the Cracow underground would smuggle themselves into Auschwitz for instructions.

A question then arises: If the Auschwitz underground was so well organized and maintained such good contact with the outside underground, why was there no mass uprising in Auschwitz on a camp scale? Why was the revolt of the Sonderkommando, a desperate last-minute act, the only significant revolt in Auschwitz?

Bruno Baum, another top underground leader, who worked closely with Cyrankiewicz on a policy-making level (later a member of the chamber of deputies in East Germany), lists the following reasons why this was so (*Wiederstand in Auschwitz,* Berlin: Kongress-Verlag, pp. 93–96):

"Realizing that there was no other way out we decided to prepare for an armed uprising. With our friends in Birkenau Auschwitz II we worked out a common plan and stepped up the gathering of weapons. Comrades outside the camp supplied us with explosives.

"We sent our plans, which included a mass breakout, to Cracow and coordinated our aims with those of the Cracow comrades. If they approved our plans they promised to give us support. With about 140,000 prisoners in the entire camp we were a very important factor for the partisan movement. After our liberation we were to carry forward, together with the Poles, the Warsaw uprising which was already a fact, into Upper Silesia.

"On the way back our courier was shot at by SS-men and taken prisoner. They found our plans he had with him and transferred him to the camp hospital. Despite the torture during interrogation he held up bravely and betrayed no one.

"After our plans were discovered we feared that a mass annihilation of prisoners would take place. But this was not the case. However, the SS took other decisive measures:

1. They reenforced the cordon of guards. Even the large cordon in the distant circle outside the camp that stood guard only in daytime and was withdrawn at night now remained for weeks throughout the night as well. Thus the camp was guarded by a double cordon of guards day and night.
2. Prisoners returning to camp from work were thoroughly searched.
3. The number of informers against us was increased.

"To our astonishment nothing else happened beyond these measures. Later however we learned that the SS employed other means to thwart our plans. Shortly thereafter thousands of Poles were suddenly transported to Gross-Rosen. The SS also began to send off large transports of Jews and other prisoners for work in various parts of Germany. . . . In Birkenau there remained, for the time being, about 5,000 men and about 15,000 women. In the mother camp, Auschwitz, there were, including the women camps I and II, another 11,000 men and about 5,000 women. . . .

"In the meantime some changes took place outside the camp. The Warsaw uprising was ebbing. Near Cracow a Polish partisan general led his division in an attack without coordination with other forces. This isolated act was doomed to failure. He was routed by the German fascists. Because of this and the situation in Warsaw the urge for an uprising in Cracow and in the area of Upper Silesia died away.

"In the light of this new situation we were compelled to draw our own conclusions. We realized that as a result of the mass transports of Poles—only several hundred remained in the Mother camp—and prisoners of other nationalities, our military strength was greatly weakened.

"We were now compelled to change our tactic. The plan for an uprising was abandoned. We said to ourselves, since we can no longer save the camp inmates we must endeavor to send some of our best forces out of the camp so that they could draw the attention [of the outside world] to our camp. . . . In a matter of one week ten of our friends were to be on their way.

"It was agreed upon that Heinz Dürmayer and I should remain in order to carry on with the resistance work in camp. Also Cyrankiewicz, who was to leave the camp, was ordered by his Polish comrades to remain."

The Jewish Partisans of Horodenka

By Joshua Wermuth

[EDITOR'S NOTE: *Horodenka, a small town in eastern Galicia (Ukraine), borders to the east on Russia and to the south on Rumania. Prior to World War II this particular region of the Ukraine was under Polish rule, though the majority of the population was Ukrainian. In 1939, as a result of the division of Poland, eastern Galicia came under Soviet rule until 1941 when Hitler attacked the Soviet Union and this region became one of the first to be occupied by the Nazis. After the war it again was made part of the Soviet Ukraine.*

During the German occupation the native Ukrainian Fascists and anti-Semites distinguished themselves by their eager collaboration with the Nazis and, in the massacre of Jews, frequently outdid their masters. They also persecuted the Polish minority. This firsthand account by Joshua Wermuth not only adds breadth to the story of Jewish resistance but is unique in yet another respect. It is the first recorded instance in which Poles, themselves menaced by Ukrainians, turned to Jewish partisans for help. In this struggle against a common enemy a unity was forged between Pole and Jew which was all too rare. It affords a glimpse of what might have been had this unity existed on a much wider scale.

Joshua Wermuth was born in Horodenka on June 16, 1916. During his wanderings in the forests as a partisan he met the woman whom he later married. After liberation by Russian troops in 1944 he set out for Israel (then Palestine), where he arrived in 1945. He lives in Haifa with his wife and two daughters, and works as a bookkeeper for a building firm.

This account, edited and translated from the Yiddish, is from the memorial volume Sefer Horodenka *(Tel Aviv: 1963).*]

———◆———

THE LAST remnants of the Horodenka Jews, seeing no other way out for themselves, decided to cross the Dniester and head for the towns of Tlust and Buczacz. Not all made the journey safely. Some were robbed on the way by bands of Ukrainians, and arrived penniless. In a matter of two weeks there were 200 Horodenka Jews in Tlust and 120 in Buczacz. The two groups were in constant touch with each other and came to the aid of those who were robbed on the way.

Three months later the Germans began the extermination of Jews in this region also, employing methods that were only too familiar to us. We began to organize ourselves for armed resistance.

It was very difficult to obtain weapons. A pistol cost between 5,000 and 7,000 zlotys (which was a lot of money then). We appealed to the local Judenrat for help, and when they refused to give us money willingly we obtained it by force. We bought several pistols and two automatic guns. Then we dispatched several groups to the nearest forest to prepare for the day when we would all leave the city.

In the meantime the Germans had initiated a large-scale extermination action in the towns of the Czortkov region, and the Jewish youth in those towns who were to have left with us for the forests were caught in the unexpected action. Our people were not yet ready for organized mass resistance and during the action only those individuals who were armed or groups who had weapons were able to take up positions in some houses and strike back. During these counterattacks our comrades killed two Germans and three Ukrainian policemen.

Only a small number of us survived the pogrom. We formed three armed groups, numbering forty people, among whom were eight from Horodenka, and headed for the nearest forest.

Our first days in the forest were very difficult. It rained without letup and we had neither shelter nor food. But soon we put up some tents and a little later dug some underground bunkers. We also learned how to provide food for ourselves. Every night several of us would go into the nearest villages and return with produce to last us for the whole day. We set up a kitchen and cooked three hot meals daily.

But our arms supply was inadequate. We discovered that pistols were not very effective in the forest. What we needed were rifles and automatic guns. We made it our first task to arm ourselves in accordance with forest conditions. By various means we were able in a short time to enrich our arsenal with five rifles.

All the unarmed Jews in nearby forests concentrated themselves around our group. They were in constant danger of attacks, mainly by the local Ukrainian population. The Ukrainians would lie in wait for them along the roads that led to the villages. Every unarmed Jew was beaten mercilessly, robbed of his money and clothing, and left completely naked.

In such instances we saw to it that these Jews got new clothing. At night we would go to the head of the village where the robbery took place and confiscate all the clothing needed by the victims.

During the first two months we had no contact with the Russian partisans. We didn't even know there were any in our area. But we rejoiced when we learned that there were Russian partisans in the nearby forests. We sent our emissaries to find them and after many days of search two girls from our group came accidentally upon a patrol of Russian partisans. The happiness at our discovering each other was mutual. We celebrated with a festive meal during which they informed us about the course of the war and their own situation. After General Kolpak's unsuccessful offensive in the Carpathian Mountains they were severed from their headquarters and so they had formed isolated groups of partisans heading east.

The Russian partisans remained with us for some time and thanks to them we were better armed. We carried out joint operations and had whatever we needed. The partisans received sufficient clothing (mainly German Wehrmacht and SS uniforms). We installed a radio on batteries and every evening heard news from around the world.

From time to time the Germans, with the aid of the Ukrainian police, raided the forest. In summer our losses were comparatively small because we had greater mobility and could withdraw deeper into the forest. But in winter this was difficult and our footsteps in the snow betrayed us. We had to adopt a new tactic. We began wandering outside the forest, changing our positions daily.

As the raids increased, the Russian partisans decided to get closer to the front, which was some several hundred kilometers away. For us such a long exposure on the roads would have meant sure death because the Ukrainians would have handed us over to the Germans. Only a few of our group joined the partisans. The rest remained, continuing the tactic of changing positions frequently, covering from twenty to thirty kilometers a night and seeking shelter by day in the huts of friendly peasants, mainly Poles. We knew eight or ten such trustworthy peasants who took us in, not out of the goodness of their hearts but because we paid them well for it.

In the winter of 1943 when it already became apparent to the Ukrainians that Hitler was losing the war they did everything possible to exterminate the armed Jewish groups. They called meetings of the local population and told them it was the sacred duty of every Ukrainian to assist the police in the liquidation of the Jewish partisans because they were the living witnesses of what had happened and they would tell the Russians how eagerly the Ukrainians collaborated with the Germans in the annihilation of the Jews.

Knowing that we moved at night the Ukrainians posted lookouts to spy. Once again we had to change our tactics. Instead of keeping close to the villages in our nightly wanderings, we marched through the fields, far away from the villages. But even now we were not free from danger. From time to time our footprints in the snow would lead the Germans and the Ukrainian police straight to the huts where we were hiding. They never found us unprepared and when we began to shoot they were the first to flee. When they discovered unarmed Jews hiding in the attics and cellars of peasant huts—emaciated and defenseless women and children— they would drag them out into the yard and shoot them on the spot. But when they met with armed force these "heroes" were the first to run.

In the last months of the war our security was under constant threat. Large groups of armed Ukrainians, the well-known Bandara bands, were determined to wipe us out completely. Now our difficulties increased because the roads (including the field roads) were occupied by German and Ukrainian soldiers, which made it practically impossible for us to continue our movements.

At the same time the armed Bandara bands also attacked the Polish population in the entire region, slaughtering whole settlements and villages. They regarded the Poles, too, as being inimical to their future.

One night while we were at one of our lodgings at the home of a Pole we knew well—a Pole who had contact with the Polish underground and who in the early days was instrumental in obtaining weapons for us— a delegation of Poles arrived headed by a Polish captain, and made us the following proposition. Since their own existence was now no less precarious than ours, and since they appreciated our armed strength and bravery which was well-known to the population in the entire area, they proposed that we close ranks and enter the Polish villages as a united group to help organize and arm the people and offer armed resistance to the Ukrainian bandits, our common enemy. They assured us that they would protect us and care for us in every way and that we would not be wanting in anything.

As I stated earlier, we ourselves were in a very critical situation at the time, so after a brief deliberation we agreed to the proposal.

One of the Polish villages gave us an impressive reception and in their welcoming speeches the leaders praised us and spoke about our heroism. Here too they repeated their call to us to fight with them side by side against our common enemy, the Ukrainian bandits.

When it came our turn to speak we felt impelled to remind them of the large number of Poles who had assisted the Germans in the murder of our brothers and sisters. In reply they said that every people had its share of individual criminal elements and the Poles were no exception, but the Polish people as a whole had great sympathy for the Jews.

It is interesting to note that despite the fact that the Poles had been a sovereign nation for the past twenty years, and that every village had its military and sport organizations, such as "Szczelec," "Sokol," and others, we found the Polish population unarmed. In 1939–1941, out of fear of the Russians, they all turned in their weapons. The Ukrainians on the other hand ignored the Russian decree and did not turn in their weapons. Now every Ukrainian had hidden a cache of rifles, automatic guns, even machine guns.

We spent several months in the Polish villages. Many Poles from nearby villages moved into the villages where we had stationed ourselves. In their attitude toward us the population lived up to their promises. Every evening they prepared a festive meal for us and gave us whatever we needed. We carried out our operations at night. During the day we kept together in certain places. Only a very few people knew of our whereabouts.

But on Sundays we would go out into the streets in broad daylight, armed with our automatic guns to guard the church that was filled with worshippers.

Before we came to this village the population could not attend church for fear of being attacked by the Ukrainian Bandara bands who in several villages had thrown bombs into churches. In our village, when the worshippers gathered, four of our partisans guarded the church outside. Before beginning the services the priest said to the assembled: "Today you can pray in peace because outside this building there is a power that is protecting us from all dangers."

We remained in that village until the liberation.

The Resistance Movement in the Ghetto of Minsk

By Yuri Suhl

[EDITOR'S NOTE: *The ghetto of Minsk, capital of the Republic of Bye-lorussia, was unique in several vital respects. The following chapter, describing the resistance there, is based on conversations I had with Hersh Smolar, both abroad and during his recent visit to this country. I have also drawn on his memoir,* About the Minsk Ghetto *(Moscow: "Der Emes," 1946), recently published in English as* Resistance in Minsk *(Oakland, California: Judah L. Magnes Memorial Museum, 1966).*

Smolar, who in the ghetto was known as Yefim Stolerovitch, was the head of the Minsk Ghetto underground until conditions made it necessary for him to escape to the forest, where he remained until the end of the war and held the following positions of leadership: deputy commander of a partisan detachment; member of the High Command of the entire zone, Stolpce-Mir, which included four partisan brigades; and editor of five partisan newspapers published in the forest.

After the war Mr. Smolar returned to his native Poland where he became vice chairman of the Board of the Jewish Cultural and Social Association of Poland, and editor-in-chief of the Yiddish newspaper, Folks-Shtimme *(People's Voice). Due to a resurgence of anti-Semitism in Poland in 1967, he was removed from his position of leadership in the Jewish community and dismissed from his editorial post.*

In 1970 he left Poland and in 1971 took up residence in Israel, becoming a Fellow at the Diaspora Research Institute at the Tel-Aviv University where he does research and writes on the political, social, economic, and cultural life of the Jews in the Soviet Union from the beginning of the revolution (1917) till the beginning of the Stalinist liquidation of that life (1930). His work will be based on his personal memoirs of the period when he was a member of the Central Jewish Bureau of the Central Committee of the Komsomol in Moscow.

His "Where Are You Comrade Sidorov?", a political memoir, written originally in Yiddish, appeared first in Hebrew translation (Tel-Aviv: 1973), followed by a Spanish edition (Buenos Aires: 1974) and a Yiddish edition Tel-Aviv: 1974) . Mr. Smolar is currently at work on another volume of

231

political memoirs which is to embrace 25 years of Jewish life in Poland after World War II.]

———————◆———————

OVER TEN thousand Jews escaped from the Minsk Ghetto to the forests to join the partisan movement, a record unmatched by any other ghetto in Eastern Europe. The exodus was organized by the ghetto underground, which carefully planned the escape of every group, providing it with arms, an experienced guide, and a specific destination.

What helped most was the early organization of the underground and its orientation. The Minsk Ghetto was set up on July 25, 1941, and one month later the first secret meeting of the underground took place.

Organizationally the basic structure of the underground was the "Tens," groups of carefully selected, trustworthy people, numbering ten each. At the end of six months the underground had twelve such groups. Together with those not in the "Tens" there were over three hundred resistance fighters.

From the very beginning the main goal of the underground leadership was to get as many Jews as possible into the partisan movement. With this single-minded aim they were constantly seeking means of establishing contact with Byelorussian partisan detachments, and the groups of ten were feverishly collecting arms and storing them away in various hiding places in the ghetto. The gun was the Jew's passport to the forest.

Since the Germans drew much of their slave labor from the ghetto population, members of the underground who worked in arms factories, weapons repair shops, and arsenals became adept at concealing whole or parts of weapons and smuggling them into the ghetto when they returned from work.

As the Germans continued their systematic decimation of the ghetto population, the sending out of combat-ready groups to the forest became more and more imperative. Not every escape, even though carefully planned in advance, was successful. There were times when a guide or courier, because of unforeseen circumstances, failed to show up at the appointed place and the group did not know where to turn. It had to wait until the guide showed up, even if it took several days. (Returning to the ghetto was tantamount to desertion.) Frequently such stranded groups were an open target for a German patrol. If ambushed, the Jews made a stand with weapon in hand. Some succeeded in fighting their way out of the entrapment; others perished before even reaching the forest.

The procurement of weapons was not the only activity of the "Tens." Members of the underground who worked in various factories and industrial establishments that produced for the Germans were under orders from their leadership to commit sabotage at every turn. As in the Warsaw Ghetto, Jewish tailors working on uniforms for the Wehrmacht sewed them in such a way as to make them impossible to wear; and shoemakers knocked so many nails into the soles of boots as to render them useless. Whole transports of leather goods and other materials were destroyed by corrosive liquids which the underground produced in its own chemical laboratory in the ghetto. An entire transport of alcoholic beverages slated for the Eastern Front was treated with chemicals to produce injurious effects on the consumer. The alcohol used by the Germans to help them overcome the Russian winter was regarded by the Jewish underground as another enemy weapon to be turned on the Germans themselves. Once, two crate loads of sawed-off shotguns about to be shipped to Berlin for an exhibit of weapons presumably taken from captured partisans (at that time the partisans had no such weapons) landed in the forest instead, thanks to the ingenuity and daring of the Jewish underground.

To counteract German propaganda and bring their own message to the people, the underground leaders set up an illegal printing press and a secret radio receiver in the ghetto. Both were acquired the same way as were the weapons. The parts were smuggled in by underground members returning from work in the evening. The receiver was concealed in the chimney of one of the ghetto houses, and the antennae were twisted to resemble a clothesline. The underground issued bulletins, sometimes daily, with news of monitored radio broadcasts.

The forging of identification papers and other documents became another vital aspect of resistance activity. The Jewish children's poet Ben Sorin was an expert at this work. He had at his disposal, in addition to the necessary implements, the underground's own photo lab. These documents were an added precaution for underground members on dangerous missions. An "official" paper of that sort would state that its bearer was on a special errand or work detail and responsible only to the undersigned German officer. Some even carried documents from the office of Wilhelm Kube, Generalkommissar of all of Byelorussia.

Various were the tools the underground fashioned for itself in its daily struggle with the enemy. But their overall use was always directed toward the single goal of getting Jews out of the ghetto.

In the beginning the Jewish groups that made it to the forest were integrated into already existing Byelorussian partisan detachments. But partisans were always on the move and as the exodus from the ghetto was accelerated it became difficult to find detachments that could absorb the evergrowing number of escapees. Necessity compelled the Jews to form their own partisan units. This required long and arduous preparations, and was fraught with many hazards. The ghetto underground would send out special couriers (usually women because it was easier for them to pose as Aryans) to study the terrain for the most suitable spot in the forest and to seek out the most reliable elements among the village population whose help could be counted on. Not every courier made it back to the ghetto.

But despite all difficulties the Minsk Ghetto Jews managed to organize seven partisan detachments on their own initiative. Of these, six eventually became mixed detachments by the inclusion of Byelorussian partisans. In some the membership remained predominantly Jewish and in all, Jews occupied the important posts of commander or commissar. The seventh, Detachment 106, under the command of the Jewish underground leader Zorin, was turned into a Family Camp, numbering about six hundred men, women, and children, and retained its Jewish composition throughout the war. Next to Commander Tuvie Bielski's [31] Jewish Family Camp, Zorin's was the largest.

Though in the main noncombatant, it made a vital contribution to the other partisan detachments in that area by supplying them with boots, clothing, and other articles of apparel that were manufactured in the forest. It also operated a central laundry, bakery, and hospital for the other detachments. In addition, the Family Camp had its own combat unit composed of the younger members who provided armed protection for the Camp and participated in various partisan operations in collaboration with other detachments.

These significant achievements of the Minsk Ghetto underground would not have been possible without the aid and cooperation of the Byelorussian population. Though the Germans found their individual collaborators among the Byelorussians, these were the exception and not the rule.[32]

The dominant characteristic of the Byelorussian population was one of friendship and sympathy toward the Jews. To cite but one of many examples: The Byelorussian Nikolai Romanovich Cashni brought food to his Jewish acquaintances in the ghetto. For one of them, Dr. Dora Aperovich, he brought a pistol. This was not the kind of article one could hand over through the barbed wire fence so he smuggled himself into the ghetto to give it to her personally. This same Byelorussian saved the lives of sixty Jewish children in his hometown Ratomka, near Minsk. He managed to get hold of the register of the Ratomka Children's Home and wherever he saw the designation "Jew" next to a child's name he erased it thoroughly and added, "Byelorussian of unknown parentage."

As Hersh Smolar points out in his memoir, *About the Minsk Ghetto:* "All who escaped from the Minsk Ghetto to the forest to carry on the armed struggle, and all who escaped to Byelorussian villages and communities to save their lives, felt at every turn that without the fraternal help of the Byelorussian population not a single Jew would have survived, and thousands did survive."

Jewish underground leaders of the Minsk Ghetto played a significant role in forming a Byelorussian underground organization outside the ghetto, and the two undergrounds worked in close collaboration and in a spirit of mutual aid and reciprocity.

The most vital help the Byelorussian underground gave the Jews was that of finding ways of moving them out to join the partisans. Most of the Jews made the journey to the forest on foot, but a good many of them, thanks to the Byelorussian underground, made it by train. Railway men who were members of the underground would hide Jews in the coal compartment of the locomotive and drop them off a few kilometers from their destination where, by prearrangement, a guide would take them to the partisan detachment. By this railroad route, over five hundred Jews reached the forest.

For its part the Jewish underground did the following: It moved its own underground printing press, together with the Jewish printer who ran it, outside the ghetto to make it possible for the Byelorussian underground to print its illegal organ. It provided the Byelorussian underground leaders with forged documents and supplied Russian prisoners of war with clothing and identification papers to help them escape to the partisans. There were times when Byelorussian underground leaders, who had reason to believe that the Gestapo was on their trail, would smuggle themselves into the ghetto, where they were hidden by the ghetto underground in secure bunkers.

In the early days of the partisan movement when medical supplies and personnel were woefully inadequate in the forests, Byelorussian partisans wounded in battle and in urgent need of medical care and surgery would be smuggled into the ghetto hospital, where they received the proper treatment from doctors who were also in the underground. Those who required a prolonged stay in the ward were supplied with forged identification papers and registered in the Judenrat as Jews. Ivan became Yankel and Piotre, Pesach. At least twenty Byelorussian partisans passed through the ghetto hospital in this way.

The fact that the entire first Judenrat of the Minsk Ghetto, as well as the chief of the Jewish ghetto police, fully cooperated with the underground and took orders from it was, no doubt, helpful in its resistance activities. For instance, the Germans quite frequently levied contributions on the ghetto, ordering the Judenrat to collect fur coats and other apparel for the Wehrmacht's winter campaign. After collecting these items from the ghetto population the Judenrat, on orders from the underground, would deliver half to the Germans and the other half to the partisans. Through the cooperation of the Judenrat the underground was frequently able to obtain advance information of the enemy's plans and act accordingly. When the Germans caught on to its activities the entire first Judenrat, except one member, was arrested and hanged publicly and was replaced by another Judenrat.

In the ghetto Smolar's official job was that of fireman in the hospital's boiler room. Eventually the boiler room became the secret meeting place of the underground leadership. The Gestapo learned of his identity through an informer and so he went into hiding and eventually fled the ghetto. His rescue by the Byelorussian underground is worth recounting not only because of its dramatic elements but also because it exemplifies the close cooperation between the two undergrounds.

One evening in the spring of 1942 Smolar was in the house of the courier Nina Liss, discussing underground matters. He then went home to his room, which was on the same street. Around eleven that night he heard a commotion—cries and shots. He emerged from his room at dawn and was immediately put to work by the ghetto police to help in the removal of corpses. As he was doing so, Hersh Ruditzer, the member of the first Judenrat who had escaped execution, ran up to him and said: "It's you they're after. Run!"

He fled and took shelter in the typhus room of the hospital because it was known that the Germans dreaded getting near a typhus ward. From there he dispatched a courier to the Judenrat to learn what had happened. The courier returned with the following report: The shooting he had heard the night before came from the house where Nina Liss lived, and the corpses he helped remove this morning were the result of that shooting.

Apparently acting on a tip from an informer, the Gestapo had come to Nina Liss's dwelling looking for Yefim Stolerovitch. Not finding him there they demanded to know where he was. Although she knew his address she would not tell. She was shot together with her five-year-old daughter. So were seventy other Jews living in that house. Moreover, the Gestapo had given the Judenrat this ultimatum: If Yefim Stolerovitch is not handed over to them by noon the entire Judenrat would be shot and part of the ghetto liquidated. The ghetto was already surrounded by Gestapo men.

Smolar summoned to his hideout two of the top-ranking underground leaders, Michael Gebeliev, link between the ghetto underground and the Byelorussian underground of Minsk (later captured by the Gestapo and tortured to death), and Motye Pruslin, in charge of the underground's propaganda apparatus (later publicly hanged by the Germans), to deliberate on a course of action. The decision was: No negotiations with the enemy. You fight the enemy.

Meanwhile the chairman of the Judenrat (who, unlike his predecessor, had no contact with the underground) took steps of his own to vitiate the German ultimatum. He made out a duplicate copy of identification papers with the name of Yefim Stolerovitch, dipped it in the blood of one of the fresh corpses, and showed it to the Gestapo, saying: This is what we found on one of the bodies shot last night. Yefim Stolerovitch is dead. The Gestapo accepted this as fact and removed its special guards that had surrounded the ghetto.

Under these circumstances Yefim Stolerovitch could not remain in the ghetto much longer. By prearrangement with the Byelorussian underground he left in July, 1942, and was sheltered under the very nose of the enemy, in the house where Generalkommissar Wilhelm Kube's guards were stationed. Kube's headquarters was across the street, and the woman who gave him shelter lived in the guards' house and worked in their kitchen.

Stolerovitch spent six weeks in that room, most of them under the bed. When he left, it was to meet an underground courier on the square who was to take him to the forest. The courier failed to show up and Stolerovitch had to find another hiding place, and then still another. At the last one, the home of a Byelorussian underground worker, there were two windows in the room from which a steep roof extended out to the courtyard. Between the two windows there was wall space wide enough for a man to press against. The arrangement was that should the Gestapo knock on the door, Stolerovitch would escape to the roof and press against the wall between the two windows.

The Gestapo did come late one night, and the woman managed to push Stolerovitch out the window but failed to do the same for her husband. After searching the room the Gestapo opened the window and looked out on the roof but did not notice Stolerovitch pressing against the wall. The Germans arrested the man, his wife, and nine-year-old daughter, took away Stolerovitch's boots and padlocked the door. The family was never heard from again.

Stolerovitch escaped to a nearby abandoned building and remained there for several days to warn other underground workers not to go near the house. Then he slipped into a column of Jewish workers returning to the ghetto. He remained in the ghetto for only twenty-four hours, and the next day, together with four armed Jews, he escaped to the forest where he remained with the partisans until the end of the war.

To document the day-to-day operations of the Minsk Ghetto partisans —their many successful missions of derailing and blowing up German troop trains speeding east; the wrecking of communication lines; the rear attacks on German convoys; the destruction of vital military equipment;

the harassing of the enemy at every turn—would require a work by itself. Here it can only be stated in the broadest general terms: These Jewish fighters of the forest dealt the enemy severe blows, and in the over-all scheme of Allied victory they have an honorable share.

At the end of the war nearly five thousand returned home. The other five thousand had fallen in battle.

Editor's Postscript

In his *Destruction of the European Jews,* Raul Hilberg devotes an inordinate amount of space to German sources describing Generalkommissar Wilhelm Kube as being soft on Jews to a point of incurring the displeasure and mistrust of other high-ranking Nazis. Among the examples of Kube's untypical Nazi behavior the following is cited: "When the Judenrat in Minsk had been ordered to prepare 5,000 Jews for 'resettlement' Kube had actually warned the Jews."

In a conversation with me Smolar denied that this had ever happened. As the leader of the Minsk Ghetto underground which had its reliable contacts in the Judenrat, he was informed of everything of importance that happened in that body. His denial was categorical.

As for Kube's so-called humanitarian impulses with regard to Jews, Smolar cited the following example of Kube's "humanitarianism." In March, 1942, all the children from the children's home in the Minsk Ghetto were buried alive in a vast pit within the ghetto. While the Germans and their helpers shoveled sand over the bodies of the young, screaming victims, Kube stood by smiling and tossing candy into the pit.

Eventually the partisan movement passed a death sentence on Kube, which was successfully carried out. David Kemach, a Soviet Jew, a parachutist and deputy commander of a partisan detachment in that region, played a leading role in working out the plans for Kube's assassination. A Byelorussian partisan, a woman, was sent to Minsk. With her she had a time bomb which she passed on to Halina Mazanik, a member of the Minsk underground who worked as a domestic in Kube's household. At the appropriate moment she slipped the bomb under Kube's bed and disappeared. That same day she and her family were taken to the forest by a partisan courier. (See Moshe Kaganovitch, *The War of the Jewish Partisans in Eastern Europe,* Central Union of the Polish Jews in Argentina, Buenos Aires: 1965, I, 83, 252–253.)

Kaganovitch, who was himself a partisan in that area, wrote: "What a wonderful feeling it was when we, already in the partisan movement, read in the Byelorussian press that the Generalkommissar of Byelorussia, the murderer of Byelorussian Jewry, was blown to bits by a bomb that was placed under his bed" (p. 392).

Raul Hilberg ignores entirely the tremendous achievement of the Minsk Ghetto underground and its role in organizing the Jewish partisan movement, as documented here. He does not even mention it. The Nazi leaders in Byelorussia knew better. In Hilberg's own book Kube is quoted as having characterized most of the Russian Jews as "partisan helpers." And in a letter to Reichkommissar Lohse in Riga, Wehrmachtkommissar Bremmer emphasized that "the Jewish population is in the forefront in propaganda, resistance, and sabotage against the Germans in Byelorussia." (See Max Weinreich, *Hitler's Professors,* YIVO—*Bletter,* Journal of the Yiddish Scientific Institute, Vol. 27, No. 2, 1946, p. 209.

*   *   *

November 20, 1941
Re: Transportation of Jews from Germany to White Russia.
To: The Reichskommissar of Ostland [Eastern Area] *Riga.*

According to a report of the 707th Division 25,000 Jews are supposed to be transported from Germany to White Russia, of whom 3,000 supposedly are intended for Minsk and 1,500 have already arrived from Hamburg.

The arrival of German Jews, whose intelligence is far superior to that of the mass of the White Russian populace, means a great danger for the pacification of White Russia. The Jewish population of White Russia is bolshevistic and is capable of any attitude inimical to Germany. In the cities of White Russia the Jews constitute the largest part of the population and the driving force of the resistance movement that is starting in some places. In the countryside, according to reports of the GFP, the Jews have tried with threats to force the farmers either not to gather the harvest or to destroy it. As everywhere, where reports about acts of sabotage, incitement of the population, resistance, etc., have forced us to take measures, Jews were found to be the originators and instigators, and in most instances even the perpetrators. Therefore the newly arriving Jews will try with all their means to contact the Communist organizations, etc., and foment trouble.

It is therefore urgently requested to arrange that no Jews from Germany will come to White Russia.

This secret German document, admitting that the Jews of White Russia played a leading role in the resistance movement of that area, is part of the YIVO archives (YIVO Institute for Jewish Research) in New York City. This photostatic copy was obtained through the courtesy of YIVO.

Wehrmachtbefehlshaber Ostland
    I c   H. Qu., 2o. Nov. 1941

Betr.: Beförderung von Juden aus Deutschland
        nach Weissruthenien.

An den

    Herrn Reichskommissar für das Ostland

                         R i g a

    Nach Meldung der 7o7. Division sollen 25 ooo Juden
aus Deutschland nach Weissruthenien befördert werden, von
denen für Minsk angeblich 3 ooo vorgesehen und 1 5oo be-
reits aus Hamburg eingetroffen sind.

    Der Zuzug deutscher Juden, die der Masse der weiss-
ruthenischen Bevölkerung an Intelligenz weit überlegen
sind, bedeutet eine grosse Gefahr für die Befriedung
Weissrutheniens. Die jüdische Bevölkerung Weissrutheniens
ist bolschewistisch und zu jeder deutschfeindlichen Hal-
tung fähig. In den Städten Weissrutheniens stellt sie den
grössten Teil der Bevölkerung und die treibende Kraft der
sich mancherorts anbahnenden Widerstandsbewegung. Auf dem
Lande haben nach Meldungen der GFP die Juden versucht, durch
Drohung die Bauern zu zwingen, die Ernte nicht mehr einzu-
bringen bzw. zu vernichten. Wie überall, wo Meldungen über
Sabotageakte, Aufhetzung der Bevölkerung, Widerstand usw.
zu Aktionen zwangen, Juden als Urheber und Hintermänner,
grösstenteils auch als Täter festgestellt wurden, so werden die neu einwandernden Juden mit allen Mitteln trach-
ten, mit kommunistischen Organen usw. in Verbindung zu
treten und zu hetzen.

    Daher wird dringend gebeten, zu veranlassen, dass
keine Juden aus Deutschland nach Weissruthenien kommen.

    Der Antransport von Juden ist m. E. mit Rücksicht
auf die angespannte Transportlage z. Zt. überhaupt nicht
möglich. Heeresgr. Mitte hat mich ersucht, die Transporte

Children—Couriers in the Ghetto of Minsk

By Jacob Greenstein

[EDITOR'S NOTE: *Jacob Greenstein escaped from Warsaw in 1939 when the Germans invaded Poland. He lived with his family in a small town near Minsk until the Germans occupied that part of Byelorussia and deported him to the Minsk Ghetto. There he joined the underground and was active in concealing weapons smuggled into the ghetto, until his turn came to leave for the forest and join the partisans.*

After his demobilization from the Red Army in 1946, Mr. Greenstein reached the DP camps in Germany where he became active in Bricha, *the organization that concerned itself with the smuggling of Jewish survivors into Palestine during the time of the British blockade, and in mobilizing Jewish youth for the Hagannah in its struggle for Israel's independence. In 1948 Mr. Greenstein emigrated to Israel where he now lives.*

Children—Couriers in the Ghetto of Minsk *first appeared in the Hebrew-Yiddish anthology,* Facing the Nazi, *Tel Aviv: 1962, and is here presented in a somewhat abbreviated version, in translation from the Yiddish. It is included in Greenstein's memoir,* Blood on Byelorussian Soil, Destruction and Resistance in Byelorussia in the Years 1941–5, *published in Hebrew by the Ghetto Fighters' House and Kibbutz Hameuchad, Tel Aviv: 1966.*]

————◆————

AMONG THE COURIERS who led people out of the ghetto, three children distinguished themselves. They were Sima, Banko, and David. Three times a week they took groups of Jews to the forests of Staroje-Sielo, covering a distance of fifty kilometers both ways. Despite their age they were fully aware of the nature of their mission and of the dangers involved.

The three children were our main contact with the forest. They came to the ghetto armed, their pistols always loaded, determined not to fall into the hands of the Germans alive. They were at ease and showed no signs of fear though they were constantly exposed to death. They carried out the orders of our general staff with strict discipline.

Sima was a twelve-year-old girl with blonde hair, blue eyes, and dimples that showed when she talked. Her parents perished in the first German pogrom. In the beginning Sima lived outside the ghetto and carried

241

out important assignments for the underground party committee. Later, when we began to lead Jews out of the ghetto, Smolar brought the little girl to the ghetto and she became our contact with the forest.

No assignment was too difficult for Sima. Before going out on a mission she listened carefully to the given instructions, then she would repeat what she was told, trying hard not to miss a single word. Her small pistol was always in the special pocket sewn into her coat. Before starting out she would always point to it and say, "Don't worry, the Fritzes will not take me alive."

On cold winter nights Sima would sneak out of the ghetto through an opening beneath the barbed wire fence. She returned to the ghetto through the cemetery. There were times when she did not succeed in getting into the ghetto at night. When this happened she would spend the night, hungry and cold, in some bombed-out building, and remain there throughout the next day. At dusk, when the Jews returned from work, she would stealthily join their column, and together with them enter the ghetto. After the liquidation of the Minsk Ghetto, Sima participated in the combat operations of the partisan detachment.

In the summer of 1944, when the Germans were driven out, Sima marched in the front lines together with other decorated partisans in the large partisans' parade in Minsk. From her youthful chest shone a silver medal, first-rank Partisan of the Fatherland war.

Banko and David were two thirteen-year-old boys who had been schoolmates and had lived on the same street. Their fathers were also friends. The boys went together to Pioneer camps. Together they hid out during the German pogroms and worked at loading coal into the freight cars at Tovarne station and together they escaped to the forest.

They wandered for weeks through the forest and villages until they came upon group of partisans called the "Stalincy." There they found Smolar, Feldman, Zorin, and other Jews of Minsk.

When Feldman called Banko into staff headquarters and ordered him to get ready to go to the Minsk Ghetto and bring out some Jews, Banko said, "I am ready to carry out your every command on one condition— that David go with me." His request was granted.

Banko's mother was still in the ghetto. All the other members of his family had perished in the German pogroms. His mother knew of Banko's activities and the dangers he was facing. But she was proud of him. Whenever Banko came for more people he visited his mother. She would put him to bed and sit near him for hours, watching him as he slept. When he awoke he would relate to her in whispers how the partisans were fighting the enemy; how they were blowing up troop trains and killing Germans.

"And when will you take me along to the forest?" his mother asked.

"I spoke to the Commander and he said the next time I'm in the ghetto I'll be able to take you along. I'd like you to be in my detachment and not in a family camp. Ours is a combat detachment; you'll have to stand guard and hold a rifle, but we'll be together. In a detachment, in a dugout, it is good to have a mother."

Banko was a small, skinny boy, who looked ten years old. The ghetto experiences had left deep marks on his elongated, youthful face. David was taller and also older-looking than Banko. But it was Banko who was in charge of their activities, and David was his companion.

David was an orphan; his entire family was killed. He was the sole survivor. His only friend was Banko. David carried out his work quietly and scrupulously, not overlooking a single detail. But he had one weakness—he did not like to remain long in the ghetto. He would become nervous and hurry Banko on by saying, "We've already been too long in the ghetto. So many Jews are waiting for us to take them out. Time is short."

Their mission was to bring combat-fit young men and women and weapons from the ghetto to the partisan detachment Parchomenko.

When Banko had gathered the people and supplies, the underground set the departure hour and selected the lookouts to guard the exists. Then Banko gave the final instructions. He addressed the people like a commander speaking to soldiers:

In two hours we will be leaving the ghetto. From that moment on you are partisans. Until I deliver you into the hands of the partisan Chief of Staff you must obey my every command. The order of the journey is as follows: I go first and you follow behind me in single file, according to the numbers I gave you. If we should run into a German patrol there is no way back because it would endanger the Jews in the ghetto. If the situation becomes critical we resist. Those who received grenades will throw them at the Germans; and those who have pistols will open fire on them. Retreat is possible only in the direction of Staroje-Sielo. The Germans will not pursue us very far because they are afraid of the night. Under no conditions must you abandon the knapsacks which you carry on your backs. Anyone who creates a panic or refuses to obey my command will be shot without warning! I hope that all will go well and that in a few hours from now you will be free people without yellow badges.

At the precise moment past midnight the two boys led the Jews out of the ghetto. As always Banko was at the head of the line, his loaded pistol in his pocket. The others followed after him. David was last. All along the way to the wide fence our people were standing guard, including some members of the Jewish ghetto police who were cooperating with the underground. The people moved quietly, holding their breath, thinking of the instructions Banko had given them.

For months these children engaged in such operations, leading out hundreds of Jews—among them practically all the doctors—and covering hundreds of kilometers. Later they participated in actual combat operations together with the others.

Here, in the natural surroundings of the forest, the children caught up on their physical growth which the ghetto had stunted. Banko grew tall and manly-looking and David surpassed him by growing a head taller. They had many friends in the Parchomenko and Budiony detachments, which they regarded as their own; and hundreds in the Zorin's family detachment where Banko's mother was. He could not persuade the commander to let his mother be with him. A combat detachment had to be combat-ready at all times, and Banko's mother had suffered too much hunger and illness in the ghetto to be able to keep up with the young partisans.

On August 15, 1943, the Germans surrounded our forest with the aim of annihilating the partisans. The Germans threw two divisions of the regular military into this operation, plus some Vlassov men and Lithuanians. A few days before the blockade they burned down the farms in the forest area. Because the peasants of these farms had maintained friendly relations with the partisans the Germans had herded them all into one house and burned them alive.

The German attack lasted fifteen days; it was prepared and carried out like a full-scale front-line operation. There were bombardments from the air; heavy and light artillery were fired without letup; mine sappers cleared the way where the military had to pass, and the Germans went into attack in three waves. Every bush, every tree, was shot at.

During the first days of the attack we offered resistance. We mined the roads, dug trenches, and engaged the Germans in minor battles. The Parchomenko detachment had mined the main Ivenic-Bakszt highway, and the first truck, carrying more than thirty Germans, was blown up as soon as it entered the forest. They were all blown to pieces together with their vehicle.

After several days our resistance collapsed. We could not hold out against a regular army. From headquarters came the command that we scatter in small groups and wait out the blockade. On September 15 the Germans abandoned the forest. At the time of the German attack several hundred partisans perished, among them between fifty and sixty Jews.

The Parchomenko detachment suffered the heaviest losses. Twenty-two men, twelve of whom were Jews, were hiding out in a cave close to the base. They were discovered because of a child in their midst and all suffered martyrs' deaths. We found them burned, some only in part, their arms pulled back and tied with barbed wire. According to all evidence they had been burned alive. We found no bullet holes on their bodies. Among the burned was Banko. His body was half-burned, his eyes open as though petrified. I untied his arms but could not straighten them out.

With clenched fists and anguished hearts we swore to take revenge on their murderers. David stood at Banko's open grave and cried bitterly. The entire detachment cried with him.

The Story of the Amazing Oswald (Shmuel) Rufeisen

By Jacob Greenstein

[EDITOR'S NOTE: *In the Archives of the Jewish Historical Institute of Warsaw I came upon Document No. 543, one of the many personal narratives of survivors who, immediately after the war, were invited by the Institute to record their wartime experiences while they were still fresh in their memories.*

Document No. 543 was related by Ber Resnik, a member of the underground in the ghetto of Mir, a town in the western part of Byelorussia, and later a partisan fighter in the forest. Resnik told how he discovered one day that Oswald Rufeisen—the interpreter to the German regional commander, Hein, who posed as an Aryan—was actually a Jew named Shmuel Rufeisen, a friend and fellow member in the same Zionist youth movement. From then on they met secretly and Oswald, utilizing his position of trust with the Germans, supplied the ghetto underground with weapons and valuable information.

Document No. 543 remained incomplete because the narrator left the country before he concluded his story. My research for this anthology led me to Jacob Greenstein's memoir, mentioned in the preceding chapter, which completes the Rufeisen story.

Resnik, Rufeisen, and Greenstein now reside in Israel.]

"AMONG THE NEW arrivals in our partisan detachment was a young blonde fellow whose odd behavior drew my attention. His name was Oswald Rufeisen. He was withdrawn and very religious. In his spare time he would move off to some corner to kneel and pray. But he was an excellent partisan, always ready to help those in need. He would rise at dawn, when the others were still asleep, fetch water, chop wood, and feed the animals. He was courageous and carried out his missions earnestly. When I got to know him well and we became intimate friends, Oswald told me the following story:

"When the Germans attacked the Soviet Union I arrived, after many wanderings, in the town of Mir, in western White Russia. Because of my Aryan appearance and excellent knowledge of German I became an interpreter for the police. In the beginning I thought only of hiding my Jewish identity and saving my life. But in the very first days I witnessed terrible scenes of German brutality. Mass executions of prisoners-of-war; peasants shot for the slightest infraction of the rules; Jews herded into the ghetto and driven to slave-labor jobs under a hail of beatings and bullets. Daily I saw the wounded and the killed. Then the idea occurred to me that while working for the Germans I might have the opportunity to save people's lives. It did not take me long to win the confidence of the Germans. Having been brought up in a German region, I knew their mentality well.

"In Turka, a town near Mir, where I worked for a while, Wehrmacht detachments arrived one day. They had suffered defeats on the Smolensk front, so they took it out on the Jews, shooting them indiscriminately on the streets. In one day alone, November 11, 1941, they shot 1,600 Jews. The next day after this horrible pogrom Oberleutnant Einhorn of the SS arrived and took the Wehrmacht commander to task for having carried out the shootings in an inhumane manner. According to German ethics, he said, people should be led to the pits, ordered to undress and then shot.

"The first person I saved was a Soviet major, whom the police had arrested. He had been in hiding for a long time, disguised as a peasant's helper. A neighbor of the peasant he worked for betrayed him to the police. For running away from the prisoner-of-war camp the penalty was death. I dismissed the police and, after a brief interrogation in the presence of my superior [Commandant Hein] the major confessed. My superior did not understand a single word of Russian. I told him that the prisoner was a peasant from a nearby farm, who got drunk yesterday, beat up his wife and created a disturbance. I began beating the Soviet major over the head with my riding crop, and as I beat him I pushed him out into the yard. Throughout, until we reached the exit, I beat him and shouted, 'Now you'll know what it means to beat a woman and create a disturbance!' My superior, who was watching this from the terrace, was beside himself with joy. In the middle of the yard, when we were alone, I whispered to the Russian: 'There are partisans 15 kilometers from here,' and continuing to beat him, shouted, 'I don't want ever to see you here again,' and pushed him past the gate.

"When I returned Hein slapped my back with satisfaction. 'Oswald,' he said, 'you're a real German. That's the only language these wild Russians understand—a good beating.'

"That was the first victim whose life I saved from certain death. From then on it went much easier. The Germans' trust in me kept increasing. They regarded me as a good Hitlerite, and parallel with my advancement grew my opportunities to do something big. I decided to save the remnant of Jews [in Mir], who numbered about 800. I was awake nights trying to figure out a way to do it.

"One day, as I was standing in the street, watching my fellow Jews being led to work under a guard of armed police, I recognized a friend of mine with whom I had once been in the same kibbutz. His name was Ber Resnik. That same evening I knocked on his door in the ghetto. I was dressed in the black Hitler uniform, and he, a ghetto Jew, wore the yellow badge on his back. He was frightened at first, thinking that his end had come. But soon he recognized me and we embraced and kissed and wept bitterly. I told him of my plan and from then on we met regularly. At that time there was already an active underground in the ghetto.

"In order for the plan to be successful the majority of the Jews had to be won over to it. And that was not an easy matter. There were some who were determined to prepare for resistance. But there were many others who were living with the illusion that they might survive the war. In the meantime I began sending weapons into the ghetto—rifles, ammunition, grenades. I had to move with extreme caution to make sure that Hein would not suspect me. The slightest misstep on my part could endanger the lives of all the Jews.

"One day I overheard a telephone conversation of Commandant Hein and learned that the total liquidation of the ghetto of Mir was to take place in three weeks. I immediately informed my friends in the ghetto. I sent them twelve rifles, two automatic guns, five pistols, some ammunition and grenades, and urged them to prepare to escape.

"At first the underground had planned to defend itself inside the ghetto. But I advised them to go to the forest instead. There one could fight and survive; in the ghetto they would kill a few Germans but all the Jews would perish. They agreed and we began to work on a precise plan.

"On the day of the planned escape I created a false alarm at police headquarters that the partisans were close to town. I mobilized all the policemen and took them in the opposite direction from the one the Jews were to take. I led them far out of town. We shot at random into the forest and they were convinced that they were shooting at partisans. . . .

"The next morning when we returned to town we learned the 'sad news' that the night before the Jews had escaped to the forest. My joy was indescribable. I was like a new-born man. Nothing else interested me anymore. 'The Jews escaped to the forest!' These words rang in my ears like a song. And to think that I had made it possible! But I soon learned that only 300 Jews had escaped, and my heart contracted in pain. For I knew full well that the other 500 were facing certain death. And so it was. On August 13, 1942, exactly on the day I warned my friends about, the local police entered the ghetto at five in the morning and took the Jews to the outskirts of town. There they were all shot."

Oswald fell silent. Tears came to his eyes. When he spoke again he said, "The one who survived was a Jew who worked in the police court-yard."

"What happened later?" I asked.

"Throughout the night I tossed on my bed. I wanted to get to the forest as quickly as possible and join my brothers. In the morning, when I came to work, my superior entered the office. He was in an agitated state. 'Imagine that!' he began to shout, 'That dirty Jew told me that you, Oswald, are a Jew! I shot him on the spot, like a dog. . . . Imagine that!' he groaned. 'He swore by his Jewish God that you helped the Jews escape from the ghetto!'

"I gaped at him, stunned. Why did he go to Hein? Why didn't he wait for me? I would have taken him to the forest. Perhaps he thought that I, too, had run away, and now they would shoot him. He couldn't hold out, one Jew among all those Germans. 'It was not his fault!' I shouted at the top of my voice, forgetting that I was standing before the Chief of Police Hein.

" 'It was not whose fault?' he shouted back. 'What are you talking about, Oswald?'

" 'Why did you shoot him?' I said. 'He told you the truth. Yes, I am a Jew,' I raised my voice again. 'And a proud Jew at that! I served you with only one purpose in mind—to save people, especially my tortured fellow-Jews. Yes, to rescue them from your murderous hands!' I suddenly felt dizzy. I clutched the chair for support and sat down.

"Hein stared at me as though stunned. But soon he regained his composure, disarmed me and left the room, banging the door behind him. I was alone now. I knew that I could not escape because Hein had most likely stationed guards at all the exits. Half an hour later my breakfast was brought to me as usual. Soon afterwards Hein entered. I was too lost in thought to notice him.

" 'Why didn't you eat your breakfast?' he asked as though nothing had happened.

"I did not reply.

"Hein began to pace the floor. Suddenly he stopped near me and put his hand on my shoulder. 'Oswald,' he said, 'we have worked together for a long time. We were always satisfied with you and never suspected you of anything. I don't believe what you told me. Think it over, Oswald. You are not a Jew. No one here heard what you said, and I haven't told a soul about it. Forget it, and let's continue working together. I shot the last Jew. There is no more Jewish problem here. I appreciate your capabilities.'

" 'Everything I told you is true,' I said. 'Have no illusions about it, I am a Jew. And as I told you before, my only reason for working for you was to be able to save the lives of people. If you quake in your boots for fear of being punished because you allowed a Jew to fool you and snatch hundreds of Jews from under your nose, I cannot help that. If you really appreciate me, give me back my pistol and let me die with honor. It will be better for you too.'

"Hein went pale. 'Think it over,' he said, and left the room.

"I remained alone with my thoughts. The idea of suicide occurred to me because I saw no other way out. Thus I sat in my office for several hours, reviewing my short life, and no one bothered me. Aid could come from only one place, I thought—the Polish family with whom I had spent my free evenings. I became very friendly with this religious Catholic family. They would do everything possible to save me if they knew the situation I was in. I resigned myself to my fate that my end was near.

"Suddenly there was a knock on the door. A policeman entered and announced that the chief wanted me to join him for lunch. Mechanically, I rose and went to the dining room.

"Everyone was there. I took my usual place. No one mentioned anything to me, as though nothing had happened. Only Hein, I noticed, kept looking furtively in my direction. The food got stuck in my throat. I had to force it down. In the middle of the meal, while the others were engrossed in their food, I rose and went out into the yard. I looked around me. No one was following me. I reached the gate; the guard let me pass. On the street I accelerated my pace. I passed through some narrow streets and was in the open field. I went faster now. Part of the field was already behind me. I cut through a small woods and was again on an open field, where hundreds of haystacks, fresh from the harvest, were drying in the sun.

" 'I am free!' I said to myself, 'I can go wherever I please!' I slowed down and continued aimlessly. The fields were never more beautiful than now. Suddenly I heard the clip-clop of horses' hoofs. I turned around. Police were pursuing me across the field. I quickly hid in one of the haystacks. A few minutes later the police galloped past me. I fell asleep from exhaustion.

"For three days I wandered around in the forest not knowing where to turn. On the fourth day, in the evening, I returned to town and knocked on the gate of the nunnery that was on the street adjacent to the Police Headquarters. One of the sisters let me in. Three months later I became converted."

Editor's Postscript

In Document 543 Resnik mentions the following two points, which help round out the Oswald Rufeisen story:

1) "There in the nunnery he suffered a nervous breakdown and adopted the Christian faith.

2) "When he left the nunnery he joined the Russian partisans, where we met again. The Russians wanted to shoot him as a former German commander. But the Jewish partisans who knew him and they whose lives he had saved, now, in turn, saved his life."

On December 6, 1962, Oswald (Shmuel) Rufeisen became the subject of a heated controversy, both in Israel and abroad, when on that day the Israel Supreme Court handed down a 4–1 majority ruling denying him the status of "Jew" under the Law of Return. The circumstances leading to this ruling are described in the following excerpt from the official record of the Supreme Court of Israel:

The decision of Supreme Court of Israel
in the case of:
OSWALD RUFEISEN, Petitioner
vs. MINISTER OF INTERIOR, Respondent

The High Court, by majority decision, discharged an order nisi calling on the Minister of Interior to show cause why he should not grant the petitioner an immigrant's visa under the Law of Return, 1950.

The petitioner, Oswald Rufeisen, known as Father Daniel, a Carmelite monk, was born in Poland to Jewish parents. He was brought up as a Jew, and belonged to a Zionist youth movement. During the Nazi occupation of Poland he rescued hundreds of his fellow Jews from the Gestapo in legendary feats of daring. While hiding from the Nazis in a Catholic convent, he was converted to Catholicism. In 1945, when the war had ended, he joined the Carmelite Order in the hope that he would be transferred to one of its monasteries in Palestine. In 1958, he was finally permitted by the Order to come to Israel. In his application to the authorities to be allowed to leave Poland he gave as his reason for wishing to go to Israel the fact that he was a Jew, albeit of the Catholic religion, and had always wanted to live in his ancestral homeland.

His application to leave was granted only after he had renounced his Polish nationality. He was given a travel document similar to those given to all Jews emigrating from Poland to Israel.

When Father Daniel arrived in Israel, he applied for an immigrant's certificate and declared himself a Jew for purposes of registration in the Register of Inhabitants. He was not registered as a Jew and his application for a certificate was refused by the then Minister of Interior, Mr. Bar Yehuda, who wrote to him saying that in his own personal opinion he was fully entitled to be recognized as a Jew but that he was powerless to grant him the certificate he sought in view of a decision of the Government that only a person who in good faith declares himself to be a Jew and has no other religion should be registered as a Jew. Mr. Bar Yehuda concluded his letter to Father Daniel with the apologetic explanation that a Minister may not act according to his own lights and concepts but must act within the existing lawful limitations while continuing to press for their amendment.

Father Daniel eventually petitioned the High Court for an order nisi which was granted him.

Section 2 of the Law of Return provides that every Jew has the right to come to Israel as an immigrant, while section 3(a) lays down that "a Jew who has come to Israel and subsequent to his arrival has expressed his desire to settle in Israel may, while still in Israel, receive an immigrant's certificate."

Though puzzled and disappointed by the ruling, Father Daniel nevertheless stated that: "The profound earnestness with which the Justices dealt with the case has given me deep satisfaction." And he defended the State of Israel from those who, on the basis of the ruling, condemned it. "My rights as a future subject of Israel have not been prejudiced in the least," he said, "and to exploit the occasion for vilifying the State of Israel is unwarranted." (*The Jerusalem Post,* December 18, 1962.)

Father Daniel continues to live in Israel and to this day maintains a warm friendship with his former fellow partisan, Jacob Greenstein.

The Little Doctor—A Resistance Hero

By Leonard Tushnet

[EDITOR'S NOTE: *No account of Jewish resistance to Nazism can be complete without mention of the role of the Jewish doctor in that struggle, especially with the partisans in the forests. Whether in strictly Jewish or mixed detachments the Jewish doctor performed his duty under the most adverse conditions imaginable. Lacking adequate facilities and medical supplies, he frequently resorted to improvisation, turning primitive tools into surgical instruments in order to minister to the urgent needs of the wounded fighters.*

But some doctors were not satisfied with just healing the fighters against Fascism, they had to be combatants themselves. Dr. Yehezkel Atlas belongs to that category. Though small in physical stature he rose to legendary heights as a commander of a Jewish partisan detachment, an intrepid fighter, and brilliant strategist.

The author of this dramatic story, Leonard Tushnet, is himself a practicing physician, residing in New Jersey. For years he has done research in certain medical aspects of the holocaust. His most recent books are To Die With Honor: The Uprising of the Jews in the Warsaw Ghetto *(Citadel, 1965), and* The Uses of Adversity: Studies on Starvation in the Warsaw Ghetto *(New York: Thomas Yoseloff, 1966).*]

———◆———

ALMOST ALL the doctors in the Polish resistance movement were Jewish. And the entire Russian partisan forces owe a great deal to a little Jewish doctor in Byelorussia.

Dr. Yehezkel Atlas was born in 1910, in Chornski Gora, near Lodz, Poland. His father was a small merchant of modest means. After a typical Jewish Orthodox education and completion of courses open to Jews in the secular schools, the young Atlas was faced with the usual

253

problem of Jews who wanted to study medicine, but who were held back by the *numerus clausus:* He could be baptized a Christian or he could leave the country for study elsewhere. He chose the latter course. He went to the University of Bologna, from which he received the M. D. degree early in 1939.

He returned to Poland just before the outbreak of World War II. When the Nazis overran Poland, Dr. Atlas with his parents and his seventeen-year-old sister Celina, a dental student, fled with thousands of other Jews into that part of the country which had been taken over by the Soviet forces. The family settled in Kozlowszczyzna, in the Slonim district of western Byelorussia. Here he began to practice medicine.

Two years of disturbed peace followed, with uncertainty mounting as the situation of the Jews under Nazi domination deteriorated. Refugees escaping across the border brought with them horrible tales of torture and genocide. Despite the Nazi-Soviet nonaggression treaty, there was an unsettled atmosphere, felt more by the Jews than by their neighbors. Finally on June 22, 1941, with the Nazi invasion of the Soviet Union, the situation of the Jews became desperate.

The Slonim district quickly fell under the attacks of the Germans. Bitter persecution followed in the form of inhuman decree after inhuman decree, reducing the Jews to the status of barely tolerated beasts of burden and culminating in the setting up of ghettos in preparation for the "Final Solution" of the Jewish problem by disease, starvation, and extermination.

In May, 1942, the ghetto of Kozlowszcyzna was liquidated. Heyk, the Gestapo leader of Slonim, arrived with a squad of Lithuanians notorious for their hatred of Jews. On his order, all the Jews of the town with the exception of Dr. Atlas were taken out to the market place and shot, and their bodies were then dumped into a mass grave.

When the extermination squad came to Dr. Atlas' house, his parents were seized immediately. There was some hesitation about his sister. When Dr. Atlas said she was his sister and not his wife, she was taken too. He was spared because doctors were badly needed by the Nazis. For the rest of his life, he reproached himself for this needless adherence to the truth; he said that had he followed Abraham's example in reverse (*Genesis:* 20:2), his sister would have been saved from the general massacre.

The German administration sent him to be the local physician in the village of Wielka Wola, on the River Szczara. The village was surrounded by dense forests, those of Ruda Jaworska, Dombrowszczyzna, and Lipiczany. For two month he carried on his duties as a doctor here, where medical services had been unavailable in the past. He became popular with the peasants, who showed their appreciation by bringing him food to supplement the official rations. Busy as he was, he could not drive out of his mind the desire to try to destroy the Nazis. The thought of vengeance seemed but a fantasy, however, while the Germans were winning victory after victory.

This period of despair ended when the peasants, realizing that he could be trusted, told him that there lived in the forests groups of former Soviet soldiers left behind in the retreat, as well as scattered active communist party members who had fled from the village. The forest dwellers were unorganized, each concerned with his own problems: to stay alive, to heal his wounds, to get arms and ammunition for defense against the exploratory and punitive raids of the Nazis into the forests.

When Dr. Atlas learned of their existence, he was enthusiastic. He saw the possibility of building a guerrilla force in the future, one that would harass and ultimately destroy the Nazis. The peasants had informed him that large caches of arms abandoned by the Soviet forces in their hasty retreat were hidden nearby. With the aid of several friendly peasants, Atlas made contact with a small band of the forest dwellers. He brought them food, applied his medical knowledge to the treatment of their wounds, and directed them to the hidden weapons.

He remained in the village, using his post as a source of information. He saw no point in joining the forest dwellers at this time. But on July 24, 1942, came the dreadful news of the liquidation of the Dereczyn Ghetto, about thirty kilometers from Wielka Wola. There, hundreds of Jews had been murdered by the Germans, their Lithuanian contingents, and the local police. Only a score of Jews, those who had been safely concealed during the slaughter, had escaped.

During the following nights, they fled across fields and swamps to nearby forests. Eleven reached the woods near Wielka Wola, where they met Dr. Atlas on one of his missions. Bella Hirschhorn, one of the refugees who later became a nurse with the partisans, described him as "a lean but handsome young man, with blue eyes and curly brown hair, wearing a peasant shirt and high Russian boots, and carrying a revolver in his belt."

The refugees told Atlas their sad tale. They informed him that they wanted to join the partisan group, which they had heard was in the forest. Atlas was forced to tell them that this group was not yet organized as a fighting partisan unit, but he encouraged them and led them into a safe clearing before he left them. He later returned with food and weapons.

The Nazi occupation forces had threatened the peasants of the vicinity with death if they sheltered Jews or gave any aid to refugees. The decree began to be enforced by public hangings. The peasants reluctantly withdrew their help from the forest dwellers, who quickly felt the effects.

Dr. Atlas sensed that the situation was becoming desperate. He left the village to live permanently in the forest. With the few survivors of the Dereczyn massacre and several other stragglers as a nucleus, he organized a Jewish partisan band, the first of many guerrilla troops to be formed in that area.

He worked feverishly, for he knew that there was little time left. The efficient German war machine was about ready to clear the forests of the "illegal" occupants. There were those who could not join the fighters because of illness or wounds. For these helpless ones, Atlas organized support but he felt that that was not his main task. The Jewish partisans were not to be a self-help organization; they were to be fighters. Arms were taken care of carefully, and supplies were gathered until the "Little Doctor" thought he was ready for combat.

His original purpose was to destroy the German garrison at Dereczyn and execute judgment on the Germans and their helpers. The increasingly strict Nazi decrees, however, had squeezed scores of Soviet soldiers out of their hiding places in the villages and forced them to seek refuge in the forests.

Solely because of their numbers, they were forced to form more or less organized groups, and soon these coalesced into guerrilla bands. A central partisan command was set up under Boris Boolet. The Jewish partisans were under the control of the central command, which was not at all glad to have them. Jews were traditionally peaceful people. But their recent tribulations had impressed many of them with the need for self-preservation at any cost, and others with a careless disregard for human lives— their own or others'. Atlas was put off when he asked for permission to act according to his plan.

He became weary of waiting. His importunities finally wore down the partisan command. On August 10, 1942, permission was granted to attack Dereczyn. Atlas set out at the head of his men. He feared that because of his medical training he would be called on to act as field surgeon. To forestall such an event, he took Bella Hirschhorn along to give first aid.

In the battle that followed, the Jewish partisans showed amazing bravery. They succeeded in driving out the Germans and seized the town. On the mass grave of the Dereczyn Jews, they executed forty-four policemen before they retired with fresh arms and equipment taken from the garrison.

This victory, one of the first in the entire partisan movement, spread the fame of Commander Atlas throughout the forests. The Russians, who had been skeptical of the fighting talents of the Jews, now accepted them fully. The Jewish partisans became known as the Atlasites. The partisan command itself had been urging Dr. Atlas to be a military surgeon because of the shortage of medical men, but now they desisted, deciding that Atlas was more valuable as a military leader.

The Jewish partisans equipped themselves well with the booty of Dereczyn. They now all had high Russian boots, leather knapsacks, and shirts, as well as good small arms and ammunition. Their fresh military appearance, no less than their initial success, welded them into a disciplined organization far different from the original bunch of despairing, ragged refugees. All young people, they felt themselves a band of avengers of their kinsmen. They were, for good reason, filled with hatred for the Nazis, and expressed it in quite dramatic ways.

Dr. Atlas . . . told his company: "We must not settle down and take things easy, lads. Our struggle only began with the defeat of the Germans at Dereczyn. Your lives came to an end in the slaughter of the 24th of July. Every additional day of life is not yours, but belongs to your murdered families. You must avenge them." He asked every candidate who wished to join the company: "What do you want?" The answer expected was: "I want to die fighting the enemy."

One episode, from a later period, illustrates the exaggerated sense of high adventure shared by Atlas and his group. He had made a vow to say Kaddish over the graves of his parents and sister. One night, together with a companion, Berik, who had had relatives in Kozlowszczyzna, he stole away from the camp. With the greatest care they made their way to their destination, where, under the very noses of the Germans, with weapons at the ready, they recited the Kaddish over the mass graves. They returned safely to camp, Atlas satisfied that his vow had been fulfilled.

This exploit made him more glamorous than before to the Jews of the forests. But his other qualities endeared him to his own group even more. To them, he was the very personification of justice and truth. Despite the fact that he was an intellectual as well as a physician—both honorable titles to Jews—he never looked down on his men, most of whom had been workers. He treated them as equals, never shouting but trying to explain and convince. He set an example for all to follow; and they did, reasoning that if an educated man could find nothing too hard or too demeaning to do, how much more should simple folk do the same things?

At this time the partisans were quite vague as to their role, other than to harass the Germans by petty ambushes or to kill isolated Nazis. The central command had not yet made contact with the Soviet forces. The idea of sabotage from the rear by derailing trains, burning bridges, or blowing up ammunition stores was discussed but no definite plans were made.

Atlas, however, did not wait for special orders. On August 15, he set out with several fighters from his group to a place twenty kilometers away, near the town of Belitza on the River Niemen. His goal was to burn the bridge over which the Germans transported military equipment eastward. On their way they met people fleeing in terror from Zhatel (Zdzientziol), where a general slaughter of the inhabitants had taken place. From them, they heard that a special German *Straf-Expedizie* was on its way. In spite of the news they pressed on, and did not turn back until they saw the bridge collapse in flames.

The Jewish partisans had plenty of small arms but needed the explosives necessary for acts of major sabotage. Atlas succeeded once in wrangling two large shells from the central command. He personally removed the detonator mechanisms so that ordinary grenade fuses could be used. His unit set out for the Rozhanka station where, on August 24, they derailed a train, the first such operation in the region. More derailments soon took place; other partisan groups followed their example.

Emboldened by their victories, the Atlasites, with additional partisan support, attacked Kozlowszcyzna. They were defeated, but the Atlasites had a new tale to tell about their commander.

The Germans were fortified in a woods near the River Szczara; the partisans were on the opposite bank. A large group of German soldiers tried to cross the river in boats, but halfway across met the withering fire of the partisans. Most of the troops drowned; the others swam back and withdrew in confusion to their own lines.

The partisans saw two Ukrainians start to wade out of the river and try to get to their posts about one hundred meters away. Dr. Atlas sprang into the stream, followed a moment later by Elijah Kowensky. Swimming rapidly, they overtook their enemies, seized and killed them, then swam back across the river under a hail of bullets.

The unsuccessful attack on Kozlowszcyzna triggered new German moves to clear the area of the partisans. An expanded guard force was sent to Ruda, a village in the heart of the forest. The presence of German troops and outposts, as well as the increasingly frequent punitive sorties into the forests, limited the movements of the partisans. It became urgent to drive out the Nazis.

The Atlasites attacked the Ruda forces on October 8, 1942. They drove out the garrison and held the surrounding area for a short time only, but long enough to gather considerable first-class arms and new equipment vitally necessary for the rapidly approaching winter.

Dr. Atlas feared the coming bitter winter of Byelorussia and the snows that would hamper the mobility of the partisans. In addition, the tracks of the partisans could be easily followed to their secret camps. There was little he could do other than preserve the health and welfare of his men and women throughout the dangerous months ahead. He ordered the digging of large underground caves; he gathered food supplies. In his new capacity as work-organizer, he led with the same fine example as when fighting.

In a very short time—much shorter than he had expected—winter quarters were ready, well stocked with flour, meat, potatoes, and dried vegetables. Arms were kept in good order. Again the farseeing military leader, Dr. Atlas decided to forestall the inevitable boredom of enforced idleness among his company. Before the winter was well under way, he started operations against the enemy. Nazi troops were ambushed, supply convoys intercepted, trains derailed.

The Germans resolved to put an end to the petty guerrilla warfare that, from their point of view, was a hopeless attempt to stem the tide of Hitler's army, but which nonetheless diverted their efforts and slowed them down in their "march to final victory." Troops withdrawn from the Eastern Front, with added fresh reserves, were concentrated in the area. On November 21, 1942, a concerted attack was made on the partisans. Although it was not completely successful, great casualties were inflicted. Among those fatally wounded was Dr. Atlas, at the head of his fighting group near Wielki Oblovic. His last words were: "Lads, I appoint Elik Lipszowicz to take my place. Pay no attention to me. Go on fighting."

The Atlasites, their number sharply reduced after this attack, became part of a Soviet partisan regiment. Dr. Atlas was posthumously awarded a Hero's Medal by the Soviet Union. He had been a military commander for less than six months, but his actions in that crucial early time of the formation of the partisan movement left behind a clear line of moral struggle for the Jewish fighters who later distinguished themselves in the war against Hitlerism.

I used the following sources for this account: (1) Zvi Szner, ed., *Extermination and Resistance: Historical Records and Source Material,* Vol. 1, Kibbutz Dohamei, Haghittavat, Israel, 1958; (2) *Sefer Ha-Partisonim,* Vol. 1, Hashomer Hatzair, Tel Aviv, Israel, 1956; (3) Moishe Kaganovich, *Di Milhome fun di Idishe Partisaner in Mizrah-Ukrain* (The War of the Jewish Partisans in Eastern Ukraine), Band 1, Zentral Farband fun Poilishe Idn in Argentina, Buenos Aires, 1956.

Diadia Misha (Uncle Misha) and His Partisans: The Blowing Up of the Soldiers' Home

By Misha Gildenman

[EDITOR'S NOTE: *By profession he was an engineer and his real name was Misha Gildenman. But in the forests of Zhitomir (Soviet Ukraine), he was known as Diadia Misha, the legendary commander of a detachment of Jewish partisans numbering in the hundreds. In his reminiscences which he wrote after the war he describes the events leading to his escape from the ghetto of Koretz (Volhynia), together with his son, Simcha, and sixteen other Jews.*[33]

"I witnessed the first 'action in our town . . . ," he writes. *"It was on a beautiful spring day on the eve of Shevuot, the Feast of Weeks. . . . Near a pit 20 by 20 meters long and three meters deep stood a table with bottles of cognac and food. At the table sits a German with an automatic gun in his hand. Frightened and despairing Jews are pushed into the pit naked, six at a time. The German orders them to lie on the ground, face down. Between one sip of cognac and the next he shoots them. Among the 2,200 Jews the Germans shot that day were also my wife and my 13-year-old daughter.*

"The massacre lasted from 4 A.M. to 4 P.M., and in the evening of that day when the surviving Jews met in the synagogue to rend their garments and say Kaddish for the dead, a voice cried out in me: 'not with prayers will you assuage our grief for the rivers of innocent blood that was spilled —but with revenge!' As soon as the Kaddish was over I banged the table and cried out: 'Listen to me, unfortunate, death-condemned Jews! . . . Know that sooner or later we are all doomed. But I shall not go like a sheep to the slaughter!' '"

From then on Gildenman concentrated on plans to escape to the forest and join the partisans. He found others who joined him, but all of their efforts to obtain weapons yielded a single pistol and five rounds of ammunition.

On September 23, 1942, when the Germans and their Ukrainian helpers again surrounded the ghetto and its liquidation was imminent, Gilden-

man held a hurried meeting with the others, who now numbered sixteen, and they decided to leave at once. They arranged to meet in the home of a friendly Gentile on the outskirts of town, and in groups of three and four they slipped out of the ghetto.

Their most urgent problem was weapons. They attacked a forester and took away his hunting gun.[34] Next they ambushed a group of policemen who were rounding up Ukrainian youth for slave labor in Germany. They killed six of them and took away their weapons. Emboldened by their success they raided a police station and came into possession of a small arsenal. And they were steadily growing in number. Other Jews who were wandering in the forest attached themselves to the group.

But they soon discovered that this area was not safe; bands of Bandarov's Ukrainian Fascists were roaming the forest.[35] Misha and his group moved on to the region of Zhitomir and there formed a partisan detachment consisting mainly of Jews.

Sometime in 1943, on orders from the Partisan High Command in Moscow, Diadia Misha recruited the local Ukrainian youth into his detachment. But he remained its commander throughout, with his son as chief of intelligence.

When the advancing Red Army reached Diadia Misha's area of operations and the partisans were incorporated into military units, Marshal Klementi Voroshilov himself, chief of the Partisan High Command, suggested to Diadia Misha that he remain behind the lines as engineer. But he declined the offer, saying: "I have a final account to settle with Hitler in Berlin proper. . . ." He went through an officers' training course and entered Berlin with the rank of captain.

After the war Diadia Misha lived for a number of years in Paris and later emigrated to Israel, where he recently died. His son, Simcha, now resides in Israel.]

AUGUST, 1943.

Every day the radio brings happy reports of hundreds of towns and villages freed by the Red Army, and of thousands of Germans taken prisoner. The partisans are elated. They feel that the difficult, abnormal life in the forests will soon come to an end, and that the hour is near when they will make contact with the Red Army.

Every night we await the Russian planes which drop weapons, ammunition, and medicine to us by parachute. The commanders of the partisan detachments have received orders from Moscow not to send any more groups on sabotage missions so that every detachment may be ready "in corpore" to merge with the Red Army.

At that time we were in the dense forests of the Ovrutch region. In all the nearby towns and villages we had our contacts who used to inform us of the moods of the Germans and the civilian population with regard to the great victories of the Red Army.

One day our Ovrutch contact, whose name was Keril, brought us the following news: A large group of policemen of the Ovrutch police station was ready to surrender to the partisans and to take with them all their arms. He also informed us that the important Greek Orthodox holiday, "Sfas" would be celebrated on August 20 and on that day one would be allowed to enter and leave the town without the special permission usually required for entering the town by the roads or the big bridge that were always guarded by German and Ukrainian police. This exception was made thanks to the intervention of the Greek Orthodox clergy in order to attract a larger number of worshippers to the big church that bore the name of the holiday, "Sfas."

I decided to take advantage of this situation and sent out that day to Ovrutch several partisans to familiarize themselves with the town, find out which institutions were functioning, which military units were stationed there and, generally, to assess the mood of the town. I had been considering the rather daring idea of making a surprise attack on the town before the Red Army marched in and of destroying the railway station and the bridge to the main artery that led from Shepetovka to Chernigov through Ovrutch.

Together with the band of partisans I sent along Motele. The least suspicious looking of the group, the boy was to get in touch with the partisans, observe them from a distance, and inform me at once if anything happened to any of them.

Motele took along his violin in the wooden violin case and he was supposed to pose as a little beggar playing in front of the church and collecting alms. As an added precaution I gave him a document made out in the name of Dimitri Rubina, son of Ivan Rubina, from the village Listvin, in the Velednik region. If questioned, his excuse was to be that he was on his way to Zhitomir in search of his father, who, presumably, was in a Russian prisoner-of-war camp. The document was properly stamped with forged stamps made by one of our partisans, a former stampmaker.

The big church, surrounded by a high white wall, looked like a medieval fortress. A whole gallery of beggars and cripples, some standing, others squatting, at the entrance of the church, tried to evoke sympathy from the holiday crowd in a variety of voices and gestures. Motele was the last in the row. He sat down, took out his violin, and placed between his legs a clay saucer he had bought in the market.

Motele knew many Ukrainian songs. He had learned them in his village, where he used to stand for hours in front of the church listening to the beggars' singing and playing. Now he tuned up his violin and in his pleasant voice began to sing the song of the "Ant." His young voice and violin playing set him apart from the rest of the beggars' chorus. A crowd began to gather around him and when he had finished the song, peasants threw lead coins into his clay saucer and peasant women put pirogy into the linen sack he carried on his back.

Suddenly a commotion arose in the crowd and people began to push back and make way for a German officer who appeared, accompanied by a German nurse. The officer walked up to the place where Motele sat and stood there, listening to his singing and playing. Motele did not notice him. When the German touched Motele's shoulder with his riding crop the boy raised his head and, seeing the officer, rose to his feet and bowed.

"Come with me," the German commanded.

Motele put his hand in his pocket to make sure he still had the document. Then he put the violin back in the case, gathered up the coins in the saucer, and followed the officer. After passing several blocks, they came to a one-story building in front of which were parked many limousines and motorcycles. A German guard stood at the entrance. They went up one flight to a large bright hall where officers sat around tables eating, drinking, and talking loudly. In one corner of the hall stood a brown piano at which sat an elderly gray-haired man, wearing a black dress coat. The officer led Motele over to the man and said something to him.

"Do you read notes?" the man asked Motele in Russian.

"Yes," the boy replied.

The pianist selected a sheet of music and placed it before Motele, who tuned up his violin and began to play with the man accompanying him at the piano. It was Paderewski's Minuet—when they had finished there was a burst of applause.

Motele was offered the job of playing in the Soldiers' Home for two hours at lunchtime and from seven to eleven in the evening. For this he would receive two marks per day, lunch and dinner.

He could not decide what to do. First, he said, he must go to Zhitomir and find his father. He also told the German that he had left a sick mother with three children at home whose sole provider he was. The officer promised him to write to the regional commandant of Zhitomir about his father and if he was really there, in the prisoner-of-war camp, he would have him transferred to Ovrutch. Motele had to agree to this proposal, and remained in the Soldiers' Home.

When he had finished playing, he went to see our contact, Keril, and asked him to inform me about the situation he was in. I ordered him to remain there, observe everything carefully, and keep me posted through Keril.

The Soldiers' Home was one of the many restaurants which the Germans had set up for their military forces, where they received the best food and the finest French wine for the cheapest prices, and they were served in more ways than one by young and pretty Ukrainian waitresses. All this was to raise the spirits of the soldiers on the way to the terrible Eastern Front from which few returned alive and unwounded.

Motele played at the restaurant and memorized the numbers of units and the types of uniforms the Germans wore on the way to the front. He eavesdropped on conversations of those who had returned from the front. Between lunch and dinner he wandered around town, read the signs on government institutions, noted the streets he was on and later relayed all this information to me through Keril. The director of the Soldiers' Home was satisfied with the talented and modest young musician. The elderly pianist, a Volks-Deutsche whose home was not far from Korosten, became very friendly with Motele and was delighted with his musical skills.

Thus, two weeks passed. One day the regional commandant, who used to spend every evening at the restaurant, ordered Motele to appear the next morning at nine in his office. When Motele arrived, somewhat frightened, the commandant gave him a friendly reception, called in the military tailor, and ordered a German uniform and cap for the boy. A few days later Motele came into the Soldiers' Home dressed as a little soldier. The pianist and the other employees seemed highly pleased.

Motele ate lunch and dinner in the kitchen, which was located in the basement. On the way down from the first floor one had to pass a dimly lit corridor. On its right were the kitchen and laundry; on its left some storage rooms. The fat cook served Motele the tastiest dishes in return for which they boy played for him his favorite song, "Rose-Marie."

One afternoon when Motele came out of the kitchen, he noticed that the door to one of the storage rooms was open. Out of curiosity he peered in and, by the dim light from a small grated window, he saw a large cellar filled with empty wine cases, herring barrels, and other useless things scattered about in disorder. He noticed that the wall opposite the entrance was cracked, apparently by a bomb explosion nearby, during a bombardment. It was a crooked crack, veering leftward.

Remembering the stories he had heard the partisans tell about their various sabotage acts an idea flashed through his mind: If a mine could be stuck in the crack of the wall, the explosion would destroy the Soldiers' Home together with the hated German officers. The idea gave him no rest, and every time he passed the corridor he peered into the basement and thought of such a sabotage act.

He wasted no time and passed on his plan to me through Keril. I, too, liked the idea and so I delegated Popov, our mine manufacturer as we called him, to meet with Motele and find out the precise details.

It was harvest time. Peasants went back and forth between Ovrutch and the fields. The guards at the town's exit were not as strict as usual. Keril piled up a wagonload of straw sheafs for binding hay and rode out into the field. The German guard who allowed Keril to pass over the bridge did not, of course, suspect that underneath the heap of straw twists lay a Jewish boy who planned to blow up the Soldiers' Home.

At the appointed place, five kilometers out of town, Popov was already waiting for them. Motele presented his plan. Popov inquired thoroughly about the thickness of the walls, whether they were brick or stone, the distance Motele would have to run after igniting the wick, and many other details. Popov figured out that it would take eighteen kilograms of the explosive available to me at that time.

A few days later Popov brought a bag full of the explosive to the same place. Keril again came with Motele, and Popov began to teach him how to assemble the little blocks of *tal* and how to make a mine, how to insert the capsule detonator, etc. All this was not entirely unfamiliar to Motele. He used to watch Popov teach the partisans how to do it. After the lesson Keril took Motele and the explosive to his house.

Now came the difficult task of transporting the explosive material to the cellar of the Soldiers' Home. But Motele found a way. In the evening, after dinner, when he said goodby to the cook, he took his violin with him. He passed through the cellar door and hurried inside. Then he took the violin out of its case and put it inside an empty barrel and left the Soldiers' Home with the empty violin case. On the second day when he came to the Home at lunchtime to play he had in his violin case three kilograms of the explosive. Before he went up to the hall to play he went as always first to the kitchen for his lunch. He looked about him cautiously, then entered the cellar, took the *tal* out of the violin case and put the violin back in. In several days he had thus transported all the eighteen kilograms of the explosive into the cellar.

Later he used every opportunity to go down to the basement and remove some stones from the wall to enlarge the opening in which to place the bomb. He followed Popov's instructions, then inserted the capsule with the long Bickford wick, and camouflaged it. All that was left to do was ignite the end of the wick and realize the act of revenge which was his dream.

Whenever he had free time, Motele worked out with Keril the details connected with the plan. They would go daily to the lake, ostensibly to catch fish or to bathe. Actually they were looking for a shallow spot that would make it possible for Motele to cross when he escaped after the explosion. They took careful note of the streets and orchards through which Motele would have to run to the lake, on the other side of which the partisans were to wait for him and take him to the woods. Everything was ready. Motele was merely awaiting the proper moment.

There was much excitement in the Soldiers' Home. High-ranking guests were expected. A division of SS was on the way to the Eastern Front to rescue the situation and to encourage the disorganized German armies after the severe blows they had received in the area of Kursk. Because of the insecurity of the railway lines—according to statistics every fifth train was blown up by partisans—the SS division was transferred at Korosten from railway cars to trucks and now it was on the way to Chernigov via Ovrutch-Mazir.

Around three in the afternoon automobiles and motorcycles began to arrive in front of the Soldiers' Home. The rooms were filled with elegantly-uniformed SS officers. They ate and drank. Above the din of clanking dishes, clinking glasses, and loud laughter, Motele's violin was heard to the piano's accompaniment. The officers amused themselves and sang. From time to time they ordered Motele and the pianist to play tangos and waltzes to which they danced. With few interruptions Motele played throughout the afternoon and evening.

At eleven o'clock the accompanist finally induced the director to put an end to the playing. There were some officers who could play the piano, so they took over and continued with the entertainment. As usual Motele went down to the kitchen to have his dinner. He was too exhausted to eat and explained to the cook that because he had played for eight hours without a stop he had no appetite. Soon afterward he said good night to the cook and left the kitchen. The corridor was dark. His hand groped for the cellar door and found it. He went inside and closed the door behind him. In the dark he found the end of the bomb wick and ignited it. He slipped out of the cellar and ran through the corridor. When he came to the exit he slowed down and approached the German guard and allowed himself a joke. He held up his right arm and called out, "Heil Hitler!"

"Ach, you little Ukrainian swine!" the German said, laughing.

Motele left the Soldiers' Home and quickly disappeared in the darkness. After running about two hundred yards he heard a powerful explosion. The earth trembled and windowpanes shattered. Moments later he heard police whistles and sirens. Red rockets lighted up the sky over the town. Both frightened and elated, Motele hugged the walls of buildings as he ran toward the lake. He entered the cold water which in some places reached his neck and held his violin above his head with both hands. He glanced back to the city and saw a big fire shooting up into the sky.

On the other side of the shore, at the foot of a small hill, a wagon waited for Motele. On it were five well-armed partisans. Ten hands reached out to hoist the boy into the wagon. With lightning speed the horses—the best in our detachment—galloped away and disappeared into the nearest woods.

For the first few minutes Motele was speechless. Gradually he calmed down and, raising his clenched fists to the red sky, said in a trembling voice, "This is for my parents and little Bashiale, my sister."

Editor's Postscript

In his account of Jewish children who displayed heroism as partisans, Kaganovich brings some additional information about twelve-year-old Motele, based on Diadia Misha's memoir. When Diadia Misha's partisans discovered a boy sleeping in the woods, he gave his name as Mitka and they thought he was a Ukrainian. Later they learned that he was Jewish, the son of a miller, and that he was born in Krasnuvka, a village in Volhynia.

"By coincidence," writes Kaganovich, "Motele was not at home when Germans and Ukrainians killed his father, mother and little sister. That same night he escaped to the woods and hired himself out to peasants as shepherd, for his room and board. In Diadia Misha's detachment the clever, daring and alert boy was utilized for intelligence and espionage work." In addition to blowing up the German Soldiers' Home, Motele is credited with, among other things, saving the lives of two Jewish children and a Russian partisan, and with shooting a German to death with his revolver. Motele fell in battle shortly before liberation. He was crawling over to a new position to warn the Soviet officers of an impending danger when he was struck by a German bullet.[36]

Diadia Misha and His Partisans: The Attack

By Misha Gildenman

FOR A LONG time we had been planning to stage an attack on the town of Rozvazhev, which is situated in the woodsy region between the Zhitomir and Kiev districts. During the long winter nights at the partisan campfires we would work out the details of this very risky operation. The precise plan of the town was drawn for us by one of two newly-arrived partisans. They also told us the streets on which the German officers were located, the number of German units and where they were billeted, as well as the safest entrances and exits to and from town.

We decided to attack on the night of December 31, 1942, past midnight on the assumption that while the military and their officers would be busy ushering in the new year their vigilance would be considerably weakened. We hoped that this attack would yield us a quantity of provisions of which, according to our information, the warehouses of Rozvazhev were full. Mainly, we needed fur coats and blankets because the temperature had already dropped to 25° below zero.

Before midnight we were already at the outskirts of the town and stopped to rest after marching twenty kilometers on the snow-covered forest paths. From a partisan's standpoint the night was ideal. The snow fell heavily from the leaden clouds that hung low, wrapping the night in a blanket of gray. A sharp eastern wind blew all around us, bringing to mind the howling of wolves.

The entire success of the operation depended on the swiftness with which it was carried out. That was why I divided my detachment into several groups, assigning to each a separate task. At a given signal they were to storm the town simultaneously.

At exactly one o'clock I gave the signal and the attack began. One group went straight to the headquarters of the Ukrainian police and tossed several grenades into the brightly lit hall where policemen sat around tables, eating and drinking. A great confusion arose. It increased when several policemen who ran out of the building were met by a hail of partisan bullets and were forced back in again. Within a matter of minutes the police surrendered. The partisans disarmed the chief and his aides, tied them up, and took them along.

A second group, the so-called liaison command, occupied the post office, smashed all the installations and cut the telephone and telegraph wires, thus isolating Rozvazhev from the rest of the world. They also destroyed the local connections.

A third group surrounded the school building in which a German garrison numbering 200 men was quartered. It was ordered to blockade the building and prevent the Germans from coming to the aid of the gendarmerie.

The fourth group had the most difficult assignment. It had to liquidate the gendarmerie, which was armed and stationed in the brick church buildings, surrounded by a high stone wall. After a bitter battle that lasted more than half an hour the partisans did not succeed in getting into the courtyard of the church. The gendarmerie set up machine guns on the roof tops and repulsed every partisan attack. The commander of the group then placed two mines under the stone wall and exploded it. In the ensuing confusion the partisans were able to get inside and commence the liquidation. Only a few gendarmes escaped with their lives by hiding in the cellars or disappearing into the darkness.

In the meantime the appropriation group emptied the military pharmacy of the medicines that we needed, and made a thorough search of the warehouses, which were stocked with flour, frozen ham, tobacco, and French wine.

When my groups set out to carry through their assignments, I and ten other partisans, including one of the two men from Rozvazhev, advanced toward the private residence of the regional commandant which was situated on a side street near the post office. I was certain that on so festive a night the commandant would, most likely, celebrate in his home with other officers.

After midnight the snowstorm had grown in force to such proportions that the howling of the wind drowned out the rifle shots and the grenade explosions as well as the noises of all the other battles fought in various parts of town. Moving stealthily along the walls of the houses, we came to the residence of the regional commandant. Near the entrance stood an armed German guard. Standing there in his big fur coat with upturned collar and his clumsy-looking straw boots with wooden soles that the Germans wore on the cold Eastern Front, he looked like an overblown puppet.

Suddenly, as though from nowhere, one of my partisans appeared before the German and, with one well-aimed blow on the head with the butt of the rifle, killed him on the spot. When I peered into the house through the frosted windowpanes I saw seated around the table nine officers, their uniforms buttoned up, their faces flushed. The table was laden with food and drinks; the room was filled with cigar smoke. The eyes of the drunken officers were on the beautiful woman, who stood in the middle of the room, singing a Russian love song and accompanying herself on a guitar.

We pushed the door open, stormed into the room, and began shooting at the officers. The attack was so swift and unexpected that only one officer managed to whip out his pistol and shoot in our direction, wounding one of my partisans. But he soon fell to the floor with a bullet in his head. Within a matter of minutes all the officers were dead. Some slid down under the table, the others remained seated with their heads in their plates. During the action the woman remained standing in the middle of the room, her eyes expressing more astonishment than fear. She was standing motionless with the guitar in her hand like a statue. Only when one of my partisans grabbed her arm and shook her vehemently did she come out of her petrified state and, in a calm voice, said in Russian, "At last you have come."

Diadia Misha and His Partisans: David of Yarevitch

By Misha Gildenman

" 'JANUARY IS NO friend!' " said David of Yarevitch. "The frost gets into your very bones, like the Sabbath horseradish that my grandmother, Mirtche, used to make." He leaned his Russian rifle with its sharp, gleaming bayonet against a tree, and held out his hands, blue from the cold, over the crackling fire the partisans had built. Smiling, he counted the people squatting around the fire, and, in a commanding tone, said, "Are all here? If so, we can get ready for the journey."

A tall young man, carrying a bundle of rags, came over to the fire. A measuring tape hung from his neck, and two needles, one with white and the other with black thread, stuck in his coat lapel. He was Abraham of Vitebsk, the tailor.

I turned to the gathering and said, "Now I will tell you about your objectives." The partisans tossed some fresh branches on the fire and moved over a little closer to me.

"Comrades," I began, "we received a radiogram from Moscow that an armored train consisting of 22 cars is on its way to Kursk. It carries several hundred German pilots who graduated from the pilots' school in Munich. They are supposed to take over the planes that are waiting for them at the airdrome. Yesterday morning the train passed through Proskurov; during the night it will pass through Shepetovka, and today, past midnight or tomorrow at dawn, it will be somewhere between Semigorod and Korosten.

"At the intersection of Semigorod Chopovitchi the train must hit the mine which you will place there. You should know that similar radiograms were also received by the partisan band, '25 Years of Ukrainia,' the 'Shytovcy,' as well as all the other detachments who operate in the forests along the length of the railway line Shepetovka-Chernigov. The train will most certainly not reach the front. But our ambition and national honor demand that the several hundred young German murderers perish from a mine laid by Jewish partisans.

271

"Well, David, you are in charge of this operation. You know the way, and you shall place the mine under the narrow little bridge which I pointed out to you the other week when we crossed the railway line. Let every one of you take along a sufficient supply of rags and when you'll get to the Ovrutch road you will tie them around your shoes. But remember, not a single piece of rag or string must be left behind. After the derailment, when you return to the road, you must quickly remove the rags and take them with you. By this tactic you will achieve a two-fold purpose: the feet wrapped in rags will leave no trace of footsteps on the hard, frozen snow. But mainly, should the Germans, after the explosion, send police dogs after you they will be able to pursue you only up to the point where you removed the rags. Then they will lose the scent and become confused.

"That is all. Be careful, be brave, do not think of death and be confident of victory. The sky is overcast. That means it will be a very dark night. Get ready, because in an hour from now you will be on your way."

The partisans peered earnestly into the fire. Night fell quickly. One of the partisans tossed some fresh pine branches on the fire. They crackled and burned brightly, illuminating the old pine trees standing nearby, their bent branches laden with snow.

David rolled a thick cigarette for himself in a piece of German newspaper and lighted up with a burning twig he pulled from the fire. Then he inhaled the strong tobacco deeply several times and the serious expression on his face changed to a genial smile. He spat vigorously and turned to his comrades: "Why are you sitting here on your haunches? Don't you know that today is the Eve of Purim? Who would have thought that David of Yarevitch, the transport worker, or David, the coachman as he was once called, would, on the Eve of Purim, be hiding out in the woods, armed with grenades, like a forest robber, and prepare to blow up a train carrying German fliers?"

Suddenly he became serious again and, staring thoughtfully ahead of him, spoke, as though to himself: "I can see my father as though he were alive, standing before me in his serge kaftan. . . . We have returned from the synagogue and brought home with us a guest. . . . The room is brightly lit, warm and spic-and-span. . . . The table is covered with a snow-white tablecloth . . . the candles are burning in the polished shining brass candlesticks. . . . On the table lies a big Purim twist . . . a platter of tasty carp and a deep bowl of compote. . . .

"My wife, Sarah," David continued, "wearing a white apron and a red headkerchief over her black curly hair, invites us to the table. . . . On my knees I hold my two dear children. . . ." David fell silent a moment and sighed deeply. "The Germans have murdered them all!" He tossed his cigarette butt into the fire and, raising his clenched fists, cried out, "Revenge! Jews, we must avenge every drop of Jewish blood spilled at the hands of the Germans!"

A hush fell over the partisans. Only the crackling of the dry branches in the fire and the howling of the wolves in the distance could be heard from time to time.

"Better let us talk of our task ahead," David said. "We are going to blow up an armored train. I can just see them, the well-fed, clean-shaven Germans, sitting in their warm compartments, the farewell speeches of their teachers still ringing in their ears. They are on their way to Kursk to take over the planes . . . they are daring, courageous. . . . They think they will enter their steel birds, with the black and white swastikas on the wings, fly over Moscow and drop their bombs. Already they see the Iron Cross and other decorations pinned on their uniforms. . . . But I, the coachman of Yarevitch, think differently. . . . And I will lay the mine under the little bridge. . . . And my report to Diadia Misha will be as follows: 'The assignment you have given me has been carried out! The armored train— its 22 cars and locomotives were blown up and the 333 German fliers have, in the honor of Purim, suffered Haman's fate. . . .'" [36]

The partisans were so spellbound by David's imaginary description of the sabotage act they were about to carry out that they remained silent for some time. Then David gave the command: "Fellows, time to go!"

The partisans rose eagerly from their places and began to tighten their belts, check their weapons, and put the rags into their knapsacks.

"And now let us say a prayer for the journey," David said, turning to his comrades. He took out a small prayer book from his leather holster and in a pleasant voice began to say: "May Thy Will Be Done. . . ." Many of the partisans repeated the prayer after him silently. It was a strange scene—a group of Jews, armed with rifles and hand grenades, praying in the secrecy of a forest.

With great fervor David repeated twice the words of the prayer. "Shield us from every foe." He then pointed to the box containing the mine, which lay near him, and said to Motele of Berznitz, "Tie the *shalachmonuth* [Purim gift] around my back, but do it so that it will not rub against my shoulders. . . . All is ready. We can go."

"May luck be with you, going and coming." With these words we said farewell to David and his group who were going out to avenge their murdered brothers and sisters.

In single file, like shadows, the partisans moved along the narrow forest path and quickly disappeared, swallowed up by the darkness of night.

Editor's Postscript

We learn from Kaganovich [37] that Diadia Misha and his partisans once staged a daring rescue of forty Jews who worked as slave laborers in a sawmill under German supervision. The woman who worked as cook for the police guards of the mill was also an underground courier for the partisans. She informed Diadia Misha that the remaining forty Jews in the mill were about to be liquidated and replaced by Russian prisoners of war. That day, at midnight, Diadia Misha himself led a group of his partisans to the sawmill and liberated the Jews.

In one of his reminiscences, Diadia Misha writes: "When we took the city of Targau (on the Elbe) we liberated a large concentration camp for women. . . . I used to observe the camp inmates as they took their first uncertain steps on German soil as free people. . . . In such moments I thought, 'It was worth suffering hunger, cold and fear as a partisan,' and now to face continuous danger on the front lines, in order to live to see that day when I . . . a son of the 'inferior Jewish race,' have with my own hands flung open the gates of German concentration camps and brought freedom to thousands of people of various nationalities." [38]

The preceding accounts were drawn from the following publications in Yiddish: "The Blowing Up of the Soldiers' Home" and "David of Yarevitch" are from *On the Road to Victory* by Diada Misha (M. Gildenman) (Paris: Yiddishe Folks Bibliotek, n.d.); "The Attack" is from *Jewish Daughters* by Diada Misha (M. Gildenman) (Paris: 1950). See also Moshe Kaganovich, *The War of the Jewish Partisans in Eastern Europe* (Buenos Aires: 1956), vol. I, pp. 170, 239–42.

The Bulgarian Jews in the Resistance Movement

By Matei Yulzari

[EDITOR'S NOTE: *Of all the Slavic countries that came under German domination in World War II, Bulgaria stands alone in her concern for the safety of her Jewish citizens. The church and the professions as well as the general population were all united in the single determination to protect Bulgarian Jewry from the fate that befell the Jewish people in other occupied countries. The anti-Jewish decrees had been issued and the cattle cars were already waiting to transport the victims to the extermination camp. But thanks to the Bulgarian people they remained empty.*

Bulgarian Jews fought bravely alongside their non-Jewish compatriots in a mighty partisan movement that inflicted heavy blows on the Nazis and aided in the country's liberation.

This little-known story is vividly described in the following documented account, written especially for this anthology. Matei Yulzari, born in Yambol in 1909, worked in the Chaim Nachman Bialik Jewish Library and was president of its board until the Fascist police closed it in 1935. He also played an active role in the trade union movement, which on several occasions led to his arrest and torture. At present he is secretary of the Jewish Educational Cultural Association of Bulgaria and a member of its Central Executive Board.]

WHEN NAZISM reached the boundaries of Bulgaria, the Nazis were not resisted, and in fact came as allies of the government of Tsar Boris III of the Coburg dynasty. The close ties between the tsarist camarilla and the Nazis severely tested the courage and dignity of the Bulgarian people. Would the Bulgarian people obediently serve as manure for the Aryan race, or would they take the hard road of resistance?

History witnessed the resolute response of the best forces of the na-

275

tion, starting with the Bulgarian Orthodox Church and the patriotic part of the army officers, and ending with the working class, craftsmen, peasantry, and intellectuals of every political shade. These trends finally took shape in the form of a Fatherland Front, as a bulwark of the resistance movement against the Nazi invaders—an attempt to regain the independence and national sovereignty of Bulgaria.

This is the general background against which the dramatic struggle developed to save the Bulgarian Jews from annihilation.

Acting under Nazi orders, the government consented to the annihilation of the Jewish population and prepared the deportation of Bulgarian Jews to death camps in Eastern Europe. The first step came in the form of a "Law in Defense of the Nation," which factually outlawed Jews. The government intended the law to whip up ill-feelings among business circles and suggest an easy way of eliminating commercial and industrial competition.

But the Bulgarian people immediately realized that the anti-Jewish legislation was only the initial step in a general attempt at their physical liquidation. They did not accept a "Law in Defense of the Nation," directed against compatriots with whom they had lived for centuries in friendship and understanding. The strong reaction of the people against the attempt to suppress the human rights of the Jewish population was expressed in floods of letters and telegrams addressed to parliament, cabinet ministers, statesmen, and social and political leaders. A wave of indignation surged throughout the country. All demanded immediate cessation of the persecution against the Jews. Street demonstrations became common and had to be suppressed by the police by brutal force, imprisonment, and reprisals.

The Union of Bulgarian Writers sent a letter to the government and parliament not to pass a law which would "enslave part of the Bulgarian people and would blemish Bulgaria's modern history." The Executive Council of the Union of Bulgarian Lawyers in a detailed exposé to the government emphasized that the proposed new law would be a blow undermining the Constitution, which explicitly prohibits any "division of the Bulgarian people into higher or lower categories." In a letter to the Minister of the Interior the Executive Council of Bulgarian Doctors expressed its dissatisfaction with the measures being planned against the Jews.

The democratic groups of the opposition also disapproved of the law. Professor Petco Stainov, a member of the Academy of Sciences, declared: "I do not believe in all this talk about the 'pure race.' The pure race is not only a mystic notion, it is a mystification. The law will mean the suspension of fundamental rights on the basis of a sui generis Bulgarian racialism. I consider this to be contrary to Bulgarian history, contrary to the spirit of the Bulgarian National Revival Period, and to the culture and dignity of the Bulgarian people. We are a tolerant people and have a feeling of national dignity."

The Bulgarian Orthodox Church in its representations said, "The draft of this law contains on the one hand grave provisions. On the other, it contains gaps which leave the door open for many dangers to our country and nation. The Bulgarian Orthodox Church feels it its duty to note that the draft of the law contains provisions which cannot be considered just or useful to the interests of the nation. . . ."

In spite of everything, the Fascist majority in parliament in December, 1940, voted and passed the hateful racialist law, which was approved by royal decree on January 21, 1941. This marked the beginning of suffering for the Bulgarian Jewish population. The law set up a Commissariat for the Jewish Problems, which daily issued orders tending to the complete plundering and ruination of Jews, depriving them of elementary rights as citizens: the right to find employment, to education, to choice of place of domicile, to marry at choice, including the right to marry people of Aryan origin, etc. All Jews were obliged to wear a yellow star in the streets, and their homes were marked with the inscription 'Jewish Home.' The law provided for eviction of the Jewish population from the capital to small provincial towns, and mobilization of the males in labor camps.

The communist, social-democrat, and agrarian parties took the Bulgarian Jews under their protection, and all other progressive forces helped in every way they could. With clandestine propaganda, they explained to the Bulgarian people the real sinister designs behind these measures. The underground radio station was used by Vasil Kolarov to tell the Bulgarian people about the mass annihilation of Jews, Poles, Frenchmen, and others by the Nazis in Poland, the Ukraine, Byelorussia, and other territories, and the dangers threatening Bulgaria.

On February 22, 1943, the Commissar for the Jewish Problems, Alexander Belev, and the SS Haupsturmführer Theodor Danecker signed the sinister "Agreement for the deportation of a first batch of 20,000 Jews to the East German Territories." When it gradually became known that the first lot of Jews from the capital and other towns in the country was about to be deported, revolutionary elements in Sofia launched an appeal to the Bulgarian people, saying: "Take your stand before your neighboring Jewish homes and do not let them be led away by force! Hide the children and do not give them to the executioners! Crowd the Jewish quarters and manifest your solidarity with the oppressed Jews!"

We shall always remember the action organized on May 24, 1943, by

THE BULGARIAN JEWS IN THE RESISTANCE MOVEMENT

Jews in Sofia, with the participation of many Bulgarians. It started from the Jewish synagogue in one of the suburbs, where the gathering was addressed by Rabbi Daniel Zion and several young men. The crowd started an impressive march, which was intended to join the demonstration of the university students and make its way to the royal palace to protest against the outrages to which the Jews were subjected. Clashes with the police were followed by numerous arrests.

This mass demonstration alarmed the authorities and they did not carry out the second stage of their deportation plan—deportation to Poland, where the Jews of Europe found their death. Fearing internal unrest, the Fascist government and the king were forced to give up their plan to send the Jews of Bulgaria to their doom in the death camps.

The strong resentment of the Bulgarian people is reflected in numerous documents in the archives of the German Legation in Sofia. Thus, the attaché Hoffman in his report to the Gestapo dated June 7, 1943, in an attempt to explain the failure of the government plan to deport the Jews, wrote:

If the deportation of the Jews from Bulgaria is taking place under special circumstances and meets with greater difficulties than in other countries subjugated by the Reich, it has to be taken into account that the Bulgarian Government is not in a position to cut the matter short, as it has to foresee and make provision for the internal and external political consequences.

The German ambassador in Sofia, Beckerle, in his report to the chancellery of the Reich, dated June 7, 1943, wrote:

I beg you to believe me that my service is doing everything possible to reach a final solution of the Jewish question in conformity with the decisions taken. I am deeply convinced that the Prime Minister and the Bulgarian Government also desire a final settlement of the Jewish problem and are trying to reach it. But they are forced to take into account the mentality of the Bulgarian people, who lack the ideological conceptions which we have. Having grown up among Turks, Jews, Armenians, the Bulgarian people have not observed in the Jews faults which would warrant these special measures against them. . . . Once we overcome the technical difficulties regarding the eviction of the Jews from Sofia, the organization of the transport for their deportation to the Eastern territories will perhaps be easier.

At this same period Germany was in the heat of battle against the anti-

Nazi coalition. Bulgaria's government had left all national resources of the country at Hitler's disposal for his military requirements. The sufferings of the people increased daily and they expressed their indignation through the clandestine press, leaflets, public demonstrations, and sabotage aiming to slow down factory production, damage goods, and put machinery out of order. They wanted to destroy goods destined for the Eastern Front.

Preparations began for an armed people's uprising. The twelve partisan (guerrilla) zones into which the country was divided counted more than 20,000 partisans and over 200,000 links. The partisan detachments inflicted telling losses on the German occupation forces. The rising tide of the partisan movement kept the government constantly engaged, and it found it impossible to send units of the Bulgarian army to the Eastern Front against the Soviet Union. Moreover, the resistance movement obliged the Germans to maintain armed forces in Bulgaria in order to protect their rear.

The Jews took an active part in the struggle of the Bulgarian people against the German occupying forces and their Bulgarian stooges, at the cost of heavy sacrifice. During these difficult years Jews joined the thousands of Bulgarians in concentration camps; among the political prisoners there were 460 Jews. Twenty-nine were under death sentences and seventeen of them were executed. Two hundred and sixty others joined the partisan detachments and 125 died in battle. Seventy-five others were sent to a special Jewish camp near Pleven only because their sons and daughters had joined the partisan detachments. The Fascists set the barracks of the camp on fire and ten Jews were burned alive. About 520 Jews were detained at the Somovit concentration camp on the banks of the Danube. They were mostly eminent social and political workers or people who had not observed some order of the Commissariat for the Jewish Problems. Three hundred and eighty were sent to the camp near the village of Chehlare near Plovdiv. All these facts show with what dedication the Jews took part in the resistance movement. They all realized clearly that the only way out was to take part in the common struggle against the Nazi occupation forces and Bulgarian Fascism.

It should be noted that in Bulgaria there was no separate Jewish resistance and partisan movement, as was the case in Poland and France, for example. The Jews had for centuries shared the historic destinies of all other Bulgarian people, and during these eventful days they joined the partisan detachments and underground movement, fighting shoulder to shoulder for the freedom of their one common fatherland. Jews of every section of the people joined the resistance movement: Communists, nonparty people, and young members of the leftist Zionist organizations.

The names of many Jewish heroes shall be linked forever with the history of the Bulgarian resistance movement to mention but a few:

Leon Tadjer (Ben David) was the first to take major sabotage action. (When Germany declared war on the USSR, he escaped from the labor camp where he was mobilized.) He found work in Rousse under an assumed name in a company supplying fuel to the German armed forces. Killing a German soldier, he set petrol tanks on fire. He was captured, tried by a military court, and hanged on December 14, 1941, without giving away any of his comrades. In his defense at court, Tadjer repeated with great courage and foresight his firm conviction that Nazi Germany would lose the war and that the anti-Hitlerite coalition would ultimately win.

Emil Shekerdjiiski was a very popular figure of the young workers' revolutionary movement. As political commissar of the "Kalyashki" partisan detachment, he and two of his comrades were surrounded on August 3, 1944, by a large military unit near Kyustendil. Asked to surrender, his little group opened fire in spite of the fact that they had only four pistols and three hand grenades. After they were spent, Emil coolly started returning the grenades which were thrown at them. He threw back nine, but the tenth wounded him slightly; the next fell at their feet. Emil reached out to pick it up but it burst and ended his life.

Violeta Yakova was already a tobacco worker at fourteen. In 1942 and 1943 she was an active member of the militant groups in Sofia, avenging the death of heroic patriots. She was in the group which liquidated the director of Fascist police, Pantev, and the German agent-provocateur Kutuza.

Violeta then joined the Trun partisan detachment and distinguished herself by her bravery and by organizing resistance groups of young people. On June 17, 1944, she came upon a group of policemen near the village of Kondofrey near Radomir. There was a rapid exchange of shots. Hit by a bullet, she was taken prisoner, but only a few minutes later she managed to run away. Chased for some 400-500 meters, she was wounded a second time and recaptured. Next morning she died of her wounds.

Menahem (Miko) Pappo, another famous name of the Bulgarian resistance movement, was born in the poor Jewish quarter of the capital. At sixteen he became an active member of the Young Workers' Union. In 1942 the police discovered his group, and he joined the underground movement as a member of one of the militant groups. He was captured during one of its actions. For two months he was severely tortured by the police but did not give away any of his comrades. The court sentenced him to death in spite of the fact that he was a minor. In his parting letter to his parents, Pappo wrote ". . . now, as I am about to die, my last thoughts are with you. I am thinking of the pain which I have caused you, but I am also thinking of the happy new life which you will soon have—a life for which I fought and for which I shall now die. . . ."

In Bulgaria today there is hardly a city without a street named after a Jewish partisan hero who fell, fighting the Nazis.

Diary of a Jewish Partisan in Paris

By Abraham Lissner

[EDITOR'S NOTE: *The Jewish resistance fighters of France, who called themselves partisans—a term synonymous with armed militancy— carried out their underground activities under conditions radically different from those of their counterparts in Eastern Europe. To fully appreciate their role in the French resistance movement the reader should familiarize himself with the play of historic circumstances that led to that difference. Hence the somewhat lengthy introduction to this chapter.*

Let us begin with the name—partisans! A partisan in military parlance is a guerrilla fighter whose base of operations is the forest; who strikes at the enemy's rear at night, under cover of darkness; who obtains his food from friendly peasants on the countryside or by force of arms from the unfriendly ones. But the Jewish partisans in occupied Paris lived·in houses and attacked the enemy on the city streets in broad daylight, as well as at night.

Being full-time partisans, and not having a countryside to depend on for food, they recieved a modest monthly salary from the Partisan High Command. Although their sabotage activities were not limited to Paris alone, their organization was known as the Jewish Partisan Unit of Paris. The group consisted mainly of immigrant Jews from Eastern and Central Europe, most of whom were from Poland, and their children. They had left their native lands to escape anti-Semitic persecution and to better their economic lot. They adopted France as their new homeland and served her loyally. Had they remained in their native countries they would have been herded into ghettos and shared the fate of the relatives and friends they had left behind. But here a different set of circumstances was operative, making it possible for them to carry out various acts of sabotage and take up arms against the enemy at a very early stage of the occupation.

In his essay "Jewish Resistance in France," [39] *L. Poliakov describes these different circumstances as follows: "Great as was the tragedy of the western Jews, it was not marked by the same brutality as in the east. The causes were various: on the one hand, the Jews in the west were more*

282

assimilated to their non-Jewish environment, they were few in number and were more widely distributed among the general population; on the other hand, the (German) enemy pursued a different policy in the west than in the east. In the west he acted with greater cunning and circumspection, to avoid shocking the native population, which was not as contaminated with the germ of anti-Semitism as the peoples of eastern Europe. The chief factor, however, was the attitude of the native population and the sympathy the Jews in the countries of the west received from their fellow citizens. The difference is most clearly revealed in the numerical comparison of the number of Jews who perished. In Poland more than 90 per cent of the Jews were liquidated, in France . . . the losses were less than 30 per cent."

To be sure the ultimate goal of the Germans with regard to the Jews was the same in France as elsewhere—the "Final Solution." What was different here was the method of its implementation. Cunningly the Germans schemed and plotted with the collaborationist Vichy regime to achieve their aim without arousing any protests from the French population.

In the early months of the occupation the Jews were not subjected to any special discriminatory decrees. This created the false illusion among many of them that there was nothing to fear; an illusion the Germans were eager to foster. Parisian Jews began returning from the suburbs and provinces where they had sought shelter, and some even came back from the "Free Zone" to which they had fled.

The first blow came in October, 1940, with the German decree ordering all Jews in the occupied zone to register with the police precincts. Most of them, especially the native-born Jews, complied, thinking that it was only a formality. Some foreign-born Jews, especially those who were recent refugees from Fascism, knew better and ignored the decree. The registrants had to fill out long forms with detailed information, which were then stamped with the word "Juif."

In the spring of 1941 the Vichy government, acceding to the Germans' demand, established the "Commissariat général aux juifs" (General Commissariat for Jewish affairs), headed by the French anti-Semite Xaviar Vallat. Soon thereafter this Commissariat set up the "UGIF"—Union Générale des Israélites de France (General Association of French Jews). Describing the UGIF as "that instrument par excellence of segregation and ghettoization . . ." Poliakov points out why the Gestapo was interested in its establishment: "Their first task was to amalgamate all Jewish activities in a manner that could be used as a foundation for the future Judenrat." [40]

The Germans were apparently successful in this respect. The Bundist

Pinkas Mintz (Alexander) writes, ". . . UGIF was a kind of French counterpart of the Judenrat in Poland. . . . I fought against the idea of cooperating with the UGIF because I regarded it as an instrument of the Nazis and the Vichy people against the Jewish population . . ." [41]

That same spring the Germans struck again, this time taking the first bold step leading to the first deportations. On May 13, 1941, they issued a decree ordering all foreign-born Jews to report at the police precincts the next day at eight in the morning, accompanied by wife or other members of the family, and with sufficient food and clothing to last for two days. About 5,000 reported. They were sent to internment camps and from there to extermination camps in Poland. (It must be borne in mind that at that time—1941 and the early part of 1942—even the Jews of Poland, who were much closer to the scene of their destruction than were the Jews of France, did not suspect that "deportation" and "resettlement" were synonymous with gas chambers.)

Three months later the ax fell again. This time the Germans did not even bother to issue a decree. It was done in typical Nazi style. At dawn, on August 20, 1941, French gendarmes, at the behest of their German masters, surrounded the eleventh arrondissement, a section of Paris thickly populated with Jewish immigrants. People were dragged out of bed, herded into vans, and taken to Camp Drancy on the outskirts of Paris. This round-up netted the Germans 5,000 victims, most of whom were later deported to Auschwitz. From then on such round-ups became a frequent occurrence.

It took the Germans in occupied France two years to get around to the Yellow Patch decree. In Poland the order that the Jews must wear the yellow Star of David came in the very first weeks of the occupation. But here they had to reckon with the possible opposition of the French population to this relic of the Middle Ages. It was one thing to stage round-ups of foreign-born Jews whom they had branded in their anti-Semitic propaganda as "spies" and "agents of a foreign power," and another thing to brand all Frenchmen of the Jewish faith this way. When the decree was issued, in June, 1942, some non-Jewish Frenchmen donned the yellow patch in open solidarity with the Jews.

"But July 16, 1942," writes David Diamant, "remains without doubt the bloodiest day in the history of the Jews of France. On that day . . . the Germans arrested 30,000 men, women, and children, and herded them into the Vélodrome d'Hiver. . . . It was the beginning of the extermination that resulted in the slaughter of 120,000 Jews of France, 25,000 of whom were children." [42]

This, in sketchy outline, is the picture of the French Jews at the time of the occupation. Another side is given by L. Poliakov, who writes, "Jews played a very prominent role in the organizations of the French resistance. It is a little known but nevertheless indisputable fact that the Jews made up 15 to 20 per cent of the active membership in those groups, although they constituted less than one per cent of the French population" (p. 261).

Not only did Jews fight side by side with their French countrymen in the general maquis movement, but they also engaged in both active and passive resistance within the framework of their own national organizations. Foremost in the ranks of passive resistance were Les Éclaireurs Israélites de France (The Jewish Boy Scout Organization of France), which is credited with having saved 3,000 adults and over 1,000 children by smuggling them across the borders to Spain and Switzerland, or sheltering them with French families in the provinces.

"Diary of a Jewish Partisan in Paris" is an account of active resistance that inflicted severe losses on the enemy. Its author, Abraham Lissner, was born in Poland, lived for a while in Palestine and came to France in 1929. In 1937 he fought with the Jewish Botvin Company against the Franco forces in Spain. Soon after the German invasion of France he became one of the organizers and leading members of the Jewish Partisan Unit of Paris.

Translated from an unpublished manuscript, this selection appears here for the first time in the English language. Mr. Lissner's latest work appeared in French under the title Un Franc-Tireur Juif Raconte *(Paris: 1969).*]

———————◆———————

MARCH 15, 1942

Minna, who is well-known among the Jewish population in the 18th arrondissement, came to my house today. She told me that someone who knows me well would like to discuss an important matter with me. The appointment was set for three days later.

MARCH 18

Met that someone. His name is Sevek. It is already forbidden for Jews to be out on the streets after 8 P.M.; nevertheless, Sevek and I continued walking past that hour and discussing what means to adopt against the modern cannibals, the German Nazis. We came to the conclusion that we must organize a Jewish Partisan Unit. Until now we had been fighting the enemy mainly with the printed word; the time had now come to talk to him in the language of weapons. For that we need Jewish partisans to attack the enemy wherever he could be found. That was the gist of our conversation.

When we had parted, I decided to abandon my legal residence and henceforth become completely "illegal."

Several days later Sevek had arranged for me to meet Leon Pakin, a man with a revolutionary past. He had spent years in the Pilsudski prisons in Poland. He had fought against Franco's forces in the Spanish Civil War, with the Jewish Botvin Company, and more recently he had been imprisoned in the internment camps of Gurs, Argelès, and Vernet D'Ariège.

I learned that he too had been assigned to organize a Jewish Partisan Unit. He told me that my task was to contact the former Jewish fighters of the Botvin Brigade. These would form the nucleus of the Jewish Partisan Unit. Some isolated Jewish groups have been in existence since 1941 but they are operating without any central direction.

The Germans have increased their repressions against the population of Paris. This is reflected by the posters that appear on the walls, issued by Herr von Schtulpnagel, which list the names of resistance fighters that were executed by the Gestapo. Among them are also the names of Jews.

APRIL, 1942

Our leadership decided that on May 1 the Jewish partisans should carry out an anti-German act of a military character by placing a time bomb close to a barracks occupied by German soldiers. Salek Bot, a young violinist, and Hersz Zimmerman, an engineer, undertook the difficult task of preparing the explosive.

APRIL 27

Today the Jewish partisans suffered a severe loss. As our two comrades were putting together the bomb, in a small hotel room in the 5th arrondissement, something went wrong. The bomb exploded, killing Salek on the spot and critically wounding Hersz. But that was not all. After the explosion the police occupied the hotel room and succeeded in arresting 17 of our comrades who, not knowing about the accident, had come to see Salek and walked into a police trap.[43]

At the present we are suffering from a shortage of weapons. This is also true of our French comrades. Nevertheless they have helped us with several revolvers with which we are learning how to shoot. For security reasons we each learn individually how to use the weapon.

MAY 16,1942

Yesterday I met the partisan Sioma, who told me that a Jew on Rue du Chat-qui-Pêche was dealing with the Germans. We decided to put an end to this shameful behavior. Today, around nine in the morning, three of us walked into his house armed with a toy pistol, which I had bought for that purpose, for several francs. Brandishing the "weapon" we told him what was in store for him if he continued dealing with the Nazi criminals. Before we left we confiscated his money, which will be used for partisan activity. We are now better organized for sabotage work and we are determined to destroy the Jewish ateliers that manufacture fur coats and fur-lined gloves for Hitler's army.

JUNE, 1942

We now have a Military General Staff which was set up at the M.O.I. (Mouvement Ouvrier Immigrés) under the control of the national F.T.P. (Francs-Tireurs et Partisans). Its aim is to coordinate and control the military operations of the individual partisan units, of which there are now four in Paris: a Jewish, Rumanian (which includes the Hungarian partisans), Italian, and Armenian. It is the responsibility of the General Staff to supply the Units with weapons, indicate the German military bases that have to be destroyed, create a center for the manufacture of explosives [44] and designate assignments in accordance with the abilities of the individual units.

The General Staff also has at its disposal a team of Jewish women whose task it is to transport weapons to various points. This work is not only dangerous, but strenuous as well. Frequently the women have to carry bombs from one end of Paris to the other, on foot.

Each Partisan Unit has its own General Staff and a woman courier, whose job it is to maintain contact with Headquarters, bring directives and return with reports. Each Unit is divided into groups of three, and in each group one partisan is in charge of the sabotage activity. In addition to acting as couriers and transporting weapons the women also provide the partisans with bread ration cards and other necessities.

The Partisan Units of the M.O.I. consist of working people and intellectuals, ranging in age from 16–50. Ninety percent of them are full-time partisans. Only a few work during the day and devote their evenings to sabotage activity.

It is not easy to join a Partisan Unit. Many try to establish contact with us and do not succeed. That is why the General Staff assigned a person to concern himself with this problem. His job is to maintain contact with responsible representatives of every anti-Fascist organization affiliated with the M.O.I. and in this way make it easier for potential underground fighters to join our ranks.

To be accepted into a Partisan Unit one has to comply with the following conditions: (1) Sever relations with everyone who is not connected with the underground organization. (2) Abandon one's legal residence and begin living alone on an illegal basis. These strict measures had to be adopted so that the partisan, if arrested, would not drag others along with him.

Full-time partisans receive a monthly wage from the organization since they have no other means of earning a living. A single partisan gets 1,600 francs [$36.54] a month; a married one with one child gets 1,900. On this salary the partisan must pay the rent for his room and eat every day in a different restaurant.[45]

A partisan must spend his entire day outdoors even when he has no special reason for being on the street. To avoid arousing the suspicion of his concierge and neighbors he has to leave his room every morning at the same time, as though he were going to work, and return in the evening, like all the other residents.

AUGUST, 1942

At 11 P.M. three Jewish partisans, Simon, Jonas Geduldig, and myself, placed a time bomb at the window of a hotel on rue Pierre de la Serbie, opposite the métro station Iéna. It was to explode six minutes later. We each entered the métro separately. Simon and Jonas took the train going in one direction and I in another. My comrades were lucky. Their train arrived soon. I had to wait for mine. Because of the lateness of the hour there were no civilians on the platform, only a German naval officer. About three minutes after we had entered the station a powerful explosion was heard, followed by a rush of dense air. The station chief on the other side of the platform began to shout and the policeman next to him blew his whistle. The German officer looked at me, as though he were about to ask me the meaning of all this. At this moment the train arrived. I reached my hideout without any mishap.

The sabotage acts of our groups are increasing both in number and in scope. It is no surprise, therefore, that the enemy's hunt for us is becoming more and more determined. The aim of the Gestapo is to discover our General Staff. Their tactic is not to arrest the individual partisan but to keep him under surveillance all day long in the hope that he would lead them to the General Staff. As many as twenty-five Gestapo agents take turns in trailing a single partisan in one day.

It is imperative that we become more vigilant. The General Staff of the M.O.I. has charged me with that responsibility. I am to check on the

reliability and trustworthiness of new applicants for the partisan movement, and to see to it that the rules of caution are strictly enforced.

Since September, 1942, there has been in Paris a group of Jewish
women partisans, as part of the Jewish Partisan Unit. Like the men, they
carry out sabotage acts, using time bombs and grenades. One day three
of these women lost their lives in the course of carrying out their duty.
As they came out of the métro station Porte d'Orléans, they were caught
in a police round-up which is a daily occurrence in Paris. One of the
women, Helen Kro, who was carrying the grenades, was the first to be
caught. The police took her home, hoping to find there a weapons cache.
While they were searching, Helen threw herself out of the window rather
than fall into the hands of the Gestapo. She was killed instantly. The other
two who were also caught by the Vichy police were later deported (most
likely to Auschwitz) and were never heard from again.

NOVEMBER 10, 1942
Today Marcel Rayman and Nathan Lemberger placed a time bomb at
the window of a hotel on Montmartre, which is inhabited by high-ranking
German officers, causing great damage.

NOVEMBER 11
Today Radios Moscow and London reported the bombing of the hotel
on Montmartre.

NOVEMBER 15
A group of Jewish partisans, led by Mayer List, today placed two
time bombs at the window of a German military barracks on rue de
Vaugirard, killing several Hitlerites while they were eating breakfast. In
this action two Jewish women participated. They carried the bombs.

NOVEMBER 26
Today the Jewish partisans have to their credit two anti-German acts:
They bombed a hotel on rue St. Florine, and they placed two time bombs
on a street not far from Place de la Concorde, where German soldiers
usually pass in groups. The bombs exploded just as the soldiers arrived,
causing severe losses in their ranks. Both acts went through without a
mishap.

DECEMBER 3, 1942
Today we suffered a severe loss. Our laboratory where the bombs
were manufactured was destroyed by an accident. It happened while
Gilbert was putting together a bomb. He barely escaped with his life.

JANUARY, 1943

The new year is off to a good start. The underground bulletin for January, issued by the General Staff, reports a number of daring sabotage acts in which Jewish partisans played a leading role. Five German military groups were attacked on the streets of Paris in broad daylight. In the town of Argenteuil a warehouse of rubber tires was burned down. Six restaurants that catered exclusively to German personnel were damaged by hand grenades. Four hotels and two antiaircraft guns were blown up. On Avenue Lavendal, in the very heart of Paris, where police round-ups occur daily, three partisans placed two time bombs in the path of a German military detachment, killing most of the soldiers.

A special team of women was involved in this attack. Their job was to walk the streets of Paris and study the movements of the German military groups. They then relayed this information to the General Staff, which assigned the partisans best suited for carrying out such an attack.

I began to suspect that my face was becoming familiar to the trailing Gestapo agents, so I vanished from the streets of Paris for ten days. I went into hiding in an attic above a French café. The owner brought me three meals daily.

FEBRUARY 3, 1943

Six Jewish partisans, two of them women, today destroyed an antiaircraft gun and attacked a barracks full of German soldiers with hand grenades. This happened in the 15th arrondissement near Quai de Passy. The women started out at six in the morning and carried the explosives on foot for a distance of six kilometers.

FEBRUARY 23

Jean Kerbel and Jacques Farber shot two German soldiers guarding a hotel occupied by high-ranking German officers on rue Pasquier, then tossed a grenade into the hotel. One partisan was shot in the leg as he fled from the scene but managed to escape.

Eighteen-year-old Paul Simon, the son of Jewish-Czech parents, carried out his first anti-German act under the leadership of Marcel Rayman. They killed two German officers on the Pont des Arts.

This was indeed an active month for our partisan units. The February bulletin issued by the General Staff lists twenty-one military sabotage acts, eleven of which were carried out by the Jewish Partisan Unit.

MARCH, 1943

An apt description for this month would be to call it "the bloody month of March." Until now the General Staff bulletins said little about arrests, and even less about partisans wounded or dead. The bulletin for March is, unfortunately, full of such bad news.

On the 10th, two Jewish partisans were killed. Jean Kerbel was about to toss a grenade at a truckload of German soldiers when the grenade exploded in his hand, killing both himself and his comrade, André.

On the 16th, the 33-year-old Paul Zilberman was fatally wounded when he hurled a grenade into a group of German soldiers standing near the movie house Rex. One day later, the Jewish partisan Cadys Sosnovski threw a grenade into a German food shop near Gare de l'Est. He was pursued by French police, shot in the leg, captured, and handed over to the Gestapo.

On the 29th, Paul Simon and another partisan attacked, with hand grenades, a restaurant reserved exclusively for German officers, in the Paris suburb Asniers. The attack was carried out at 1 P.M. when the restaurant was full of diners. While escaping, young Paul was arrested and later shot by the Gestapo.[46]

The Jewish partisans retaliated. Our losses did not go unavenged. One day in March, when a group of German soldiers on a week-end leave to Paris were returning to their barracks in Versailles, they were attacked by two Jewish partisans. They were scheduled to leave from the Alma Marceau station. Just as it began to move, one of the partisans, young Wolf Wajsbrot, tossed a grenade into the car especially reserved for German soldiers. With this act he avenged not only his comrades felled in Paris but also his parents who perished in the Auschwitz gas chambers.

APRIL–MAY, 1943

These were perhaps the busiest two months to date for our partisan units. The underground bulletins read like battlefront communiqués: Four high-ranking German officers shot. Sixteen German military groups attacked with hand grenades in various parts of Paris. Five garages set on fire. Nine hotels destroyed. Altogether, thirty-four sabotage acts, fifteen of which were carried out by the Jewish Partisan Unit.

All this activity led to stepped-up police surveillance. By the end of May the Gestapo had tightened its ring around the Jewish partisans to a point where we had to act quickly or perish. It was decided to disband the Unit and disperse the individual partisans to various farms around Paris. The aim was to get the enemy accustomed to the idea that the underground fighters had disappeared from the city. I was assigned by the General Staff to carry out this program and to supply the partisans with money and bread rations.

In order not to lose contact with them I am to see one of the partisans every other day. On a less frequent basis I am to be in touch with the partisan groups of other nationalities. This condition will be maintained for three weeks. Then each partisan will be reassigned to a sabotage group. Though the enemy succeeded in demobilizing us for about a month, victory is ours. We remained intact.

JUNE, 1943

The bulletin for this month no longer mentions the Jewish partisans as a separate unit. They are now serving as cadres in other national units and participated in many of the anti-German acts listed in the June bulletin. These include: Six truckloads and five marching groups of German soldiers attacked with hand grenades. Two traitors and one German general (Abt) shot. Three troop trains derailed.

JULY, 1943

A daring anti-German act was carried out today in Clichy, a suburb of Paris. The Germans reserved one hospital in Clichy exclusively for officers of the Luftwaffe. Every morning at eight, a busload of these officers are brought to the hospital. A partisan unit consisting of Rumanians, Hungarians, Armenians, and Germans, under the leadership of the Jewish partisan Joseph Clisci, was assigned to attack the bus with grenades. The attack was to be carried out in the municipal garden of Levallois-Perret, a town bordering on Clichy. The weapons were to be brought by the Jewish woman partisan Golda Bancic.

After the attack the retreating partisans were pursued by several French gendarmes who opened fire on them. As chief of the operation, Clisci did not leave the scene until all of the partisans had escaped. While covering their retreat he was wounded in the leg but managed to hobble into an abandoned courtyard and hide in a cellar.

The Germans carried on a search for him until five in the afternoon, without results. But a Frenchwoman betrayed him to the Hitlerites, who then surrounded the house and, through a loudspeaker, ordered him to surrender. Each time a German officer or soldier approached Clisci's hiding place he was met by a hail of bullets. In this way Joseph shot five Germans. With the last remaining bullet he shot himself rather than fall into the hands of the Gestapo.

JULY 9–10

A German troop train speeding on the Paris-Cherbourg line was derailed by the partisans. That night the ambulances in that area were kept very busy. It is the second derailment this month.

Owing to a provocation the Gestapo succeeded in arresting a number of underground fighters, including some Jews. But despite this mishap July was a busy month for the partisans. They have to their credit nineteen anti-German acts which, both in scope and importance, surpass some of their previous activities.

AUGUST, 1943
A troop train was derailed on the Paris-Reims line, killing and wounding many German soldiers.

AUGUST 17–18
A trainful of German soldiers going on furlough was derailed on the Longwy line.

AUUGUST 19
The partisans had discovered that a certain German commandant took a leisurely stroll every morning through the Parc Monceau. This morning he took his last walk. He was shot by two partisans, Alfonso, a Spaniard, and Marcel Rayman, a Jew.

AUGUST 26–27
The third derailment this month. This one on the Paris-Troy line. The result: One locomotive and fourteen carloads of weapons destroyed. All three derailments were carried out under the leadership of the Jewish partisan Boczov, who is a specialist in these things. These derailments dealt the enemy a severe blow, not only in the loss of men and equipment but also in disrupted railway communication, which at times lasted for as long as seventy hours.

SEPTEMBER, 1943
All of Paris is agog today with the news of Dr. Ritter's execution. Karl Ritter, Fritz Sauckel's gauleiter, has deported hundreds of thousands of Frenchmen to Germany for slave labor. The High Command of the partisan movement condemned him to death and assigned the following three partisans to carry out the execution: Alfonso, a Spaniard; Marcel Rayman, a Jew; and a German anti-Fascist. They waited for him, at nine in the morning, on rue Pétrarque, in the 16th arrondissement. As Ritter's automobile was emerging from his garage Alfonso fired at him. Ritter tried to leap from his car, but just then Rayman pumped three bullets into him, killing him on the spot.

The Ritter execution was sensational but by no means the only anti-German act that our partisans carried out in September. We also have to our credit the destruction of seventy-five railway cars and their locomotives, carrying German troops and weapons. In addition, several military groups were attacked with hand grenades on the streets of Paris. The following Jewish partisans played a leading role in these anti-German acts: the 37-year-old Boczov, who is as skilled in the art of throwing hand grenades as he is in train derailments; the Hungarian Jew Robert, another specialist in blowing up and derailing German troop trains. His wife was arrested by the Gestapo but he continues with his sabotage activities; the 19-year-old Thomas Elek, who gave up his studies during the occupation to devote himself fully to underground activity; the 24-year-old Jonas Geduldig, who was one of the first to join our Jewish Partisan Unit in Paris.

OCTOBER 1, 1943

Our General Staff learned that every evening at nine a busload of German aviators started out, from a place near Porte de Choisy, for their airbase in Orly, after a day's furlough in Paris. The Italian Partisan Unit was assigned to carry out an attack, with the aid of the German-Jewish partisan Marcel, who spoke German perfectly. Today the attack was carried out successfully.

Marcel walked over to the open window of the bus and began a conversation with one of the fliers. While he was talking with the German officer Marcel held his grenade wrapped in his beret. As soon as the bus began to move he tossed it inside through the open window. The officers who escaped death pursued him but gave up because his retreat was successfully covered by the other partisans.

There were several sabotage acts on the railway lines this month, but the one on the Paris-Troy line stands out in importance. In this one act the partisans destroyed fourteen tanks and several carloads of rice, sugar, and sardines which the Germans had robbed from the French to send to the Wehrmacht on the Soviet front. Unfortunately, we lost four men in this operation. They fell into the hands of the Gestapo during their retreat, while passing the town of Melun. Two of them were members of the Jewish Partisan Unit of Paris. They were Leon Goldberg, 19, whose parents had been deported (most likely to Auschwitz), and Willy Szapiro, 33.

These sabotage acts enraged the enemy. The Gestapo struck back and, with the aid of the Vichy police, succeeded in arresting some of our partisans. But the real blow came as a result of a betrayal in our own midst. On October 20, a member of our General Staff was arrested. He broke down during questioning and betrayed all of us to the enemy, hoping thus to save his own skin.

The Gestapo put him into one of their police cars and rode through the streets of Paris so that he could point out to them the places where the partisans used to meet. As a result many partisans were arrested. The few who eluded the Gestapo still managed to maintain contact with one another.

Like the others I had to abandon my dwelling place. The first night I spent in a hotel on Avenue Poincaré where a Jewish friend of mine worked, on forged papers. The hotel's restaurant catered to high-ranking German officers. I succeeded in escaping this hell thanks to my French comrades from Clichy-Levallois who offered me a hiding place during those tragic days. The situation became so critical that those who had eluded arrest had to leave Paris and continue their partisan activities away from the capital.

JANUARY, 1944

Early this month I left Paris and headed for the districts of Nord Pas de Calais, a region inhabited by Polish, Hungarian, and Italian immigrants, and other nationalities the majority of whom worked in the many coal mines in that area. My underground contact in that region was the Jewish partisan Gilbert, from Paris. I met him in the town Hénin-Liétard. In addition to its other inhabitants the town was surrounded by camps of deported Ukrainians who worked in the coal mines under military and Gestapo supervision. It was a center of Hitler's war machine, and it was necessary to bring to these workers our rich experience of struggle against the enemy, which we had acquired in Paris, so that they would smash the Hitler machine as quickly as possible.

FEBRUARY, 1944

I was in Douai when the walls of the houses were covered with posters the Gestapo had distributed all over France under the heading "The Army of Criminals." I saw the faces of my comrades-in-arms, swollen and distorted from all the tortures they had endured. I recognized Manouchian, Boczov, Grzywacs, and all the others. It is difficult to describe what I lived through when I read the text on that hateful poster.[47] I thought: My dear, unforgettable comrades. Your young lives were cut down by the enemy now, an hour before victory, but your sacrifice was not in vain.

Thousands of others are following your example, and are doing everything to complete as quickly as possible the great work you have begun.

JUNE 6, 1944
The Allied Armies have landed on the beaches of Normandy!

The partisans are stepping up their sabotage work and are regrouping themselves to attack the retreating German armies from the rear.

Events are moving swiftly now. The Allied Forces are scoring ever greater victories. Passing through the towns and villages of the north, one could hear through the open windows the radios announcing the latest communiqués from the cities liberated by the Allied Armies. One day, while passing an open window, I heard that Paris was liberated. Oh, how I envied my fellow partisans in Paris! We, here, are still in the enemy's hinterland. In addition, I have the feeling that I have completed my task here. It is no longer difficult to find a night's lodging, and in practically every house one comes upon a group of recently organized patriotic militia that has its own leadership and is beginning to represent a mass movement. Seeing all this, I experience a warming sense of pride that I, together with my fellow partisans, Jewish and non-Jewish, have made a modest contribution to this struggle.

Table of Sabotage Acts Carried Out in Paris by Immigrant Partisans in Collaboration With Jewish Partisans From March, 1942, to End of November, 1943.

29 hotels damaged by time bombs, 33 hotels damaged by hand grenades, 15 German recruiting bureaus set on fire, 16 garages burned down, 78 ateliers and warehouses containing war materials set on fire, 123 military buses destroyed, 19 busloads of Hitlerites attacked by hand grenades, 11 traitors shot, 31 military groups attacked by hand grenades, 2 antiaircraft guns destroyed, Dr. Ritter shot, 4 high-ranking German officers shot, 17 groups of German officers attacked by hand grenades, 7 military barracks attacked by hand grenades.

Altogether over 3,000 Hitlerites were killed and wounded between March, 1942, and the end of November, 1943. In those above-mentioned operations the Jewish Partisan Unit has to its credit the following acts: 19 hotels, 13 warehouses, 23 military buses, 16 German military groups. In addition, Jewish partisans participated in the train derailments, and in sabotage acts carried out by other nationality groups.

Marcel Rayman's Last Letters to His Family [48]

Fresnes, February 21, 1944
My dear aunt, uncle and cousins:
  When you read this I'll no longer be alive. I'm going to be shot today at three o'clock. I regret nothing that I've done. I'm completely tranquil and calm. I love you all and I hope that you'll live happily. You'll give these few words which follow to Mother and Simon, if they ever return, which I hope.
  My dear aunt, I should have liked to see you again, as well as my youngest little cousin whom I've hardly known. I'm presently reunited with three of my comrades, who await the same fate that I do. We just received a package from the Red Cross and we're eating like a bunch of kids all the sweet things that I like so much. I embrace all of you for the last time. Fernande, my little Madeleine and also my little Elise. Here we are all in . . . [illegible]
  I'm certain that this will cause more pain to you than to us.
                                                            MARCEL
My dear little mother:
  When you read this letter, I'm certain that it will make you very unhappy, but I'll have been dead for some time and you'll be comforted by my brother who will live happily with you and give you all the joy that I should have liked to give you. Forgive me for not writing at greater length, but we're all so joyous that it becomes impossible when I think of the pain you'll have. I can only tell you one thing; it's that I love you more than anything in the world, and that I wish I could have lived if only for you. I love you, I embrace you, but the words cannot convey what I feel.
  Your Marcel who adores you and who thinks of you to the last minute. I love you, and long live life.

My dear Simon:
  I count on you to do everything that I myself cannot do. I embrace you, I'm happy, live happy, make mother happy as I would have liked to do if I had lived. Long live the beautiful and joyous life that all of you will have. Tell all my friends and my comrades that I love them all. Pay no attention if my letter sounds mad, but I can't stay serious.
                                                            MARCEL

The Destruction and Resistance of the Jews in Italy

By Masimo Adolfo Vitale

[EDITOR'S NOTE: *Unlike France and Belgium, Italy did not have an independent Jewish resistance movement. Jewish resistance fighters in Italy were part of the general Italian partisan movement, and distinguished themselves in such underground groups as "Freedom and Justice," "Garibaldi," and other organizations.*

Masimo Adolfo Vitale was born in Turin and currently resides in Rome where he is president of "Comitato Ricerche Deportati Ebrei" (Committee for Research on Deported Jews). During World War II Mr. Vitale served on the intelligence staff of the Allied Forces. He is a historian and the author of five volumes on the history of Italy's Armed Forces both at home and in her African colonies, published under the auspices of the Ministry of Foreign Affairs. The following appeared in Yiddish in YIVO BLETER (Journal of the Yiddish Scientific Institute), vol. xxxvii, "The Period of Recent Catastrophe" (New York: 1953), pp. 198–204.]

THE TRAGEDY of the Italian Jews in the last holocaust bore a greater similarity to the tragedy of the German Jews than to that of other countries. In other countries the holocaust was brought about by a foreign enemy who invaded the land, with or without a war declaration. But in Italy, as in Germany, the troubles of the Jews stemmed from their native anti-Semites.

In his attitude to the Jews, Mussolini was just as two-faced as he was in many of his other attitudes. Even before he came to power he publicly declared himself an adherent of racism. At the third National Fascist Congress, which took place in November, 1921, he stated: "I want you to know that the racial question is very important to Fascism. The Fascists must make a strong effort to safeguard the purity of the race, because race makes history. . . ." At that time he made no mention at all of the Jews.

After the Fascist victory in October, 1922, Mussolini realized that the racial question was not appropriate to the time and conditions prevailing in Italy and so he bypassed it. As a result of the concordat with the Vatican in February, 1929, the Jewish question was raised in the Italian press. Mussolini's reaction was expressed in a speech to the Chamber of Deputies on May 14, 1929. He said: "Jews have lived in Rome since the days of the Caesars. They have asked to be permitted to weep at the graves of the Caesars. . . . There exists no difference between them and the adherents of other religions." [49]

In 1933, after Hitler had come to power and made racism a central feature of his politics, Mussolini, in an interview with Emil Ludwig, again stressed his friendly attitude toward Jews. A year later, when the Nazi persecutions of the Jews were in full swing, Mussolini stated on September 6, 1934, at the opening of the southern fair in Bari: "Thirty centuries of history permit us to view with contempt certain teachings propagated on the other side of the Alps by the offspring of those who were still wild tribes when we already had a Caesar, a Virgil, an Augustus. . . ." [50]

Mussolini at that time not only spoke well, he even acted well. The Jewish refugees from Germany were welcome in Italy. Even in 1937 when Mussolini was beginning to negotiate a pact with Germany, he declared in an interview with Generoso Pope of the New York daily newspaper *Il Progresso Italo-Americano:* "Every report about a change of attitude on the part of the Italian government toward the Jews has no basis in fact and is inspired by foreigners who have a resistance to and hatred of this government." [51]

But at the same time Lieutenant Farinaci, who later called himself the "Italian Streicher," initiated an anti-Jewish campaign in his journal, *Il Regime Fascista,* where he wrote: "International Jewry is anti-Fascist. Never has a Jew uttered a word of veneration or thankfulness for fascism. . . ."

Other Italian newspapers, such as the *Corriere della Sera,* emulated him and there began a sharp anti-Jewish agitation in the press which only echoed government policy. But Mussolini was once again being deceptive when he stated: "The articles which appear in the press are only an expression of the editors' opinions and have nothing to do with the government."

The Italian ambassador to Washington, Fulvio Suvich, repeated to Dr. Stephen Wise, president of the World Jewish Congress, almost word for word what Mussolini had said the year before when he was interviewed by Generoso Pope.

As soon as the Nazis had taken over Austria in March, 1938, the Fascist party made the following declaration: ". . . The majority of the Italian population is of Aryan origin and its civilization is Aryan. . . .

Jews do not belong to the Italian race. They are the only ethnic group that has never assimilated itself with the rest of the Italian population because it is composed of racial elements who are not European, and are totally different from those elements who have given the world the Italian race. . . ."

On August 5, 1938, there appeared the Manifesto of Racism in which an attempt was made to define the difference between Jew and Italian and which became the ideological basis for future racist decrees. The manifesto was signed by ten scholars.[52]

One month later the first racist decree (number 1390) was issued. All Jewish teachers were to be dismissed from their jobs in government schools, and all Jewish students were forbidden to attend such schools. From then on decrees were issued, one after another, each worse than the previous one. Jews were expelled from all government jobs, the liberal professions, the press, business and, finally, practically all their possessions were confiscated.

It cannot be said that the anti-Semitic blow came unexpectedly to Italian Jews, but they were not prepared for it. Before 1937 there was practically no anti-Semitism in Italy. Altogether Italy had between 45,000 and 50,000 Jews. In the southern parts of the country there were no Jews at all. So how could there have been a "Jewish question?" The Italian people could not comprehend the change in the government's attitude to its citizens of the Jewish faith. They reacted to the first racial laws with very little enthusiasm. Their sympathy was definitely on the side of the persecuted.

The severity with which the government carried out its anti-Jewish campaign, the persecution of those who expressed sympathy for the Jews, the self-aggrandizement of some elements who made capital of the Jewish tragedy—all this had its effect. And the number of people who had the courage to show their antipathy to the new laws grew smaller and smaller.

The most difficult period for Italian Jewry came after the truce of September 8, 1943. Italy was divided in two parts, with Marshal Badoglio ruling the southern part. The northern part was under the control of the Republican Fascist Party and the Germans. Unfortunately, most of the Italian Jews were in the northern part. On November 17, the Republican Fascist Party branded the Jews as "enemy number one." [53] Those were the fearful days, when the enormous contribution of fifty kilograms of gold was levied on the Jewish community of Rome (September 16, 1943); the great hunt of October 16, 1943, when 1,127 Jews were rounded up—among them 800 women and children—and dragged off to Birkenau (only fourteen survivors returned: thirteen men and 1 woman);

the continuous deportation of Jews to concentration camps (6,000 Italian Jews were sent to Auschwitz alone).

Italian Jews were deported not only to Germany and Poland. They also filled the native prisons and camps. They were tortured in the St. Vittore prison in Milan, in the Marasi prison in Genoa, in the St. Sabo prison in Trieste, and in the concentration camp, Fossoli, near Modena. At this point the Italian people came to their aid. They sheltered Jews in the villages or smuggled them into the southern part of Italy. Although the Italian church as a whole had, in the beginning, made little effort to save Jews, individual priests of various orders, in the smaller communities, sheltered Jews in the churches and convents. Later the church as a whole began to help the Jews.[54]

The only bright light in this hour of darkness was the Jewish resistance movement. In Italy it was concentrated in two centers: In the north a para-military organization came into being which consisted of several brigades—the "Garibaldi" group and the group that called itself "Freedom and Justice." These numbered about 6,000-7,000 persons. In central Italy Rome was the center and the movement concentrated its activity in the areas of Rome, Naples, Abruzzi, Tuscany, and in the markets.

The number of Jews that participated in the resistance movement was somewhat over a thousand.[55] They took part in the most dangerous missions and acted as liaison between the Italian underground movement, the French maquis, and the Allied Armies. They maintained an underground press and radio stations, helped Allied prisoners of war escape from prison camps, carried out acts of sabotage and, whenever possible, gave aid to the persecuted. It is believed that the first partisan who fell in a bitter battle with the enemy was a Jew. He was twenty-three-year-old Sergio Diena, a member of the group "Freedom and Justice." He was killed on December 4, 1943, and was posthumously awarded the Silver Medal.

The Italian Jews paid dearly for their participation in the resistance movement. One hundred fell in bloody battle with the enemy. Others were tortured to death in prisons or shot. Generally speaking, Jewish participation in the Italian resistance movement was very prominent. Of the 45,000 Jews who lived in Italy before the war, close to 6,000—most of the young people—left the country when the anti-Jewish decrees were promulgated. Over 10,000 were dragged off by the Germans for deportation. Of the remaining 30,000—which included elderly people, women, and children—over 1,000 joined the resistance movement. This is a high percentage.[56]

The Jewish partisans came from all segments of the population.

Among them were doctors, lawyers, engineers, university professors, students, manufacturers, workers, and clerks. The number of women in the movement was also considerable. In the third regional command of the second division of "Freedom and Justice" there were thirty Jewish women. Although most of the partisans were young people, born and educated under the Fascist regime, there was also a considerable number of elderly people, veterans of the First World War. The youngest Jewish partisan, Franco Cesana, was barely thirteen years old. He fell in the mountains near Modena while carrying out an important mission.

For a more comprehensive picture of the Jewish resistance group and its role in the Italian resistance movement we are citing here a few brief biographical notes about some typical Jewish partisans and their achievements. Take Eugenio Curiel, for instance. A mathematician and philosopher, a veteran anti-Fascist, he lived for a while in France as a refugee. In 1938 he returned to Italy. He was immediately interned on the Ventotente Island (in southern Italy). After the fall of Mussolini he went to Milan where he organized the "Youth Front," became the manager of the journal *La Unita,* and was, generally, the leading spirit of resistance. He was recognized by a spy who informed on him. He was arrested at once and shot. He was one of thirty-four Italians who were later awarded by the government the golden medal for bravery.

Eugenio Calo was wounded in battle. He fell into the enemy's hands and was tortured to make him reveal the names of his comrades. He refused to name them. On July 14, 1944, the Germans buried him alive.

Mario Yacchia, born in 1896, was a decorated veteran of World War I and a veteran anti-Fascist who, together with others, such as Fari and Amendola, founded the "Committee for National Liberation" and organized the group "Freedom and Justice." He was commandant of the partisans in the region of Emilia. Once, while attending a meeting of partisans in Parma, the gathering was betrayed by an informer and the house was surrounded by the enemy. He could have saved himself but he saw to it that the others escaped. Then he began to destroy important party documents. He was caught and tortured but maintained silence. On August 20, 1944, he was shot. The government posthumously awarded him the golden medal for bravery.

Ildo Vivanti, of the group "Free Italy," fell in April, 1944. Later the brigade of Jeso Valley took his name and he was celebrated in partisan songs such as "The Well-Known Partisan."

The Jewish women in the partisan movement also distinguished themselves for their self-sacrificing dedication. The only woman partisan to fall in battle was twenty-three-year-old Rita Rosani, a teacher, who founded the partisan group "Eagle," and participated in the bitterest battles. She died fighting on September 17, 1944. She was posthumously awarded the golden medal for bravery. A monument was erected on the place where she fell. In Verona a street was named after her and in the Memorial Park of Trieste a monument was erected in her honor.

Silvia Elfer, together with her brother Eugenio, were active in the Abruzzi mountains where they found thousands of Allied prisoners of war who had escaped from their camps. Silvia sought to provide them with food, clothing, and other needs. Her brother was caught by the Germans and shot on the spot. Silvia was shot accidentally by an American sentry.

We see then that Jewish participation in the Italian resistance movement was very substantial, both in terms of numbers and achievements. Jews were prominently represented both in the organization and in the leadership of the movement. They played an important part in the printing and dissemination of partisan propaganda literature. The price they paid was high, but the Italian people appreciated the contribution of the Jews to the liberation of their country. Many of the highest medals were awarded to Jews and a number of streets in various cities bear the names of Jews who fell in battle. In some places monuments honor their memory.

One of the streets of the Eternal City of Rome is named after Leone Ginsburg, a literary critic who was among the first anti-Fascist fighters in the partisan movement. He was arrested in an illegal printing shop where propaganda material was printed, and was held in the "Regina Coeli" prison, where he was questioned and tortured. He died under torture without revealing any information about the partisan movement.

The Jewish Resistance Movement in Belgium

By Jacob Gutfreind

[EDITOR'S NOTE: *The Jewish resistance fighters of Belgium, like their French counterparts, called themselves partisans and operated as an independent underground organization which collaborated with and received support from the general Belgian resistance movement. And, like the French Jewish partisans, most of them were Yiddish-speaking Jews from Eastern European countries who had emigrated to Belgium.*

Jacob Gutfreind belonged to that category. He came to Belgium in 1938, a political refugee from his native Poland, which was then under the rule of a semi-Fascist regime. At the end of 1941 he was the organizer and commandant of the first Jewish partisan groups in Belgium. In 1957 he emigrated to Israel, where he now resides with his family (his wife survived Auschwitz), and holds a position in one of the ministries of the Israeli government.

His firsthand account of the Jewish resistance movement of Belgium was submitted especially for this anthology.]

———◆———

WHEN THE Germans marched into Belgium on May 10, 1940, the roads leading to France became clogged with Belgian refugees, including most of that country's Jewish population (about 90,000), which headed for the south of France. But three weeks later the Germans caught up with them when, on June 22, Marshal Pétain capitulated to Hitler's Wehrmacht. Early in August the French administration decreed that all Jewish refugees be interned in refugee camps.

In the meantime reports were filtering through from Belgium that life there was normalizing itself, and that the Germans were not molesting the Jews.

304

These two factors—the internment of the Jewish refugees and the news from Belgium—motivated about 45,000 Jews to return to Belgium. The rest had managed to settle in the south of France. Many of them were later deported to Auschwitz together with the French Jews.

With the return of the refugees Jewish parties and organizations came to life again—this time under conditions of illegality. The only legal organization was the Jewish Community Council headed by H. Rotgiel. But it did not last long. It was replaced by a Gestapo-appointed Judenrat at the head of which was Rabbiner Ullman. It was dominated by people to whom Jewish communal life was alien, especially the life of the immigrants, who comprised between 80 and 90 percent of the Belgian Jewish community.

Only two organizations remained active in Jewish life at that time. They were the progressive, left-wing, "Solidarité," and "Fraternal Aid" of the Left Poale-Zionist. It fell to these two organizations to play the historical role of raising the banner of resistance against German Fascism. And it should be stated that the "Solidarité" was in the vanguard of the anti-Nazi struggle, especially where it concerned armed resistance. The majority of the Jewish partisan fighters came from its ranks. The fact that the more than twenty graves on Tier National (the place in Brussels where the Germans used to execute resistance fighters) are occupied by its members, speaks for itself.

The German tactic with regard to the Jewish population could be divided into two phases:

1) The preparatory phase which lasted from May, 1940, to July, 1942.

2) The deportation phase which began in July, 1942, and continued until it was completed.

In the main this was the tactic the Germans applied to the Jewish communities in Western European countries. In the beginning their approach was one of greater "moderation" than they showed to Jews in Eastern Europe. Here they had to take into account the sentiments of the general population whom they wanted to win over to the "New Order." It must also be borne in mind that anti-Semitism was not as rabid in the Western countries as in the Eastern. That is, perhaps, the reason why Hitler did not set up any ghettos and concentration camps in the West. Finally, the subtle calculation behind the tactic of "moderation" was to tranquilize the vigilance of the Jewish population.

Slowly but systematically the Hitler apparatus to destroy the Jews lumbered forward.

In October, 1940, came the first Nazi decree, giving a "scientific" definition of a Jew and ordering all Jews to register with the Belgian municipalities and have the word *Jude* stamped on their identity cards.

That same month a second decree made mandatory the registration of enterprises owned by Jews and prohibited their owners from disposing of them as they saw fit. Beginning with 1941, Jews were barred from the press, radio, educational institutions, and the legal profession.

On June 10, 1941, further economic restrictions were decreed against Jews. Jewish firms had to bear a sign saying, "Jewish Enterprise" and had to deposit their capital in only one designated bank. Aryan overseers were put in charge of the enterprises. That same month another decree forbade Jewish doctors and dentists to practice.

On August 29, 1941, the Germans slapped a curfew on the Jewish population. Jews were not allowed on the streets between 8 P.M. and 7 A.M.; and they were permitted to live in only four cities—Brussels, Antwerp, Charleroi, and Liége.

On November 25, 1941, the Germans appointed a Judenrat called the Association des Juifs de Belgique, a tool in the hands of the Gestapo to facilitate the deportation of the Jews.

The final decree in this first phase of anti-Jewish laws came in May, 1942, when all Jews were ordered to wear on their breast the Star of David on a yellow patch with the word *Jude* in the center, in black letters.

The cunning Nazi tactic of piecemeal persecution was not without its psychological effect on the Jews. They adjusted to each new decree, hoping it was the last. Thus, for instance, when, on December 31, 1941, the Nazis issued a decree barring Jewish children from public schools they began to attend Jewish schools set up by the Judenrat. A medical aid society was formed where Jewish doctors and dentists, deprived of general practice, treated only Jewish patients. And in time one got used to the evening curfew.

Adjustments to the new conditions fostered delusions in a substantial segment of the Jewish population, which were stumbling blocks in the path of resistance and had to be overcome. But there were those who saw very early through the Nazi deception. These Jews defied the curfew and went out in the evenings to plaster the walls with anti-Nazi slogans and to stuff letter boxes with anti-Nazi literature. Through its two illegal Yiddish publications, *Our Word* (Left Poale-Zionist) and *Our Struggle* (Solidarité), the Jewish underground organizations exposed the true character of the Nazi anti-Jewish decrees and exhorted the Jews not to work for the German war machine, not to work on fur coats for the Wehrmacht and, later, called for a struggle against the Judenrat.

In the meantime the general resistance movement of Belgium, embracing such diverse elements as Catholics and Communists, had made its impact on the country and gave rise to the National Front of Belgian Independence. The Jewish population was particularly in need of such a front. The two existing Jewish organizations joined the Front, and a National Committee for the Defense of the Jews affiliated with it was set up. This happened around the end of 1941.

The general secretary of the Jewish community, Rotgiel, a man of high moral principles, joined the Jewish defense committee. The Germans tried to utilize his prestige by forcing him to become a member of the Judenrat, but he categorically refused and instead combated that body. For this he paid with his life in one of the German concentration camps.

Local Jewish defense committees were also set up in three other cities: Liége, Antwerp, and Charleroi. The composition of the Jewish defense committee as well as its local affiliates reflected a broad representation of both the right and the left, the religious and the nonreligious, the intellectuals and nonparty people. Together they formed a united national fighting front within the Jewish community.

The aims of the Jewish defense committee were manifold. In the first place it was essential to be able to rely on the help of the Belgian population, to obtain the aid of both institutions and prominent individuals. Without that support it would have been difficult, if not impossible, to carry out a program which included the setting up of separate sections for the following purposes: (1) to make false identification papers, (2) to gather finances, (3) to be in charge of publications and propaganda material, (4) to administer communal aid, (5) to provide aid to partisans.

But the most important section was to be the one in charge of children. Under prevailing conditions the functioning of this section was highly complicated. It entailed establishing contact with Belgian institutions, children's homes, churches, Catholic clergy, and hundreds of Belgian families. Mothers were not allowed to know even the names and addresses of the institutions or families where their children were hidden.

Had this far-flung underground apparatus not been set up in good time the Jewish community would have found itself in a hopeless situation when the Germans struck the final and most decisive blow, the deportation decree of July, 1942. Thanks to its existence and the effective aid it was able to give Jews, especially those with little financial means, many were able to hide and survive the war.

One of the most notable achievements of this underground apparatus was its activity in the area of saving children. This work, fraught with many dangers, required the utmost concentration of energy and the involvement of many organizations and courageous individuals. In the end 3,000 Jewish children were saved from certain death.

Though organizationally the Jewish partisans were independent of the Jewish defense committee, they were, for all practical purposes, the armed branch of the committee, which provided the partisans with vital information and links for certain of their actions, provided the partisans with forged identity papers, found shelter for their children, and gave material aid to the families of partisans who were arrested or who fell in combat.

Armed Struggle

The increasing attacks of the Germans and the emergence of local traitors and collaborators made it necessary to enter into armed struggle with the enemy. The first group of Jewish partisans came into being at the end of 1941. By January-February, 1942, the number had grown to three groups (in principle there were theree men to a group). In the first half of 1943, battalion strength was reached with four companies, including intendants, an intelligence service, a laboratory, numbering about seventy people altogether. This did not include the considerable number of Jews who participated in the general Belgian partisan movement as well as those who were members of some smaller non-Jewish group. But the main burden of defending the Jewish community rested on the armed Jewish partisan groups. They conducted their struggle along the following two lines:

1) They ferreted out and eliminated the Jewish informers, combated the Judenrat, fought against the manufacturers who produced for the Germans, and gave armed assistance to the Jewish defense committee whenever it was necessary.

2) They sabotaged the German war machine by setting fire to factories, derailing trains, attacking garages, carrying out death sentences imposed by the underground on certain Nazis and their collaborators.

In July, 1942, the deportation decree became law and created confusion and panic in the Jewish community. For the Jews the burning question was whether to appear or not to appear at the place where they were ordered to assemble for deportation. The Judenrat sent out youthful messengers to Jewish homes urging the Jews to appear. They were met with curses and some were beaten and chased away.

The Jewish underground organizations conducted a campaign against appearing for deportation, imploring the people not to believe the Judenrat that they would be sent to work and urging them to go into hiding instead. Some Jews heeded the advice of the underground and found shelter with some friendly Belgians. But a considerable number of Jews responded to the Judenrat call signed by Rabbi Ullman, believing that they would be sent to work as the call stated and that by appearing voluntarily they would save the other members of their families from deportation since the Germans applied the rule of collective responsibility and threatened to punish an entire family for the failure of one member to heed the deportation order.

It was then that the three commanders of the existing three partisan groups—Weichman, Rakower, and myself—met in a café in the center of town, to discuss means of resisting the deportation drive and striking out at the Judenrat for its traitorous role. It was decided to raid the Judenrat headquarters and destroy the list of names and addresses they had planned to hand over to the Gestapo. Since time was short the plan was to be carried out the next day.

The Judenrat headquarters was situated on Boulevard du Midi, one of the lively Brussels boulevards, opposite the large Catholic youths building which was then occupied by the German Wehrmacht. The next day, between three and four in the afternoon, two of our partisans, posing as German security agents, entered the building and with drawn revolvers gathered all the Judenrat officials into one room and ordered them to be quiet and not to make a move. At the same time two other partisans equipped with bottles of gasoline slipped into the headquarters, poured the gasoline on official documents and lists of names, and set them on fire. In a matter of minutes their task was completed. The four then left the building and lost themselves amidst the passersby on the boulevard, while two remained outside for a moment to cover their retreat. The act went through without a mishap.

The news of the attack on the Judenrat spread quickly among the Jewish population. It was a serious blow to the prestige of that institution. Some members got frightened and left the Judenrat. The leaders, however, remained on their jobs and continued to collaborate with the Germans. The first transport left for Auschwitz on February 9, 1942, carying 1,000 Jews. Every few days another transport departed. In the first five weeks 10,000 Jews were deported. On the 29th of the month the partisans struck again. A notorious member of the Judenrat was shot dead in broad daylight on one of the Brussels streets.

Despite the strict secrecy surrounding the departure of transports, the Jewish partisans succeeded in learning that on April 19, 1943, the very first day of the Warsaw Ghetto uprising, a transport carrying 1,500 Jews was to leave Belgium for Auschwitz. They obtained this information at the very last hour, and time did not permit for the elaborate preparations required to stop the transport. The Jewish defense committee and the partisans had to act quickly.

They enlisted the aid of the Lifshitz brothers, both of whom had long battle and sabotage experience in the general Belgian partisan movement.

(The two were later executed in the Belgian camp Breendonck.) Dr. George Lifshitz and his brother Alexander went out to the Tirlmunt region with their group of partisans. In the evening they took up positions on the railway line. As the train approached, George started to signal the engineer with a red lantern. The train slowed down and finally came to a stop. The partisans rushed up to the cars and pulled the doors open. Jews started to leap from the cars and ran in the direction of the nearby forest. Immediately the Germans began to play the reflectors throughout the length of the train and opened machine-gun fire on the fleeing Jews. At the same time Germans pursued the escapees. The partisans managed to withdraw. Between 600 and 700 Jews had jumped from the cars. The Germans succeeded in catching half of them. Over twenty were shot while fleeing. Ten were wounded. Eight of these were taken by the Germans to the Tirlemont hospital.

The Jewish defense committee was determined to save these eight wounded Jews from being deported with the next transport. The rescue was carried out by the Jewish partisans. On May 2, 1943, three automobiles left Brussels for Tirlmunt. One of them belonged to the Belgian Red Cross and was confiscated for that purpose. At 4:30 P.M. the three vehicles were at the appointed spot. Two partisan groups forced their way into the hospital, overpowered the guards, tied them up, helped dress the wounded, and in a matter of minutes the eight Jews were out of the hospital and the three cars were speeding back to Brussels.

The first automobile, carrying partisans armed with machine guns, was to clear the way for the other two. As they approached the center of Tirlmunt their path was blocked by German field police. The partisans in the first automobile opened fire with machine guns and revolvers, cutting the roadblock and making it possible for the other vehicles to escape through side streets. The partisans sped off, leaving behind some German dead. They were, however, compelled to abandon their bullet-ridden car and escape to a nearby forest. From there they made their way safely back to their base in Brussels the next morning. Unfortunately the ending was not a happy one. One of the chauffeurs, it turned out, was an informer. Some of the wounded were subsequently rounded up by the Gestapo and deported.

One day Paul Halter, a leader of one of the Jewish partisan groups, learned that the Gestapo had discovered the hiding place of nineteen Jewish children—a church in the center of Brussels—and was planning to raid the church that very day. There was no time to contact the commandant of the partisans. Halter had to act independently. He mobilized his group, entered the church, and evacuated the children. The partisans divided the children among themselves and found temporary shelter for them with trusted Belgian families. Later the Jewish defense committee placed them in more permanent hideouts. Later that day the Gestapo came to the church with a truck to seize the children, and left with it empty.

There was a German couple in Brussels, both Gestapo agents, whom the underground condemned to death. Three Jewish partisans—Weichman, Potashnik, and Rosenzweig—were assigned to carry out the death sentences. On the morning of January 7, 1943, the three went to the couple's residence, accompanied by a Belgian official of the Municipal Gas and Electric Utilities whose presence was needed to gain entrance into the house. Weichman, wearing a gas and electric worker's cap and carrying a bundle of tools slung over his shoulder, ascended the stairs while the other two remained as lookouts below.

They knocked on the door.

"Who is it?" the woman called out.

"We're here to check the gas meter," the Belgian replied.

She let them in. While the official was busying himself with the meter, Weichman scanned the rooms for the husband. The woman was handed papers for signature and as she was about to sign one of them said: "Excuse me. The man of the house has to sign." She went to another room and Weichman followed softly behind her. As the husband reached for the papers Weichman shot him on the spot. The woman threw herself on Weichman, scratching his face and screaming. She too was shot dead.

Weichman, his face still bleeding from the woman's scratches, and his Belgian companion ran down and disappeared in the crowd. The two partisans who were to cover their escape also disappeared. The next day the press carried a front-page communiqué from the German military forces offering a half a million francs to anyone who would lead to the arrest of the assassins.

Months later the three partisans were caught and arrested in the course of their underground activities. Despite the tortures they were subjected to they did not reveal any secrets.

On September 9, 1943, at 5 A.M., a Nazi execution squad ended the young lives of Weichman, Potashnik, and Rosenzweig.

These are but a few episodes in the life of the Belgian Jewish underground during the German occupation.

Notes

1. CHAIM WEIZMANN (1874-1952), Zionist leader; first President of Israel.

2. DAVID ABRAMOVITCH, "Jews in the Walcze-Nora Forest," *Face to Face with the Nazi Enemy* (Tel Aviv–Jaffa: 1961).

3. YITZCHAK RIMUN, "Heroism of Russian Jews in the Anti-Nazi Struggle," *Keneder Odler* (August 21, 1964).

4. RAUL HILBERG, *The Destruction of the European Jews* (Chicago: Quadrangle books, 1961), pp. 662–69.

5. HANNAH ARENDT, *Eichmann in Jerusalem, A Report on the Banality of Evil* (New York: Viking, 1963), p. 108.

6. *The New Leader* (August 5, 1963).

7. Peoples Guard, the partisan arm of the Polish Workers Party (Communist), later renamed People's Army. (Small in 1942–43, it grew to a force of 50,000 in 1944–45 and toward the end it was much better armed than the Home Army.)

8. GÜNTER WEISENBORN, *Der lautlose Aufstand. Bericht über die Wiederstandsbewegung des deutschen Volkes 1933-1945* (Hamburg: 1953), pp. 164–65.

9. Published partly in WALTER SCHMIDT, *Damit Deutschland lebe* (Berlin: 1959), pp. 311–13.

10. On November 7, 1938, Ernst von Rath, third secretary of the German Embassy in Paris, was shot to death by Herschel Grynszpan, a seventeen-year-old Jewish youth whose parents, together with ten thousand other Jews, had been herded into cattle cars and deported to Poland. In reprisal for the boy's act of revenge, two days later, on the nights of November 9 and 10, the Nazis staged a pogrom against the German Jews. They burned down synagogues, looted Jewish shops, and beat up and arrested Jews, by their own admission killing at least thirty-six. The damage caused by the smashed windowpanes alone ran to five million marks ($1,250,000). The pogrom aroused world-wide protest, and that night became known as "Crystal Night." WILLIAM L. SHIRER, *The Rise and Fall of the Third Reich* (New York: Simon and Schuster, 1960), pp. 430–37.

11. See note 7.

12. Land Army, the largest Polish underground movement, directed by the Polish Provisional Government in London. It was permeated with anti-Semitic elements and frequently attacked Jews.

13. Published by the Central Association of Polish Jews in Argentina (Buenos Aires: 1948), pp. 341–43.

14. *Notes from the Warsaw Ghetto* (Warsaw: Verlag Yiddish Buch, 1963), II, 214.

15. Dr. Szymon Datner, *The Fight and Annihilation of the Bialystok Ghetto* (Lodz: Central Jewish Historical Commission, 1946).

16. *Notes from the Warsaw Ghetto* (Warsaw: Verlag Yiddish Buch, 1963), II, 290–91.

17. *Ibid.,* pp. 301–2.

18. Simcha Poliakiewicz, *Days Without Light* (Tel Aviv: I. L. Peretz Publishing House, 1963).

19. *Ibid.*

20. Without a certificate or working permit, it was impossible to exist in the ghetto. A Jew who did not possess a certificate was always liable to be picked up in an "action" which frequently meant death. To confuse the Jews and lull them into a false sense of security, the Germans kept changing the color and value of the certificates. Yellow Certificates, issued primarily to craftsmen, were regarded as the most important of all and were sometimes referred to as *Lebens sheinen* ("life certificates"). But in the end, these also proved to be worthless.

21. Aaron Schworin, "Lachwa, Part I," *From the Last Extermination* (*Journal for the History of the Jewish People During the Nazi Regime*) (Central Committee of Liberated Jews in Bavaria [U.S. Zone]: 1946), No. 3, pp. 3–7; Chaim Shkliar, Abraham Feinberg, "Lachwa, Part II," *ibid.* pp. 8–11; Chaim Michali, "Revolt in Lachwa Ghetto," *Folk and Zion* (Jerusalem: Jewish Agency, March-April 1964), pp. 57–59.

22. According to Eber Cheiffetz, *Jewish-Journal* (July 16, 1945), the number of Lachwa Jews who succeeded in joining the partisans was 300.

23. Wilhelm Boger, inventor of the Boger torture rack, was a defendant at the Auschwitz trial in Frankfurt and sentenced to life imprisonment.

24. Szmulewski took these photographs in August, 1944. Jan Sehn, *Auschwitz-Birkenau* (Warsaw: 1957), p. 130.

25. Crematorium III.

26. Every nationality in Auschwitz was represented in the camp's underground. The Jewish section numbered about 300.

27. Israel Gutman, *Auschwitz Zeugnisse und Berichte* (Frankfurt am Main: 1962), pp. 273–79.

28. Moishe Kulka, *Memorial-Book of the Ciechanow Jewish Community* (Tel Aviv: 1962), pp. 386–90. *See also* Noah Zabladowicz, *ibid.,* pp. 338–39.

29. One survivor of the Sonderkommando revolt, Filip Müller, now lives in Prague. Recently he appeared as a witness for the prosecution at the trial of twenty SS men held in Frankfurt.

30. MOISHE KULKA, *Memorial-Book of the Ciechanow Jewish Community*, see above.

31. TUVIE BIELSKI was the legendary commander of the largest Jewish partisan detachment in World War II. It numbered close to 1,500 Jews, most of them noncombatants. When it became known that Commander Bielski accepted into his detachments the old as well as the young, the armed as well as the unarmed, Jews who escaped from the ghettos of Lida, Novogrudek, and other towns in western Byelorussia beat a path to Bielski's detachment in the Naliboka forest. As more and more Jews flocked to this detachment, a whole community grew in the heart of the forest, working and producing for other partisan units. While running the "Family Camp," Bielski was also the commander of a combat detachment which distinguished itself for its daring missions and the punishment it inflicted on the enemy. Bielski is also credited with having been among the first to organize a partisan movement in that area as early as 1941. Of his two brothers, Zushi and Eshol, also partisans, Eshol fell in battle. After the war, Bielski left for Palestine and fought in Israel's War of Independence. He now resides in New York.

32. Frequently, collaborators in that area were western Ukrainian nationalists and Fascists whom the Germans promised an independent Ukraine after the war. Some were brought back from Berlin, where they had been trained by the Nazis.

33. *The Destruction of Koretz* (Paris: 1949); *Jewish Daughters;* also see Moshe Kaganovich, *The War of the Jewish Partisans in Eastern Europe* (Buenos Aires: 1956): I, 170, 239–42.

34. Foresters, as a rule, collaborated with the Germans in their hunt for partisans.

35. One of several factions of Ukrainian Fascist nationalists who collaborated with the Germans. Their slogan was: "Against the Poles, the Jews, and the Red Partisans."

36. MOSHE KAGANOVICH, *The War of the Jewish Partisans in Eastern Europe*, I, 136–38.

37. *Ibid.*, II, 262–64.

38. *Jewish Daughters*, pp. 91–92.

39. "Studies on the Epoch of the Jewish Catastrophe, 1933-1945," *YIVO Annual of Jewish Social Science* (New York: 1953), p. 252.

40. *Ibid.*, p. 254.

41. *In the Years of Destruction and Resistance of the Jews of France (A Personal Memoir)* (Buenos Aires: 1956), pp. 131–32.

42. *Héros Juifs de la Résistance Française* (Paris: 1964), p. 14.

43. They were all executed by the Gestapo except one, the student Masha, who was deported to Auschwitz and perished there.

44. Later the manufacture of explosives was completely decentralized. Each unit had to have its own laboratory. This system had a double advantage: It speeded up the supply of weapons and permitted the individual units to carry on their sabotage in case of a raid on the laboratory.

45. Since food prices were constantly rising, the partisan's monthly pay was raised in 1943 to 2,300 francs.

46. After the liberation, the city council of Asniers named one of the town's streets Paul Simon.

47. The writer refers here to the twenty-three partisans, eleven of whom were Jews, who figured in the famous trial of the "23." Before they were photographed for the poster which was to be displayed all over Paris and in other parts of France, they were tortured by the Gestapo for three months. As a result, their faces looked puffed up and distorted. At the trial, the young Jew Marcel Rayman proudly said to his executioners: "I am a Jew, and as a Jew I could not live without fighting against you." On February 21, 1944, all twenty-three were shot by the Nazis on Mount Valérien. On their tombstones hang the decorations of the French Government with the inscription THEY DIED FOR FRANCE.

48. *Héros Juifs de la Résistance Française* (Paris: 1962), pp. 163-64.

49. Parliamentary Reports, 28th legislature.

50. *Giornale d'Italia* (September 6, 1934).

51. *The New York Times* (June 24, 1937).

52. As Mussolini's son-in-law, Count Ciano, relates in his diary, the Manifesto was the work of Mussolini himself. The professors merely signed it. *Ciano's Diary 1937-1938* (London), p. 150.

53. Article 7 of the resolution adopted by the Republican Fascist Party at the conference in Verona-Castelveccio.

54. The role of the Vatican in helping Jews is a separate subject about which much has already been written.

55. In her unpublished manuscript Jews in the Italian Resistance Movement, Mrs. Gina Formiggini of Naples, Italy, cites the figure of Jewish participation as "more than two thousand." She writes: "Many Jewish historians stated that only one thousand Jews were in the Italian Resistance movement. The difference between this figure and the one that we cite may be attributed to the following facts: (1) The present is a more recent work and therefore more data was available, and (2) the figure one thousand probably refers specifically to partisans who participated in armed resistance, whereas non-combat members of the resistance participated as well.

56. The information about the number of Jews in the resistance movement, as well as the biographical sketches of the partisans who fell in battle, was

taken from the following sources: National Association of Italian Partisans of Rome, Milan, and Turin; Association of Partisans (Gielle) Turiné Italian Communist Party in the region of Vercelli; Jewish communities of Rome, Milan, and Turin; organ of Italian War Department; letters from relatives of those who fell in battle.

INDEX

About the Minsk Ghetto, 231, 234
Abraham of Vitebsk, 271
Abramovitch, David, 313
Abramovitch, S., 71
Abruzzi, 301, 303
Abt, 292
Action Reinhardt, 141
Ainsztein, Reuben, 115, 116, 136-43
Aizenshtat, Berl, 162
A.K., *see* Armia Krajowa
Alef, G. (Bolek), 54
Aleichem, Sholem, 114
Aleksandria, 169
Alfonso, 293
Amendola, 302
André, 291
Anielewicz, Mordecai, 86-91, 94, 95, 101, 106, 108, 109, 112, 116, 118
Antek, *see* Zuckerman, Yitzchok
Anti-Fascist Fighting Bloc (Bialystok), 139, 140, 142
Antwerp, 183, 188, 306, 307
Aperovich, Dora. 234
Aran, 163
Arendt, Hannah, 4, 313
Argelès Internment Camp, 286
Argenteuil, 290
Armia Krajowa (Polish Home or Land Army), 2, 6, 45, 47, 73, 76, 105, 106, 115, 116-17, 118, 139, 140, 143, 313
Arndt, Rudolf (Rudi), 57, 60, 61
Asniers, 291, 316
Association des Juifs de Belgique, 306
Atlas, Celina, 254
Atlas, Yehezkel, 253-59
Auara (German Press), 152
Auschwitz, 2, 45, 68, 107, 114, 128, 179, 182-88, 189-95, 196-218, 219-25, 284, 289, 291, 294, 301, 309, 314; Museum, 193
Austria, 7, 128, 299

Bachnar, Alexander, 181
Badoglio, Pietro, 300
Baku, 16
Balevicius, Jonas, 162
Bancic, Golda, 292
Bandara, 229, 230, 261
Banko, 241, 242-45
Banovce, 181
Banska Stiavnice, 178
Baranowicze, 47, 130, 173; Ghetto, 172
Barasz, Ephraim, 138, 141
Bari, 299
Baruch, 20, 21, 22, 24, 25, 31, 32, 34, 36, 47

Baum, Bruno, 193, 223
Baum, Herbert, 59-68
Baum, Marianne, 59, 60, 64, 65, 68
Baum Group (Baum-Gruppe), 1, 55-68
BBC (British Broadcasting Corporation), 213, 215
Bebravou, 181
Beckerle, Adolf Heinz, 278
Beitar, 138
Belev, Alexander, 277
Belgium, 304, 305, 309
Belitza, 258
Belzec, 107, 142
Benario, Olga, 57
Benny, 34
Berezne, 169
Berg, Ernst, 33, 35
Berik, 257
Berkowski, 173, 174
Berlin, 1, 4, 11, 46, 47, 55-68, 202, 233, 261
Berlinski, Hersh, 115
Berman, Adolf, 115, 124
Bezdany, 156
Biala-Podliaska, 79
Bialystok, 18, 130, 157; Ghetto, 136-43, 150
Bielski, Tuvie, 174, 175, 234, 315
Birkenau (Auschwitz II), 182-87, 190-95, 196-218, 219-25, 300
Birnbaum, Heinz, 61, 63, 65
Bleter Far Geszichte, 55
Bloch, 90
Boczov, 293, 294, 295
Boehm, Arno, 197, 211
Boger, Wilhelm, 314
Bohemia, 198, 201, 205
Bohumin, 202, 203
Bologna, University of, 254
Boolet, Boris, 256
Bor-Komorowski, Tadeusz, 118
Boraks, Elijah, 139
Borisov (Kleinman), 3
Borisov (town), 9
Borodin, 220
Boroš, Pavel, 177, 178
Borowski, 174
Borowski, Chiena, 154
Borzic, 207, 210
Borzykowski, Tuvia, 104
Bot, Salek, 286
Botvin Company, 286
Brandt, 95
Bratislava, 179, 180, 206, 207, 209, 210, 211, 214
Brauze, Moshe, 152
Breendonck, 310
Bremmer, 239

Brener, 70
Brest, 44
Brussels, 306, 309, 310, 311
Brzecki, 21, 22, 25, 28, 29, 30, 31, 32, 33, 34, 35, 38, 39
Brzesko, 183
Buchenwald, 57, 60
Büchler, Jozef, 178
Buczacz, 226, 227
Budapest, 179, 216, 217, 218
Bug, 43, 44, 137
Bulgaria, 129, 275-81
Bulgarian Jews, 275-81
Bulgarian Orthodox Church, 276, 277
Bund, 70, 113, 138, 150, 153
Burbiszki, 151
Byelorussia, 128, 141, 160, 161, 163, 165, 172, 173, 231-39, 246, 247, 253, 254, 258, 277

Čadca, 206
Çalo, Eugenio, 302
Čánský, 206
Capajev, 180
Carmelite Order, 251
Carpatho-Russia, 208
Çashni, Nikolai Romanovich, 234
Černý Dunajec River, 209
Cesana, Franco, 302
Chaiffetz, Eber, 167, 314
Chamberlain, Neville, 176
Charleroi, 306, 307
Charlottenburg, 63
Chehlare, 279
Cheiffetz, Asher, 167
Cheiffetz, Chaim, 167
Cheiffetz, Moshe-Leib, 167
Chelm, 7, 40, 43, 46, 47
Chelmek, 208
Chelmno, 142, 145
Chemical Institute (Berlin), 64
Cherbourg, 292
Chernigov, 262, 266, 271
Chobot Forest, 167
Chorazyski, Julian, 131, 133, 134
Chornski Gora, 253
Churchill, Winston, 125
Chvonik, 155
Ciano, Galeazzo, 316
Ciechanow, 219, 220
Clichy, 292
Clichy-Levallois, 295
Clisci, Joseph, 292
Codex Judeorum, 176
Commandant of Auschitz, 45
Committee for National Liberation (Italy), 302
Communist Party, Poland, see Polish Workers Party (PPR)

Communists, 58, 59, 62, 64, 116, 138, 139, 150, 154, 177, 178, 180, 239, 279, 306
Constance, 202, 205
Corriere della Sera, 299
Council of Bulgarian Doctors, 276
Cracow, 119, 208, 223, 224
Crystal Night, 56, 59, 313
Curiel, Eugenio, 302
Cwoidzinski, Antoni, 121
Cyrankiewicz, Jozef, 189, 192, 193, 219, 223, 225
Czechoslovakia, 7, 12, 39, 128, 129, 135, 187
Czepik, 47
Czestochowa, 118, 132; Ghetto, 69-76
Czortkov, 227

Dachau, 3, 57, 69, 194
Daladier, Edouard, 176
Danecker, Theodor, 277
Dankner, Hans, 57
Danube, 279
Datner, Szymon, 314
David, 241, 242-45
David of Yarevitch, 271-73
Davidov, 163-64
Days Without Light, 146, 314
Degenhart, 71
Dejaco, Walter, 195
Denbiak, Kazik, 78
The Deputy, 2
Dereczyn Ghetto, 255, 256, 257
Dessler, Salek, 154, 155, 156, 157, 158
The Destruction of the European Jews, 3-4, 44, 115, 134, 238, 313
Devinska Nova Ves, 180
Diadia Misha, see Gildenman, Misha
Diamant, David, 284
Diena, Sergio, 301
Dnieper, 20
Dniester, 226
Documents and Materials About the Warsaw Ghetto Uprising, 115
Dombrowszczyzna Forest, 254
Donbas, 13, 34, 44
Douai, 295
Drancy (camp), 284
Drecksler, 182
Drepski, Israel, 167
Dresden, 57, 59
Dror, 138, 139
Dunkirk, 179
Dworzecki, Mark (Dvorjetsky), 154, 158

Eastern and National Information, 114
Les Éclaireurs Israélites de France (the Jewish Boy Scout Organization of France), 285
Edelman, Marek, 103, 113

Eden, Anthony, 118, 211
Eichmann, Adolf, 190, 198, 199
Einhorn, 247
Einhorn, A., 121
Eisenbach, Aaron, 125
Eisenbletter, Charlotte, 57
Eisenman, Jonah (Kaniewski), 80
El Salvador, 217
Elbe, 274
Elek, Thomas, 294
Elfer, Eugenio, 303
Elfer, Silvia, 303
Ella, 223
Elotchka, 13
Der Emes, 9
Emilia, 302
Engel, 38
Engels, Friedrich, 137
England, 61
Epstein, Paul, 204
Erlichman, 173
Esther, 223
Estonia, 157, 158
Eszterhazy, Janos, 176
Exnăr, Ladislav, 178
Extermination and Resistance, Historical
  Records and Source Material, 119, 125,
  259

Farber, Jacques, 290
Farber, Josef, 194
Fari, 302
Farinaci, 299
Father Daniel, see Rufeisen, Oswald
Feinberg, Abraham, 165-67, 314
Feinberg, Ber, 18
Feiner, M., 115
Feldman, 242
Feldman, Joseph (Georg Pesenka), 3
Felhendler, Leon, 45
Fells, 98
Ferleger, M., 71, 72
Feyner, Isadore, 71, 72
Ficht, 40
Fighting Warsaw, 116
Fishelevitch, Mendel, 71, 72
Fleischman, 98
Fleischmann, Gisi, 207
Folks-Shtimme (Warsaw), 125, 231
Folman, Marek, 74
Formiggini, Gina, 316
Fossoli, 301
Foxman, Abraham, H. 148-59
Foxman, Joseph M., 148, 172-75
FPO· (Fareinikte Partisaner Organi-
  zatzie), 150-58
Fraenkel, Edith, 67
France, 7, 12, 39, 63, 66, 209, 279, 282,

283, 284, 302
France Dimanche, 217
Franco, Francisco, 194, 286
Frank, Hans, 101, 114
Franke, Joachim, 64, 66
Franke Group, 64, 65, 66
Frankfurt, 217, 314
Franz (Sobibor), 13, 14, 15, 16, 21, 27,
  29, 31, 33, 35, 38, 39, 41
Franz (Treblinka), 131
Frayman, Hersh, 71
Fresnes, 297
Freud, Sigmund, 121
Freud's Theory of Dreams (Cwoidzinski),
  121
Freundlich, Feliks Israel, 63, 65
Freundlich, Margaret, 63
Fried, Anatol, 155
Frieder, 207
Friedman, Philip, 6, 118, 155, 159
Frimmer, 113
Frubel, Stanislaw, see Poliakiewicz,
  Simcha
Frumer, Chaim, 104
F.T.P. (Francs-Tireurs et Partisans), 287
Fudin, Regina (Lilitch), 110
Fuerst, 207
Fun Letzten Churbon, 168

Gajek, 110
Galasz, Edward, 128
Galewski, 129
Galicia, 226
Galinski, Edek, 183, 185, 186, 187
Gallows humor, 125-27
Geduldig, Jonas, 288, 294
General Sikorski Institute (London), 116
General Zionists, 70, 87
Geneva, 213, 214, 217
Genick, 25, 29, 32, 35
Genoa, 301
Gens, Jacob, 153, 154, 155, 157
German Federal Republic, 50
Gersht, Fried, 57
Gersht, Yitzchok, 57
Gestapo, 1, 51, 52, 53, 54, 78, 80, 124,
  141, 142, 169, 170, 182, 183, 202, 205,
  251, 254, 278; Berlin, 55, 56, 58, 59,
  64, 65, 66, 67; Czestochowa Ghetto,
  69, 72, 73, 74; Minsk Ghetto, 235, 236,
  237; Paris, 283, 286, 288, 289, 290,
  291, 293, 294, 295; Vilna Ghetto, 150,
  154, 155, 156, 157
Geto Yediot (Ghetto News), 156
Gilbert, 289, 295
Gildenman, Misha, 3, 260-74
Gildenman, Simcha, 260, 261
Gilinsky, Yossl, 162

Ginsberg, Leone, 303
Glazman, Joseph ("Abram"), 150, 153, 155, 156
Glicksman, William, 69-76
Globocnik, Odilo, 141, 142
Glos Warszawy, 115
Goebbels, Joseph, 6, 62, 63, 68, 196
Goettinger, 33, 36
Goldberg, Leon, 294
Goldkorn, Dora, 105
Goldmann, Nahum, 120
Goldschmidt, 135
Gomerski, 11, 15, 35
Gowarczow, 81
Great Britain, 215
Greece, 49, 128, 129
Greenstein, Jacob, 241-52
Greischutz, 27, 28, 33, 36
Grisha, 25, 26, 36
Grodno, 138, 161, 162, 164; Ghetto, 150
Gross, 169
Gross-Rosen, 224
Grot-Rowecki, General, 115, 116
Grunwald Cross, 54
Grynszpan, Herschel, 313
Grzywacs, 295
Guderian, Heinz, 137
Günther, Hans, 199
Gurs Internment Camp, 286
Gutfreind, Jacob, 304-11
Gutman, Israel, 220, 221, 222, 314
Gwardia Ludowa, see People's Guard

Hach, 40
Hagen, 49, 50
Halter, Paul, 310
Hamburg, 23, 239
Hanoar Hatzioni, 89, 138, 183
Hanu Sovice, 180
Hanysh, 76
Hap, Leon, 61
Harcesz (Polish Scouts), 88
Hartenstein, 205
Hasag labor camps, 70, 75
Hashomer Hatzair, 79, 85, 86, 87, 88, 89, 90, 138, 139, 177, 180, 219, 223, 259
Haulstich, Friedrich, 34, 38
Hauser, 203
Hausner, Gideon, 134
Hein, 246, 247, 248, 249, 250
Hekhalutz, 138, 149, 150
Helm, Erbert, 36
Hénin-Liétard, 295
Hermlin, Stephan, 65
Hertmann, 200
Heshen, Heinz, 57
Heydebreck, 198
Heyk, 254

Heymann, 65
Hilberg, Raul, 34, 44, 45, 115, 134, 237, 238, 313
Himmler, Heinrich, 7, 45, 92, 93, 97, 106, 114, 141, 200
Hirsch, Fredy, 198, 211, 212
Hirsch, Hella, 67, 68
Hirschhorn, Bella, 255, 256
Histadrut ha Hovdim, 207
Hitler, Adolf, 1, 6, 10, 21, 23, 52, 55, 56, 57, 58, 59, 60, 65, 67, 68, 88, 126, 127, 137, 141, 142, 176, 228, 261, 299
Hitler's Professors, 239
Hlinka, 176
Hochhuth, Rolf, 1
Hoess, Rudolf, 45, 185
Hoffman, 278
Hokes, Katie, 40
Holland, 7, 12, 24, 31, 39
Holtzer, Charlotte, 56, 66
Holtzer, Richard, 56, 65, 66
Holy See, 214
Holzer, Leo, 202, 204
Home Army, see Armia Krajowa
Horodenka, 226-30
Horodyszcze Ghetto, 172
Horodziej Ghetto, 172
Horthy, Miklos, 207, 215
Hoth, Hermann, 137
Humenne, 177
Hungary, 2, 66, 177, 179, 193, 196, 208, 215, 216, 217

I Cannot Forgive, 194
I.G. Farben, 59
In the Dispersion, 121
Innsbruck, 195
International Auschwitz Committee, 190
International Brigade (in Spain), 286
International Red Cross, 197, 198, 199, 202, 203, 204
Iramas cigarette factory, 57
Israel, 251, 252, 261; Supreme Court, 251
Istanbul, 207, 211
Italy, 298, 299, 300, 301, 302
Itzik, 152
Itzkowitch, Michael, 34, 37, 43

Jacob, 222
Jadamowitz, Hilde, 59, 66
Jakub, 31, 36
Jan Zizka Brigade, 181
Janek, 25, 31, 33-5
Janowitz, Leo, 197
The Jerusalem of Lithuania in Struggle and Destruction, 154
Jerusalem Post, 252
Jewish Agency, 2, 207

Jewish Council, see Judenrat
Jewish Cultural Organization, see YKOR
Jewish Fighting Organization, see ZOB
Jewish Frontier, 2
Jewish Historical Institute of Warsaw, 55, 117, 125, 246
Jewish Journal, 167
Jewish Labor Organization (Warsaw), 117
Jewish Military Association, 93, 94, 95, 100, 111, 115
Jewish National Committee, 117
Jewish Quarterly, 116, 136
Jewish Social Self-Help, 122
Joachim, Hans, 61, 64, 65
Joint Coordinating Committee (Vilna Ghetto), 149
Judenrat, 56, 82, 84, 227, 284; Belgium, 305, 306, 307, 308, 309; Bialystok Ghetto, 137, 138, 139; Lachwa Ghetto, 165, 166, 167; Marcinkonis Ghetto, 160, 161; Minsk Ghetto, 235, 236; Theresienstadt Ghetto, 197, 202, 204; Tuczyn Ghetto, 169; Vilna Ghetto, 153, 154, 156; Warsaw Ghetto, 101, 109, 124
Jusik, 47
Justice in Jerusalem, 134
Juzef, 31, 36

Kaganovich, Moishe, 238, 259, 267, 274, 315
Kahn, Shoshana, 158
Kalimali, see Shubayev, Alexander
Kanal, Israel, 113
Kaniewski, see Eisenman, Jonah
Kaplan, Yosef, 89
Kapustin, 162, 163
Karmil-Krasňanský, 206, 207, 209, 210, 215
Kastner, Rudolf, 207
Katowitz, 203
Katowski Forest, 170
Katsherginski, Shmerke, 158, 159
Katzenelson, Yitzhok, 90
Katzovo, Edita, 181
Kaufman, 71
Kawe, Joseph, 139
Kelbasin, 161
Kemach, David, 238
Kempner, Vitka, 152
Kerbel, Jean, 290, 291
Keril, 262, 264-66
Kielce, 119
Kiev, 46, 267
Kirshner, Harold, 218
Kittel, 154, 157, 158
Kittner, 131

KKO (Communal Bank), 53
Kleinman (Borisov), 3
Klepnitzki, Moshe, 167
Knieža, Emil F., 176-81
Kobrovsky, Ahron, 161, 162
Kobrovsky, Bentsiyon, 161, 162
Kobrovsky, Khayim, 163
Kobrovsky, Yitzhok, 163-64
Kochmann, Martin, 59, 60, 64, 65, 68
Kochmann, Sala, 59, 60, 64, 65, 66, 68
Kolarov, Vasil, 277
Koldyczewo Camp, 172-75
Kon, Stanislaw, 133
Kondofrey, 280
Koniuchowski, Leyb, 160-64
Konyetopol, 75, 76
Kopecký, 213, 214
Korbonski, Stefan, 116
Korchak, Reizl, 159
Korczak, Janusz, 84
Koren, 173
Koretz, 3, 260
Korn, Lea, 110
Kornischoner, 47
Korosten, 264, 266, 271
Kostolna, 180
Kostopol, 169
Koszcz, 169
Kotre, 163
Kovacz, Tibor, 207
Kovner, Abba ("Uri"), 150, 155, 157
Kowalski, Isaac, 151, 152, 159
Kowensky, Elijah, 258
Kozlowszcyzna, 254, 257, 258
KPD (Kommunistische Partei Deutschlands), 59, 66
Krakow, see Cracow
Kralovany, 180
Krasnuvka, 267
Kremenchug, 9
Kripo (Kriminal Polizei), 63
Krirzanowski, Jegor, 169
Kro, Helen, 289
Krüger, Friedrich-Wilhelm, 92, 97, 106, 114
Kruk, Herman, 159
Krupp, Alfried, 220
Kube, Wilhelm, 233, 237, 238
Kulka, Erich, 196-218
Kulka, Moishe, 221, 222, 314, 315
Kursk, 20, 266, 271, 273
Kusznier, 173
Kutuza, 280
Kyustendil, 280

Lachwä Ghetto, 6, 165-67, 314
Lammers, Hans Heinrich, 101
Landau, Ludvik, 111
Langsfeld, Hugo, 213

Láník, Josef (Alfred Wetzler), 205, 206, 207, 208, 210
Laufschner, Ruzenka, 213
Lautz, 103
Lazar, Chaim, 159
Lederer, Siegfried, 201, 204, 205
Left-Poale Zionists, *see* Poale-Zionists (Left-wing)
Leichert, 131, 134
Leifer, Joshua, 220, 221, 222
Leipzig, 59
Leitman, Shloime, 11, 12, 13, 17, 19-26, 28-35, 37-41
Lemberger, Nathan, 289
Lenin, Nikolai, 137
Lerner, Sala, 57
Lerski (Lerner), 105
Lev. Misha, 47
Levallois-Perret, 292
Levinbuk, Zelig, 173
Lichtheim, R., 213
Liège, 306, 307
Lifshitz, Alexander, 309, 310
Lifshitz, George, 309, 310
Lipiczany Forest, 254
Lipschitz, 57
Lipszowicz, Elik, 259
Liptovsky Mikulas, 209
Liss, Kalman, 122
Liss, Nina, 236
Lissner, Abraham, 282-97
List, Mayer, 289
Lithuania, 148, 160
Litten, Hanz, 57
Litvinovski, Yefim, 46
Lodz, 38, 47, 52, 138, 169, 253; Ghetto, 216
Lohse, Hinrich, 238
London, 6, 58, 65, 207, 211, 214, 215
Longwy, 293
Lopatin, Dov, 167
Löwy, Hilde, 67
Lubetkin, Zivia, 113, 115
Lubinskinski, 63
Lublin, 47, 125, 141, 178, 206, 207
Ludvipol, 169
Luka, 23, 25, 26, 27, 28, 29, 37, 38, 40, 41, 42
Lukaszenia, Vladimir, 173
Lukiszki Prison, 148
Lukov, 178
Luniniece, 166
Lurie, N., 9
Lustgarten, 63, 64

Maccabees (Prague), 211
Maccabees (Slovakia), *see* Makabi
McClelland, 213
McCloy, John J., 216

Macedonia, 128
Mach, Sano, 209
Mackiewitz, Icke, 152
Madaiska, Sonia, 154, 155
Magun, Liza, 151
Maidanek, 84, 107, 206
Makabi (Slovakia), 177, 180
Malines, 183
Malkinia-Siedlece, 129
Mandel, 188
Mangel, 209
Manifesto of Racism, 300
Mann, Mendel, 168-71
Manny, 25, 31
Manouchian, 295
Mantella, Georges, 211, 217
Maquis, 285
Marasi Prison, 301
Marcel, 294
Marcinkonis, 160-64
Marconi, Leonardo, 114
Mario, 210, 211
Mark, Ber, 54, 55-68, 77, 92-115, 116, 125
Mark, Esther, 77-81
Markovic, Jakub, 181
Markus, Alexander, 178, 179
Martin, 200
Martyrs and Fighters, 118
Marx, Karl, 137
Masaryk, Thomas G., 134
Massarek, Rudolf, 134-135
Mauthausen, 178
Mazanik, Halina, 238
Mazurkiewitch, Semion, 43
Melun, 294
Mendelson, Hela, 139
Mersik, Zvi, 139
Meyer, Gerd, 64, 65
Michali, Chaim, 165-67, 314
Michalovce, 177, 178
Milan, 301, 302
Milkanowitzki, 155
Minna, 285
Minsk, 7, 9, 11, 17, 20, 48, 242; Ghetto, 231-45
Mintz, Pinkas (Alexander), 284
Mir, 246, 247, 248
The Miser, 121
Mlawa, 208
Moabit Prison, 67
Modena, 301, 302
M.O.I. (Mouvement Ouvrier Immigrés), 287, 288
Molczadz Ghetto, 172
Molière, Jean Baptiste Poquelin, 121
Moll, 191, 192
Monek, 47

"Monter," Colonel, 105
Moravia, 198
Mordowicz, Czezlaw, see Podulka, Petr
Moscow, 20, 24, 58, 63, 261, 262, 273
Moses, 57
Moszkowicz, Daniel, 139, 140, 142
Motele, 262-67
Motele of Berzsnitz, 273
Moytek, 74
Müller, Filip, 198, 314
Munich, 57, 59, 176, 271
Murer, Franz, 158
Murmelstein, Benjamin, 204
Mussolini, Benito, 298, 299, 302, 316
Musteika, 162
Myslovic, 203

Nadrzeczna 66 (youth group), 71, 72, 73
Naliboka, 174
Naples, 301
Narocz Forest, 156, 158
National Front of Belgian Independence, 306
Nedeca, 209
Neged Hazerem, 87
Dos Neie Leben (Lodz), 54, 133
Nellie, 12-13
Neugebauer, 156, 157, 158
Neumann, Oscar, 207
Neumann, Renée, 201, 203
Neumann, Robert, 50
Neustadt, Meilech, 54
New Berun, 198
Nicolas-Kraus (Mikos), 218
Niehaus, 198, 199, 200
Niemen River, 174, 258
Nohorodek, 166
Nord Pas de Calais, 295
Norman, 174
Normandy, 296
Notes from the Warsaw Ghetto, 4, 51, 122, 125, 126, 314
Novaky, 181
Novogrod, 149
Novy Targ, 208
Nowa Wileika, 156
Nowaky, 206, 207
Nowi Mir, 3
Nowogrodek Ghetto, 172
Nowogrodzka, Judith, 139
Nowy Kurier Warshawski (New Warsaw Courier), 53
Nuremberg laws, 176

Olshtin, 73
Omastina Valley, 181
Oneg Shabbat, 123, 124
Oranienburg, 202, 205

Orly, 294
Oswiecim, 142
Otwock, 122
Our Struggle, 306
Our Word, 306
Ovrutch, 262, 264, 265, 266, 272

Pakin, Leon, 286
Palestine, 177, 211, 218, 252
Pantev, 280
Pappo, Menahem (Miko), 280
Paris, France, 261, 282-97, 313
Parma, 302
Partisan groups: Atlas Partisan Detachment (Byelorussia), 256-59; Budiony Partisan Detachment, 244; children as partisans, 241-45, 260-67; Davidov Partisan Group, 163-64; Diadia Misha's Partisans (Ukraine), 260-74; "Eagle" Partisan Group (Italy), 302; Forois (Forward) (Bialystok), 140, 142; "Fraternal Aid" (Belgium), 304; "Free Italy," 302; "Freedom of Justice" (Italy), 301, 302; "Garibaldi Group" (Italy), 301; Horodenka Partisan Groups (Galicia), 227-30; Jewish Partisan Unit of Paris, 1, 282-97; Jewish Partisans in Belgium, 304-11; Jewish Partisans in Bulgaria, 275-81; Jewish Partisans in Italy, 298-303; Jewish Partisans in Slovakia, 177, 178, 179, 180, 181; "Kalyashki" Partisan Detachment (Bulgaria), 280; Kobrovsky Brothers Partisan Group, 161-64; Levi Partisan Detachment (Poland), 80-81; Minsk Partisan Groups, 232-38; Parchomenko Partisan Detachment (Byelorussia), 243, 244, 245; "Solidarité" (Belgium), 304, 306; Stankevich's Partisan Company, 164; Trun Partisan Detachment (Bulgaria), 280; Tuvie Bielski's Jewish Family Camp, 234; Tuvie Bielski's Partisan Group, 174-75; "The Vengeance," Jewish Partisan Units (Vilna), 156; Zorin's Family Detachment (Byelorussia), 244
Pechersky, Alexander (Sasha), 7-44, 45, 46, 47, 48, 49
Peissach, 173
People's Guard (Gwardia Ludowa), 53, 73, 79, 80, 105, 110, 113, 115, 312
Peretz, Shloyme, 163, 164
Perle, Shia, 90
Pesenka, Georg (Joseph Feldman), 3
Pestek, Victor, 201, 202, 203
Pétain, Henri Philippe, 304
Petschauer, Jirka, 202
Pewinska, Eva, 80

Peysack, H., 71
Pietrasza, 137
Pilevsky, Efrayim, 163
Pilsen, 202
Pilsudski, Jozef, 286
Pinkas Synagogue (Prague), 135
Pinsk, 174
Piotrkow, 118
Pius XII, Pope, 210, 214, 215
Pleven, 279
Plovdiv, 279
Poale-Zionists (Left-wing), 58, 70, 87, 124, 305, 306; (Right-wing), 87
Podulka, Petr (Czezlaw Mordowicz), 208, 209, 210
Poland, 1, 2, 6, 7, 12, 17, 39, 52, 128, 129, 141, 161, 176, 177, 189, 208, 215, 251, 252, 253, 254, 277, 278, 279, 282, 283, 284, 286, 301
Polesia Forest, 174
Poliakiewicz, Simcha, 146-47, 314
Poliakov, L., 282-83, 284-85
Polin, 167
Polish Communist Party, see Polish Workers Party (P.P.R.)
Polish Home Army, see Armia Krajowa
Polish-Jewish Relationships During the Second World War, 111, 125, 144
Polish Land Army, see Armia Krajowa
Polish Provisional Government (London), 6, 115, 117, 313
Polish Socialist Party (P.P.S.), 192
Polish Workers Party (P.P.R.), 53, 70, 71, 87, 109, 113
Ponary, 149, 150, 156
Pope, Generoso, 299
Popov, 265
Porges, Šimon, 180
Potashik, 311
Povroznik, Chaim, 40
Poznan, 47
Praga, 53
Prague, 180, 214, 216, 314
Pripet River, 166, 167
Il Progresso Italo-Americano, 299
Proskurov, 271
Pruzany, 137

Radio London, 289
Radio Moscow, 289
Radom, 80, 81, 118
Radomir, 280
Radomsko, 72
Rahm, Karl, 204
Rajzman, Samuel, 48, 128-32, 134
Rakov, 75
Rakower, 309
Ran, Leizer, 159

Rapoport, Fayvl, 161
Rappaport, Nathan, 126
Rath, Ernst von, 313
Ratomka, 234
Ravensbrück, 57
Rawicki, 173
Rayman, Marcel, 289, 290, 293, 297, 316
Red Army, 20, 46, 47, 141, 143, 171, 179, 193, 261, 262
Red Cross, 193, 195; Belgian, 310; German, 197, 198, 199, 200; International Committee, 200; Slovakian, 197
Regina, 223
"Regina Coeli" Prison, 303
Das Reich, 62
Reich, Boby, 209
Reichstag, 47
Reichsvereinigung von Deutschen Judentum, 56
Reiman, 28
Reims, 293
Remba, Nachum, 82-84
Republican Fascist Party, 300
Resnik, Ber, 246, 248, 251
Resnik, Nisel, 154, 155
Return Undesirable, 47
Reutte, Austria, 195
Revisionists (Zionist), 150
Riegner, 197, 213, 214
Riga, 239
Rimun, Yitzchak, 313
Ringelblum, Emmanuel, 4, 5, 6, 51, 84, 85-96, 111, 121, 122, 123-25, 126, 128, 133, 144, 145
Ringelblum Archives, 123-25
Ripshtayn, Kuba, 76
Riters, 188
Ritter, Karl, 293, 294, 296
Robert, 294
Robinson, Jacob, 159
Robota, Rosa, 2, 193, 219-23
Rochtchin, Yitzchok, 166, 167
Roháč, Jan (Arnöst Rosin), 208, 209, 210
Rohn, 72
Romanow, 76
Romanowitch, 104
Rome, 300, 301, 303
Romek, 174
Roosevelt, Franklin Delano, 211, 216
Rosani, Rita, 302
Rosenberg, Walter, see Vrba, Rudolf
Rosenthal, Leo, 207
Rosenzweig, 311
Rosin, Arnöst, see Roháč, Jan
Rostov-on-the-Don, 9, 11, 34, 44, 46
Rotgiel, H., 305, 307
Rotholz, Heinz, 65, 66, 67

Rotholz, Lotte, 67, 68
Rousse, 280
Rovno, 168, 169, 171
Rozenfeld, Semyon, 46, 47
Rozhanka, 258
Rozsi, 212
Rozvazhev, 268, 269
Rozyne, 70
R.S.H.A. (Reichssicherheitshauptamt),
   196, 198, 199, 203, 205
Ruda, 258
Ruda Jaworska Forest, 254
Rudi Arndt Group, 60
Ruditzer, Hersh, 236
Rudnitska Forest, 158
Rufeisen, Oswald (Shmuel), 246-52
Rusk, Bishop of Innsbruck, 195
Russia, see Soviet Union
Ryba, Walter, 34, 38

Sachsenhausen, 57, 65, 194
St. Sabo Prison, 301
St. Vittori Prison, 301
Sammern-Frankenegg, Ferdinand von, 92,
   95, 96, 98
Sasha, see Pechersky, Alexander
Sauckel, Fritz, 293
Sawin, 47
Scheingut, Tuvia, 106, 110
Schliesser, Otto, 202
Schmerling, 83
Schmidt, 16, 30, 38
Schmidt, Anton, 157
Schmidt, Walter, 313
Schnabel (Sobibor), 47
Schnäbel (Warsaw Ghetto), 93
Schönfeld, Julius, 180
Schtulpnagel, 286
Schultz, 104
Schulze-Beusen-Harnak Group, 63-64
Schwalb, Nathan, 207, 213
Schwartzbart, I., 115, 117-18
Schwartzman, Getzl, 169
Schwarzhuber, Hans, 198, 207
Schworin, Aaron, 165-67, 314
Second Bloc (Bialystok), 138
Sefer Horodenka, 226
Semigorod, 271
Senie, 36
Sered, 180, 206, 212
Seredy, Primasz, 207
Sevek, 285, 286
Sheinbaum, Jechiel, 152, 157
Shekerdjiiski, Emil, 280
Shepetovka, 262, 271
Shershniewski, Berl, 154
Shidlovski, 76
Shilka, 163

Shirer, William L., 313
Shkliar, Chaim, 165-67, 314
Shubayev, Alexander (Kalimali), 16, 25,
   26, 34, 35, 36, 41-3, 46
Siemens Electrical Motor Plant (Berlin),
   59, 60, 61, 62, 66
Sikorski, 112
Silesia, Upper, 224
Sima, 241, 242
Simon, 288
Simon, Paul, 290, 291, 316
Sinelnikov, A., 47
Sioma, 286
Siudak, Pawel, 117
Skalite, 206
Skolsky, Lipe, 163
Slonim, 89, 138, 254; Ghetto, 172
Slovak Jews, 176-81
Slovak People's Party, 176
Slovakia, 128, 176-81, 204, 205, 206, 208,
   209, 210, 215
Slutzki, Abraham, 167
Smolar, Hersh (Yefim Stolerovitch), 231.
   234-38, 242
Smolensk, 3, 247
Snina, 208
Sobakince, 161
Sobibor, 2, 7-50, 142
Socialist Party, Polish (P.P.S.), 192
Socialists, 58
Sofia, Bulgaria, 277, 278
Sokol, 230
Sokolow, 128
Sola River, 208
Solomon, 89
Somovit Concentration Camp, 279
Soport, 72
Sorin, Ben, 233
Sosnovski, Cadys, 291
Sovetish Heimland, 46, 47, 49
Das Soviet Paradis (The Soviet Paradise)
   Exhibit, 63, 67
Soviet Union (Russia), 3, 7, 11, 12, 20,
   22, 39, 46, 61, 129, 137, 140, 165, 226,
   247, 254, 259, 260, 279, 294
Spanish Civil War, 286
Spartacus, 77, 78
Staf, Leon, 122
Stainov, Petco, 276
Stalag 337, 172
Stalin, Joseph, 3, 137
Stalingrad (Volgograd), 20, 176
Stará Spisská Ves, 209
Staroje-Sielo Forest, 241, 243
Stawki, 43, 44
Steinbrink, Werner, 63, 64, 65, 66
Steiner, Ernst, 206, 207
Sternfeld, Mikuláš, 210

Stern, Ursula, 40
Stillman, Elsa, 61, 65
Stolpce Ghetto, 172
Stolpce-Mir, 231
Streicher, Julius, 299
Stroop, Jurgen von, 93, 97-107, 109, 113, 115
Sudowicz, 132
Suhl, Yuri, 51-4, 82-4, 144-47, 189-95, 219-25, 231-39
Sutzkever, Abraham, 152, 159
Suvich, Fulvio, 299
Svatý Júr, 210, 211, 215
Svirska, Minna, 155
Swienciany, 153
Swierzen Ghetto, 172
"Swit," 109
Switzerland, 179, 200, 207, 211, 218, 285
Szapiro, Willy, 294
Szczara River, 254, 258
Szczelec, 230
Szenicki, 174
Szmulewski, David, 189-95, 314
Szner, Zvi, 259
Sztandar Wolnosci (Flag of Freedom), 152
Szypper, Yitzhok, 90

Tadjer, Leon (Ben David), 280
Taflik, 170
Tamara, 96
Targau, 274
Tarnow, 182
Tchubak, Tuvia, 170
Teitelboim, Niuta (Wanda), 51-4
Tencer, H., 71
Tenenbaum, Joseph, 45, 159
Tenenboim-Tamarof, Mordechai, 139, 140, 142, 149
Theresienstadt, 68; Family Camp (Birkenau), 203; Ghetto, 197-218. For "Council of Elders" see Judenrat, Theresienstadt Ghetto
Third Reich, 56, 57, 58, 60, 62, 160
This Is How It Was, 83, 121
Tirlemont, 310
Tiso, Jozef, 176, 179, 180, 210
Tcebbens, Walter C., 104
Tomberg, 90
Tomin, V., 47
Topolčianky, 180
TOZ (Society for the Protection of Health), 70
Trafida, 155
Travcic, 202
Trawniki, 98, 125
Trebišov, 179

Treblinka, 2, 5, 44, 45, 47, 48, 52, 70, 79, 84, 91, 107, 121, 124, 142, 146, 220; Uprising, 128-35
Trembatch, 90
Trencin, 180
Trieste, 301, 302
Trifon, Riszard, 110
Trnava, 205
Troy, France, 293, 294
Tsar Boris III (Bulgaria), 275
Tsibulsky, Boris, 13, 17, 27, 28, 34, 35, 36, 41, 42, 43, 46
Tuczyn Ghetto, 168-71
Turka, 247
Turkow, Jonas, 83, 121, 122
Tursky, Louis, 2
Tuscany, 301
Tushnet, Leonard, 253-59
Tyrol, Austrian, 195

UGIF (Union Générale des Israélites de France), 283, 284
Ukraine, 3, 46, 168, 277
Ullman (Belgium), 305, 308
Ullmann (Auschwitz), 213, 214
Umschlagplatz, 82, 87, 95, 104
Uncle Misha, see Gildenman, Misha
Underground, 45, 159
Union of Bulgarian Lawyers, 276
Union of Bulgarian Writers, 276
La Unita, 302
United Anti-Fascist Bloc (Bialystok), 138
United States, 61, 216

Vaispapir, Arkady, 36, 41, 42, 43, 46
Vallat, Xaviar, 283
Vatican, 207, 211, 215, 299
Vernet D'Ariège Internment Camp, 286
Verona, 303
Verona-Castelveccio, 316
Versailles, 291
Veselák, Vaclav, 202
Vichy Regime, 283, 284
Vilna, 68, 88, 89, 137, 138, 148, 149, 150, 151, 154, 157, 164; Ghetto, 148-59. See also Judenrat, Vilna Ghetto
Vilner, 89
Vinné, 177, 178
Vitale, Masimo Adolfo, 298-303
Vitke, 152
Vittenberg, Itzik, see Witenberg, Isaac
Vittenberg Day, 153-56
Vivanti, Ildo, 302
Vlassov, 244
Volga, 39
Volgograd, see Stalingrad
Volhynia (Ukraine), 3, 168, 171, 260, 267

Voroshilov, Klementi, 44, 261
Vrba, Rudolf (Walter Rosenberg), 194, 205, 206, 207, 210, 217

Wajsbrot, Wolf, 291
Waks, 10
Walter, Irene, 62, 64, 65
Wanda, see Teitelboim, Niuta
The War of the Jewish Partisans in Eastern Europe, 238
War Refugee Board, 216
Warsaw, 11, 17, 48, 50, 51, 52, 53, 70, 72, 73, 79, 80, 85, 88, 92, 128, 129, 137, 138, 189, 190, 224; Ghetto, 1, 4, 5, 6, 51, 52, 53, 54, 70, 75, 77-9, 84, 85, 121-27, 128, 133, 150, 233, 240, 313; Ghetto cultural life, 121-22; Ghetto house committees, 78, 122; Ghetto humor, 125-27; Ghetto Monument, 127; Ghetto Uprising, 85, 91, 92-121, 133, 134, 136, 139
The Warsaw Ghetto Uprising, 92, 115
Washington, D.C., 216
Wasser, Hirsh, 124, 125
Wehrmacht, 4, 52, 53, 107, 141, 165, 227, 233, 247, 294, 306, 309
Weichman, 309, 311
Weichselmetal-Union (Auschwitz), 216, 220, 221
Weidmann-Group, 202
Weimar Republic, 57
Weinberg, Khayim, 164
Weinberg, Shloime, 173
Weinberg, Zelma, 40
Weinreich, Max, 239
Weisblum, Giza, 182-88
Weisenborn, Gunter, 55, 56, 65, 313
Weissensee, 56, 61
Weissmandel, 207
Weizmann, Chaim, 2, 211, 313
Welker, 203
Wengrov, 128, 131
Wengrov, a Monument to the Perished, 134
Werkleute, 58, 59
Wermuth, Joshua, 226-30
Wesse, Suzanne, 62, 64, 65
Westerburg, 40
Wetzler, Alfred, see Lénik, Josef
White Russia, see Byelorussia
Wiadomosci (News), 125
Wiederstand in Auschwitz, 193, 223
Wielka Wola, 254, 255
Wielki Oblovic, 258
Wiernick, Yankel, 133, 134
Wiesel, Eli, 4
Winicki, 137
Wise, Stephen S., 120, 299
Wishunski, Yankel (Wiga), 79

Witebski, Werner, 57
Witenberg, Isaac, 150, 153-56
Wladka, 75
Wlashov, 19
Wlodowa, 7, 40
Wojskowska, Rebecca, 139
"Work-Camp Birkenau," 197, 198, 199
World Jewish Congress, 120, 215, 299
World Zionist Organization, 120, 121
Wuppertal-Elberfeld, 57

Yacchia, Mario, 302
Yad Washem, 199
Yakova, Violeta, 280
Yamaika, Zofia, 77-81
Yanov, 47
A Year in Treblinka, 133
Yechiel, 98
Yehuda, Bar, 252
Yekaterinoslav-Dniepropetrovsk, 3
Yiddishe Kultur, 125
Yivo Annual of Jewish Social Science, 160
Yivo—Bleter, 239
YKOR (Jewish Cultural Organization), 122
Yohimek, 71
Yutzari, Matei, 275-81

Zabladowicz, Noah, 220, 222, 223, 314
Zakopane, 208
Zandman, 87
Zbraslav, 204
Zdzieciol Ghetto, 172
Zeger, Leibel, 173
Zeimer, Mirek, 204
Zhatel (Zdzientziol), 258
Zhitomir, 260-61, 262, 268
Zilberman, Paul, 291
Zilbermann, 47
Žilina, 179, 206, 209
Zimetbaum, Mala, 2, 182-88
Zimmering, Max, 57
Zimmerman, Hersz, 286
Zion, Daniel, 278
Zionists, 58, 59, 150
Zlate Moravce, 181
Zloty-Potok, 73
ZOB (Jewish Fighting Organization), 70, 71, 72, 73, 74, 75, 87, 89, 90, 91, 93, 94, 95, 99, 101, 103, 104, 106, 107, 109, 110, 112, 113, 115, 116, 118, 127
Zorin, 234, 242, 244
Zoska, 72
Zuckerman, Yitzchok (Antek), 101, 108, 119
Zylberberg, Mordecai, 71
Zygelboim, Szmul, 118, 119

126 - Jokes